PRAISE FOR *STONEWALL*

"ONE OF THE MOST IMPORTANT BOOKS ABOUT LESBIANS AND GAYS TO EMERGE SINCE STONEWALL."
—*Seattle Weekly*

"THRILLINGLY ZEROES LIKE A LASER ONTO TEN DAYS THAT SHOOK THE WORLD . . . six viewpoints artfully melted into one voice . . . moves like fiction toward a volatile climax. I couldn't put it down, and learned so much."
—Ned Rorem

"A POWERFUL AND COMPELLING BOOK that will make it harder for future 'sixties' books to ignore the gay liberation movement."
—*The Nation*

"THE WORK OF A MAJOR HISTORIAN, just the kind of book you want to read: the real lives, the feel of the time, the experience of the struggle, the individuals who brought freedom and changes."
—Kate Millet, author of *Sexual Politics*

"ENGROSSING . . . a long overdue look at one of the seminal events in the history of gay activism. Important and absorbing."
—*Kirkus*

"PACKS THE DRAMATIC WALLOP OF A FAST-PACED NOVEL . . . shows individuals engaging in all the conflicts that emerged in the first years of the modern movement . . . demonstrates that the personal is historical and exciting."
—Jonathan Ned Katz, author of *Gay American History*

MARTIN DUBERMAN, historian and playwright, is the author of fifteen books, including his highly acclaimed biography *Paul Robeson; Cures: A Gay Man's Odyssey*, (Plume); and (as co-editor) the Lambda Award–winning *Hidden from History* (Meridian). He is currently Distinguished Professor of History at Lehman College and the CUNY Graduate Center, and founder and director of the Center for Lesbian and Gay Studies at CUNY.

BOOKS BY MARTIN DUBERMAN

Cures: A Gay Man's Odyssey (1991)

Mother Earth: An Epic Drama of Emma Goldman's Life (1991)

Hidden from History: Reclaiming the Gay and Lesbian Past, co-editor (1989)

Paul Robeson (1989)

About Time: Exploring the Gay Past (first edition, 1986; second edition, 1991)

Visions of Kerouac (1977)

Male Armor: Selected Plays, 1968–1974 (1976)

Black Mountain: An Exploration in Community (first edition, 1972; second edition, 1993)

The Memory Bank (1970)

The Uncompleted Past (1969)

James Russell Lowell (1966)

The Antislavery Vanguard, editor (1965)

In White America (1964)

Charles Francis Adams, 1807–1886 (1963)

MARTIN DUBERMAN

STONEWALL

A PLUME BOOK

PLUME
Published by the Penguin Group
Penguin Books USA Inc., 375 Hudson Street,
New York, New York 10014, U.S.A.
Penguin Books Ltd, 27 Wrights Lane,
London W8 5TZ, England
Penguin Books Australia Ltd, Ringwood,
Victoria, Australia
Penguin Books Canada Ltd, 10 Alcorn Avenue,
Toronto, Ontario, Canada M4V 3B2
Penguin Books (N.Z.) Ltd, 182–190 Wairau Road,
Auckland 10, New Zealand

Penguin Books Ltd, Registered Offices:
Harmondsworth, Middlesex, England

Published by Plume, an imprint of Dutton Signet,
a division of Penguin Books USA Inc.
Previously published in a Dutton edition.

First Plume Printing, May, 1994
10 9 8 7 6 5 4 3 2 1

REGISTERED TRADEMARK—MARCA REGISTRADA

LIBRARY OF CONGRESS CATALOGING-IN-PUBLICATION DATA:
Duberman, Martin B.
Stonewall / Martin Duberman.
p.   cm.
Originally published: New York : Dutton, c1993.
Includes bibliographical references and index.
ISBN 0-452-27206-8
1. Stonewall Riot, New York, N.Y., 1969.   2. Gay liberation
movement—United States—History.   3. Gay men—United States—
History.   4. Lesbians—United States—History.   I. Title.
[HQ76.8.U5D85   1994]
305.9′0664′0973—dc20   93-45838
CIP

Printed in the United States of America
Original hardcover designed by Steven N. Stathakis

AGAIN AND ALWAYS—
    FOR ELI

Becoming human is becoming individual, and we become individual under the guidance of cultural patterns . . . which give form, order, point, and direction to our lives. . . . [But] we must . . . descend into detail, past the misleading tags, past the metaphysical types, past the empty similarities, to grasp firmly the essential character of not only the various cultures but the various sorts of individuals within each culture, if we wish to encounter humanity face to face.

—CLIFFORD GEERTZ
The Interpretation of Culture

CONTENTS

ACKNOWLEDGMENTS

My greatest debt is to the six people who trusted me to tell their stories and endured the multiple taping sessions needed to make that possible: Yvonne (Maua) Flowers, Jim Fouratt, Foster Gunnison, Jr., Karla Jay, Sylvia Ray Rivera, and Craig Rodwell. I sent the completed manuscript to all six to check for factual inaccuracies, and listened carefully to their occasional disagreement with this or that emphasis —but all understood that finally I could not surrender to them the authorial responsibility to interpret the evidence. Unless otherwise noted (which happens with some frequency), all the quotations in this book are from the transcripts of those taped interviews with my six subjects, together totaling several hundred hours; I'm alerting the reader here to the source of most of the quotations in order to avoid having to make repetitive citations throughout the book itself.

I have also been fortunate in being allowed to use several major archival collections still in private hands. In this regard, I am especially indebted to Foster Gunnison, Jr., and William B. Kelley. My ability to tell the story of the pre-Stonewall political movement in some detail has largely hinged on having access to those two extraordinary collections. In addition, the rich International Gay Information Center (IGIC) Papers—formerly known as the Hammond-Eves Collection— in the New York Public Library Manuscript Division has recently been processed and contains invaluable records and correspondence.

All of this material has proven to be so fresh and informative that

I have paused at certain points in the book to convey it. But not, I hope, paused too long; wherever I felt the documentary details threatened to overwhelm the narrative and convert the book into a traditional monograph, I have relegated them to the (sometimes lengthy) footnotes—which I have in turn relegated to the back of the book.

I am grateful to a number of people (other than the six subjects themselves) who allowed me to tape-record their recollections and thereby flesh out a number of critical points in the narrative: Martin Boyce, Nick Browne, Ryder Fitzgerald, Robert Heide, Robert Kohler, Sascha L., Thomas Lanigan-Schmidt, Chuck Shaheen, Jim Slaven, Gregory Terry, Joe Tish, and Ivan Valentin. I am also indebted to Steven Watson for providing me with tapes and transcripts of interviews he did in the late seventies with Marsha P. Johnson, Minette, Sylvia Ray Rivera, and Holly Woodlawn.

For assorted other favors, source materials, encouragement and leads, I'm grateful to Mariette Pathy Allen, Desmond Bishop, Mimi Bowling, Renée Cafiero, Barry Davidson, Richard Dworkin, Dan Evans, Barbara Gittings, Eric Gordon, Erica Gottfried, Liddell Jackson, Marty Jezer, Kay "Tobin" Lahusen, Tom McGovern, Joan Nestle, Duncan Osborne, Jim Owles, Gabriel Rotello, Vito Russo, Bebe Scarpi, Bree Scott-Hartland, La Vaughan Slaven, Mark Thompson, Jack Topchik, Jeffrey Van Dyke, Paul Varnell, Bruni Vega, Rich Wandel, Fred Wasserman, Thomas Waugh, and Randy Wicker. For the Stonewall chapter, I am indebted to Dolly and Leo Scherker for permission to consult materials that their son, Michael, had gathered for a planned oral history of the Stonewall riots that was tragically aborted by his premature death. I have included only a few brief remarks from Scherker's interviews (so cited in each instance in the accompanying footnote), but hearing in full his twenty or so tapes has broadly informed my own work.

Finally, my manuscript has greatly benefited from the careful readings Jolanta Benal, Matthew Carnicelli, John D'Emilio, Frances Goldin, Arnie Kantrowitz, William B. Kelley, and Eli Zal gave it; their cogent responses caused me to rethink any number of sections in the narrative. The pioneer activist Jim Kepner—whose encyclopedic knowledge of the gay movement is unrivaled—provided me with a detailed, incisive commentary that saved me from error and deepened my understanding at many points. I have also been extremely fortunate to have had Arnold Dolin of NAL/Dutton as the book's editor and Frances Goldin as its agent. Both have guided *Stonewall* through its various incarnations with the dedication and skill for which they are already well known.

Finally, to my partner, Eli Zal—to whom this book is dedicated—I owe the priceless gift of sustained, loving support.

PREFACE

"Stonewall" is *the* emblematic event in modern lesbian and gay history. The site of a series of riots in late June–early July 1969 that resulted from a police raid on a Greenwich Village gay bar, "Stonewall" has become synonymous over the years with gay resistance to oppression. Today, the word resonates with images of insurgency and self-realization and occupies a central place in the iconography of lesbian and gay awareness. The 1969 riots are now generally taken to mark the birth of the modern gay and lesbian political movement —that moment in time when gays and lesbians recognized all at once their mistreatment and their solidarity. As such, "Stonewall" has become an empowering symbol of global proportions.

Yet remarkably—since 1994 marks the twenty-fifth anniversary of the Stonewall riots—the actual story of the upheaval has never been told completely, or been well understood. We have, since 1969, been trading the same few tales about the riots from the same few accounts—trading them for so long that they have transmogrified into simplistic myth. The decades preceding Stonewall, moreover, continue to be regarded by most gays and lesbians as some vast neolithic wasteland—and this, despite the efforts of pioneering historians like Allan Bérubé, John D'Emilio and Lillian Faderman to fill in the landscape of those years with vivid, politically astute personalities.

The time is overdue for grounding the symbolic Stonewall in empirical reality and placing the events of 1969 in historical context. In attempting to do this, I felt it was important *not* to homogenize experience to the point where individual voices are lost sight of. My intention was to embrace precisely what most contemporary historians have discarded: the ancient, essential enterprise of *telling human stories*. Too often, in my view, professional historians have yielded to a "sociologizing" tendency that reduces three-dimensional lives to statistical cardboard—and then further distances the reader with a specialized jargon that *claims* to provide greater cognitive precision but serves more often to seal off and silence familiar human sounds.

I have therefore adopted an unconventional narrative strategy in the opening sections of this book: the recreation of half a dozen lives with a particularity that conforms to no interpretative category but only to their own idiosyncratic rhythms. To focus on particular stories does not foreclose speculation about patterns of behavior but does, I believe, help to ensure that the speculation will reflect the actual disparities of individual experience. My belief in the irreducible specialness of each life combines with a paradoxical belief in the possibility that lives, however special, can be shared. It is, if you like, a belief in democracy: the importance of the individual, the commonality of life.

For the six portraits in the book, I have deliberately chosen people whose stories were in themselves absorbing odysseys, and yet could at the same time speak to other gay men and lesbians. Jim Fouratt's struggles to remain within the Catholic Church, for example, or to gain entrance into the world of the New York theater, do not *duplicate* anyone else's religious or artistic experiences, yet should prove sufficiently similar to illustrate them broadly. Yvonne Flowers's ambivalence, as a black woman, about white lesbian bars, is not *precisely* anyone else's reaction to the bar scene, yet will be familiar enough to many to call out comparable feelings in them.

The six people I ultimately decided to profile seemed to "fit" well together. Their stories were different enough to suggest the diversity of gay and lesbian lives, yet interconnected enough to allow me to interweave their stories when, in the second half of the book, the historical canvas broadens out into the Stonewall riots, gay politics, and the first Christopher Street Liberation Day March.

This is not to say that these six lives represent all possible variations on gay and lesbian experience in the Stonewall period. To only *begin* to enumerate the many absent possibilities, these stories say nothing about rural or village, Chicano- or Italian- or Asian-American gay lives—nor anything about what it was or is like to be a gay postman, a lesbian pharmacist, a bisexual pop star. No group of six

could possibly represent the many pathways of gay and lesbian existence. But they can suggest some of the significant childhood experiences, adult coping strategies, social and political activities, values,
perceptions and concerns that centrally characterized the Stonewall
generation.

If the first sections of this book, with their focus on individual
lives, are designed to make past experience more directly accessible
than is common in a work of history, they are decidedly not designed
as "popularized" history—by which is usually meant the slighting of
historical research or the compromising of historical accuracy. My
emphasis on personality might legitimately be called novelistic but,
in contrast to the novelist, I have tried to restrict invention and remain
faithful to known historical fact. As in my previous books, I have
searched diligently for previously unknown or unused primary source
materials (and have been lucky enough to have found them in abundance), and have scrupulously adhered to scholarly criteria for eval-
uating evidence. Just as dull, abstract prose is no guarantee of
reliability, so lively human representation is no indicator of slovenly
scholarship.

My hope is that the focus on individuals and on narrative will
increase the ability of readers to identify—some with one story, some
with another—with experiences different from, but comparable to,
their own. I know of no other way to make the past *really* speak to
the present. And gay men and lesbians—so long denied any history
—have a special need and claim on historical writing that is at once
accurate *and* accessible.

MARTIN DUBERMAN
October 1992

THE CAST

CRAIG RODWELL: Raised in a Chicago school for troubled boys, he arrived in New York as a teenager, emerged as a radical figure in the Mattachine Society, opened the Oscar Wilde Memorial Bookstore and spearheaded the first Christopher Street Liberation Day March.

YVONNE FLOWERS: The only African-American child attending an all-white grade school in New Rochelle in 1942, she grew up to become a jazz fanatic, a devotee of nightlife, an occupational therapist and teacher, and one of the founders of Salsa Soul Sisters.

KARLA JAY: Born in Flatbush and a graduate of Barnard, she joined the feminist collective the Redstockings, as well as the Gay Liberation Front, subsequently completed a doctorate in comparative literature, authored a number of books and earned a full professorship.

SYLVIA (RAY) RIVERA: Hustling on Times Square at age 11, she became a street transvestite, a fixture in the Times Square area, a fearless defender of her sisters, and the founder of STAR—Street Transvestite Action Revolutionaries.

JIM FOURATT: Brought up in Rhode Island, a teenager of precocious intelligence, he joined and left the priesthood, became a New York actor, hipster, antiwar protestor, and a major spokesperson for the countercultural Yippie movement.

FOSTER GUNNISON, JR.: The privileged scion of a wealthy yet emotionally distant family, he forsook business and academic careers, plunged into the pre-Stonewall homophile movement, became its archivist, and helped plan the first Christopher Street Liberation Day March.

PART
ONE

GROWING UP

CRAIG

Marion Rodwell had been reluctantly boarding out her young son, Craig, during the week. Divorced and working in Chicago as a low-paid secretary, Marion hadn't known what else to do; she couldn't afford to stay home and she didn't have enough money to hire a competent baby-sitter. For several years, Craig lived during the week—Marion reclaiming him on weekends—with Mrs. Ryberg, a kindly woman who took in a number of neighborhood children. As soon as he was old enough, Mrs. Ryberg gave him chores to do, including the job of kneading yellow coloring into the margarine to make it look more like butter (this was wartime, with butter unavailable). Craig liked Mrs. Ryberg so much that he hadn't minded the work, though it was strenuous and he was little more than a toddler.

But when Craig was five, Marion decided he should be in a more stimulating environment, and she turned to an inexpensive day-care center on Chicago's North Side. But it quickly became apparent that the low rates reflected the minimal individual attention given. Marion felt at her wit's end when a Mrs. Merkle, who sometimes worked at the day care center and had taken a shine to Craig, told her that she would board the boy full-time if Marion would pay her a small sum each week. Marion agreed, hoping Mrs. Merkle would be able to give Craig the daily affection and attention he needed.

Attention he got, but very little affection. Mrs. Merkle also took in laundry to piece out an income, and she put Craig to work running sheets and towels through a mangle, watching hawk-eyed to make sure the five-year-old didn't slack off. Craig worked in constant terror of getting his fingers caught in the mangle, and he soon grew to hate Mrs. Merkle. But she found the arrangement profitable and began to play with the idea of adopting Craig as her own son (or indentured servant). Word of Mrs. Merkle's intention reached Marion and threw her into a panic. Mrs. Merkle had a husband, and Marion feared the courts might equate that with "having a stable home." Desperate, she confided in her boss. A devout Christian Scientist, he had connections with the church-affiliated Chicago Junior School for "problem" boys, and before long he had arranged for Craig to be admitted there free of charge.

Craig never forgot that fall day in 1947 when his mother drove him out to Chicago Junior. At age six, he didn't entirely understand what was happening to him, but his fright was palpable. The school was located some fifty miles outside of Chicago, set deep in the country between the towns of Dundee and Elgin. A complex of old, marginally maintained buildings, Chicago Junior was surrounded by woods and sealed off by a chain-link fence. Before leaving Craig off, Marion did her best to comfort him, assuring her son that with some forty other boys as playmates, he would be happy at the school. She promised that she would unfailingly come to see him on the third Sunday of every month, the only day visitors were allowed on the grounds.

But Craig had not been reassured. During his first month at the school, he cried himself to sleep every night. And every morning at breakfast, he threw up the unfamiliar hot cereal. A housemother cured him of the crying by sternly lecturing him about how unhappy his mother would be should she learn of his "bad" behavior. Another housemother cured him of the vomiting by picking him up by the neck from the breakfast table, marching him into the bathroom and forcing him to stand over the toilet and *eat* the vomit.

The housemothers came in two basic varieties: the stern ones who mechanically kept to the rules (and kept the boys at arms' length), and the warm surrogate mothers. Mrs. Wilkins, the music teacher, who doubled as a substitute housemother, quickly became Craig's favorite. The students lived in three dormitories, twelve to fifteen boys in each, and a housemother slept in a small room adjoining each dorm. Whenever Mrs. Wilkins was in charge, she let the boys do pretty much as they liked—make noise, and stay up past their bedtime—and usually refrained from checking up on them in the middle of the night.

She would also read them stories. Craig had two favorites. One was about a pair of boys who wanted to be brothers so badly, they pricked each other's fingers and formed a "blood bond." The other was "The Happy Prince." As Craig retells that story, it took place in a poor middle-European city that had a richly jeweled statue of Prince Somebody or Other in its main square. One day, a pigeon sitting on the Prince's shoulder noticed that a tear had formed in his eye. When the bird asked the Prince why he was unhappy, the Prince explained that the people in the city were starving because of poor crops, and he urged the pigeon to take the emerald embedded in his eye and sell it to buy the people food.

On and on the story went: The Prince would cry, would encourage the pigeon to sell the diamonds on his sword handle, the rubies on his breastplate—and so on—to provide coal for the people's stoves, warm clothing to put on their backs—and so on. At the story's close, all the jewels are gone, but the Prince is happy in the knowledge that the people no longer suffer. Craig adored the story and contended in later years that it had taught him important lessons about the need to share worldly goods with those less fortunate. (He also learned in later years that the story was written by Oscar Wilde.)

There were only two men on staff at the Chicago Junior School. One was Mr. Lazarus, who had himself been a student there and who in summer months would take some of the boys out for a midnight swim in the ancient concrete pool on the grounds and then astonish them by diving underwater, pulling off his bathing suit, and letting his ass shine naked in the moonlight. No one, so far as Craig knew, was ever invited to touch it.

The only other man at the school was its superintendent, the hated Mr. Kilburn. He enjoyed pitting the boys against each other in competition for his favor and each night would award the most "deserving" student the supreme honor of carrying a huge dinner tray to him and his wife in their apartment on the top of the classroom building; the bearer's reward was a Baby Ruth candy bar. Craig never once got to carry the tray. For after getting over his initial fright and settling into the school's routines, he had quickly become something of a rebel—the boy who challenged authority and "sassed" back.

That would alone have earned Kilburn's dislike. What intensified it was his conviction that Craig was a sissy. Two hours of sports were mandated at Chicago Junior for every student every day of the year. Craig, as the tallest boy in his group, was good at basketball, but inept in baseball—scandalously so, in Kilburn's view. Deciding he would teach Craig how to throw the baseball "like a real boy," Kilburn made him trudge a mile to the baseball field after dinner each night to get the appropriate coaching.

What convinced Kilburn that Craig's prospects in life were dim was his discovery that Craig had been sending away for autographed pictures of movie stars, had managed to collect several dozen, and—scandalously, again—had been sharing them with the other boys. Kilburn promptly confiscated the collection and thereafter opened all of Craig's incoming mail to make sure it contained no offending material. To underscore the horrendous nature of Craig's crime, Kilburn meted out his favorite punishment: Craig was given "one hundred burdock"—that is, assigned to dig up a hundred of the burdock plants that dotted the grounds; the burdock had long, deep roots, and to kill it one had to laboriously dig out every last piece.

This was but one of several Dickensian features of the school. Corporal punishment, including paddling, was commonplace; one teacher's favorite method was to beat offending students with an electric cord. The boys themselves did almost all the work on the place, keeping up the grounds, helping in the kitchen, serving the food. They marched in formation to meals in the dining hall, had to sit on the front part of their chairs to keep their backs stiff, and during breakfast were forbidden to speak. Strictly enforced prayer sessions began with Bible study at five A.M. and were reinforced periodically throughout the day, even during football huddles. When Craig didn't understand something in the Bible, or in the writings of Mary Baker Eddy, which the boys were also made to study, he would raise his hand and say so. Most of the teachers treated this as a form of defiance. They sternly warned Craig that he was being "difficult," and his reputation as a rebellious child spread.

The draconian spirit at Chicago Junior produced a variety of bans. No incoming phone calls were permitted; the one phone on the place was locked up in the laundry room. Entertainment consisted of an occasional bonfire in fall and an occasional swim in summer, plus carefully monitored television once a week (the boys were allowed to watch only *I Remember Mama* and Sid Caesar's *Your Show of Shows*, and the set was turned off during commercials for fear the cigarette and beer ads might prove too appealing). And any boy being punished for any reason was automatically denied his monthly visiting day—which meant Craig sometimes didn't get to see Marion for months at a time.

Among the boys' few diversions were occasional square dances, which they would perform for the Evanston Women's Club and other local groups as a fund-raising device. Half the boys would dress in regular clothes, and the other half would don little skirts and halters, which the housemothers had sewn for them. As a reward for the performance, each boy would be given a stocking filled with candy, fruit, and pennies.

There was also a Halloween party every year in the gym. The housemothers would again make costumes for the boys; one year Craig went as a fat lady, with a pillow stuck under his dress and lipstick smeared on his face. (When the boys lined up to have Craig give them kiss marks on the cheek, Mr. Kilburn ordered a halt.) The thirteen-year-old seniors were taken into the town of Elgin once a month to learn the fox-trot and the waltz—though the boys viewed this as punishment, not entertainment.

Despite these rigors, Craig was happier than not during his seven years at the Chicago Junior School and retains "wonderful, vivid memories" of the place. They center, not surprisingly, on the intensely emotional, sometimes erotic friendships that developed among the boys themselves.

Craig's first crush, when he was seven, was on an older boy (aged eight) named Bob Palmer. Bob's talented piano playing made him something of a school star and Craig "just worshiped" him. Epiphany came on a cold winter night. In the freezing, drafty dorms each boy kept an extra blanket at the foot of his bed, and Craig awoke one morning to discover that his blanket had been pulled up over him. He "just knew" Bob Palmer had done it, had gotten up in the middle of the night to make sure his little friend was warm.

Craig was the first boy in his age group to reach puberty, and in the showers the others never tired of staring in amazement at his emerging pubic hair. Harry, a slightly older boy, moved matters to the next logical stage. He took Craig out to one of the gigantic oak trees in the woods that the boys (disobeying the rules) loved to climb, and when they were standing at the top of the tree, he unzipped Craig's pants and said he was going to show him something. Craig immediately got a roaring hard-on and Harry masturbated him. To Craig's astonishment, "white stuff" flew out of his penis, great gobs of it covering his jeans—followed by panic over how to explain the stains to his housemother. Craig and Harry finally concocted a tale about "finding a can of white paint while playing in the woods."

Not all the boys were as winning as Harry. Chicago Junior, was, after all, a school for "disturbed" youth, and a few of the boys really did have problems beyond being overweight or having rejecting parents. When Ted invited Craig for a romp in the woods, the scenario moved quickly beyond white paint: Ted wanted to stick a pin up the opening in Craig's penis. Craig had the good sense to jump up and run. Ted tried to give chase, but he was a large, clumsy boy and Craig easily outdistanced him. Eventually Ted was sent to St. Charles, the nearby state reformatory. "We're going to send you to St. Charles" was a standard threat at Chicago Junior, though one infrequently carried out.

Most of the sex play among the boys involved kissing and masturbation, though "cornholing" was known to happen, and oral sex was frequent enough for rumors of it to reach Mr. Kilburn. He at once convened an assembly—always a weighty event at the school— to express his indignation over rumors that boys were "inserting their penises into other boys' mouths." He demanded that each boy submit a statement to him, declaring whether he had or had not ever committed that mortal sin.

Craig had deeply internalized the Christian Science notion that "truth is power and that truth is the greatest good," and he forthrightly declared in his statement that he had indeed engaged in the forbidden behavior. Worse, his tone was not defensive and he made no apology. Yet to his surprise, Kilburn did not punish him, even though some of the boys who confessed *were* put to pulling burdock or breaking up rocks. Craig supposes that Kilburn had already written him off as hopeless—after all, he had been the only person in the school to favor Stevenson over Eisenhower in the 1952 election—and was probably afraid Craig would make even more trouble if punished. The episode confirmed Craig's belief—which was to be central in his life—that "telling the truth" was in the end always the best policy.

The boys, of course, went right on having sex with each other. Not everybody participated, but none of them looked askance at the activity. Intense friendships and frequent touching were so integral to the special environment they inhabited as to seem utterly natural; even the nonsexual boys would walk back and forth to the dining hall unself-consciously holding hands. Occasionally a housemother would tell them they "shouldn't" do that, which made Craig aware for the first time that some people regarded his feelings as wrong—infuriating him, even at that early age.

The boys generally ignored "spinsterish" injunctions, and as soon as the lights under the housemother's door went out at night, they would jump into each other's beds. According to Craig, there was "no sense of shame about it and we always knew and talked about who was going with whom." Craig had sex with nearly half the boys in his own class of ten; several of them, in later years, did self-identify as gay.

In seventh grade, when he was eleven, Craig got himself a "steady." He and Tony were passionately in love, but only incidentally sexual—kisses, massages, and hand-holding were about the sum of it. But they spent as much time together as possible; if Craig had dishwashing duty after dinner, Tony would wait for him outside the hall so they could walk back to their dorm together.

One day, daringly, the two boys decided to play hooky. Both were avid baseball fans—Craig adored the Chicago Cubs, Tony the Milwaukee Braves. When they learned that the Cubs and Braves were due to play a doubleheader against each other at Chicago's Wrigley Field, they decided they *had* to go, and Tony somehow got hold of enough money to buy them train tickets to Chicago. They planned to stay for only the first game so that they could get back to the school before dark and not be missed. But once the excitement got hold of them in Wrigley Field, they forgot about their resolution and stayed till the doubleheader was over. That meant catching a late train that stopped a full three miles from the school. They walked the distance in the dark along the scary railroad tracks and, to keep up their courage and to avoid falling between the trestles, held hands the whole way.

When they arrived at the dorm at eleven that night, Mr. Kilburn was waiting for them, "just livid." The boys tried to prove how responsible they'd been by telling Kilburn they had carefully held hands during the entire three-mile walk. Mrs. Kilburn, who was present for the interrogation, said something snide about "faggots," and Craig and Tony were not only punished but split up into different dorms. That might have been bearable, except that Tony, soon after, abruptly stopped speaking to Craig and acted as if he no longer existed. Tony never did explain why, but Craig surmised it had something to do with having been frightened by the accusation of "faggot." The rejection deeply upset—and puzzled—Craig for many years thereafter.

YVONNE

Yvonne's mother set her jaw, and the family knew that one more immovable decision had been reached: the youngest of two daughters, Yvonne (generally called "Chickie") would *not* go to the segregated Lincoln Elementary School, but rather to the all-white Daniel Webster Grammar School. In 1942, blacks were not expected, not in New Rochelle, New York, any more than in the South, to make militant demands. But Theo Flowers had never let herself be guided by timid counsels. She had joined the Communist party nearly a decade earlier, impressed by the role it had played in defending the Scottsboro Boys—those nine hapless black youths falsely accused of raping two white women in 1931—and convinced that no other political group gave a damn about black people. She was far too independent ever to become a dutiful party functionary, yet she was never shy about acknowledging her political sympathies. When New Rochelle passed an ordinance requiring Communists to register, Theo, not about to deny her affiliation, marched down to the town hall and registered.

So when Theo said no to the segregated Lincoln School, her ten-year-old daughter, Yvonne, though "a nervous wreck" at the likely amount of high-volume public anger that lay ahead, felt certain that the New Rochelle authorities had already lost the battle. After all, her very birth had been successfully contested; because Theo had refused to deliver in a hospital that practiced overt discrimination, Yvonne had been born in the nearby Mount Vernon Hospital rather than in New Rochelle.

The school board tried to thwart Theo by redrawing district lines so that the street on which the Flowers family lived would fall outside the Daniel Webster School zone. But Theo brought formal charges of gerrymandering and won her case in court. And so, just as Yvonne had anxiously predicted, she took her place in the fifth grade class at Daniel Webster in the fall of 1942. (Nearly twenty years later, in 1961, the New Rochelle school system became the site of the North's first court-ordered desegregation, at which time a Federal judge ordered the closing of Lincoln Elementary, with its 94 percent black student population. That order was resisted for two more years, but in 1963 a new school board ordered Lincoln razed and its students bused elsewhere.)

Yvonne was the only black child attending Daniel Webster in 1942, but she already knew many of her classmates from the neighborhood and never felt harassed or even isolated while at Webster. Yet despite her friends and her obvious intelligence, Yvonne never became an A student. Later in life she would recall the teacher who told her that she was "a C student and would always be so," and that she should never think of anything so out of her league as a college education. "On some level, I believed her," Yvonne says, and describes herself as an "underachiever" throughout her life.

Yet she ascribes that, overall, less to racism than to the intimidating effect of growing up with a high-powered mother she felt unable to measure up to. For Theo Flowers not only was politically aware, but also spoke five languages, read voraciously, had had a promising concert career as a singer of German lieder (a bout with tuberculosis forced her to give up singing), and was something of a local "griot" —a wise woman—consulted for political advice and courted for support throughout the city of New Rochelle.

Many of the black people in town were related, being descended from two large families that had settled there generations ago. And in the thirties and forties, a village atmosphere still prevailed. The goat man and his herd came down Yvonne's block twice a week, and the vegetable sellers and fish peddlers even more frequently. Almost all the blacks in New Rochelle knew one another, so when Theo went to the store on Saturday morning, the family knew not to expect her back until late in the day; everybody had to talk to her about something, and a cup of coffee or a drink could go on for hours.

Theo also loved to party. Indeed, it wasn't illness alone that had ended her singing career, but also an unwillingness to make the necessary sacrifices or endure the needed discipline. She had been attracted to her first husband, Yvonne's father, in part because, as a boxer (his brother was Bruce Flowers, a well-known fighter in the twenties and thirties), he lived a fast-lane life—so fast-lane that he died of alcoholism when Yvonne was four.

Theo's second husband, with whom Yvonne grew up, managed bars and always had a bottle of scotch nearby. He was an easygoing man, a life-of-the-party type who knew how to keep everybody laughing. He did sympathize with Theo's political views, and especially her blunt pro-black stance, and at dinner the family conversation often revolved around what President Roosevelt had said that day and what the impact was likely to be on black people. But he lacked Theo's dynamism and felt awed, sometimes overwhelmed, by her energy. Theo was unquestionably the dominant figure in the house and her husband knew better than to try to curtail her. When her love of gambling sometimes kept her out at the neighbors all night playing poker (or "pokino," the local favorite), he might pace the floor and fret—but he refrained from walking the two blocks to tell her to come home.

Theo's own parents were scandalized at their daughter's independent views on religion. They had both come from devout homes in the border states, and together ran a restaurant in Yonkers. (Cooking had long been a family specialty: Yvonne's great-grandfather and great-granduncle had been cooks in the U.S. Navy at the turn of the century.) Theo's mother was an ardent Catholic who practiced African spiritualism on the side, and her father was a devout Baptist. They had compromised by bringing Theo up Episcopalian, but could never compromise over her secularist bent as an adult; they refused to accept the Sunday morning habit in the Flowers home of listening to the famed Wings Over Jordan Choir on the radio as a legitimate equivalent for going to church.

At their insistence, Theo agreed to send Yvonne to Sunday school, but her own secularism rubbed off on the child. When it came time, at age twelve, for her baptism, Yvonne—who had also inherited her mother's independent spirit—refused to go through with it because she "didn't believe." But unlike Theo, confirmed in her secularism by her radical-minded friends, Yvonne felt deeply troubled at her lack of belief and the way it isolated her from her dutifully baptized peers. She talked with her minister, who showed annoyance at her stubborn insistence on *understanding* the Creation and at her confessed discomfort at going on her knees to Jesus, a white man. It wasn't until her mid-twenties that Yvonne would finally find the compatible God she had long sought.

She was equally stubborn about her sexuality. Entering high school in 1946 at age fourteen, she quickly acquired a steady boyfriend. They loved each other and stayed together throughout the four years of high school, but when Yvonne was fifteen and he sixteen and they attempted to have sex, she said he was "too big" and the act went unconsummated. Since he was also her best friend, she confided to him that she had felt erotically attracted to other girls from an early age—could remember standing in front of a mirror at age six or seven and defiantly shouting that "when I get grown, I am going to have all the girlfriends I want to have."

She didn't have to wait that long. While still in her early teens, she started to "mess around" with a friend of her mother's, a beautiful woman who looked like Lena Horne. Though Theo had a number of gay friends in her sophisticated circle, and though Yvonne had always felt able to confide in her mother, she kept the affair a secret. Yet in a more general way, she did try to tell her family about her attraction to women. Indeed, she was no more than twelve or thirteen when she abruptly announced it one night at the dinner table.

Her family's reaction was the equivalent of "pass me the peas" —as if she hadn't said anything at all. She next tried putting the news in a letter, which she read aloud at the dinner table. Again, nobody said a word, as if they hadn't heard her. It was only years later, after Yvonne had left home, that she and her mother finally talked openly about her sexuality. Theo accepted her daughter's insistence that she was lesbian once she understood that it wasn't going to keep her from getting an education or having a career, wasn't going to stop her from having "plans and dreams." In Yvonne's view, much of the homophobia that exists in the black community is a function of middle-class aspirations, and the taking on of the narrow values of that class. Theo had a radical's disdain for mere assimilation and scorned white bourgeois provincialism. Her politics of inclusion made it necessary for her to accept and applaud differences of all kinds—though in regard to her own daughter's lesbianism, the best she could manage was tolerance.

Yvonne was no less precocious in her early obsession with jazz. She had grown up around music, but by age twelve had (abetted by Frank, a clerk in the New Rochelle record store who shared her zeal and fed it with weekly releases) developed her own special taste for bebop—for Dizzy Gillespie, Charlie Parker, Tadd Dameron and, above all, for Thelonious Monk. She tortured her family by playing her 78s over and over at top volume, until everyone knew every line on every Thelonious Monk record. By the time Yvonne was fifteen she had become so immersed in bebop and progressive jazz that she researched and wrote a ten-page "history of jazz." It was for her own edification, not to fulfill a school assignment.

It was also at fifteen that she persuaded "Aunt" Janet, one of her mother's hell-raising friends, to take her to the New York City jazz clubs—the Royal Roost, Birdland, and the other hangouts that dotted

Fifty-second Street, then the jazz mecca of the world. Yvonne had had her first drink at twelve, and had quickly taken to it, but she never viewed the jazz clubs as places to party. She was one of those dead-serious fans who listen to music with such intensity that they become nearly oblivious to the drinking and seduction scenes taking place on the periphery. Nobody dared mess with her; she was there to *listen*. Later, when her particular favorite, Thelonious Monk, played at the Five Spot for two years, Yvonne became a fixture at the club. One night she went straight up to Monk and told him he was the only man she would ever marry. He gave her a silly, spaced-out smile.

KARLA

Karla's parents told her that Jews were "the Chosen People" and the *goyim* were not to be trusted ("the minute something goes wrong, they'll turn around and call you a kike"). Such cultural assumptions aside, Abraham and Rhoda Jay saw themselves as, if anything, *anti-religious*. Abraham's grandfather, a tyrannical, ultra-orthodox rabbi, used to drag his grandson out of bed at four o'clock in the morning to help make a *minyan*. It turned Abraham off religion for the rest of his life, and Karla never remembers setting foot in a synagogue (the one time Abraham took his children to temple to experience a *seder*, the presiding Reform rabbi—to Abraham's chagrin—skipped the service). Karla knew she was Jewish, but had no real idea what that meant—"except that other kids had Christmas trees and we didn't."

When his two children were born, Abraham was so determined to avoid giving them traditional Old Testament names—indeed, he disliked his own name, preferring to be called Eddie—that he simply looked at the shipping schedule in the newspaper and chose from the list of ships arriving or departing. Fortunately for his daughter, a Danish freighter, the *Karla Dane*, was docking on the day she was born, so she was spared being called Lusitania for the rest of her life—or, God forbid, Queen Mary.

Abraham's mother, Becky, was the only grandparent Karla got to know at all well. Becky had come to the United States with her parents in the late nineteenth century to escape the pogroms in Russia. On their way across the Atlantic, their boat had sunk and they had

had to spend several days in a rowboat. The experience left Becky frightened of water for the rest of her life—and caused her to forget where precisely in Russia she had come from. Or so she claimed. For whatever reasons of her own, she refused to talk about the old country. She spent her life raising children and cooking food in the back of the saloon her husband owned.

Not that Karla ever learned much more about her mother's family. "It was like a wall of silence," Karla later said; "my parents never spoke about the past. They were very closemouthed." The sum of what she was told about her maternal grandmother was that she had been born in the United States; and about her grandfather, that he had been born in Austria and had run a fruit stand in Brooklyn before retiring.

And it was only as an adult that Karla discovered that her own exceedingly beautiful mother had had, as a teenager, a first marriage. Rhoda had fallen deeply in love with a fellow student at Erasmus Hall High School in Brooklyn; though told he had a "rheumatic heart" and only a short time to live, she had insisted on marrying him. In a desperate effort to save her young husband, Rhoda took him to Florida, where he soon died. To compound the tragedy, his family blamed her for his premature death.

For the rest of her life, Rhoda would be a deeply unhappy woman: frequently ill and barricaded in her room; known as quarrelsome and difficult. She waited until she was thirty to remarry and then chose Abraham, whom she did not love, because it seemed as if he would be a good provider. Abraham, at five feet two and nearly two hundred pounds ("He had been brought up on sour cream," Karla later quipped), wasn't physically attractive and, though forty, had never married. But he was a bright, jovial, good-tempered man, if inclined to be stubborn. (Stubbornness, Karla says, "is almost like a disease in my father's family.") Abraham was apparently in love with Rhoda but later, perhaps to cover his pain at the unhappy union, would joke that he had married her because she was thin and he had wanted to give his kids a fighting chance.

Abraham was a hard worker. He had dropped out of school at age twelve to help out in his father's saloon, had thereafter been a truck driver, and had then—at the time Rhoda met him—gone to work at his uncle's dunnage company on the docks. In those years, dunnage firms handled the bins and containers in which all overseas freight was shipped; Abraham's job was to count and haul lumber.

It was backbreaking work, and life on the docks could be dangerous —he was shot at least once—but his salary was enough to support his mother and two sisters.

He and Rhoda were married in 1942. Their son, Paul (Karla thinks maybe her father was reading a list of Christian saints on the day he chose her brother's name), was born in 1943. Karla was born four years later—during a blizzard that trapped her father and brother in a Long Island railroad car for twelve hours while her mother was in labor in a hospital (an ordeal that they all frequently reminded Karla of in later life). Neither parents nor siblings got along well. Karla insists that throughout their childhood her brother had precisely three expressions: "Shut up," "Drop dead," and "Get out of my room."

Abraham and Rhoda were more talkative—or rather, argumentative—with each other, but not much more friendly. They dealt with each other primarily through evasion (a childhood friend of Karla's reports that all she can remember of Rhoda is a closed door). With Rhoda taking to her bed for long stretches and Abraham working seven days a week on the docks (though he was decidedly interested in his children when he *was* present), Karla might well have suffered severe emotional deprivation had it not been for the timely appearance of Nene.

Nene (a nickname her brothers and sisters had settled on when they couldn't pronounce "Lulubelle") was a black woman in her late twenties hired by the Jays as a live-in maid when Karla was four. Nene was married, but her husband was older, liked to drink, and could be abusive, so Nene (who had no children of her own) welcomed the live-in job. When she arrived, Karla was still sleeping in a crib, and she had a lot of trouble adjusting to the bed that Nene now insisted on. But Karla had no trouble at all getting used to Nene herself. She was a warm-hearted, loving human being of immense goodwill, with a wonderful sense of humor, a great smile, and a happy laugh. Nene, unlike Rhoda, was never depressed—indeed, she was the only person who could get along with Rhoda, which she accomplished by simply shrugging at her angry outbursts. Small and slim, Nene was agile and energetic, but always slowed her quick pace so that young Karla could keep up without effort. Nene became, in essence, Karla's primary parent.

Nene's passion was baseball. At every possible opportunity, she would take Karla to Ebbets Field to watch the Dodgers play (Paul rarely came along; he was a sickly child, afflicted with asthma). The first thing Karla remembers reading is baseball scorecards, which she

and Nene (who couldn't read well) would pore over. Karla loved
Ebbets Field more for the peanuts than for the baseball, but she was
a good-natured, uncomplaining child who felt absolutely content as
long as she could be with Nene. "It never occurred to me as a small
child," Karla would later say, "that I was not going to grow up black
like Nene. It never occurred to me that we were different. I did get
some strange looks, though, after I started elementary school. I
sounded like the only black kid in an all-white school."

Karla was also lucky in having a wonderful aunt (by marriage)
living two houses away from the Jays in Flatbush. Aunt Betty, nick-
named Queenie, had been a vaudeville singer, had married several
times, cursed like a truck driver, told dirty jokes, had a raucous sense
of humor, and sang at all the family gatherings—usually accompanied
by her dachshund, Judy. Queenie had no patience with the notion of
a woman learning her proper, antiseptically limited, place. Not only
did she drive a car—which was then highly unorthodox for a
woman—but she played touch football with the boys in the street,
and thought nothing of jumping in to rescue Paul when, as happened
often, he fell prey to the other kids in the neighborhood. Betty was,
like Nene, a rescuer by nature—and Paul and Karla needed all the
help they could get.

If Karla took her optimistic good nature from Nene, she showed,
like Queenie, an early impatience with traditional female roles. As
far back as she can remember, Karla was called a tomboy. Queenie
told her that she had been a tomboy, too, and to pay the label no
mind. But everybody else kept nervously reassuring Karla that she
would "outgrow it." Many years would pass before she would be able
to define fully what "it" was, but what Karla knew early on was that
she would rather be playing punchball with the boys in the street
than jumping rope or playing house with the little girls.

Karla's mother was decidedly disappointed in her. Though ill
and withdrawn during much of Karla's childhood, Rhoda would rouse
herself to clean the house (obsessively, over and over: "Jewish
women," Queenie would sardonically say, "cleaned as a substitute for
sex"); to prepare an occasional gourmet meal (Nene usually did the
cooking); to play an occasional game of canasta; and, above all, to
shop. Rhoda liked dressing well almost as much as she liked a good
bargain, and with a true shopper's fanaticism would return over and
over again to Loehmann's famed bargain store to watch hawk-eyed
until the price fell to the lowest possible level. She later admitted that
she spent money to get back at her husband, whose earnings had

begun to slip. Along with buying herself clothes, Rhoda would periodically bring home pretty little Ginny or Barbie dolls for Karla, and a proper doll carriage to carry them around in.

Karla wouldn't go near the dolls. But nothing could discourage Rhoda from continually adding to the collection, not even the insistent way Karla would unceremoniously dump the dolls from the carriage and install her beloved, battered teddy bear in their stead. Her best (and lifelong) friend, Jessica, on the other hand, adored the dolls and good-natured, generous Karla let her play with them to her heart's content. That annoyed Rhoda still more. "She simply couldn't see from behind her own eyes," Karla later said. "She saw this child she wanted to have. This child was not me."

If Karla's tomboyishness alienated her mother, it did not isolate Karla in the neighborhood; the role, she later recalled, "wasn't all that unacceptable"—in Flatbush, anyway. Her cheerful nature helped make her popular. Though she was given to playing practical jokes and pranks, there was nothing malicious or mean-spirited about her. She would never hurt anyone intentionally, and she disliked physical fights; but if she never started one, Karla, who was strong and knew it, usually finished it. Her Flatbush neighborhood was essentially middle-class Irish, Italian, and Jewish, but it grew rougher as she grew older, and by the time she was ten she had joined one of the proliferating gangs as its sole female member. They used an abandoned shed behind a bakery as a clubhouse, and periodically fought other gangs in the neighborhood—but nobody then had guns, and serious injury was rare.

Though Karla preferred to run rather than fight, she did get into a fair number of brawls. She was once attacked by a group of girls and burned with cigarettes, and another time a girl ripped open the back of her leg with a compass. When one of the neighborhood boys hit her in the face, Karla smacked him back—and broke his jaw. When another little boy came after her, she got him in a leg lock and cracked several of his ribs. Her disposition was friendly, but from an early age, Karla proved a tough, stoic little kid, a determined survivor.

Karla's athletic ability also contributed to her acceptance, especially since her skill was marred by clumsiness. She was good enough at running and at punchball to join the boys in the street, yet a puzzling lack of depth perception made her terrible at touch football and stickball; all this made her an accomplished, likeable klutz rather than an awesome superwoman. She fell down so often and got so many scratches and cuts that her father at one point started good-naturedly calling her Stitch.

Most of her awkwardness was due to extreme nearsightedness that for a long time went undiagnosed; if she bumped into a wall, her parents simply ascribed it to her being "the worst clod who ever walked the earth." When she started public school in Brooklyn, she was given an eye test, but when the technician pointed to the chart and Karla said she couldn't see anything, it was thought that she was "clowning around again." That, combined with poor reading skills, got her put in a class for slow learners—a nightmare experience which lasted some four years and from which she barely escaped in time to make up for lost skills.

Her class of mostly delinquent, emotionally disturbed children (as adults, a number of them ended up in Dannemora prison) was considered unteachable. At the beginning of every day, the reluctant teacher assigned to them would put lists on the blackboard which the children were told to memorize; in one column were the characteristics of a "good citizen," such as cleanliness; in the other were those of a "bad citizen," with special emphasis on "communism."

The children were thought too stupid to learn their own names, so each was assigned a number. Karla's was 36. She became so used to responding to it that at home Nene could sometimes get her attention only by calling out "Thirty-six!" When it finally was discovered that Karla's vision was 12,000/300, and she won a transfer to a regular class, she found herself way behind the other kids. But once she did begin to read—as a fourth-grader—she turned to books avidly: Because of her nearsightedness, she had never developed any alternative interest in television.

Starting at age five, Karla was sent away summers to Camp Swatonah in the Catskills; Abraham thought it wise to give her a break from family squabbling. Rhoda was usually too ill to visit, but Nene and Abraham came up periodically to check on how Karla was doing. They needn't have worried. She took to camp immediately, never felt a twinge of homesickness, and went back happily every summer until she was twelve. She was mystified at the kids who would cry for their parents and mope miserably around the bunk. The only time Karla cried was at the end of the summer—when she had to go home.

She had terrible crushes on the female counselors. "It was my first awareness," she later said, "that I was gay," though at the time, of course, she lacked that descriptive vocabulary. The counselors were mostly Southern teenagers with stark "duck" haircuts, and in retrospect Karla has little doubt that most of them were lesbian. All she knew at the time was that when she first saw these women, she said to herself, "I am more like them than I am like my mother or even Nene." "I knew I was different as a little kid, but when I saw these counselors I knew I was like them in some fundamental way. I had no words for it. I don't know whether I defined it as being athletic or what, but I felt an immediate identification with them."

But when—aggressive little kid that she was—Karla tried to crawl into their beds, she scared them half to death; they'd respond, at most, with an affectionate wrestle/cuddle before quickly kicking her out. Karla had better luck with her fellow campers. They were in and out of each other's beds constantly, and Karla was able to expand considerably on her growing knowledge of the female body and sex organs—knowledge she had begun to accrue at home by enticing the neighborhood girls to let her play doctor with her brother's toy medical kit.

But her happy summers at camp came to an end when her parents decided the money would be put to better use by enrolling Karla in private school. Her parents put a high value on the education they themselves had never had. After an older boy on the block got stabbed in the back at Walt Whitman Junior High School (where Karla was due to go), Abraham and Rhoda immediately enrolled her instead, as an eighth-grader, in the all-girl "Bromley Institute."* Bromley was as close to an upper-class finishing school as Brooklyn had to offer, and there were only twenty-eight students in Karla's class. Always quick to adjust, she took to the school from the start—and not simply because she now found herself in an all-female atmosphere.

Ray was only three when it happened, but he remembers what was playing on the television set in the background (*Have Gun, Will Travel*), what his mother was wearing (a strapless turquoise dress) and

---

* Wherever names have been changed, quotation marks are used at first reference in order to indicate a pseudonym.

the brand of rat poison (JR). She mixed the poison into two glasses of milk, drank one herself, then put the other down in front of him and told him to swallow it. He tried to, but the taste was so bad he stopped after a few sips. His mother got angry; she poured sugar into the glass and again ordered him to drink. When he gagged, she impatiently took the glass out of his hand and drank it down herself. Then she went into the bathroom, came out a few minutes later with her makeup on, started to cry—and then suddenly ran out of the apartment to the neighbors'.

The next thing Ray remembers is the hospital: orderlies rushing to pump his stomach, his mother vomiting uncontrollably. She lingered for two days and then—aged twenty-two—died. When Ray saw her laid out at the funeral parlor, he figured she was sleeping, and Grandma Viejita told him that that was right. Later, at the cemetery, Viejita tried to throw herself into the open grave and had to be restrained.

For years afterward, she denied that her daughter had killed herself—until Ray finally confronted her with a truth he had long since accepted: "She killed herself and I know that!" Ray screamed at his grandmother. "I remember the look on her face when she was doing it! I remember everything. . . ." By then, ten-year-old Ray even had a theory as to why she had tried to take him with her: "Moms knew I would have to suffer a long life, and I would be completely different than anybody else."

Viejita took Ray and Sonia, his two-month-old sister, from their apartment in Spanish Harlem to live with her in Jersey City. Ray's natural father, José Rivera, had disappeared years ago; his mother's second husband, a drug dealer who had fathered Sonia, showed no interest in the children. José reappeared only once, when Ray was four. Viejita called him into the room one day, pointed to a stranger sitting there, and said, "This is your father." When José tried to kiss him, Ray yelled, "I don't have a father!" kicked him in the shins, and ran out of the apartment. José never came by again.

Nor did he ever send child support. Viejita (an affectionate term for "Old Lady") had to bring them up on her own. Born in Venezuela, she had raised her own daughter alone in New York—her Mexican husband having deserted her when she got pregnant. Now in her mid-forties and employed as a pieceworker at the Pickwick Mills factory, Viejita was lucky if she could bring home fifty dollars a week. Yet she did her determined best to keep the refrigerator full and clothes on the children's backs—that is, until Sonia's father reappeared one day and took her off to live with a couple he knew who, like himself, were Puerto Rican.

Viejita was never the same. Sonia had reminded her of her own daughter, and that made the loss doubly devastating. After years of trying, she finally tracked down Sonia and her adopted family in Brooklyn. But when Viejita and Ray went there for dinner, the evening proved a disaster; annoyed that Sonia kept calling her adopted mother Mommy, Ray finally blurted out, "That's not your mother! You're my sister and you don't even know that! Your moms is dead!" Sonia's "mommy" politely ushered Viejita and Ray out the door. It was years before they were invited back again, and Viejita threatened Ray with death if he so much as mentioned the past. Ray managed to hold his tongue, and the day went off well. Thereafter, Viejita was occasionally allowed to visit, and she periodically sent Sonia gifts and money; but Ray never saw his sister again.

Viejita seemed to blame him for the separation. She told him he was a "troublemaker," that she had only wanted Sonia, not him. When he left a spot of dirt after cleaning the apartment, or when he failed to iron her blouse just so, she would beat him. Ray didn't doubt that Viejita loved him in her own way, but he turned increasingly to Sarah, an upstairs neighbor who had known his mother and was herself childless. Sarah would buy him little things that his grandmother couldn't afford, and she would listen to him talk about his unhappiness.

In 1958, when Ray was seven, Viejita fell ill and sent him off to St. Agnes, a Catholic home for boys. She felt well again within six months, but delayed bringing Ray back home until the nuns strongly recommended that she do so. But she didn't seem to want him around anymore and started to board him out on weekdays. She at first sent him to people she knew in the neighborhood and then, for a long stretch when he was nine, to Elisa, a Colombian friend whom Viejita had sponsored as an immigrant. Elisa and her husband lived in a nice house in Sea Cliff, Long Island—they were the only Hispanic family in the town—and they sent him to the local Catholic school. Elisa was good to Ray most of the time—as long as he meticulously completed the many chores she gave him—but when she got in "one of her moods," she would beat him for the slightest infraction, or for no reason at all, and not just with a belt but with a two-by-four plank. She also beat him on the day she invited him, aged ten, into her bed and he refused to go.

On weekends, holidays and during the summers, Ray would return to Viejita, who had moved to Manhattan's Lower East Side. She was never too happy about his return. The neighbors had begun to tease her about Ray's effeminacy, predicting he would soon be a full-fledged *maricón*. What they didn't know was that he had already, at age seven, had sex with his fourteen-year-old cousin—and by age ten was having sex regularly with a married man down the block.

Returning from the man's apartment one evening with hickeys on his neck, Ray couldn't understand why Viejita was staring at him so fixedly. At first he thought it must be his eyebrows again. He had taken to trying on Viejita's clothes when she wasn't home, sashaying around the house in padded bras and panties. Then one day he had gotten the idea to shave his eyebrows, but he had botched the job and had to paint them over with Viejita's eyebrow pencil. That night, completely forgetting, he had washed his face thoroughly and gone into the living room to say good night to his grandmother. "Where are your eyebrows?" Viejita had asked evenly. Faced with disaster, Ray had mumbled something about having lost them down the sink and had said he would go look for them. Viejita had held him fast, but to his surprise had not beaten him. She had quietly gotten out her eyebrow pencil and had repainted Ray's face.

But this time, seeing the hickeys on his neck, she was not so benign. Where did he get them? she demanded. Thinking fast but not exactly well, Ray said he got them from Millie, the girl down the hall. "She tried to attack me downstairs!" Sure, sure, said Viejita, try telling me another—and she hauled off and whacked him. "Next thing I know," she screamed, "you'll be hanging out with the rest of the *maricónes* on Forty-second Street!" It was not the first time Ray had heard Forty-second Street mentioned. When he, Viejita, and a group of neighbors from the block had passed the Times Square area on their way to Coney Island for the day, he had heard them make snide comments about the "fags" who hung out there. He had stored the information away, not yet fully understanding it, not quite ready to have a firsthand look.

But then more trouble developed at school. Ray had started wearing face makeup in the fourth grade, but for a couple of years nobody had seemed to notice, or care. (Nobody, that is, except for his fifth-grade teacher, a married man with eight children who had taken to driving Ray home from school and then one day had seduced him in the backseat.) Perhaps Ray's athletic abilities in track and gymnastics had given him some protective covering, for if he was effeminate, he was also wiry and tough, widely known as someone you didn't mess with.

But in the sixth grade somebody did. He was skipping rope one day with the girls, and wearing what was then called "full face" makeup (eyeliner and mascara), when a classmate named Glen called him a faggot. Ray whirled on him—"You don't call *me* no faggot!"— and although Glen was two heads taller, beat him up right then and there in the playground. Called into the principal's office, Ray explained what Glen had said. "Now do I look like a faggot, Mr. Sloan?" Ray demanded—which took some bravado, since he was dressed in skintight pants and was still wearing makeup. Mr. Sloan, for whatever reasons of his own, agreed that Ray did not. He suspended Ray for a week—and Glen for a month.

But that marked the end of Ray's formal education. In 1962, at age eleven, tired of Viejita's beatings and the neighborhood mockery, he left home for good. He headed straight for Forty-second Street.

J   I   M

Jim's family life shifted so often before he was five years old that he ended up feeling he had no family at all. And he would later let stand some of the rumors that surrounded him about being the son of the chairman of the board of Pepsi-Cola (thus conveniently making Joan Crawford his stepmother), or about his father having been a circus performer. "Circus" is in fact an apt invention and metaphor for the emotional acrobatics that surrounded Jim's childhood.

His mother, Connie, ran away from a convent school in New Jersey when she was fifteen to live with thirty-five-year-old James Fouratt, Jim's father. Connie and James never married: she refused to wed outside the Catholic Church, and he refused to wed in it. She left him after giving birth within a three-year period in the mid-forties to three boys (one of whom died in infancy); ever after, she deflected all questions about that period of her life.

When Connie, not yet eighteen, decided to leave James Fouratt and start over, she went to the state of Washington to live with her own mother, Florence. Descended from an upper-class French family, Florence, too, had early realized that her first marriage was a mistake, had divorced Connie's father (a butcher whom she accused of being a drunk) and had quickly remarried. When Connie went to live with Florence, she left young Jim in New Jersey with James, telling the boy that she would be sending for him shortly.

But she and Florence soon concluded that leaving Jim with his father had been a mistake, that James might not later be willing to give the boy up. Deciding to take no chances, they concocted a kidnaping. Florence and her husband simply appeared one day when Jim was on his way home from school, and told him to get in the car. Since he knew his grandmother, he obliged; but later, safely resettled in Washington, he cried bitterly over the new puppy he had been forced to leave behind. It was only some thirty years later, in the seventies, that Jim reconnected with his father—briefly, since the hoped-for knight in shining armor turned out to be a bookie and an alcoholic, an ill, bigoted old man who lectured Jim about his "sick" values.

Connie's new life in Washington started well. Still young, and very attractive, she entered a state beauty contest—and won. Then it was discovered that she had two sons and had been "divorced" (to conceal Connie's nonmarriage, Florence had somehow arranged bogus divorce papers). Stripped of her crown, Connie nonetheless had a millionaire suitor to fall back on. That is, a conditional suitor: He wanted to marry her but refused to raise her children. Florence urged Connie to accept the proposal and offered to adopt the two boys herself—a solution that would not have sat well with Jim, who had developed considerable antipathy for his grandmother.

Just as Connie was agonizing over her options, her own father, whose second wife had recently died and left him with a daughter younger than Jim—is it any wonder that the confusions of Fouratt family history fed the need for plausible invention?—invited her to live with him in Rhode Island. Connie decided that was her way out, and, leaving the younger boy with her mother, she took Jim, now aged five, and understandably bewildered at yet another shift in the family configuration, to her father's house in East Providence.

He lived in a neighborhood that was basically working-class Irish-Portuguese-Italian, and strongly Catholic. (Connie herself, though a believer, only became devout later in life.) Within two years of moving in with her father, Connie married Bill Malone, a short-order cook, the son of an Irish cop and a telephone operator. In adulthood, Jim would come to think of his immediate family as having been dysfunctional—his mother doting on him more than on her husband.

But Connie and Bill tried to do well by him, pinching pennies to send him to a good (and as it turned out, liberal) parochial school. Clever, bright, eager to learn, Jim took to his new school immediately and, encouraged by some of his more freethinking teachers, was soon reading the progressive Catholic publication *America*, as well as materials put out by Dorothy Day's radical Catholic Worker movement. Precociously articulate, Jim could stand on his feet and talk rings around his contemporaries, and he also had highly developed social skills that quickly thrust him into leadership positions. Yet, puzzlingly, he was behind his peers in spelling and writing and had trouble committing anything to paper. Only years later, in his twenties, did he finally discover that he was dyslexic.

That was not the only way he was different. His family, perhaps as awed as his contemporaries by his perky verbalness, tended to treat him like an adult—his mother, after all, was only fifteen years older, and her husband was a year younger than she. Jim was also an unusually beautiful boy, somewhat undersized and slight, but perfectly featured, an angelic blue-eyed blond so pretty that as a three-year-old he had been chosen to be a "Whitcomb baby" in the famous series of ads that illustrator John Whitcomb designed for Gerber baby foods.

Jim's prettiness would often be mistaken, especially as he got older, for blandness or passivity, the surface stereotype belying the complex inner reality. He was, in fact, an intricate mix of sweetness and dynamism, and his cherubic mask misrepresented an assertive temperament. "My sensibility was much more female than male," he later said, "but my Gestalt was male." Often called "girl" or "faggot," he identified with neither, though his "gay spirit" (as he later liked to call it), his sense from an early age of being different, did make him compassionate toward other outsiders. Since most people need to hang on to the illusion that others are one-dimensional—that makes them *seemingly* more comprehensible and manageable—the complex Jim would all his life be puzzled by the way people reacted to him as if he were *either* (and only) a passive boy or a warrior male.

He was further set apart by illness. As a youngster he had rheumatic fever twice, and then leukemia, and didn't go to school for two years. Given massive doses of cortisone—the drug had just come on the market and not much was known about its properties—he blew up to three hundred pounds (and never did develop an Adam's apple). Bedridden for more than a year, he lived in a world apart, putting on little shows in his room with stick figures, endlessly watching television and listening to soap operas on the radio.

He became so adept at performing that after he recovered, and while still a teenager, he was chosen to emcee *The World Around Us*, a local television show devoted to current affairs. And his fluency in public speaking led to his election as president of the Rhode Island chapter of Junior Achievement, a national organization founded to teach teenagers about the wondrous workings of capitalism by encouraging them to set up their own little businesses (Jim ended up winning the National Junior Achievement sales award for a French dressing he created).

He was even pro-McCarthy. At the tender age of seven, Jim was signing people up for membership in the Committee of One Million, founded to support Senator McCarthy. He dutifully carried petitions from door to door soliciting members, and when the door sometimes got slammed in his face, he would complain to his mother—he describes himself as a "self-righteous priss" in those years—that such people were refusing to be "good Americans." She finally put an end to his canvassing by ripping up the petitions—not out of political progressivism (she really had no politics) but out of some powerful fear of "making trouble." "My whole subsequent political life," Jim later said, "has been a form of atonement for my McCarthy petition."

By the time Jim was in high school, his numerous activities had him crisscrossing Providence. To save money, he would hitchhike and before long discovered that blow jobs were one of the side benefits. Men would pick him up in their cars and, in exchange for sex, drive him anywhere he wanted to go. He soon found out that certain street corners were favored, and thereafter confined his hitching to those. He never feared getting into a car; as a survivor in his own family, he felt he had developed extrasensory instincts about potential danger.

But once, in his late teens, those instincts failed him. A truck driver, perhaps attracted to his long blond hair and delicate features, picked him and drove him to a place where other truckers gathered. Together five of them raped him, brutally ripping open his rectum; then they left him, bleeding, on the side of the road. A cop car finally came along but, instead of being helpful, the cops ridiculed him as a "faggot" and told him that he had asked for it. He ended up in a hospital for several days.

In 1960, when still a junior in high school, Jim won early admission to Harvard. It seemed a dream come true; he had already vowed *never* to go to a local school, like Providence College or Rhode Island College, never to become "the working-class kid stuck in a trap." But then reality hit: His family simply couldn't afford the

Harvard tuition, and somehow nobody, neither his teachers nor his parents, suggested that he apply for scholarship money. Crushed, Jim, aged sixteen, decided to quit high school and become a priest.

As a moralistic, at times self-righteous young man, he was attracted to the do-gooding part of a priest's life, but had never been a fully convinced believer or felt certitude about the validity of Catholic dogma. The particular order he chose had been founded in the nineteenth century by Isaac Hecker (a baker at the transcendentalist community Brook Farm, who had later become a priest), and among its glamorous celebrants were the two "show-business priests," Father Norman O'Connor ("the jazz priest") and Father Elwood Kaiser (who produced movies for television and Hollywood). Given the order's showy tolerance for nonconformity, it seemed to Jim—in his own words, "a precocious, smart-assed" young man—just the right place for him. But as it turned out, only certain kinds of nonconformity were tolerated, which Jim—in some ways deeply innocent—was slow to discover.

Though he had gotten his fair share of blow jobs while hitchhiking across Providence, Jim only kissed a man for the first time when visiting New York City during the summer following his first year in seminary. Soon after that momentous occasion came another. At a poetry reading, he fell in love on the spot with the poet himself and went to bed with him—only to discover, when back in the seminary the next day, that he had caught crabs. Not that he had any idea what the squiggly little moving dots on his body were, or where they had come from; in his naïveté, he went to the head of the seminary to ask him about the strange visitation. The head, who had been a marine chaplain, sternly told Jim to shave every hair off his body— and would say no more.

But Jim's English teacher, with whom he had gotten friendly (and who was himself homosexual and would later leave the order), took Jim aside and tried to warn him that he was on dangerous ground. He explained that two members of the order had recently petitioned to be ordained as openly homosexual priests—and had not only been turned down, but had been thrown out. Something like a homosexual panic had ensued in the order, he warned Jim, and the issue had become extremely sensitive. Just how sensitive, Jim soon found out.

Another seminarian, angry at Jim for having made fun of his tiny penis in the showers, reported to the authorities that Jim had pictures of nude men in his desk. As indeed he did. Called in by the ex–marine chaplain to explain, Jim said he found the pictures "aesthetically pleasing." Was he a homosexual? the chaplain demanded. Yes, Jim said, he thought he was—but added that he saw no conflict between that and becoming a priest. Like Craig Rodwell, Jim had been brought up to believe that if you were honest, all would turn out well. He now learned otherwise. The chaplain told him he would have to leave the seminary at once, and gave him fifteen dollars for bus fare back home.

Jim was stunned and humiliated; he had become used to being treated like a winner. And as a winner, he refused to believe that his feelings were "sinful" or that his relationship with God had in any way been compromised. He was very clear about that, indeed had always been clear about that: He *knew* when he had done wrong and he had never felt that way about his sexuality. Telling his parents, however, was quite another matter. Sex was not something discussed openly in his house (though years later, when Jim did tell his mother that he was gay, she was supportive, only asking that he not inform his stepfather, whose uncle Freddy, a transvestite, was already more than the family could handle). So Jim said something vague to his mother about having decided that seminary was "not right" for him after all. And then he did what he had wanted to do all along: He went to Harvard.

Not as a matriculating student, but to live with two friends of his from East Providence whose families *had* been wealthy enough to pay their tuition. Jim simply moved into their room in Adams House and started sitting in on classes. It was a poignant time: He got close to becoming part of something he had long aspired to, yet he remained at a distance from it—an auditor, not a full participant. What made it all bearable was falling in love. He met a man who did promotional work for the Phoenix Theater (in the early sixties, among the most innovative and prestigious of theatrical companies) and, at the man's urging, decided to move to New York to be with him.

Jim arrived in the Big Apple in 1961—the same year Ray Rivera, aged eleven, left his grandmother's apartment and headed up to Times Square. Jim's excitement about starting a new life soon dissipated: The man he had followed to New York, it turned out, already had a live-in lover. He did at least make good on his promise to get Jim a job with the Phoenix, placing him in the subscription department; from there Jim quickly earned a promotion to stage manager and bit player with the Phoenix Traveling Theater, a troupe that performed in high schools. It may not have been the new life Jim had anticipated, but the world of the theater would in fact become exactly that for him. He soon moved in with two gay men connected with the Phoenix who were eager to share expenses on a West Eighty-seventh Street apartment, found that he could live on his fifty-dollar-a-week salary by restricting his diet to pizza and Coca-Cola, and resolved, true to the "show-business" Catholic order that had kicked him out, that he would become a Broadway star.

The Gunnison home on Hampshire Circle, in the wealthy New York suburb of Bronxville, was notable for its grand staircase, its squash court, its sunken garden (which could be filled with water during winter for ice skating), and its butlers' rooms—complete with a Filipino butler named Dabby. Foster Gunnison, Sr., had built the house during the Great Depression. He had inherited some money, and on his own had made a good deal more in his double career as lighting designer and builder. The lighting career had come first. A pioneer in the use of glass brick and carved structural glass—indeed, in the whole concept of what is today known as "architectural lighting"— he had started the firm of Cox, Nostrand and Gunnison when he was twenty-three. It specialized in Art Deco design and handled many of the largest installations of the 1920s and early 1930s, including the President's office and Cabinet Room in the White House, the Empire State Building, the Center Theater (now demolished) in Rockefeller Center, the Chrysler Building, the Waldorf-Astoria, Radio City Music Hall, the RCA Building, and the Daily News Building.[1]

In the following decade, Gunnison launched a second career. Impressed with Henry Ford's mass-production techniques, he decided to apply them to building prefab houses in modular parts that could be shipped anywhere and reassembled. He bought an old furniture factory in New Albany, Indiana, used his designer skills to turn out inexpensive, assembly-line homes, and applied his sales skills to set up a national dealership system. Before long he had sold enough Gunnison Homes to build a modern plant; he eventually became known as the founder of the prefabricated-housing industry in America.

Handsome, driven, gifted, he married a woman whose beauty and surface charms were a match for his own, though her more modest lineage was not. Whereas Caroline McAllaster's family had been in the United States a mere three generations, the first Gunnison, Hugh, had arrived in Boston in 1631, and had ultimately become a judge and a deputy to the Massachusetts General Court. The succeeding four generations of Gunnisons were shipwrights, carpenters (one served in the revolution, under John Paul Jones) and farmers, giving way in the fifth generation to ministers and army officers, and in the sixth to Herbert Foster Gunnison, who became publisher in the late nineteenth century of the *Brooklyn Eagle*, the distinguished newspaper that had earlier been edited by Walt Whitman.

Though Foster Sr. had little regard for Caroline's family (twenty years later he characterized her father, with derisive exaggeration, as a man who "never did a tap of work until he was thirty years old because he spent all of his time gambling"), he and Caroline do seem to have been in love when they married in 1918. But by the time Foster Jr. was born, in 1925, the ardor had decidedly cooled. Intensely preoccupied with his work, Foster Sr. had never had a deep investment in family life, and from the early years of the marriage had gotten involved in a series of side affairs—not all of them, apparently, with women. Both his wife and son eventually came to suspect that Foster Sr. was a bisexual and that his live-in "assistant" down at New Albany was in actuality a male lover.

At any rate, Foster Sr. was neither a devoted husband nor a consistently caring father. He spent an increasing amount of time living apart from his family, absorbed in supervising his new business in Indiana. By the early thirties, Caroline and Foster Jr. were, except for occasional visits, essentially living alone in Bronxville during the winters and at Gypsy Trail Club, an exclusive residential community outside Carmel, New York, during the summers.

Foster Jr. did, in the 1940s, spend several long vacation periods with his father at New Albany, where he was proudly exhibited to Senior's friends and business associates as the forceful, super-achieving chip off the old block that the inhibited, troubled youngster was decidedly not. Moreover, the father's overemphatic doting on his son in public contrasted sharply with the stern lectures he gave Junior in private about the boy's assorted shortcomings—lectures that alternated with constant admonitions to those "moderate habits of living" Foster Sr. had trouble incorporating into his own life.

Foster Jr. was, in his phrase, "a victim of well-intended overmanagement"—a charitable interpretation of what seems on his father's side to have been essentially a driven determination to shape his offspring into an acceptable image. Foster Jr. would later ruefully claim that "my father put me on a pedestal way beyond anything that I merited." But that assessment, too, seems dubious, seems to reflect a combination of wish fulfillment (the pedestal) and a habit of self-deprecation ("beyond anything that I merited") that his father's hectoring reproofs had helped to engender. Much closer to the mark is Junior's suggestion later in life that his abilities had "always been underestimated"—the negative appraisal of his gifts having been early internalized, and thereafter communicated to others.

His mother was far worse at nurturance. Like her husband, Caroline was a charming, popular companion to her peers, but a cold, endlessly critical, domineering parent. She was obsessed with being liked and with being socially correct, and was far too self-centered to give a child sustained affection. When alone with Foster Jr. she would, far more than her husband, castigate the boy for his imperfections. She was not above recounting the "terrible time" she had had giving birth to him (two other pregnancies had ended in miscarriages), or repeating how much she had hoped for a nice little girl. Caroline always kept her word, paid her debts like clockwork, and was generally admired for her honesty and reliability. But she was also a volcano of buried resentment: She menaced Foster Jr. with a knife several times; suggested (when he was six) a double suicide pact; and periodically threatened to call the police and have him taken away.

Not surprisingly, Foster Jr. had frequent illnesses that confined him to bed, and when he was four or five, he developed a severe case of asthma. The family first tried sending him to Bermuda, where he got worse, and then to Richmond, Massachusetts, where he got no better. Finally, when he was nine and so underweight that serious doubts about his survival arose, the doctor suggested he be sent to board at the recently opened Thomas School in Arizona, a place that catered to children from well-to-do families. Most of the children at Thomas suffered from psychological or physical problems—it was an upper-class version of the combined school-and-orphanage that Craig Rodwell was to attend near Chicago a decade later.

The school was set in a beautiful, barren stretch of desert on the eastern outskirts of Tucson, surrounded by the distant Santa Catalina hills, with the nearest structure, the picturesque adobe ruins of old Fort Lowell, nearly two miles away. Foster Jr. was accompanied out West by his parents, but when school started in late September 1934, they left. Foster was assailed by homesickness throughout much of his first year. But he soon fell in love with the desert, and gradually became acclimated to being away from home.

The Thomas School had only forty students, divided between day students and boarders, and its young male teaching staff had been recruited almost entirely from Ivy League colleges. The school also kept a stable of horses (and a stablemaster). Foster quickly learned how to ride, and went out nearly every afternoon after classes to explore the desert terrain, chasing jackrabbits and rattlesnakes (he threw up the first time he watched the stablemaster skin one of the snakes to make a belt). The woman who operated the school, perhaps predisposed in Foster's favor by his father's gift of a library, turned him into something of a pet, letting him come into her room early each morning to snuggle in her bed with a puppy she owned while she got ready for the day. She was not a particularly warm person—indeed, she could be something of a disciplinarian—but Foster thrived on the special attention. Well before the end of his five-year stay in Arizona, his asthma had entirely disappeared.

After he returned home in 1939, his father decided to build the largest model Gunnison Home for his own family in the Gypsy Trail compound, and for the next three years Foster Jr. and his mother were nearly year-round residents there. He attended the local Carmel high school and then spent two years at Culver Military Academy in northern Indiana, where his father had once been a summer cadet. Unpredictably, Foster Jr. enjoyed Culver: He was able to continue his riding there and, although he never achieved any substantial military rank at the school, he felt, "as a person dependent upon authority," that the structured, disciplined, subordinate life suited him well.

After graduating from Culver, he entered Haverford College in the fall of 1944. Foster Senior had handpicked the Pennsylvania school as suitably small and prestigious. But Foster Jr. never took to it, and in his first term very nearly flunked out. He got a 42 in physics and a 54 in government (with 60 as a passing grade)—and his *highest* grade was a 68 (in English). His father, for once, handled the situation with some tact. While pontificating in his usual way about "the need to complete whatever one starts," and while managing parenthetically to deplore Junior's sloppy handwriting in his letters, Foster Sr. was nonetheless able to emphasize the positive: It was now clear, he wrote his son, that Junior's bent lay in liberal arts, not in engineering or scientific subjects—however much father and son might have hoped otherwise—and he urged Junior to be grateful that he had learned in the nick of time what his strengths were, and could therefore play to them in planning his future professional life.[2]

But Junior's unhappiness in fact encompassed more than a few uncongenial courses. He confessed to his father that he had been in "a constant state of depression" since arriving at the school. He found "every phase" of life at Haverford disagreeable: The food wasn't to his taste; the boys—mostly Quakers—had a set of ideals he did not share and could not fathom; there was no high-powered sports program; and, perhaps worst of all, he had discovered that his roommate "exhibited several glaring tendencies toward Communism." Foster felt wretched, lost fifteen pounds, and had "a constant tired feeling." Realizing that his father might ascribe those ailments to malingering, to a lack of "stick-to-it-iveness," he shrewdly played to a set of complaints Foster Sr. might find more congenial: He needed a school, he wrote his father, that was closer to home and that placed more emphasis on "college spirit" and on fraternities; and he confessed to a special hankering to be on a campus that had a chapter of Beta Theta Pi (the family fraternity for several generations).

Foster Sr. took the bait. Misreading his son as usual, he announced that he had hit upon exactly what was needed to pull Junior out of the doldrums: a coeducational college. It would give Junior "a brighter life," and that in turn would stimulate success in his studies. But Senior refused to consider a transfer until his son had satisfactorily demonstrated that he could "conquer all your problems at Haverford—even though you are unhappy." With the promise of release in the wind, Junior studied around the clock and in the second term of his freshman year achieved "a very creditable average." Fulfilling his side of the bargain, Foster Sr. allowed his son to transfer to Columbia, which accepted him on condition that he repeat his freshman year.

In the late forties, Columbia had one of the best football teams in its history, and Foster Jr. became a rabid fan, experiencing near delirium when Columbia pulled "the upset of upsets" in breaking Army's long undefeated string of victories. With a new lease on life, and trying his best to fit the collegiate mold, he did join his father's old fraternity, Beta Theta Pi, and in fact enjoyed the camaraderie— including the repeated trips he and a group of brothers took to Union City, New Jersey, or to the Globe in Boston to catch the burlesque shows. It was the comedy Foster liked, not the sex.

Indeed by now, aged twenty, Foster was well aware—though he had done only a little adolescent experimenting with friends—that his orientation was homosexual. At Columbia he sometimes dated to keep up with his peers, but fled in alarm at the occasional discreet

signal from a fraternity brother that some kind of sexual advance might
be welcome. When one of them (a man later well known in publishing)
directly propositioned Foster, he was so shocked and self-protectively
"incensed," that he grabbed a dry mop and chased him out of the
room. Indeed, Foster's uncertain footing in matters of sex was to result
in a pattern of lifelong celibacy. Once, in his mid-forties, he got an
"expertly administered, absolutely delightful" blow job; that would
be the sole sexual experience of his adult life. Which helps to account,
perhaps, for the special zeal with which he embraced every opportunity to bury himself in organizational work, to toil, with vast en-
joyment, and semi-anonymity, on behalf of a cause he believed in.

He discovered his penchant for organizational work even before
he graduated from Columbia. On one of his visits to New Albany in
the mid-forties, his father had taken him to visit the local chapter, in
nearby Louisville, Kentucky, of a recently founded national men's
singing organization designed to preserve what was viewed as the
disappearing folk art of barbershop quartets and choruses. The Louisville chapter was made up largely of local businessmen, and it was
the networking, not the music, that had drawn Foster Sr. But the
barbershop bug immediately bit Junior and became a lifelong passion
with him. For a few years he sang in a male chorus, but later found
that he enjoyed the business end even more; he helped to organize
local, then district, then national programs, and took special satisfaction, one spring day in 1961, at being present for the formal ceremony
in the office of Governor John Dempsey of Connecticut that proclaimed April 8–15 a week for officially celebrating the venerable
institution of barbershop quartet singing.

In 1949, the year Foster graduated from Columbia, his father
and mother, already long separated, finally decided on a formal divorce. But the settlement proved protracted and acrimonious, with
each parent trying to enlist Foster Jr. as an ally. For a time, his father
would have the advantage. Foster Sr. saw that his son, after graduation, was floundering, uncertain what kind of work to take up and
where his aptitudes might lie, and so offered to set him up with a
Gunnison Homes dealership in St. Petersburg, Florida. He assured
Junior that he would accumulate considerable capital in short order.
That alone had appeal, but what appealed still more was the possibility
that his father might finally, after years of doubt about his son's
commonsense abilities, find in him something like a worthy business
associate.

YOUNG ADULTHOOD

YVONNE

Yvonne's sister had gone to college in Georgia, but Yvonne was having no part of it. There was no way, she told her mother, that *she* was going to go south to college. *No* way. Theo couldn't argue with her too much; having brought her daughter up in her own outspoken image, and having imbued her with proud, pro-black attitudes, she realized Yvonne might be right in predicting that she would end up dead in a Southland still rigidly insistent on segregation.

But why in heaven's name, Theo wanted to know, had Yvonne settled on Seattle University? Was the Far West the only possible alternative to the Deep South? Yvonne said something sly about how pleased Grandma would be because Seattle was run by the Jesuits, and then, more seriously, insisted on how well suited the school was to her own burgeoning interest in philosophy; what could be better than the chance to read scholastic philosophy with the people who invented it? "But what will you *do* there?" her mother asked in mock horror. "It's tucked off nowhere, way out in the left-hand corner!" Yvonne tried to reassure her that since her childhood friend, the studious Freddy, was already enrolled at Seattle University, the two of them could concoct some plot or other.

Theo couldn't help but smile; she'd been considered wild herself all her life, and took some vicarious pleasure in her daughter's high-spirited decision to shock the neighbors—this was 1950—with the spectacle of a seventeen-year-old girl going off to school at the other end of the country. That Freddy would watch over her was thought a dubious blessing; he was already suspect in the neighborhood for his "swell-headed" bragging that he intended to study Russian and become a diplomat (what he hadn't announced was that he, too, was gay).

To the neighborhood's satisfaction, Yvonne lasted only two years at Seattle University (though Freddy graduated with honors). She did well academically—thanks to how bright she was, not to how diligently she applied herself. And she dutifully joined the prestigious Alpha Kappa Alpha black sorority. But then, as an antidote to that conventional social scene, she got in with an older black crowd that included Patti Bown (later well known as a pianist) and spent much of her time, as she had in high school, in the jazz clubs—and also in pursuing a love affair, the last she would have with a man. Moreover—and without really needing the money, but attracted to the thrills—she set up an inventive fence operation in which she sold (at a 50 percent commission) the booty some of her navy friends won while gambling aboard ship.

Yvonne enjoyed the edgy secrecy of moving in and out of disparate worlds, some of them clandestine, some of them proper. And that included the gay world. While still back in New Rochelle, she had managed to connect with a few very discreet lesbians in the surrounding towns, but when she set out to explore gay life in Seattle, she soon found that there was little to explore.

The West Coast certainly had its share of bars; although there were not more than thirty exclusively lesbian clubs in the whole country in late 1963, the West Coast had for several decades boasted a fair number of them—as well as the ubiquitous undercover agents and surprise police raids that were their invariable accompaniment. Mona's in San Francisco, which opened for business in 1936, was probably the best known of the early lesbian bars. Their number increased during and after World War II, with the If Club and the Star Room in Los Angeles becoming especially popular.[1]

But Seattle lagged far behind. Yvonne did locate a few places *rumored* to be gay, but she had scant success in meeting other lesbians or getting connected to a gay network. Not that she felt at all desperate; she was "having a ball" exploring a variety of worlds, and felt content in not committing to any of them.

During the summer vacation following her second year at Seattle, when she was back in her family's house in New Rochelle, Yvonne suddenly broke out in an acute case of acne. She had never had so much as a pimple before; now her face was a mass of bumps and sores. Her mother took her to a well-known dermatologist, who promptly prescribed a series of X-rays—the then-touted experimental treatment. The X-rays literally burned the face, leaving patches of black skin that slowly peeled off. Yvonne felt so disfigured after the treatments that she decided not to return to Seattle, and indeed rarely left the house for a year. The experimental X-ray treatment for acne soon fell out of favor with dermatologists, but not before, in Yvonne's view, it had inflicted hidden internal damage that may well have contributed to the string of physical problems, and especially lupus, that would subsequently plague her.

Even before the X-ray treatments, she had seemed unusually susceptible to physical ailments. At twelve she had had a mild form of polio, which thereafter made her tire easily whenever she tried to play sports—though her tight, wiry body made her look like a natural athlete. Then at fourteen she had developed dysmenorrhea—painful cramps accompanying menstruation—later followed by endometriosis, which predisposed her to vaginal cysts and tumors.

None of this had kept her from being her mother's daughter—a high-energy, can-do person who could party till dawn. But two or three days a month, when the cramping and medications got her down, Yvonne took to her bed; the only up side was that her physical problems turned her into a lifelong reader. She was especially drawn to Faulkner, Nietzsche, Sartre, and Hesse. Ibsen's *A Doll's House* excited her incipient feminism, and Orwell's *Down and Out in London and Paris* her wanderlust (though his descriptions of rat-infested pantries kept her from eating in restaurants for years).

When the acne finally receded, and Yvonne was willing to venture out of the house, she enrolled at New York University in Greenwich Village to complete her B.A. Billy, a gay male friend, took her on a tour of the Village clubs, and she quickly became a regular. She went occasionally to a few places on Eighth Street, including the famed Bon Soir, but soon developed a special fondness for Lenny's Hideaway and, somewhat later, the Grapevine, an interracial, upscale bar, just off Seventh Avenue, that had dancing and catered to both men and women. But there weren't many such places in the Village; the barriers of race, class, and gender that centrally characterized mainstream American culture in the fifties were also decidedly in place, though perhaps marginally less noticeable, in the gay subculture.

As Yvonne became increasingly comfortable with a lesbian identity, she continued to travel—much more than most—between several worlds that straddled racial and class divides. She spent at least as much time in the working-class bars and after-hours places of Harlem and Brooklyn as in the middle-class Greenwich Village clubs. A lesbian subculture seems to have developed earlier in Harlem than elsewhere, probably because blacks, knowing the pain of being treated as outsiders, had developed an attitude toward homosexuality relatively more tolerant than was characteristic of white heterosexual circles, with their unrelieved insistence on "sickness" and "degradation." Harlemites might ridicule stereotypic bulldaggers or drag queens, but in the twenties especially, bisexuality had a certain cachet in sophisticated circles, and in the world of show biz the rumored lesbianism of such favored entertainers as Bessie Smith, Ma Rainey, Alberta Hunter, and Ethel Waters tended to be ignored as irrelevant.[2]

Given this complex set of attitudes, heterosexual Harlem was sometimes willing to share nightclub and bar space with gays and lesbians. That included, in the 1920s, such well-known hangouts as Lulu Belle's, Connie's Inn, and the Clam House (which featured the 250-pound, tuxedo-clad singer Gladys Bentley belting out her raucous double-entendre lyrics), as well as the drag balls that attracted thousands to the huge arenas, like Rockland Palace, in which they were staged. Subsequently, Harlem clubs like Snooky's, the Purple Manor, and the Dug-out continued to mix straight and gay, thereby providing homosexuals with a proportionately greater number of gathering spots than were available in the more uptight downtown white world. When Yvonne arrived on the scene in the early fifties, these traditions, though diluted, were still intact. One of her favorite Harlem hangouts, the Wellsworth, on 126th Street and Seventh Avenue (just behind the Apollo Theater), was in fact two bars: a straight bar in front, and then behind it, with a separate side entrance, a black lesbian bar.

Harlem became a retreat from the endemic racism of the Village scene. Going into one of the few lesbian bars in the Village—the Seven Steps, Bagatelle, Swing Rendezvous, Pony Stable, Page Three, Laurel's (famed for its free Chinese food on Sunday afternoons)— meant essentially going into a white women's bar and finding herself ignored or treated like an oddity. That is, if in the first place she got by the Mafia thugs at the door, who often turned away, and sometimes insulted, anyone with black skin. The male bouncers were supposedly there to keep out straight men keen to convert a "lezzie," but it was also their job to keep out "undesirable" women.[3]

One night in the Bagatelle, Yvonne and her friends Tootsie and Debby were talking together at the bar when a white woman sitting nearby tried to flirt with them. When they ignored her, she went up to the thug on the door and said the three women had been bothering her. He, in turn, told them that they would have to leave the club, but Yvonne and her friends were so outraged at the injustice that they refused. The thug then tried to evict them forcibly, a furious fight ensued, and Yvonne had to threaten him with a broken beer bottle before they could edge their way out of the place.

The tough, divey Swing Rendezvous, and the Seven Steps on Hudson Street, were more likely to admit black lesbians than was the upscale Bagatelle, which, with its tiny dance floor, was the most popular mid-fifties lesbian bar in the Village. But even in the Swing, the scene was essentially the same: a few black women in a sea of white faces. Nor did black lesbians necessarily form bonds of solidarity. The writer Audre Lorde, Yvonne's contemporary and later her friend, thought for a time that she was the *only* black lesbian living in the Village, and even after she met more black lesbians in the bars, they formed few friendships among themselves. In Lorde's words, "We recognized ourselves as exotic sister-outsiders who might gain little from banding together. Perhaps our strength might lay in our fewness, our rarity."

For Lorde, part of the trouble was the tendency of black lesbians, even more than white, to get into heavy butch/femme roles. As a "kiki" (or "Ky-Ky," as Lorde spells it)—that is, someone who refused to label herself in an either/or way—Lorde was considered unacceptably "AC/DC," a confused "bluff" (a combination of "butch" and "fluff"), unwilling or unable to find a suitably clearcut identity.

Yvonne was more comfortable than Lorde with the strict roles lesbian bar culture enforced, and herself leaned toward the butch side (her butch name was Vonne, short for Vaughan). As she put it years later, "I cross-dressed primarily to take on the power of the other gender; and also to make a clear statement to women what my preference was and a clear statement to men that I was not available to them." Yet she shared Lorde's misgivings, if not her vehemence, about the bar scene being a "reflect[ion of] all the deprecating attitudes toward women which we loathed in straight society. It was a rejection of these roles that had drawn us to 'the life' in the first place . . . we recognized oppression as oppression, no matter where it came from."

In the fifties and sixties, middle-class and upper-class lesbians relied less on the bars for a social life than working-class women did—just as they were less invested in butch/femme role dichotomies. Yvonne was again atypical in the way she socialized across class lines. She would sometimes be invited as a token black to an otherwise all-white cocktail party of professional women, or to Fire Island, a summer playground that only wealthier lesbians could afford. And Yvonne would go, pleased to be part of so many different worlds. But she would deliberately dress down in sneakers and jeans, in those years decidedly déclassé, eschewing "respectable" Bermuda shorts.

Nor did she often date across racial lines. Only once in these years did she get seriously involved with a white woman, and then it was with someone who traveled almost entirely in the black lesbian world. Not that Yvonne was much interested in settling down with *anyone*; though intensely romantic, she was also intensely wary—a trait that often comes as second nature to those brought up in an alcoholic environment of erratic or excessive emotion that needs to be defended against. Yvonne would later describe herself as "frightened of intimacy," unable to handle closeness, afraid of being smothered —or abandoned. And she would herself increasingly use alcohol and drugs as a way of holding those fears at bay.

In 1956, following a protracted argument with her mother, Yvonne decided to get her own apartment in New Rochelle. After moving in, she supported herself by doing everything from babysitting to running numbers to driving factory workers back and forth to their jobs in Mamaroneck and Pelham. She was now in her mid-twenties, still hell-bent on catching every jazz set, on closing every club, on burning every candle at every end. The relentlessness of her partying naturally put a crimp in her studying, and it was not until 1959 that she was able to complete her B.A. at NYU.

CRAIG

In 1954, when fourteen-year-old Craig graduated from the Junior School, he went back to live with his still-struggling mother, Marion, in Chicago and enrolled as a freshman in Sullivan High School. That alone proved traumatic. The intimate, rural, all-boy atmosphere of the Junior School abruptly gave way to the urban anonymity of a big-city high school with twelve hundred students, male and female, mostly Jewish—a bewildering kaleidoscope of shifting faces. To compound Craig's feelings of dislocation, he had to contend with a new surrogate father, his mother having recently remarried.

Hank, an ex–Golden Gloves champion who worked in a print

shop, was "the sweetest guy in the world" when sober, but one of the nastiest when drunk, which was often. He and Craig's mother would get into shouting matches, but he interfered very little in Craig's own life. On the rare occasions when he tried to, Craig, though pint-sized, quickly put him right. One night after dinner, when Craig was about to leave the house, Hank abruptly said, "Where do you think you're going?" Craig said he was going out; Hank said he was not; Craig repeated that he was. Then Hank pointedly said, "When I was your age we used to go down to Diversey [a gay area in a then rough neighborhood] and beat up queers." Craig may have been surprised, but he wasn't intimidated. "You big, brave man," he said, glaring at Hank—and walked out of the house.

Hank *had* been on to something. Craig had been leaving home after dinner nearly every night for exactly the reason Hank had guessed: to cruise the gay areas. It had all begun, and quite accidentally, soon after he had come to live in his mother's apartment.

Craig had been interested in politics from an early age; at the Chicago Junior School he had avidly pored over the *Christian Science Monitor*, the only newspaper the boys had been allowed to read, and at thirteen he was subscribing to the *Democratic Digest*, a publication of the Democratic National Committee. For Craig, the daily newspaper was an absolute necessity—both to follow politics and to see how his beloved Cubs had done.

One night, after he had been living with his mother for about a month, he went out to Howard Street to get the evening paper. It was raining lightly; as Craig headed back home, a man suddenly started to walk next to him and then said something about how it was too wet out even for the ducks. Craig instinctively knew the guy was coming on to him, and he wanted him to, but he was scared—he guessed the man was at least twenty-three years old. Yet he gave him his home phone number and told him to call from three to six in the afternoon, when his mother would still be at work.

The man did, and Craig agreed to go for a ride in what turned out to be a yellow MG convertible. They drove out to the cornfields near Skokie, had sex in the car, and started to head home—only to discover that the car was stuck in the mud. They tried putting corn husks under the wheels, but to no effect, and the man had to walk to a gas station and hire mechanics to haul them out. "I'll never forget the look on their faces," Craig said years later, with a laugh—"a mixture of amazement and disgust."

But for Craig it was high adventure—the first time he had ever had sex with someone older than himself. That is, give or take some furtive experiences at Comiskey Park, which to Craig, a fanatical Chicago Cubs fan, had become a kind of second home. He would let men pick him up in Comiskey and then, apparently fearless, would either give out a phone number or go directly with the pickup to one of the bathrooms in a deserted area of the stadium. From one of the men he learned the technique of avoiding detection while getting a blow job in a stall by standing in two shopping bags.

But it was from the man who owned the MG that Craig first heard the word "gay" and first learned that there were gay cruising areas all around Chicago—around Clark and Division streets, Bughouse Square, Wilson Avenue, Howard Street, Rush Street, the Clark Theater (in the top two balconies one could even have sex), department-store bathrooms (especially at Marshall Field's, Carson Pirie Scott, and Goldblatt's), and, in summertime, the gay beach at Oak Street.

There was even a coffee shop on the corner of Division and State, called Marx's, that was a hangout for gay high school kids. Craig, and the friends he soon made at Marx's, would sit in booths drinking Coca-Cola while eyeing the older guys walking by to cruise them. If the eyes connected, that could lead to renting a room at the Lawson YMCA or in one of the cheap hotels dotting the Loop, or to hours of driving around and parking in the older men's cars.

Craig loved the cruising and loved the sex, but even at that age would never go with anyone he didn't feel drawn to in other ways; he was always "hot to fall in love, to form an attachment." And to make himself look older—he usually claimed to be seventeen—he wore a leather jacket and engineer boots and chain-smoked cigarettes. But at least once, Craig badly miscalculated. One night on Howard Street he met Dave, a Loyola University student in his early twenties, and started to see him with some regularity in the afternoon, when Craig's mother was at work. Dave always wanted to fuck Craig, and Craig always said no. Finally one afternoon Dave grabbed and raped him, hurting him badly. But Craig couldn't scream for fear the neighbors would discover what was going on. He told Dave he would never see him again.

A few weeks later, when reading the *Chicago Daily News*, Craig came across Dave's picture along with an article describing how the police had come to his room after a thirteen-year-old had reported him, and had found pictures of young boys—at which point Dave had gone to the dresser, pulled out a gun, and shot himself in the mouth, dying instantly. Craig was terrified that his mother would see the article; he had told her Dave's name and address and had made up some story—that Dave was the high school track coach, or some such—to explain his visits to the apartment. Craig cut the article out of the paper and when Marion asked why, he said, "I needed it for biology class."

Sometimes Craig walked the streets till one o'clock in the morning; when he got home his mother was usually waiting up for him, and furious. He'd make up long stories about losing track of the time while playing chess, or about the subway breaking down, or about being caught up in a bowling competition. Since he was usually out three nights a week, the stories wore a bit thin, but if Marion suspected anything, she kept her own counsel, probably out of the realization that Craig's will was too strong and he had been living by it for too long to brook interference now.

And if Hank had any plans to rein the boy in, those soon came to a halt. Afraid that Hank might physically hurt his mother during one of their shouting matches, Craig bought himself a knife, "just in case." Sure enough, one night he heard glass breaking and his mother screaming. Craig burst through the door brandishing the knife, yelling "I'll kill you!"—but was stopped by his mother grabbing hold of his wrist. But that was the end of the marriage; Marion asked Hank to leave.

Since Marion couldn't control Craig, she gave him the silent treatment when he did something that displeased her. At one point she didn't speak to him for months, and even Craig acknowledged that in that instance she had reason. It all began with one of his casual pickups. Frank, a dishwasher in his thirties and a gentle, sweet man, took Craig back to his tiny slum apartment one night, gave him a blow job, and then kindly offered to walk him to the subway. In the 1950s Chicago had a ten o'clock curfew for those under seventeen; Craig had always kept an eye peeled for the cops but had never had any run-ins with them.

This night was different. As Craig and Frank reached the corner of Clark and Schiller, two blocks from the subway station, three or four police cars suddenly roared up from different directions. They quickly separated Craig and Frank and questioned them individually on the sidewalk. The first thing they asked Craig was how old he was, and he said seventeen. Then they asked him for his mother's name and phone number and Craig—having been trained to tell the truth—gave both. Marion was allowed to take him back home, but that was hardly the end of it.

Both Craig and Frank had to stand trial. The prosecutor tried to coax Craig into testifying that Frank had given him money for sex but Craig resolutely refused to embellish the truth. Though the prosecutor was furious, he still managed to put Frank away for five years on the charge of committing "a crime against nature." He then tried to get Craig sent to a reformatory, but Marion cried and begged so piteously that the prosecutor relented; Craig was put on probation for two years on condition that he see a psychiatrist for six months.

Once again Craig's luck held. In the fifties, psychiatry was united behind the notion that homosexuality was diseased, pathological behavior that—this was supposed to be the good news—could be cured. In those years there were very few dissenters from that view, yet Craig, almost miraculously, found himself in treatment with one of them, Calvin Fentress. Instead of trying to change Craig's sexual orientation, Fentress told him about the ancient Greeks and their acceptance of same-gender love as natural; and he told the probation officer that Craig was dating girls and progressing well. Fentress tried telling Marion the same thing, but since she had been forced by the court to foot the psychiatric bills on her meager salary, she remained obdurately angry with Craig and for months subjected him to the silent treatment. As for Frank, Craig never saw him again, though many years later he thought he caught a glimpse of him washing dishes in a cafeteria.

Craig continued, of course, to cruise. Within a few months, still only fifteen and still too young to get into the bars, he met a man named Harry at the Oak Street Beach. Harry proved to be different in several critical ways. He was in his forties. He never seemed to want to do anything more with Craig than kiss. And he had an intriguing stack of magazines on his coffee table, including issues of *ONE* and *The Mattachine Review*. Craig didn't know either publication, and Harry explained that they were put out by an organization of homosexuals.

Craig had never heard of homosexuals organizing, let alone to promote their rights, and was instantly "thrilled" at the news. Harry told him where he could buy *ONE*—only a single newsstand in all of Chicago carried it—and also showed him a listing in *The Mattachine Review* of local chapters of the parent organization. To Craig's delight, there was a branch listed for Chicago, and the very next day, with typical assertiveness, he went down to the building on Dearborn Street to sign up. But when he got there, he could find no reference to a Mattachine Society on the directory, and he realized with a sinking heart that the Chicago listing was a mailing address only—and one he could not write to, since the mail would come to his mother's apartment and he *was* still on probation.

But Craig made up his mind right then and there that he would save up his money and go to New York to live. He had heard for years that more queers lived in New York City than anyplace else on earth, and Harry told him that Mattachine had a large branch there. To help save money, he worked in the mail room of a Chicago law firm, took a summer job with Kaiser Aluminum as an office boy, walked to school every day to avoid the expense of carfare, and when anybody asked him what he wanted for Christmas or Easter, always said "cash." By the time he graduated from high school, Craig had saved nearly six hundred dollars.

But then Marion refused to let him move to New York. So Craig hit on a subterfuge. He had been studying ballet, in a desultory sort of way, since he was six years old and now announced that he intended to become a ballet dancer. Marion, who had apparently silently accepted by this point that Craig was gay, agreed to his career choice —but thought it could be best pursued in Boston. And so, in late summer of 1958, she went with Craig to enroll him in the Boston School of Ballet, and saw to it that he would live in a rooming house specializing in genteel old ladies.

Craig hated ballet school from the beginning, but solaced himself with exploring the gay scene in Boston. In the late fifties it was just as furtive and small-scale as Chicago's, but at least had the advantage of being unfamiliar. On the very day Marion left to go back to Chicago, Craig went out cruising on Commonwealth Avenue and the Boston Common—then notorious meeting spots, and dangerous ones (within weeks, Craig had to flee from a gang of toughs throwing rocks and screaming "Faggot!" at him). That first night, he met three different guys, gave each of them his phone number, and before long had discovered the few gay bars that then existed: the piss-elegant Napoleon Club and the two rougher bars, the Punch Bowl and Jacques.

But the drinking age in Boston was then twenty-one, and Craig had trouble getting into the bars, though he sometimes managed to ease his way in with a crowd. One way or another he quickly succeeded in meeting people, and one of his new friends soon got him a furnished apartment, springing him from the genteel boarding house. He also managed a mini-affair with a Native American who lived in Salem and had a morning radio show devoted to local news and obituaries.

None of this was enough to hold Craig's interest, and after a few months he decided to get out of Boston. He told his mother that if he was ever going to make it in ballet, he would have to go to New York to study. Reluctantly, she gave permission, and Craig packed his suitcase and took the next bus out. He arrived in New York not knowing a soul, but having somehow heard that the Thirty-fourth Street Sloane House YMCA was "simpatico." He immediately checked in there.

KARLA

Karla was astonished when, years later, she found out that most of her classmates at the Bromley Institute had bitter memories of the place. There were reasons enough, as even Karla—who felt Bromley had saved her life—acknowledged. The school was not merely strict, but hawklike in its scrutiny of the girls' behavior. Only certain kinds of clothing, preeminently white blouses and skirts decidedly below the knee, were deemed appropriate for young ladies being "finished." If a girl was caught teasing her hair, or smoking, or playing Beatles records, she was likely to be expelled. When Richard Burton came to Broadway in *Hamlet*, the school forbade the girls to see it: "Richard Burton is a divorced man." Karla went anyway, and got away with it.

The curriculum was entirely prescribed, with no electives to allow for individual tastes (when one teacher overstepped the bounds and encouraged the girls to read Updike's *Rabbit, Run*, she was promptly fired). Chapel was mandatory twice a week (the school was Protestant, though most of the girls were Catholic or Jewish). All the girls were required to play sports, and even their diets were closely supervised. When the Good Humor ice cream truck came by Bromley's iron fence, the girls were refused permission to buy—not for nutritional reasons but rather, as headmistress Mrs. Moore explained, because the school was in a Hispanic area of Brooklyn and the man selling the Good Humor bars was undoubtedly slipping drugs into them. Karla wondered what drug you could buy for fifteen cents and decided Mrs. Moore meant aspirin.

None of these rigors and deprivations much bothered Karla. Though Bromley restricted her body, the school opened up her mind, and she would always be passionately grateful to it for showing her how smart she was and for fostering her intellectual development. Thanks to small classes, every student at Bromley got close individual supervision—which Karla (if not many of the others) welcomed. Her English teacher told her she had talent as a writer, her French teacher praised her skill with languages; and her math teacher was so impressed with her gifts (her father Abraham was also a wiz at numbers) that Karla was sent to NYU to take an advanced course (she got a 98).

Bromley was intellectually nurturing not least because all the teachers were women (the only man at the school was the janitor), and a girl was *always* the smartest person in class and *always* editor-in-chief of the school newspaper. And the students, all of whom were white, got on well with each other. From Karla's perspective anyway, "there were no outcasts. . . . It didn't seem to me on looking back that anyone was particularly mean to anybody else. . . . There was no one who was ostracized for any reason, either because a kid was fat or a kid was unattractive. Everybody seemed to be friendly."

If that smacks of a rose-colored retrospective, it suggests that for Karla, anyway, Bromley was indeed "wonderful." And although she "still didn't have any words for what I was feeling," being at Bromley also gave her at least a rudimentary start at understanding her own sexuality. A lot of the girls had boys' nicknames for each other, sometimes those of well-known male actors. Only two of her classmates, Karla later learned, openly identified as lesbians, but labeled or not, there seems to have been a fair amount of homoerotic activity at Bromley, with necking and petting something of a commonplace.

Karla never developed any sense that such activity was "wrong." But two of the Bromley girls did overstep an ill-defined line. They were among the school's wealthy contingent; they lived in fancy houses and were driven to school in chauffeured cars. The two had been inseparable friends since elementary school, but by junior year at Bromley their behavior became notably more "eccentric"—to the point where even Karla felt confused and embarrassed by it. During lunch hour, when everyone else ate together at long tables, the two girls would sit ostentatiously apart, constantly touching, loudly calling each other "dearest" and "darling." They even appeared in ties now and then.

Finally, Headmistress Moore called the mother of one of the girls and pointedly asked whether her daughter came home for the night or spent it at the other girl's house. The mother's purported answer

—"None of your fucking business"—spread like gleeful wildfire throughout the school, giving the girls enormous pleasure. (Mrs. Moore was not well liked.) But the daring twosome's blatancy continued to make Karla nervous: "I felt sort of threatened by them because I felt they might endanger all of us, could cause the school to crack down on all of us." She learned later in life that both girls had married men—and had gone right on seeing each other and spending nights alone together. Perhaps, Karla mused, the relationship represented a special category of "upper-class lesbianism"—no labels, no apologies, no guilt, no remorse.

Bromley held periodic dances with Poly Prep, the boys' academy in Brooklyn, but few of the girls dated more than occasionally. Rhoda expressed some mild concern at Karla's apparent lack of interest in boys, but retreated when Karla pronounced them "boring"; that was still about the limit of her vocabulary. But by junior year at Bromley, Karla had discovered the locked case at the local library, and had discovered, too, that the librarian *would* allow her to read the books in it—though insistent on rattling her keys loudly to alert everyone in the room that another dirty-minded young girl had revealed herself.

About the first book Karla fell upon—it was a prototypical lesbian discovery—was Radclyffe Hall's *The Well of Loneliness*. But unlike so many other lesbians in these pre-liberation years, Karla did not feel a shock of recognition, nor was she filled with relief at the realization that other women like herself existed. She hadn't felt tortured enough for that, hadn't been guiltily hiding the desperate secret of her sexuality from herself and others. In this regard, the all-girl environment of Bromley had served her much as the all-boy environment of Chicago Junior School had served Craig Rodwell: Same-gender intimacy came to seem utterly natural to them. About all that Karla got from *The Well of Loneliness* was a newly depressing awareness that a lesbian lifestyle could be centrally characterized by confined options and negative consequences.

Again unlike so many lesbians in these years, Karla never read the lesbian pulp novels that began to appear in abundance in the fifties. Many of the books portrayed loneliness, alcoholism and suicide as the common lesbian lot. Some women found such desperation to be no more than an accurate reflection of their own unhappy lives, and took some solace in knowing that their misery was shared. But many other women have cited the pulps as having given them what limited empowerment they were able to find back then. For not all the novels were filled with wretched, self-hating "inverts." In Claire Morgan's

1952 novel, *The Price of Salt*, for example, the women are presented as complex, admirable figures insisting, against great odds, on their own worth and on making dignified lives for themselves.[4]

Karla seemed to have arrived at comparable self-esteem without benefit of the pulps. Her double distinction in the classroom and on the playing fields gave her, by the time of her graduation from Bromley, a settled self-confidence that she had previously lacked. She had a wall of trophies in athletics (in college she would become a semi-professional bowler), and in her senior year she won a coveted Regents Scholarship and graduated second in her class. It was quite a road for "Number 36" to have traveled.

The Regents Scholarship came in the nick of time. Up until the early sixties, Karla's father had been part-owner of the dunnage company he worked at, and he had made a fairly good living on the docks. His job status might have been blue-collar, but his income was middle-class. Karla never felt that she lacked for anything while growing up, though throughout high school she contributed what she could through baby-sitting and dog-walking jobs. But then, with the opening of the St. Lawrence Seaway, an alternate shipping route, Abraham's fortunes started to decline. He told Karla he would be unable to finance a college education for her.

He was ambivalent anyway about a girl getting too much book learning—he *did* manage to find the money to send his son, Paul, to college. But Karla was determined on more education. The Regents Scholarship, which paid well in those years, made that plausible. The money wasn't enough for her to go to her first choice, Vassar, where charges were too expensive for her means, but it proved just enough for Barnard. Besides, a cousin had gone there and had raved about it. So Barnard it was. Abraham pledged ten dollars a week, and the scholarship covered tuition. Not enough money was left over for a dormitory room, however. And it was not at all clear how Karla would eat.

FOSTER

Shortly before the end of World War II, U.S. Steel was casting about to find new uses for the metal in the coming postwar period. Foster Gunnison, Sr., a superb salesman, managed to convince the company that it could substitute steel for wood in his prefabricated houses, turn out models in the $2,800-to-$5,000 range, and thereby open up a huge new market, comparable to that for automobiles. Persuaded, U.S. Steel bought out Gunnison Homes for two million dollars, kept Foster Sr. on as its president, and also put him on the parent company's board of directors.[5]

By the early fifties, Foster Sr. had become convinced that U.S. Steel was making a botch of things; it might have been a giant company but its managers had no experience in the highly specialized housing field, and they seemed unwilling to rely on his. U.S. Steel, for its part, gradually became convinced that it had bought a white elephant; the company never built a single house with any steel in it, and soon discontinued Gunnison Homes, turning the plant into a warehouse. In 1950, before that final debacle, Foster Sr. decided to step down as president of Gunnison Homes (while remaining on the board of U.S. Steel) and to set up a prefab-house dealership in St. Petersburg, Florida, run by his son.

Foster Jr., now in his mid-twenties, had been floundering since his graduation from Columbia in 1949. Struggling to get a handle on a possible career, he decided to undergo a series of psychological, aptitude, and intelligence tests at the New York University and Columbia University counseling centers. The results were revealing, though somewhat disquieting. Foster's scores for general intelligence surpassed those of over 99 percent of twenty-six-year-olds, and on the verbal sections his performance was rated "truly outstanding." That alone had to be a comfort to someone who had barely survived his freshman year at Haverford.

But the rest of the news seemed to confirm what his father viewed as Junior's "maladjustment." The test results portrayed a somewhat formal, meticulous man, obsessive about detail work yet generally lacking in confidence. The report described him as "extremely sensitive, moody, unstable and rather immature," and ominously concluded, as well, that "he is not at present making a favorable sexual adjustment." The experts recommended a prolonged course of psychotherapy. Foster opted for Florida instead.

His father had bought up several blocks of land in north St. Petersburg, had had his prefabricated homes shipped down there from the plant in Indiana, had put them up, and had then sold houses and lots together, at 2 percent financing, for little more than six thousand dollars. Though Foster Sr. didn't himself move to Florida until 1953, about a year after his son, he handled most of the sales himself, leaving

Foster Jr. to take care of the dealership's internal business affairs. In all, some three dozen houses got built in a two-year period, with handsome profits for the father-son team. Foster Jr. accumulated enough capital, further parlayed through investments, to become financially independent.

But the work itself never captured his interest—though, as always, he did enjoy being behind the scenes in a structured situation that emphasized detail work. By the time Foster Sr. moved to Florida in 1953, following his marriage to his secretary (after a long-standing affair), Foster Jr. had decided he wanted to leave the firm to pursue an academic career. That hardly seemed a logical choice, given his mediocre undergraduate record, but, with the psychological testing results to bolster him, Foster felt that his previous under-par performance had been due to boredom with the subject matter of his courses. Of recent years he had begun to develop an interest in psychology, and as he did so, apathy toward academic study had given way to enthusiasm. Foster decided to enroll at Trinity College in Hartford, Connecticut, for a master's degree. His intention was to continue on to an eventual doctorate and to a life in academia.

But his reentry into the academic world was not easy. He found himself unable to concentrate for very long. His mind wandered when he read, and his interest wavered from subject to subject. No sooner had he enrolled at Trinity than he began to increase his involvement with barbershop quartets. No sooner had he started out in psychology than he began to take elective courses in philosophy.

By the mid-fifties he was spending more time with barbershoppers than with academics, and he began to doubt whether he was really cut out to be a student and scholar after all. But he did get confirmation and encouragement from various quarters. His professors gave him uniformly high grades, and as one of the college officials wrote Gunnison Sr., "Foster's record here speaks for itself. I think I need not tell you that few people achieve such excellence."

Moreover, one of the most touted young professors in the school went out of his way to praise Foster's abilities. Paul W. Kurtz, an assistant professor of philosophy at Trinity, had only gotten his own doctorate at Columbia in 1952, yet was already regarded as one of the guiding lights behind the emerging movement of humanism—and as an inspiring teacher as well. His sympathy for metaphysical speculation, at a time when logical positivism had taken over philosophy, appealed both to Foster's penchant for the "big questions" and to his pronounced psychological identification with the underdog. Though

Kurtz was very nearly the same age as Foster, he played a major role in arousing Foster's dormant academic abilities and interests. He might even be said to have become something of a surrogate father—except that this time, the father's interest seemed genuine. When Kurtz went to Venice in the summer of 1958 to attend the International Philosophical Congress, he took Foster with him and the two did some traveling together en route to the congress. Foster seemed at last to have found a congenial mentor and an academic home, and by 1958 he had formally enrolled as a student in both psychology and philosophy.

But the college dean had begun to suggest that he was being dilatory in completing his master's degree in psychology. Foster had chosen to make his thesis an evaluation of Adorno's study of the authoritarian personality, drawn to it, perhaps, as a way of better understanding the context of his own upbringing. But it was not until 1960, his sixth year in graduate school, that he was finally able to complete the thesis and earn his degree. The psychology faculty awarded him a grade of 97—the thesis apparently contained a genuinely original mathematical formula—but then reduced the grade to a 90 because of the inordinate amount of time he had taken.

With the master's in psychology behind him, Foster continued to pursue a second degree in philosophy with Paul Kurtz. But just as he was about to begin his thesis, Kurtz announced that he was leaving Trinity to teach elsewhere. He later encouraged Foster to join him in promoting the burgeoning humanist movement, but by then Foster felt too rooted in Hartford to leave. Besides, he may have been experiencing, on a level too deep to be fully conscious, a rejection that Kurtz had never intended; he may have been feeling that the surrogate father had turned out, after all, to be much like the original: willing to enlist Foster in his own projects, while controlling the terms of the relationship from a safe distance.

In 1961, the same year Kurtz left Trinity, Foster's own father died, succumbing at age sixty-five after a decade's struggle with heart trouble and diabetes. Foster's ever more difficult mother never remarried; a lifelong health fanatic, she concentrated her energies on a daily routine of walking and dieting. She announced her determination to live to be ninety—and did, by seven days. On Foster's infrequent visits to her at Gypsy Trail, she continued to subject him, between dollops of brewer's yeast and vitamin supplements, to her unpredictable, explosive mood swings.

In a farewell letter to Foster, Kurtz offered him some parting advice: He would be "much better off," Kurtz wrote, if he "resituated" himself. "You have too much to offer, and you should have every opportunity to make the most of it." But for now this was not a message Foster could hear. After a brief spell of academic success, he lapsed back into his long-settled self-image as someone marginally gifted whose existence didn't much matter. He reverted to lessons he had learned as a youngster: *not* to call attention to himself, *not* to attempt distinction that was "clearly" beyond his grasp. As a child Foster had survived life with his demanding, domineering parents by becoming, on the surface, unobjectionably "nice." But beneath that accommodating surface lay dormant discontent that had not yet found an expressive channel. For a while longer, Foster would settle for working semi-anonymously in a non-profit environment free from demanding responsibilities. But by the mid-sixties, when in his forties, he would finally find a "cause" able to call out to the full his uncommon talent for nurturance and his tenacious dedication.

J I M

Jim could never bring himself to sleep with people in order to get parts. He thought of himself as a romantic: sex was "a big deal," a way to get to know someone with whom he planned to spend the rest of his life. Not that he didn't pick people up in bars for casual sex on occasion, or go to Everard, the gay Turkish baths; but even in those places he was searching for a boyfriend, for tenderness and connection. He didn't "do" a lot of sex, though not—as an eighteen-year-old, stereotypically pretty blond—for want of opportunities.

He was, in fact, constantly fending off passes—and not always in a way that (at least in retrospect) pleased him. He thinks he may have been too arrogant and haughty when rejecting a proposition— "How dare you!" indignantly written all over his face. It was not simply a matter of priggishness, though; Jim was also angry at being approached as merely another pretty boy (at eighteen he looked twelve), at his pursuers' consistently ignoring what he knew was his complexity and intelligence.

He blames himself most for having sometimes led people on. He was, he can now admit, "a fabulous cock-tease." Once he accepted a director's invitation to vacation in Puerto Rico, with the stipulation that he would have his own bedroom; when Jim discovered, on arriving, that the two of them were sharing a bed, he made a huge stink about it, withdrawing into huffy chastity. "I shouldn't have gone in the first place," Jim now says. "I knew perfectly well what would happen if I did."

Paula Strasberg, the wife of Lee (head of the Actors Studio), and herself a respected coach, once said to Jim, "I don't care *how* you get the part. It's only when you get the part that you know if you can do any good work." Jim wasn't able to proceed on that advice, but he came to cherish nearly everything else he heard at the West Forty-sixth Street Actors Studio. In the early sixties, it was decidedly *the* place for theater people; every actor wanted to be accepted as a member of the hallowed Studio. In Jim's case, he won admission by a hair.

During the interview, Lee Strasberg told him peremptorily that he was underage, and then asked him who his two favorite actors were. Despite his mask of naïveté, Jim could be shrewdly calculating; he answered "Marilyn Monroe," knowing that she was close to the Strasbergs. Then he named Montgomery Clift, and said that whenever Clift performed "something unusual happened." (He omitted telling Strasberg that on first arriving in New York, he had found out Clift's address, gotten wildly drunk, and crooned "Monty, Monty" under his window; he had awakened the next day in Clift's guest room, but never got to meet him.) Jim added that he had first heard about the Actors Studio after asking one of the Phoenix Theater actresses he most admired where she had studied. Strasberg was apparently taken with all of Jim's answers, and decided not only to admit him to his own private classes held at Carnegie Hall, but to give him a full scholarship.

Jim ended up studying with Strasberg for nearly seven years. Where others found Strasberg self-aggrandizing and pretentious, Jim found him almost wholly admirable, something of a surrogate father. "Lee changed my life," Jim says simply. "I was a very smart kid, and a sensitive kid, but I was very much out of touch with my own feelings." Going to class became more important to him than anything else in his life, more important than holding down a job and eating, even more important than going for an audition. Strasberg sent him to other teachers besides himself: to Master Chang, a t'ai chi teacher on Canal Street, and to Sevilla Fort, a black dancer who taught Jim that he didn't have to wait until he could do something perfectly, or better than anyone else, before taking a chance; it was okay to do the best he could, so long as it *was* his best.

Jim briefly found "true love" in Strasberg's class—with Frank, a fellow student. They lived together for a while in a twenty-nine-dollar-a-month garden apartment on Forty-sixth Street (sublet from Richard Hepburn, the brother of Katharine Hepburn). When he and Frank broke up, two of Jim's heterosexual friends decided that he needed a girlfriend, and for a while Jim had an affair with the woman they introduced him to. But he never pretended to be straight, and in the world of the Actors Studio never had to. Homosexuality was commonplace among members of the Studio, though no one talked openly of it, or ever publicly declared—in the later style of gay liberation—his or her orientation. In the early sixties, to be a declared homosexual would have been like asking to be an unemployed actor.

The same attitude held even in the far-out reaches of the Living Theater, which Jim got connected with in 1962, a year after joining the Actors Studio. By then, the earlier distinction between Broadway and off-Broadway theater had blurred, and avant-garde work had started to move from off-Broadway to the coffeehouses, lofts, churches, cellars, and storefronts that Jerry Tallmer, drama critic of *The Village Voice*, had labeled in late 1960 "off-off-Broadway." In the world of the avant-garde—still fermenting in the early sixties, but soon to burst forth—Judith Malina and Julian Beck's Living Theater ("The Living" in the jargon of the cognoscenti) was considered by many the most radically innovative. It was self-consciously political, prided itself on its interracial company, combined communal living with theatrical experimentation in its Fourteenth Street space, and mounted a sweeping assault on mainstream American values.

Yet even at the Living Theater, homosexuality was more practiced than spoken of. By 1962 Jim was sharing an apartment with the Living Theater's stage manager and performing in its production of Auden and Isherwood's *The Dog Beneath the Skin*, but he almost never heard any open talk about the same-gender love and lust being played out all around them. Still, he valued his stint with the Living Theater. He had known few Jews or blacks while growing up in East Providence—blacks lived on South Main Street, not in his neighborhood, and Jews were rich people who owned big houses on Blackstone Boulevard; now he finally got intimate exposure to both, and took easily to both (indeed, in Jim's view, gay people have a sixth, sympathetic sense that draws them naturally, compassionately to other outsiders).

He was particularly drawn to Joe Chaikin, a member of the Living Theater who had made a strong impression in the company's pathbreaking play about junkies, *The Connection*. In 1963 Chaikin would form his own group, the Open Theater, with which Jim would get involved and which, in the minds of many, would come to epitomize the theatrical ferment of the decade. Jim credits Chaikin with actually saving his life at a point when he was feeling down about being gay. Chaikin simply took him to bed, cuddled and kissed him, made him feel good about himself.

Still, there was only one avant-garde theater in New York in the early sixties where it was thoroughly okay to be gay: the Caffè Cino, the earliest (1958) of all the off-off-Broadway experimental groups and a significant if rarely credited crucible for an emerging gay male sensibility. The Cino was the brainchild and alter ego of Joe Cino. Born in Little Italy, he had originally intended to become a ballet dancer, an unlikely aspiration for an Italian-American boy, but when he was in his twenties that passion had given way to a *somewhat* more seemly preoccupation with theater. (In the early-morning hours after the Caffè had closed its doors to paying customers, Joe Cino, stark naked and by then overweight, would perform solo dances under the stage lights in nostalgic tribute to his youthful dreams.)[6]

The Caffè Cino, at 31 Cornelia Street in Greenwich Village, functioned as a coffee shop cum performance space and was essentially an extension of Joe Cino's own apartment (he usually slept on a mattress in the back room). He packed the small Caffè with assorted *chotchkês*, glitter, and crystal, hung paintings by Kenny Burgess (a Cino waiter) on the walls, and constructed a tiny (twelve-foot) stage surrounded by tables and chairs that accommodated no more than fifty people.

A large espresso machine stood on a counter off to the side. It produced the countless pots of brew that, together with sandwiches and sodas, provided the Caffè's fare (and sustenance—it never got a dime in arts grants). The wall behind the espresso machine was covered with pictures of movie stars, opera divas, and unidentified beauties of both genders. Each evening Joe Cino, usually dressed in a trademark black cape, would start the performance with a flourish— "It's magic time!"—and would then retreat behind the espresso machine to serve up coffee and, now and then, to follow along (audibly) with the proceedings onstage.

A number of gay male theater artists who later became well-known—Lanford Wilson, Tom Eyen, Marshall Mason, Robert Patrick, Jean-Claude Van Italie, Paul Foster, William M. Hoffman, Tom O'Horgan, Neil Flanagan, H. M. Koutoukas, Doric Wilson, and Ronald Tavel (not to mention nongay playwrights like John Guare and Sam Shepard)—worked at some early point in their careers at the Cino, as did a bevy of future stars, including Bernadette Peters, Harvey Keitel, and Al Pacino.

Joe Cino encouraged a kind of gay-hip atmosphere. Years before an emergent gay movement helped to legitimize such subjects, Cino's favorite injunction to gay male playwrights was "Get real, Mary!"— that is, "Let's bring the gay thing out into the open!" The result was a large number of plays with gay male themes or characters, including some—like Lanford Wilson's *The Madness of Lady Bright*, Tom Eyen's *Why Hanna's Skirt Won't Stay Down*, and Robert Dahdah's campy, if not overtly homosexual, production of *Dames at Sea*—that have achieved the status of classics. And the message that it was okay to be gay filtered out beyond the Cino circle itself. Arthur Bell, later a prominent gay activist and *Village Voice* columnist, recalled that for him and others, the Caffè "exemplified the freedom that was to come. . . . The Cino group made me want to assert my own gayness to the world."[7]

Jim Fouratt found his way to the Cino in the early sixties. He performed the role of a Mae West–like spider in *Fairies I Have Met*, a play based on the poems of Oscar Wilde (the playwright, Allen James, later committed suicide), and acted in several plays by Joe Bush, who in the fifties had written the first "outing" book, *Famous People Who Are Gay*. Ondine, born Robert Olivo and later a Warhol star, was part of the Cino while Jim was performing there, and much talked of as the possessor of the largest cock in North America. Intrigued, Jim accepted Ondine's invitation one day to view his prodigious organ in the bathroom. When they got there, the cock proved to be prodigious indeed, but all Ondine wanted to do with it was shoot it up with a hypodermic needle. Apparently he couldn't get off unless someone was watching.

The experience scared Jim. He was not yet twenty, and did not want to become part of the endemic drug-taking at the Cino. Indeed as the sixties wore on, Joe Cino, always drawn to intensity and ecstatic abandonment, himself became increasingly addicted to speed—and increasingly paranoid. When his lover, John Torrey, the Cino's elec- trician, was electrocuted while doing a lighting job in New England, a despondent Joe moved closer to the edge. On March 31, 1967, he carved up his own body with a kitchen knife. A hundred and twenty people gave blood at St. Vincent's Hospital in an effort to save him, but he died three days later, aged thirty-six. Friends and associates tried to keep the Caffè Cino going, but it closed its doors for good in 1968.

Jim acted at the Cino during its heyday, and although he never became a central figure in its operations (or its mythology), he did a number of eye-catching turns—including a pathbreaking nude scene ("I was primarily worried about how my dick was going to look") in which he was sexually abused by, among others, Jesus, Mary, Dale Evans, and Roy Rogers, and which ended with him ecstatically fucking a TV set.

Robert Heide, one of the Cino playwrights, thought Jim was "incredibly pretty, something like the famous photo of himself that Truman Capote put on the back jacket of *Other Voices, Other Rooms.*" And he also thought Jim was a good actor, a hypertheatrical, incandescent presence, with an almost "Marilyn Monroe aura about him." Heide was among the few who also recognized that Jim was "super-intelligent," even if he himself wasn't admitting to it much, preferring the then current "Let's be cool" style.[8]

Jim and Bob Heide never had anything more than a brief flirtation, but did hang out together for a time. They shared much: the notion that theater was somehow going to save their lives; sardonic amusement at all the "straight" Actors Studio–Living Theater types who were somehow available for gay sex; and, too, some mutual friends—Jim Spicer, the Living Theater's general manager, who ran its Monday night "new playwrights" series at the Cherry Lane Theatre, and Ron Link, the stage manager and director with whom Jim shared an apartment for a time.

Hanging out in the Village in the early sixties meant a mix of bars and coffee shops. There were far fewer gay bars than in later years, and those that did exist were run by the Mafia and subject to frequent police raids. Jim, Bob Heide and their friends frequented (as did Yvonne Flowers) Lenny's Hideaway, a cellar bar on Tenth Street off Seventh Avenue South, as well as the popular gay dancing bar (about the only one in existence at the time) that adjoined the Cherry Lane Theatre on Commerce Street. Sometimes, too, they would go to the Old Colony, Mary's, and the gay and straight artists' hangout, San Remo, on MacDougal Street, which specialized more in drama than in sex (Jim Spicer's habit of draining black Russians and throwing the glass on the floor barely raised an eyebrow).

Coffee shops were also places to rendezvous. Mother Hubbard's in Sheridan Square was a special favorite. Open all night, it was famous for its apple pie and its generosity to actors. Owner-manager

Adele Speare (the gay crowd called her Mildred Pierce in tribute to her Joan Crawford–like looks and her Cadillac) offered a hamburger, apple pie, and coffee for ninety-five cents—or for nothing if you were one of the out-of-work actors she favored. Around the corner from Mother Hubbard's was Pam-Pam's, where another generous woman, Clara, let Bob Heide and Ron Link run up a $500 tab at one point. And across the street was Riker's, where a large gay crowd would go after the bars closed.

For those single-mindedly on the prowl for sex, there were the all-night Everard Baths, the balcony at the Regency Theater (which showed old movies) on Sixty-sixth Street, the men's rooms at assorted subway stops and at Rockefeller Center, the working-class Howard Baths in Newark, and the McBurney and Sloane House YMCAs (Stella Adler, with whom Heide was studying acting, would archly tell her classes, "Now, I don't want my boys running around the YMCAs!").

Alcohol was still the preferred drug in gay circles in the early sixties, but mescaline and LSD were finding advocates. One Living Theater actor specialized in mixing mescaline and apricot nectar, and Johnny Dodd, a waiter and co–lighting designer at the Cino (he died of AIDS in 1991) would throw periodic LSD parties in his apartment on Cornelia Street—the apartment from which in 1964 Freddie Herko, a dancer with the James Waring company, made a naked ballet leap out the sixth-story window to his death. When Bob Heide showed Andy Warhol the spot on the street where Herko had landed, Warhol nonchalantly said, "I wonder when Edie [Warhol's superstar, Edie Sedgwick] will commit suicide. I hope she lets us know so we can film it!"[9]

A favorite cure for drug excess was a visit to the Lemon Guru —Dr. Soltonoff, a chiropractor with offices on Houston Street who developed a devoted following that included Bob Dylan and Joe Louis. Soltonoff insisted that lemon juice in a glass of hot water three times a day, in combination with fasting, would cure just about anything. But should it not, there was the still-sanctified path of psychotherapy. Dr. Robert Akeret was a particular favorite with theater people. Working closely with Rollo May, Akeret developed his own special technique of "photoanalysis" in which he would analyze old family pictures in order to diagnose interfamily tensions and relationships.

Also much consulted was the gay psychoanalyst Dr. Karl Goldman, who had survived internment in a concentration camp during the war. Goldman's apartment on Waverly Place became a drop-in salon; of an evening you could ring his bell and usually find a congenial group gathered in the living room. He sometimes cooked for the more "interesting" gay men he collected—including, occasionally, Jim Fouratt and Bob Heide—discoursing at length after dinner on existentialism or the meaning of paranoid psychosis. A genuine intellectual, Goldman was also tight and aloof, literally hunched over with tension and incapable of looking anyone directly in the eye. He could be archly patronizing, effectively using his wide-ranging knowledge to cow those who were younger or more impressionable (but really to establish his own right to exist). Goldman was later found handcuffed and dead in his bathtub, drowned by an ex-con he had been treating as a patient.

Lee Strasberg told Jim that his success in the theater would depend not on his abundant talent—which by itself could prove an obstacle —but on the extent of his ambition and his perseverance. Though Jim became addicted to neither drugs nor sex, he did become something of an excitement junkie, always wanting to be where the action was, and preferably at the center of it. His early years in New York coincided with the fading influence of one oppositional culture, the Beats, and the gradual emergence of a new one, with several strands—from hippie to New Left—that would coalesce by the middle of the decade around the issue of the Vietnam War. Jim, barely twenty, managed to meet some of the luminaries of the older protest movement and to participate in some of the earliest manifestations of the newest one.

In 1963, the IRS seized the Living Theater's Fourteenth Street space for failure to pay taxes, and rather than bow to pressure from the state, the company decamped for Europe. Saul Gottlieb, variously connected to the Living Theater as writer, director, and fund-raiser, and his lover, Dale Evans, who would later become a significant figure at the SDS publication *New Left Notes*, decided to drive cross-country to San Francisco; they invited Jim to go along with them.

Though the car broke down in Montana and they had to pull an elaborate airline scam to afford a flight the rest of the way, the trio did manage to arrive in San Francisco. Gottlieb had ties to the beatnik enclave there, and during their two-month stay Jim had dinner at Lawrence Ferlinghetti's house, and met everyone from the poet/playwright Michael McClure, to the poet John Wieners, to the avant-garde jazz musician Cecil Taylor, to then-beatnik Phyllis Diller (who had gotten her start at the Purple Onion, a beat hangout).

When he returned to New York, Jim soon found himself, almost inadvertently, involved in the incipient antiwar movement. In 1962 the radical Students for a Democratic Society (SDS) had issued its touchstone "Port Huron Statement," a searching critique of American life that indicted as well the country's colonialist posture on the world scene and its willingness to go to war in the name of countering a bogusly inflated Communist "threat." By 1963, moreover, the black civil-rights struggle was in high gear, with hundreds of demonstrations that year in dozens of cities. And after Lyndon Johnson's ascension to the presidency in late 1963, American involvement in Vietnam seemed poised on the verge of escalation.

Marketta Kimball, a fellow student at Actors Studio with whom Jim was preparing a scene for class presentation, asked him one day to meet her in Times Square before starting to rehearse. Jim agreed without giving the matter any thought. He arrived to find himself in the middle of one of the first demonstrations in New York against U.S. participation in the escalating Vietnam War. About sixty people had gathered, and all of them were arrested.

In the weeks before the case came up, Jim gathered a variety of letters, including one from Senator John Pastore of Rhode Island, testifying to his "good character." Nonetheless, he was found guilty, and given a suspended sentence. He felt "a little had" by Marketta, but the entire experience proved a milestone for him. Up to that point Jim's only real politics had been a kind of moral imperative, derived from his Catholic training, to "tell the truth." But now he had discovered—just as had Craig Rodwell, with his own brand of Christian Science truth-telling—that if you spoke truth, everything did *not* come out all right. He had been pulled off the street by FBI agents and branded explicitly a criminal and implicitly a traitor. That infuriated him—and would soon propel him into a radical activism that would push *stage* acting to the periphery.

R   A   Y

Gay hustling had been centered in the Times Square area for a long time. In 1948, the popular pulp *Salute* published an article entitled "Nightmare, USA" that lamented the "sad decline" of what, until the 1920s, had been the glamorous heart of New York's theater district.

Of late, the article contended, the Times Square area had become the scene of a well-entrenched, "horrifying" spectacle in which "dozens of twisted, money-mad kids, aged ten to eighteen, daily offer themselves to homosexuals." *Salute* insisted that "none of the lads is homosexual" ("possibly excepting a few of the older youths"); they were hustling out of dire necessity, disgusted at their "grisly profession, revolted at what they do."[10]

When Ray Rivera, eleven years old, scrawny but beautifully proportioned, with high, dramatic cheekbones and almond-shaped, languid eyes, arrived at "Forty-two" in 1962, he was decidedly one of the younger hustlers—but he was hardly heterosexual and hardly felt "disgusted." "Elated" was closer to the mark. When a man offered him ten dollars to have sex his very first night on the street, Ray was ecstatic: "Ten dollars?! Wow! Ten dollars of my own! Great! Let's go!" Needless to say, his grandmother, Viejita, didn't share his enthusiasm; when a neighbor reported spotting Ray on Forty-second Street, Viejita threatened him so violently—at that point he hadn't yet left her house for good—that the next day, after she had gone to work, he swallowed a whole bottle of her medication.

Someone called an ambulance, and Ray spent the next two months on a ward in Bellevue Hospital. Convinced that he was going to die, Viejita tried to take the cross that had belonged to her daughter (Ray's mother) from around his neck. When Ray fiercely held on to it, Viejita yelled, "But you're going to die!" "So I guess," Ray shot back, "I'm going to need it"—and refused to relinquish his grip.

As soon as he got out, he was back on Forty-second Street, more euphoric than ever at discovering that so many queens hung out and hustled there, determined this time to move out of Viejita's apartment for good. She tried to stop him by getting him recommitted to Bellevue, and from there sent to a foster home in Central Islip on Long Island. But after a few months Ray ran away, ran back to Forty-second and back to "Gary," an eighteen-year-old hustler he had fallen in love with. He and Gary took an apartment together on Seventy-third Street and Columbus Avenue and, against all the odds, stayed together for seven years, both of them hustling, both of them getting high on black beauties and bennies, both of them becoming well known and well connected in the Times Square world of queens, pimps, hustlers, and addicts.

Before long, Ray even had a new name. All the queens on the street renamed themselves; it was part of assuming a new life and a new identity. After Ray decided that he belonged among them, that he had finally found his real family, one of the old-timers told him, "Well, there's no Sylvia. There's no Sylvia right around at this realm. If there is, we don't know about it. You'll be Sylvia. What's that other name you like?" "Lee," Sylvia answered.

So Ray became Sylvia Lee Rivera. And she was formally re-christened. The ritual took place in someone's apartment uptown, with fifty friends from the street in attendance, most of them Hispanic and black but with a sprinkling of white queens. Sylvia was decked out in a white gown, a preacher from one of the Pentecostal Hispanic churches performed the christening ceremony, and afterward every-one partied. "It was just like being reborn," Sylvia later remembered. "You knew you were going into a different life. And I remember the preacher saying when he put the water on my head, 'Don't forget: This is going to be a hard life.'"

Among those present for the rechristening was "Miss Marsha P. Johnson" (Malcolm Michaels, Jr.), one of the very first people Ray had met on the street. Marsha was a black queen some five years older than Sylvia, who had started out as a boy hustler and now mostly worked in "full face" makeup. In Sylvia's words, "Marsha plugged in the light for me." On the day Sylvia first spotted her, Marsha was panhandling on the corner of Forty-second Street and Sixth Avenue, still dressed in the waitress pants and white shirt she wore on her job in Childs' restaurant. Ray felt immediately drawn to her and went right up to Marsha and started talking.

Marsha explained that yes, she did work Forty-second Street, but right now was just trying to get some spare change so she could get herself a dinner over at Romeo's—a special deal: spaghetti and meatballs for ninety-nine cents. "Mind you," she told Sylvia, jiggling a pocketful of money, "I made out good on tips today at Childs', but you never can be too sure. Besides, I might get lucky standing here, and pick up a trick."

"What *is* this queen talking about?!" Sylvia thought to herself, simultaneously confused and mesmerized. "What's your name, chile?" Marsha demanded. "Ray," the not yet rechristened Sylvia said. "Oh Miss Ray, you so *young*! How old are you?" "Eleven and a half," Ray answered. "Chile, you should be home with your mama!" "Well, how old are you?" Ray shot back, even at eleven not easily silenced. "Oh honey, don't worry about it," said seventeen-year-old Marsha with a yawn. "They call me the old queen, I've been around for so long. Did you eat today, chile?"

When Ray said he wasn't hungry, Marsha briskly took him in

hand. "Come on, I'm going to buy you somethin' to eat. I made tips. I made a few dollars. We'll go sit down and eat at Romeo's." And down they went to Forty-second and Seventh, every queen and most of the boy hustlers on the way calling out greetings to "Miss Marsha." At Romeo's, too, everybody seemed to know her. "Hey Marsha girl, how ya doin'?" the cashier called out. "How ya doin', girl?" the straight counterman repeated. Marsha nodded regally and gave her commands: "The usual, the ninety-nine-cent special. We'll have two of those. And make sure the plate's clean. We don't want no greasy plates."

For much of the next decade, Sylvia and Marsha were there at the important events in each other's lives, and toward the end of that decade were together at many of the central events in the early days of the gay liberation movement. In the beginning, Marsha was a guide for Sylvia, showing her the ropes, counseling her to "show a happy face all the time, not to give a fuck about nothing, not to let nothing stop you." Later on, politically, it would be Sylvia who took the lead and in fact far outdistanced Marsha in energy and commitment, who, applying Marsha's early advice literally, "refuse[d] to let anything stop her, refuse[d] to take any shit from anybody."

But in the early sixties, Marsha played the big-sister role, teaching Sylvia how to apply face makeup skillfully (in those years full drag was only for special occasions, not for hustling); getting her a part-time job as a messenger for Childs' restaurant (Sylvia later won promotion to billing clerk and then, working in suit and tie and full face makeup, to the accounts payable department); showing her how to rap to potential clients; and instilling the rules of the street: "Don't mess with anyone's lover; don't rip off anyone's dope or money." And that went for wigs, too. When Luisa, a Spanish queen, grabbed Marsha's wig off her head one night, Marsha ran screaming after her, finally catching up with her in Bryant Park, where she read her the riot act.

And it was Marsha who tried to prevent Sylvia's first arrest. One night, Marsha was stationed on Eighth Avenue by the Blarney Stone (the boy hustlers tended to stay on Forty-second Street proper; the queens usually hustled around the corner on Eighth), when Sylvia came down the avenue on her way to see some friends on Forty-second. "Don't go down there, girl," Marsha warned. "They're going to arrest people tonight; I feel it in my bones. Stay up here with me." But Sylvia, just turned twelve, insisted she *had* to "see some people" and down she went to Forty-second.

Thirty years ago, as Sylvia remembers it, the Times Square scene wasn't nearly as dangerous as it later became. "The street actually belonged to gay people back then. If anything jumped off, it jumped off with us knowing about it." To some extent that included police harassment. The paddy wagon would back up with such predictable regularity to Bickford's, in the middle of Forty-second Street, to take on a load of arrested queens ("Aw right, ladies, let's go!") that the event took on mixed overtones of boredom and mirth ("It was almost like something you look forward to"). The police would hold the queens overnight in the Tombs, near the Centre Street Courthouse, and then release them the next morning to return again to Times Square.

But the police were not *that* predictable. As Sylvia sauntered onto Forty-second that night, she saw a whole slew of hustlers and queens being crammed by the police into a narrow space in the middle of the street between one of the movie theaters and a hot dog stand; a few of the queens were busily tearing up their parole cards and sticking the pieces between the grates. Undaunted, Sylvia went right up to the crowd—and was promptly scooped up along with the rest into a waiting paddy wagon.

At the station, Sylvia told them she was sixteen and gave her name as "Robert Soya" ("I couldn't even spell it!"). Never having been arrested before, Sylvia found the whole thing vastly amusing. When the arraigning judge looked down on the crowd of some fifty queens and hustlers in front of him and said out loud to the assistant D.A., "The names you read are all male names, but I see quite a few females here," Sylvia burst out laughing, thinking the judge had made a deliberate joke.

He hadn't. "Oh, so you think that's funny?" the judge said, glaring at Sylvia. "Then I suppose you'll also think it's funny that I'm locking the whole lot of you up till Monday morning." That meant three days in the Brooklyn House of Detention, and the other queens were no more amused than the judge. They came down hard on Sylvia, and at the end of the three days, with all those "noisy and tacky queens on my case, I was glad to get out of there." Sylvia told Marsha that "the next time you tell me not to go anywhere, I will not go anywhere."

By this time, Sylvia and her eighteen-year-old-lover, Gary, had moved to the Aristo Hotel on Sixth Avenue in the Forties. For twenty-five dollars a week, they got a big room with private bath, and Sylvia, who had learned to cook as a child, hooked up a hot plate. It was "something like having a home," and their many friends from the street used it as headquarters. To complete the sense of family, Sylvia would often go with Gary to visit his mother and father in Flushing ("his parents were very accommodating"), and would take in Gary's brother for a few days when he was out on a pass from reform school.

But when Viejita met Gary, the reception was quite different. Sylvia had been visiting Viejita regularly every few weeks, and had also been sending her money (though Viejita never spent it and later returned it all to Sylvia—by then a tidy sum—denouncing it as "blood money"). When Sylvia told her about Gary, Viejita at first refused to meet him, convinced that Gary had talked Sylvia into hustling. When Sylvia protested that Gary was "a nice boy and hadn't made me do nothing," Viejita yelled, "You can't love another man!" After she belatedly accepted that Sylvia could and did, Viejita shifted to a new complaint: that Gary was white. "Why can't you have a Spanish boy?" she would yell at Sylvia, and Sylvia would shout back, "Oh, sure, sure—so I can go kill myself like my mother did?" When Viejita finally agreed to come to dinner one night, she sat stony-faced through the meal.

Sylvia did love Gary—more than any other man she would ever meet—and felt he "really did help my mind; he was there when I really needed him." They would sometimes "beat the shit out of each other," but they also had a great sex life—"I remember one time it got so good that we bent the rods on the fucking bed, the metal bars." They began to turn tricks together, too—for more money, not pleasure. Stoned on black beauties, they were willing to perform almost any scene, if the price was right.

But whether with Gary or alone, Sylvia tried to keep an eye out for danger. "I didn't want no problems. I just wanted to turn a trick, make my money, and go on about my business." Nor did she ever have much trouble. Gifted with a voluble, forceful personality (even at age twelve), and the ability to make quick, shrewd judgments of people, Sylvia never went with a client or climbed into a car until she had a chance to size the person up for at least a couple of minutes.

But after she started to wear more drag, at about age fifteen, the odds got somewhat worse. People did pull guns on her several times and did try to rip her off, though she outsmarted them by keeping only twenty or so dollars in her purse and putting the rest into a slit she had made in the hem of her miniskirt. And when hustling as a woman rather than as a boy, she managed to get over on almost all of her johns. If a trick got suspicious and asked her right out if she was a man, Sylvia, pretending indignation, would say, "Oh, so you think I'm a man, huh? So here, so go ahead and stick your hand in my crotch—c'mon, put it down here!—and tell me if I'm a man!" She'd be wearing a G-string that brought her balls up on her stomach and her dick halfway up her ass—"in the beginning it was painful" —and, to fool the client further, had sewn wig hair onto the G-string; to the touch, the wig hair was indistinguishable from pubic hair.

Almost everyone bought it. But one night when she was in drag she agreed to go home with an unusually young and attractive john. When they started to make out, Sylvia got turned on; the force of her erection popped the G-string, and her dick fell out. The john jumped out of bed, screaming "You fucking faggot!" at the top of his lungs, and started to hit her. One blow was so powerful it sent Sylvia flying across the room. She reached for her purse—friends had given her a gun to carry "just in case"—thinking the sight of it would slow the guy down. But when Sylvia pointed the gun at him, instead of backing off he lunged at her in a rage—and she fired. Not waiting to find out how badly he was wounded, she grabbed her clothes and ran.

That was not the end of it. Recovered, and determined on revenge, the man toured the Times Square area night after night, with two policemen in tow. When he finally spotted Sylvia, the cops arrested her. In the station, she got on the phone to Viejita, who came down to the precinct and did a tearful-grandmother bit, getting Sylvia released to her custody. On the advice of their Spanish lawyer, Sylvia washed off the makeup, cut her hair, enrolled in school, and on the day of the trial appeared in court as a model clean-cut teenage boy. "I ask you, your honor," Sylvia's lawyer intoned, "does this look like a street hustler or a transvestite?" The judge agreed it did not, and Sylvia beat the case.

THE
EARLY
SIXTIES

Resistance to oppression takes on the confident form of political organizing only after a certain critical mass of collective awareness of oppression, and a determination to end it, has been reached. There are always isolated individuals who prefigure that awareness, who openly rebel before the oppressed community of which they are a part can offer them significant support and sustenance. These individuals—the Nat Turners of the world—are in some sense transhistorical: They have somehow never been fully socialized into the dominant ideology, into its prescriptions and limitations; they exist apart, a form of genius.

Resistance, of course, can take many forms short of open defiance. The day-to-day resistance of African-American slaves who deliberately broke their hoes, feigned illness, slowed their work pace, or ran away—and the development of vehicles, especially religion and music, to express their unique experience—may never have reached Nat Turner's level of dramatic visibility, but did nonetheless provide outlets for "refusal."

In the years before World War II, gay men and lesbians, too, developed subcultural forms of daily resistance—from Walt Whitman's encoded language of "adhesiveness," to the female "support networks" that emerged with the settlement-house movement, to distinctive forms of dress, body language, and "camp" argot. Now and then an individual voice would be raised publicly—Edward Carpenter's in England, Magnus Hirschfeld's in Germany—to argue for the "naturalness" of homosexuality or to make an overt plea for greater public acceptance. In the United States, there is at least one documented instance of an individual in these years openly protesting homosexual oppression.

His name was Henry Gerber. He had emigrated to Chicago from Bavaria when he was twenty-one, and as an American soldier during World War I had returned to Germany. There he discovered Hirschfeld's homosexual-emancipation movement and decided to attempt a similar organization in Chicago. But Gerber's Society for Human Rights, founded in 1924, lasted less than a year. Although Chicago in the 1920s had a well-developed gay male subculture centered in "Tower-town," few came forward to join the Society. Gerber, as well as those who signed the Society's articles of incorporation, were arrested, and Gerber spent his life savings of two hundred dollars to cover their trial expenses. The "scandal" subsequently cost him his job with the post office. He then reenlisted, served several years on Governors Island in New York, and continued his sporadic, often lonely, protest.[1]

But if the United States lagged behind Weimar Germany or Edwardian England in the pre–World War II period, the experiences of gay men and lesbians during that war went a long way toward creating the needed critical mass of consciousness in this country that could eventuate in an organized political movement. During World War II many men and women who had grown up in rural areas or small towns and had regarded themselves as singular freaks, discovered in military service legions of others who shared their sexual orientation. The experiences and bonding that followed led many gay men and lesbians to decide, after the war, against returning to their hometowns and in favor of settling down in one of the subcultural enclaves that existed in the large cities, and particularly on the two coasts. Their presence helped to fuel a proliferation of gay and lesbian bars in the postwar period; several mid-sized cities like Richmond, Kansas City, and San José opened their very first ones. And the bars, in turn, became primary social institutions for gay men in general and for working-class lesbians, allowing for increased contact and cooperation.

And then, in 1950, the Mattachine Society (the name taken from a medieval secret fraternity) came into existence in Los Angeles. A small group of left-wing gay men (including Rudi Gernreich, later famous as a fashion designer), some of whom were self-described Communists, formed around the early leadership of Harry Hay. They put together an elaborate, hush-hush skeleton organization that in its hierarchical, cell-like structure reflected the order of the Freemasons, and in its secrecy reflected the realities of a Cold War climate that had made deviance of any kind subject to swift repression.[2]

The Mattachine analysis of homosexuality was, at its inception, startlingly radical. This small group of some dozen men pioneered the notion—which from mid-1953 to 1969 fell out of favor in homophile circles, only to be picked up again by gay activists after 1969—that gays were a legitimate minority living within a hostile mainstream culture. They further argued that most gays had internalized the society's negative judgment of them as "sick," that such "false consciousness" had to be challenged, and that political struggle was the best vehicle for doing so.[3]

Someone in Mattachine suggested that they needed a magazine to get their message out, and to create such a publication, a committee began meeting independently of Mattachine. In January 1953 it put out the first issue of *ONE*, a small monthly that would last until 1968 (with a brief revival in 1972). Several women were active in publishing *ONE*, especially, in the early years, Ann Carrl Reid and Joan Corbin, but Mattachine itself remained overwhelmingly male (and white).[4]

In 1955 a group of women, led by Del Martin and Phyllis Lyon, decided to launch Daughters of Bilitis (DOB), the first lesbian organization. DOB initially put heavy emphasis on meeting social needs—on ending the profound isolation and invisibility of lesbians—but it did gradually involve itself in education and law reform. Throughout the fifties, the Big Three—Mattachine, DOB, and *ONE*—maintained sometimes strained but essentially friendly relations, even though *ONE* periodically attacked Mattachine for being too conformist and assimilationist.

And indeed Mattachine had quickly shed its initial radicalism. Most of those who joined in the two years after its founding were far more conservative than the originators and by 1953 had wrested control of the organization from them. The newcomers were primarily interested in winning acceptance on the mainstream's own terms, not in challenging mainstream values; they regarded themselves as patriots and good Americans; and they preferred to rely on "experts" rather than on political organizing to plead their cause—having internalized the view of that era's prime experts, the psychiatrists, that their "condition" was pathological. Mattachine's original organizers had soon found themselves isolated; Harry Hay resigned and the conservative newcomers took over the organization.

CRAIG

By the time Craig Rodwell arrived in New York City in the late fifties, Mattachine had long since ceased to be a radical voice. Its dominant message to other gays had become an assimilationist one: Reform your own image so that it comports with respectable, middle-class sensibilities. But if Mattachine had become too conservative for its radical founders, it remained too radical for the vast majority of gays and lesbians, who had been cowed by the experts into a negative self-image, and were fearful that membership (even though pseudo-nyms were used) could threaten the loss of jobs, friends, and community status.

Only the most intrepid would consider joining Mattachine or DOB in these years. In 1960 Mattachine had only 230 members, and DOB had enrolled less than half that number.[5] But the spirited, mettlesome Craig Rodwell, though just eighteen when he arrived in New York from Boston in the summer of 1958, could hardly wait to join up—though he reluctantly accepted the fact that he would first have to find a place to live and get a job.

The Sloane House YMCA, on Thirty-fourth Street, provided a good, inexpensive start (along with a fair amount of action in the shower room), and Craig soon met someone there, Collin, with whom he became friendly. Like Craig, who had gotten a scholarship to the School of American Ballet, Collin was a dance student, hopeful of becoming a chorus boy on Broadway. Along with a friend of Craig's from Chicago, the teenagers took an apartment together—two tiny rooms—on Sixteenth Street and Seventh Avenue. It soon became a camping (in both senses) ground for the raft of street strays they began to meet; on some nights eight or nine people would be sleeping on every available inch of floor space.

Next came the problem of getting a job. All Craig had was a high school diploma and a few clerical skills. So he did what generations of the young have always done to survive in the big city: took a restaurant job. In a sense he was lucky; he was hired (even if only as a lowly salad boy) at Aldo's, the popular gay restaurant in Greenwich Village. His job was to stock up the two-tiered salad cart—local mythology insisted it had been donated by Christine Jorgensen—with a big bowl of lettuce, assorted dressings, and smaller bowls of condiments such as olives, tomatoes, and watermelon rinds, and move from table to table, serving the mixture of choice.

As befitted the camp atmosphere, Craig would sing out on arrival at each table, "Roquefort, garlic, or gasoline?" but in fact he hated the job from the start. Stanley, the man who ran Aldo's, was clearly Mafia, and the line of division between the straight, homophobic bartending and managerial staff, and the gay waiters and salad boys, was sharp. Having grown up in an all-boy atmosphere where same-gender affection was part of the natural flow of everyday life, Craig, unlike so many gays in these years, hadn't internalized his full share of homophobia. The condescension of the staff, in combination with the self-deprecation of some of the waiters and the uppity airs of some of the customers, put him in a state of simmering rage.

One night he decided he'd had it—and also decided that he was going to leave in style. He went to the kitchen, got some packing straw from the melon crate, and substituted it for the lettuce on the salad cart. After the customer made his choice of dressing, Craig obligingly put it over the salad/straw and served it. This went on for nearly an hour, with Craig serving almost the entire restaurant before anyone complained—intimidated either by Craig or by lifetime gay training in swallowing abuse without complaint. It was finally Stanley who caught wind of something being wrong and confronted Craig. He, in turn, called Stanley a "Mafia pig"—and stormed out.

That meant job-hunting again. Fortunately, Craig had taken typing in high school and had gotten good at it. Even so, he had to tip the man doing the hiring before he could get a clerical job in a plastic-flower factory, where he mostly did shipping work and typed invoices. About the only good thing that could be said for the job—aside from the fact that it paid the rent—was that the factory was located off Union Square on Sixteenth Street, near Craig's apartment.

By that point, Craig had already made his first trip to the Mattachine Society of New York at 1133 Broadway. In the tiny third-floor office he found one person at work—the president, "Al de Dion" (almost everyone in those years used a pseudonym). De Dion was cordial and pleasant, but when he found out that Craig was only eighteen, informed him that he had to be twenty-one before he could officially join Mattachine. Craig had never anticipated such a barrier and was crushed. But de Dion cheered him up by saying he *could* subscribe to the newsletter, volunteer to help out in the office, and also attend Mattachine's West Side Discussion Group, which met

once a month in the basement room at Freedom House on Fortieth
Street.

Attending his first meeting of the West Side Discussion Group
soon after, Craig had mixed feelings of elation and dismay. He was
thrilled to be in a room with several dozen people willing to attend a
public meeting on the subject of homosexuality, but was alarmed to
find that almost all of them were men over forty in business suits,
and paying what to him was far too much deferential attention to the
speaker of the evening—a stodgy psychiatric "expert" who pontifi-
cated at length about the entitlement of homosexuals to civil rights
even though their sexual development might have been distorted by a
"faulty" family configuration.

The more meetings Craig attended, the more his dismay grew.
He discovered that New York Mattachine had decided to confine its
operations to two areas, education and research, and had disclaimed
political agitation as counterproductive. Yet as Craig got to know more
and more of the individuals involved, he found many whom he liked
personally and even a few who shared his view that Mattachine should
become more activist and visible. "George Desmannes," editor of the
newsletter, was among the people Craig grew fondest of—"a warm
and wonderful" man who quickly and gratefully put Craig to work
doing pasteup, editing, and production of the newsletter.

Craig turned out to be an ideal volunteer. Not only was he an
enthusiast with seemingly limitless energy, but he could actually type
on the massive old IBM which had defeated everyone else. Craig even
insisted on justifying right-hand margins; he would spend days counting up the number of letters by which each line was too long or too
short, assigning pluses and minuses, and then laboriously retyping
copy. He loved doing it, and George loved having him do it. Over
time, Craig got more and more involved on the editorial side and by
1961, when he reached twenty-one and became an official Mattachine
member, he had pretty much taken over the newsletter—though,
typically, he never cared about being listed as its editor and getting
credit for his work.

As Craig became increasingly active, George advised him to use
a pseudonym to avoid having the FBI come snooping around his
apartment. Craig dismissed that as paranoia, but bowed to his fondness for George and let him put "Craig Phillips" among the other
names on the masthead. But he felt awful about giving in to what he
viewed as cowardice and for hiding what he was in fact proud of. So
within a few months, he started using his real name, scandalizing the

many conservatives in Mattachine who lived in constant fear of police reprisals.

They were even more frightened when Craig and several others decided to join a gay picket line in front of the draft board on Whitehall Street in protest against its policy of releasing information on sexual orientation to employers. The night Craig "casually" mentioned the plans, the two other volunteers working in the office at the time looked as if they "were both going to have heart attacks." "You can't do that!" one of them yelled, "Mattachine will lose its incorporation. Our charter forbids *any kind* of political activity—you'll ruin us if you do anything militant like that!"

Others later warned Craig that the last thing Mattachine wanted was press coverage, that publicity of any kind would lead not to additional recruits (as Craig claimed) but to the police shutting down the office. But they had no power to *forbid* Craig from acting in an individual capacity, and besides, they were a little intimidated by this seemingly fearless young dynamo. In the upshot, only half a dozen people joined Craig, and only one other (Renée Cafiero) was affiliated with Mattachine.

The small band included two young firebrands of the day, one of whom was straight. Jefferson Fuck Poland (he insisted the name was on his birth certificate) was the founder and head of the League for Sexual Freedom, and he brought along his girlfriend of the moment, who in turn brought along a baby. The other (who had been the chief organizer of the event) was "Randy Wicker" (Charles Hayden), who had joined Mattachine on arriving in New York in 1958 but had found its tone so tepid that he had formed his own one-man organization, the Homosexual League of New York, and had been using it to achieve some breakthrough coverage on homosexuality in the previously indifferent radio and print media.

Randy's lover, Peter, and Renée Cafiero's lover, the children's-book writer Nancy Garden, brought the group up to seven (not counting the baby). They may have been brave, but they were also scared. In the early sixties, the climate of Cold War conformity had lifted, but countercultural protest and challenge did not yet rend the air. People simply did not picket draft boards—let alone a mere handful of people acting in defense of a despised sexual minority. There seemed a fair chance that they would be summarily arrested, carted off to jail, and possibly beaten.

What in fact happened was that they walked back and forth in front of the draft board, and tried to hand passersby a flyer they had made up. But it was a rainy Saturday and only a few people were on the streets. The sergeant stationed in front of the building glared at them from time to time, but nobody else seemed to notice them much. It was something of an anticlimax, and yet they felt euphoric. They had done something different and daring, made a beginning. And they believed bigger and better actions would soon follow.

Craig was hardly all work and no play. In his early years in New York, his friends were mostly street queens, although—unlike Sylvia Rivera and her friends up on Forty-second Street—few of them hustled for a living; the only coinage in Craig's crowd was fantasy talk of meeting a rich sugar daddy. Their circle consisted of a rotating dozen or so late-teenagers, half of them black, with a smattering of Puerto Ricans and whites. In those years being a queen meant wearing eyeliner and mascara, and sometimes "doe eyes," with dark black lines on the top, and bottom lids filled in to a point. Anything more—that is, jewelry, teased hair, or drag—not only would have invited arrest, but would have meant debarment from many of the gay clubs. Even in modest mascara, Craig's friends were often either denied entrance or (as happened in the Club Fifty) marched straight into the bathroom to wash their faces.

Not that bars were their chief hangout. Craig and his friends might stop in on Sundays at the Wishbone on West Fifty-eighth Street to get free hot dogs and macaroni salad, but generally they were too poor to afford the inflated prices of gay clubs. And besides, in the early sixties, the outdoor scene was much more in vogue than the bars. The three most popular downtown places were Greenwich Avenue, Eighth Street, and Washington Square Park (the railing along MacDougal was known as the meat rack). On Greenwich Avenue on a given night, hundreds of gay men would sit on doorsteps or car hoods watching the promenaders move back and forth. An eye always had to be kept out, of course, for the cops. They never let anyone stay still for long; "Keep moving, faggot, keep moving," they would growl, poking their nightsticks into the men's ribs. At one point, the city cut down all the bushes in Washington Square Park and imposed a curfew in order to rid the area of "undesirables."

It was in Washington Square Park, when Craig was out cruising alone one night, that three plainclothes cops jumped him. Acting as if he were an escaped serial murderer, they screamed epithets, slapped him in handcuffs, and took him down to the old Sixth Precinct on Charles Street. Sitting in the squad room, surrounded by cops, the teenage terror of Mattachine let them know that he was no ordinary frightened faggot. Furious at the way he'd been treated, he started to harangue the cops, demanding to know by what right they had dragged a citizen off the streets. Indignant at having a "pervert" talk back to them, the cops took Craig into a side room and beat the shit out of him. The next day, his roommate Collin got him out, but Craig then had to appear at FBI headquarters on Sixty-ninth Street with his draft card to prove he was properly registered.

When Craig and his friends went out together, it was not primarily to cruise but to have fun. Part of that fun was "going wrecking"— taunting straights. That was pretty easily accomplished; the mere sight of two men holding hands on the street was enough to produce instant apoplexy in most heterosexuals. But if any of them made the mistake of trying to rough the faggots up, they were in for a rude surprise; some of the doe-eyed sissies were in fact tough street kids who didn't let anybody mess with them. The powerfully built Johnny Italiano was notorious for his quick fists; a straight who came at Johnny rarely walked away under his own power.

Sometimes, daringly, Craig and his friends went "wrecking" outside the gay areas. On one romp (thirty years before Queer Nation supposedly invented such noisy escapades) they went to a live broadcast of *The Carol Burnett Show*. Arriving at the studio in full face makeup, they created a deliberate stir in the balcony and—to nobody's surprise—got thrown out. They were also fond of spending an entire evening riding the subways (bargain entertainment at a fifteen-cent fare). Poured into blue jeans or chino pants made deliberately too tight by endless soakings in hot water, singing in loud falsetto the saccharine popular tunes of the day, they would, when feeling particularly exuberant, form a chorus line, kick their legs in the air and, to the tune of "It's Howdy Doody Time," perform their own special lyric:

> *We are the Village queens,*
> *We always wear blue jeans,*
> *We wear our hair in curls,*
> *Because we think we're girls.*

Perhaps because they seemed fearless, or perhaps because people thought they were lunatics, they rarely got hassled. On the contrary, a few fascinated young guys would usually end up tagging along during the evening.

Craig's daring caught up with him one day at Riis Park, the beach in Queens that was popular with gays. A local ordinance banned "suggestive" bathing suits on the beach, but the police, using the ordinance as a means of harassment, enforced it only against gay men. The cops would appear on a Sunday or a major holiday and station themselves near the refreshment area on the boardwalk above the beach. When word spread that they were there, a gay man going up on the boardwalk for a hot dog or a trip to the bathroom would dutifully cover his bikini with a towel—often making a major camp production out of the compliance.

Craig decided one Sunday to shift from camp indirection to straight-out protest. Hearing that the cops had arrived, he marched up to the boardwalk—*without* a towel over his bikini—and simply walked past them. They were initially startled, then angry. The police were used to gay men humbly begging their pardon and meekly promising never, never, never to do that (whatever it was) again. They stopped Craig in his tracks and asked him what the hell he thought he was doing. Running, as always, against type, Craig returned anger with anger, berating the cops for antigay harassment.

They responded by dragging him off to a small police room behind the bathhouse and demanding his name and address, which he quickly provided; but to badger him further, they kept asking for the same information over and over. Tiring of the game, Craig finally refused to answer again. This was astounding impertinence, and the outraged cops proceeded to knock Craig around. Still, he refused to break his silence. The cops then loaded him into a van, took him to the local precinct in Queens, and locked him up. Around midnight they brought him, in handcuffs, down to Criminal Court at 100 Centre Street for arraignment.

By this time Craig had lost his shoes and shirt; he appeared before the night court judge dressed only in shorts. The judge took him into his chambers and asked sympathetic, fatherly questions. He told Craig that because he was under twenty-one he would have to appear in juvenile court in two weeks; there, the judge predicted, he would almost certainly be let off with a ten- or fifteen-dollar fine. Two gay men who had been sitting in on night court (then a popular diversion), and had heard the testimony about what this defiant gay boy had done, drove Craig back home in their car.

But the trial two weeks later did not go according to the judge's script. When Craig arrived, he learned that charges of resisting arrest and inciting a riot had been added to his bathing-suit violation. He tried to argue his case before the presiding judge, insisting that he had not resisted arrest and could not have "incited a riot" since the police had taken him off almost immediately to their room behind the bathhouse. Then, his own volatility again getting the better of him, he heatedly told the judge that the police harassment of homosexuals at Riis Park was cowardly and indefensible.

Up to that point, the judge had been blank and uninterested. But with the mention of homosexuals, his face turned beet red, the realization having finally dawned that the teenager in front of him was one of "those" people. He banged down his gavel as Craig was in mid-sentence, and threw the book at him—which, since the judge had already dismissed the resisting-arrest and rioting charges, amounted to three days in jail or a twenty-five-dollar fine. Having been told two weeks earlier that the fine would be no more than fifteen dollars, Craig had brought exactly seventeen dollars with him. The judge banged down the gavel again and told the bailiff to take him away.

He landed in the Brooklyn House of Detention, where Sylvia Rivera, that same year of 1961, had suffered her own first incarceration. On arriving, Craig was brought into a large holding cell filled with both cops and prisoners. Suddenly a bruiser of a cop strode to the center of the room and said, "Awright, who's the one who's refusing to speak?" Before Craig could decide whether, against all experience, he should once more tell the truth, several of the other policemen pointed him out. Without another word, the burly cop strode over and hit Craig so hard on the side of his head that he landed up against the wall. Then the cop grabbed Craig's wallet and scattered the contents on the floor, yelling, "Pick them up, faggot. *Now!*" By then Craig was dripping blood and in tears. He picked up the stuff from the floor, answered when asked what his name was, and was locked up in the notorious "Queens' Tank."

Craig spent much of his three-day sentence teaching ballet to the thirty or forty street hustlers—doubtless some of them friends of Sylvia's—locked up with him. He was a huge hit. The queens loved learning the graceful movements, and were fascinated with Craig; it seemed unfathomable that a clean-cut, educated white boy was being treated the same way they were. Which for prisoners in the Queens' Tank, as Craig quickly learned, meant no commissary privileges, no movies, and no recreation beyond the walk from their cells to meals.

When released after his three-day stint, Craig, still traumatized, went directly across the street to a hamburger joint, gobbled up several burgers in a row and then, too upset to be thinking clearly, left the luncheonette without paying his bill. When he realized what he'd done, he was terrified that "they" would somehow come after him again and throw him back in jail—so terrified that instead of returning to the luncheonette and paying, he simply ran in the opposite direction as fast as he could.

But if the jail experience had unnerved him, it had hardly made him contrite. He went back to his friends, back to Mattachine, back to cavorting on the subways and streets. And everywhere he went, his volatility went with him. One night in the gay Tic-Toc bar on Second Avenue, he threw a glass of wine at Farley Granger after the actor had patted his ass uninvited and made some "friendly" comment about its attractive contours; Craig took it as an insult comparable (he was also a proto-feminist) to the way straight men pawed women, and he had come to the conclusion that *nobody*, straight or gay, was entitled to put him down.

It was an attitude that deeply unnerved the man who in 1961 became Craig's lover. They first met at the popular outdoor cruising area along Central Park West in the Seventies and Eighties, immediately started to see each other on a regular basis, and soon decided that despite all their dissimilarities—the man was ten years older than Craig, had a prestigious job as an actuary, dressed in Brooks Brothers suits and had conservative political values to match—they were very much in love. The man's name was Harvey Milk.

He was a romantic, enveloping personality, and he swept Craig off his feet. As soon as Harvey got to work every morning, he would call Craig to wake him for ballet school, usually with a joke. Three or four nights a week Harvey would take him out—his treat—to assorted ethnic restaurants; Harvey loved the cultural mosaic of New York and was determined to experience at least its culinary aspects. Alternatively, he cooked Craig elegant meals in his own apartment, which was only eight blocks from Craig's. And he was quick with bouquets of flowers and gifts. Hearing that Craig, between classes, ate his sandwich-and-soda lunch on a rock in Central Park, Harvey presented him with a miniature porcelain vase, complete with paper flower, to put on the rock next to him while eating.

They had already been seeing each other when Craig got arrested at Riis Park. The episode frightened Harvey; he was afraid it might get in the papers and he might somehow be implicated. He had already been made nervous by Craig's activities at Mattachine, and his voluble insistence that *all* gay people had to stand up for themselves. When

Craig and his friend Collin hand-made some flyers for a meeting of the West Side Discussion Group and stuffed them in every mailbox in the neighborhood where two men or two women were listed as living together, Harvey was furious. He told Craig that the flyer would scare some people to death: they'd assume that the truth about them was known and their whole lives would be ruined. Craig shouted back that Harvey was simply afraid that his own cover might be blown. (Yet Craig was chastened by remembering that when he had done the same thing back in Chicago, everyone had assumed that two nelly hairdressers in the neighborhood had been responsible for the mailbox stuffings, and they had been evicted from their apartment.)

But when the relationship finally disintegrated, it was over sexual fidelity, not politics. Craig, twenty years old, found it impossible to be monogamous, whereas Harvey required monogamy as a *sine qua non*. One night when they were dining out at an Indian restaurant on Ninety-sixth Street and Broadway, Harvey—ordinarily full of playfulness—became very serious and told Craig there was something he had to discuss: He had gonorrhea. Since he hadn't been with anybody else, he held Craig responsible. Craig acknowledged that he had slept with other men, and promised that he would stop, but the relationship never really recovered. Harvey started calling every *other* morning, and then gradually, over the period of a few months, stopped calling altogether.

Craig was grief-stricken. Harvey had been the love of his life, and the loss drove him to despair. Without a satisfying job, much education, or a career, "the future now looked a total blank." He quit ballet school, stopped seeing his friends and going to Mattachine, and finally decided to kill himself. He had attempted suicide once before, in his early teens, after he and Frank had been arrested on the street and Frank sent to jail. Put on probation, frightened, and with no one to talk to, Craig had swallowed a handful of aspirins with a Coca-Cola, having read somewhere that the combination was lethal. He had gotten sick but survived.

This time, Craig planned more carefully. He gave notice to his landlord, to his roommate Collin, and to his employer (at the time, an advertising agency). He bought a bottle of Tuinals on the black market, waited for Collin to go out to the movies one night, and then wrote him a formal note with instructions to call his aunt so she could tell his mother.

Then he began to take the pills. He had gotten through about half the bottle when he remembered that he hadn't put the note on the chair by the door so that Collin would see it first thing on arriving home. So he jumped off the couch and left the note on the chair. Then suddenly, before he could get back to the couch, he blacked out, hitting his head on the fireplace as he fell to the floor. The last thing he could remember was lying on the floor, desperately trying to reach the rest of the pills.

For some miraculous reason, Collin came back early from the movies. Finding Craig on the floor and thinking him dead, he dialed the police, the fire department, and an ambulance. The ambulance arrived first and took an unconscious Craig to Harlem Hospital, where he was given a shot of adrenaline and where he woke up strapped down to the bed. The first thing he saw when he opened his eyes was a cop, and he became instantly enraged, actually breaking loose from one of the straps. Then he passed out again, and when he next woke up, he was in the psychiatric ward at Bellevue.

They kept him there for a month, the worst month of his life. Each day began with the hospital's terrifying "morning lineup": All the patients on the floor had to stand in the corridor to hear a list read off of who was going to have electric-shock therapy that day. Craig's name was never called. Nor was he given psychotherapy. But he did get plenty of experimental drugs, which he quickly learned to put under his tongue and then, after the nurse had left, to spit out. The doctors asked Craig's father, whom he hadn't laid eyes on in years, to come down from Boston, and his mother to fly in from Chicago; when they arrived, the doctors told them that they would release Craig only if he were transferred to a private institution. Craig's father reluctantly agreed to foot the bill, and Craig was sent to the psychiatric ward at St. Luke's.

In Craig's words, "it was like going from Bed-Stuy to Park Avenue"—only two to a room, bedspreads, gourmet meals, television, and recreational therapy. To complete what felt like a restoration, Harvey came up to visit one day along with Collin; but Harvey proved uninterested in a reconciliation and it took another five years before even a distant friendship could develop.

Part of the agreed-upon deal in getting Craig out of Bellevue was that he be in psychiatric treatment for at least six months, starting while he was still in St. Luke's. From the first session, Craig adopted his silent strategy, and since the doctor never said a word either, there was no exchange between them at all. That is, until some time later, when Craig announced he was quitting and the doctor threatened to notify the police. "You go right ahead," Craig said, and walked out. His bluff was never called.

After three weeks in St. Luke's, Craig was released to a relative's house in Pleasantville, New York, where he stayed for a few months and then returned to Manhattan. He got a new job, this time doing clerical work for Marine Transport Lines, and his life seemed on the mend. But then Marine Transport got a big contract with the navy, requiring security clearances for all employees. Since Craig's homosexuality was a matter of police record, he couldn't get a clearance and was let go. So he went back to live with his mother in Chicago and took a job at an enameling factory. After years of being on his own, he found close-quarters living with his mother intolerable and, on impulse, accepted an invitation from a sometime admirer to join him in California. As soon as Craig stepped off the bus in Los Angeles, he knew he'd made a mistake; within a month he decamped for New York.

Arriving in the city in January 1964, he immediately plunged back into political work. Mattachine had begun to shift somewhat away from its previous conservatism, and Craig was eager to do everything in his power to accelerate the process.

YVONNE

Yvonne Flowers sometimes went to the Village poetry cafés that had sprung up in the late fifties, and especially to the Gaslight on MacDougal Street, where Allen Ginsberg, her favorite poet, was known to give impromptu readings. (What she didn't know was that Ginsberg, in turn, idolized her other hero, Thelonious Monk.)[6]

To accommodate her penchant for nightlife, and her part-time job as an attendant in the psychiatric ward at St. Vincent's Hospital, Yvonne had arranged to take all of her classes in the late morning or early afternoon. She would sometimes arrive at NYU without having had any sleep at all, and still high from club crawling. After class, she would crash at home for a few hours and then rush to her four-to-midnight shift at St. Vincent's. There she could easily cop a "dexie" (Dexedrine, an amphetamine pill popular in the sixties) and rev herself up again. Though she worked as an attendant, her job was in fact not very difficult and she was surrounded by buddies. In the early sixties, numbers of students, actors, and writers worked part-time at St. Vincent's and some of the people Yvonne partied with by night worked on the same floor with her by day. Other party friends appeared regularly in the emergency room, victims of drug overdoses and suicide attempts.

Drugs were not then kept under careful lock and key, nor guardedly counted out pill by pill, and Yvonne and her friends had fairly open access to the stockroom. Doriden (a hypnotic similar to that later popular favorite, Quaalude) was especially in vogue, and usually taken with wine. Dexamyl was also available. But as casual as Yvonne's attitude toward drugs was, she drew the line at anything experimental. In the early sixties, some research on LSD was being done at St. Vincent's, in conjunction with the U.S. Army; the LSD was given to psychiatric patients as an alternative to electric-shock treatment. Some of them flipped out and stayed out, so when the hospital employees were asked to serve as a control group, Yvonne firmly declined.

On weekends when she wasn't working or in class, Yvonne went to lesbian softball games—that defining institution of working-class lesbian life. These were the years in which lesbian softball teams and leagues (and to a lesser degree, the winter substitute, basketball) were all the rage. Yvonne didn't actually play—her assorted physical ailments made her tire too easily—but she enjoyed the scene. She loved cheering on the Montereys or the New York Aces, and loved the partying that followed the games (the teams were usually sponsored by bars). She especially liked watching the New York Aces' eighteen-year-old first basewoman in action; a fierce ball player who hooked her mitt onto her trousers "like the last little butch," she later became a celebrated newscaster (though not the sports commentator she had dreamed of becoming).

As an alternative to the bars, a number of black women specialized in throwing house parties. Yvonne herself gave one every few months, going in with friends who had a big loft on Second Street and Second Avenue. Dozens of people (mainly women) would pay a dollar each to get in to dance, drink, eat, and gamble, and Yvonne made a tidy profit. House parties were a venerable Harlem tradition, going back at least to the 1920s, when they were called rent parties. They were raucous, merry affairs that managed all at once to pay the landlord and keep the participants dancing till dawn.

Yvonne's friend Audre Lorde later contrasted on several levels the parties black and white women gave. The latter never had enough food (they offered a little bowl of sour cream and onion dip rather than hearty cornbread or fried chicken wings and potato salad); they never had music that could be danced to, or hard liquor (they preferred "sophisticated" wine), or laughter. The subdued tone at white lesbian parties always put Lorde off: "Mostly, women sat around in little groups and talked quietly, the sound of moderation . . . thick and heavy as smoke in the air . . . I always thought parties were supposed to be fun."

Yvonne, too, much preferred black lesbian gatherings, but being a party animal, she didn't turn down many invitations of any kind. And neither finding God nor falling in love slowed Yvonne's pace. The spiritual revelation came first—swiftly and suddenly. She had always wanted to believe that there was a God who made the world, that somebody was in charge, and her search had included, for a time, attendance at Zen Buddhist gatherings. But for years she "couldn't get it." Then one day, walking along Ninth Street from the Lower East Side to the Village, talking to God as she frequently did, she said, "I want to believe. I really *want* to believe." And just like that, she did. She quite suddenly "understood," finally believed in her heart "that there was a creator and this world was not a joke, not an accident."

Talking about God was not a hip thing at that time in Yvonne's circles, so she kept her revelation to herself. Nor did she take her newfound conviction into the fold of the black church. She found the level of homophobia there too high—about equal to the level of hypocrisy. It was perfectly clear that the black church was filled with gays and lesbians, yet their presence was either denied or denounced. *That* kind of Christianity, Yvonne felt she could do without. She had found God, and would not contaminate His loving presence in her life with the prejudices of those who purported to speak in His name.

She felt something similar about black civil rights organizations. Part of the dissonance was temperamental: Yvonne was a loner, most comfortable when *not* attempting to involve herself with others. But whenever she did make a feint in the direction of joining up, she ran smack up against the endemic homophobia that characterized the black political movement in these years. The case of Bayard Rustin—the man who organized the 1963 March on Washington and had been a close associate of Martin Luther King, but was shunted to the background once it had been publicly revealed that he was gay—was merely the most famous example of how the religiously oriented civil rights movement tried to distance itself from the "taint" of homosexuality.[7]

Yvonne thought of herself as inclined toward socialism, toward the vision of a classless society in which, as a black person, a woman, and a lesbian, she would no longer be excluded and forced to choose among her several identities. Much of her struggle during the sixties—juggling, not committing, observing—was at bottom an attempt to work out for herself the possibility of freeing all three of the identities she embodied, and to learn how, when they sometimes seemed to conflict, to establish appropriate priorities among them.

She did go to a fair number of rallies and meetings, including the 1963 March on Washington. Her stepfather had died just a week before the march, but Yvonne and her mother felt they *had* to be there. Saddened with grief, they barely talked during the trip, but they were both glad they had gone. "It made me *very* proud," Yvonne later said. "I *knew* it was a historic moment. And it gave me a lot of hope—it showed things *could* happen."

And although she continued to be wary about committing to organizational work, at parties she would frequently go around the room and collect money for a particular cause—for the Patrice Lumumba Collective, say, or for almost *anybody*'s defense fund. Among the groups she felt closest to was Women Strike for Peace, which began late in 1961 with a call for disarmament and a protest against the resumption of nuclear-bomb testing. Yvonne would, in a nearly anonymous way, without knowing anybody else involved, simply get on one of the WSP buses loading up in Union Square to go down to Washington, and add her body to the rally count.

Then, in 1963, came the death of one of her coworkers at St. Vincent's. He was a Haitian immigrant named Bernie, who had joined the army as the only way he could think of to save up enough money for medical school. He was among the first American soldiers killed in Vietnam, and when Yvonne saw his name listed on the TV nightly news she was enraged that such a sweet, gentle man had been wasted in so inexplicable a war. She vowed to enlist more actively in the antiwar movement that was beginning to gather strength, and went down to Washington for one of the earliest demonstrations.

It proved a frightening experience. Tear-gassed and chased by police, she tried to climb a lamppost to take photos and discovered she barely had the strength to shinny up. During subsequent winter demonstrations, she had trouble getting her hands and feet warm, no matter how stout her boots or heavy her gloves. Years later she realized that these episodes marked the beginning of the physical problems that would eventually be diagnosed as lupus. But at the time, she simply put her puzzling symptoms out of her head, determined to continue living life at full tilt.

But full tilt was not the equivalent of full commitment—may, indeed, have been a substitute for it. There were only so many hours in the day, and Yvonne's devotion to partying left little time over to pursue her degree, to work steadily in a political movement, or to get deeply involved with another human being. Even when she found herself in love, she did her considerable best to sabotage the relationship, telling herself that she was too highly sexed ever to settle into monogamy.

She first saw Anne from a car window, saw a beautiful, pregnant black woman "strutting down the street." Who is *that?* Yvonne thought, never dreaming that within days she would be meeting her. Anne, it turned out, was the next-door neighbor of one of Yvonne's good friends. She had recently left her husband, was raising their son on her own, and would soon give birth to a daughter. She didn't see herself as lesbian, but decidedly did respond to Yvonne. It wasn't long before the two became lovers; soon after that, they decided to live together. And they would stay together for seven years.

But they were not easy years. Anne smoked a little pot and drank a little wine, but didn't consume nearly the amounts that Yvonne did—perhaps because she didn't have the same level of pain. Nor did Anne share Yvonne's passion for jazz and nightlife; she much preferred quiet domesticity. Yvonne might have, too—she deeply loved Anne—but her demons kept her on the go, kept her away from the apartment they had taken together in Brooklyn, away from the threatening closeness of the relationship, away from sharing herself in any consistent way.

Anne never fought with Yvonne about her late hours, her drugs, her affairs, her seeming preference for hearing jazz above anything else. She took Yvonne as she found her, knowing any alteration would have to come from within. But Yvonne, at least in retrospect, bitterly blames herself, and carries to this day considerable guilt and regret over what she insistently labels her "destructive" behavior. She *wanted* to do it differently, had clear values about what was the right way to live, and knew that she wasn't measuring up to her own view of what a relationship should be.

She felt certain that she wanted to live with Anne for the rest of her life and help raise Anne's two children, yet she couldn't get a grip on her own fear of being "trapped," her panic at the prospect of being "captured and smothered, or rejected and abandoned." And so she persisted in staying out all night, in pretending she could handle her escalating drinking and drugging, in juggling several simultaneous affairs on the side. She hated her own dishonesty. She knew she was hurting herself and hurting Anne.

Finally, in 1963, when one of Yvonne's side affairs looked as if it was getting serious, Anne picked herself and her children up and left. Yvonne was crushed, but well aware that she had pushed Anne to the breaking point. She missed the two children desperately, and on top of that, she worried about the subsequent effect on them of being raised around so much pot and alcohol. (Years later, Anne's son did develop a drug problem.) Yvonne knew that she had repeated her own parents' pattern, had let the need to get high prevent her from being consistently present emotionally.

Later, Yvonne and Anne would try—unsuccessfully—to reconstitute their relationship. But in 1963, filled with regret, Yvonne got an apartment of her own in Brooklyn and decided to try and get her life in order. She was thirty-one years old, still unsettled in a career, still "ripping and running" through several worlds without getting much succor from any of them. Within a year she had made the decision to pursue occupational therapy as a career and to go back to school to get a master's degree.

THE
MID-SIXTIES

At the close of 1963, *The New York Times* published a lengthy article entitled "Growth of Overt Homosexuality in City Provokes Wide Concern." The title said it all: The "concern" was that of psychiatrists, religious leaders, and law-enforcement officials; the "growth" was in visibility, in the perception that homosexuals were emerging from "the shadows" (the *Times*'s term), with a small number of militants openly agitating for increased acceptance. Predictably, the *Times* gave over the bulk of its article to the dominant psychoanalytic view of the day, preeminently associated with the theories of Irving Bieber and Charles Socarides, that homosexuality was a pathological disorder. The article even allowed Socarides the closing quote: "The homosexual is ill, and anything that tends to hide that fact reduces his chances of seeking and obtaining treatment." The "good news," according to the article (and the psychoanalytic profession), was that through psychotherapy the homosexual could be cured.[1]

The *Times* piece, despite being weighted toward a traditional, negative view, was a marker in ending public silence. In various media, the years 1962 to 1965 saw a sharp increase in the amount of public discussion and representation of homosexuality. Lesbian pulp novels appeared in far greater numbers than previously; male pornography, thanks to a Supreme Court decision clearing physique magazines of obscenity charges, proliferated; both best-selling fiction (such as James Baldwin's *Another Country*) and popular films (*The L-Shaped Room*, *Li-*

lith, *Darling*) continued to emphasize negative images but, at least peripherally, began to offer some sympathetic portraits.

The new frankness about homosexuality was part and parcel of a much larger cultural upheaval. The conformity and dutiful deference to authority that had held sway during the fifties were giving way under the hammer blows of the black civil rights struggle, the escalating war in Vietnam, and the emerging ethos of a counterculture that mocked traditional pieties and valorized "doing your own thing." A rapid-fire succession of events from 1963 to 1965 marked a seismic shift in national consciousness. The number of civil rights demonstrations in 1963 alone reached 930; they were highlighted by "Bull" Connor turning his police dogs loose on demonstrators, the bombing of Birmingham's Sixteenth Street Baptist Church, which took the lives of four little black girls, and the massive civil rights march on Washington (in which Yvonne and her mother, Theo Flowers, participated). And the year closed with the assassination of President Kennedy.

During 1964, local insurgencies continued to spread. And riots in Harlem; the murder of civil rights workers Michael Schwerner, Andrew Goodman, and James Chaney; and the refusal of the Democratic National Convention to seat the Mississippi Freedom Democratic Party delegation further dramatized the national upheaval. When, in August of that year, President Johnson used a series of episodes in the Gulf of Tonkin to win a free hand from Congress to "take all necessary measures" for the protection of American forces in Vietnam, the stage was set for a greater upheaval still.

Then in rapid succession in 1965 came the dramatic civil rights march from Selma to Montgomery, the bombing of North Vietnam, the rioting in Watts, and the emergence of black nationalism as symbolized in the "black power" slogan. Compared to these large-scale events and the substantial number of people enrolling in one or another national protest, the budding homophile movement remained minuscule—even when adding to the earlier Mattachine, ONE, and Daughters of Bilitis organizations the prominent new (mostly West Coast) Council on Religion and the Homosexual, the Tavern Guild, and the Society for Individual Rights.

Yet the homophile movement did both reflect and further contribute to the general assault on traditional values and, with respect to homosexuals themselves, represented the first glimmers of a possible improvement in status. To a greater extent than is usually credited, the homophile movement in the early sixties did challenge the dominant psychiatric view of homosexuality by arguing—contra Bieber and Socarides—that sexual orientation was inborn, was only *possibly* a disorder (the matter was much debated *within* homophile organizations), and in any case was *not* susceptible to "cure" and not deserving of the severe social and legal strictures imposed on it.

Resistance to oppression did not begin in 1969 at Stonewall. The West Coast had given birth both to Mattachine and the Daughters of Bilitis in the 1950s and, in the 1959 mayoral election in San Francisco, candidate Russ Wolden had made a political issue of homosexuality for the first time by accusing his opponent, the incumbent George Christopher, of making the Bay Area national headquarters for sexual deviates. All three dailies condemned Wolden for "stigmatizing" the city, and Christopher easily defeated him in the election.

In 1961, openly gay José Sarria, a charming, inventive drag performer at the venerable Black Cat bar, ran for city supervisor in San Francisco and polled more than three thousand votes—a decade before Jim Owles attempted a comparable run in New York. In 1964, police harassment of San Francisco's gay bars led to the formation of the Society for Individual Rights (SIR) which, thanks to its willingness to meet the social as well as political needs of gay men, had enrolled a thousand members by 1966, thus becoming the largest homophile organization in the country.

An important turning point for the movement in San Francisco came on New Year's Eve, 1964. A four-day conference between gay activists and progressive Protestant ministers in May of that year had led to the formation of the Council on Religion and the Homosexual. To spread word of the new organization and raise funds for it, a New Year's Eve dance had been announced at California Hall on Polk Street. The police had agreed to let the dance proceed on the stipulation that anyone appearing in drag be instantly whisked inside the hall, out of public view.

But on the night of the dance, five hundred gay men and lesbians arrived in their formal clothes to find that they had to walk through a gauntlet of police photographers. Thereafter, at roughly twenty-minute intervals, police inspectors entered California Hall on the pretext of needing to make a fire inspection or check the liquor license. When, after an hour or so, their right to enter the hall was challenged ("Where's your invitation?" one man demanded of the police), a scuffle ensued and arrests were made. The next day, the outraged ministers held a press conference to denounce the police—and the *San Francisco Chronicle* featured it on page one. When the case came to court, the presiding judge threw out all charges against the gay defendants and lectured the police on their dereliction of duty.

In several senses the California Hall incident marked a turning point: Heterosexual ministers had spoken up not to denounce gays but to defend their humanity; the courts had sided with homosexuals; the police, previously behaving as if invested with a natural right to harass gays, had been reprimanded and curtailed; and gay activists had learned the precious lesson that open, organized defiance could yield positive results. Ted McIlvenna, the minister who had spearheaded the Council on Religion and the Homosexual, was perhaps justified in his later assertion—after nearly all the credit for gay liberation had gone to the 1969 Stonewallers and those who followed—that "the Harvey Milks and those people were Johnny-come-latelies."

In New York City, too, resistance was mounting. Randy Wicker, main organizer of the protest in front of the Whitehall Street draft board, had continued—as had Craig—to resist the frightened conservatism of New York Mattachine's leaders; Wicker also served as a media gadfly, calling public attention to the harassment and discrimination under which gays suffered. The old guard, both in Mattachine and the Daughters of Bilitis, was to retain control in New York for several more years, but in Washington, D.C., Franklin Kameny's leadership of the local Mattachine Society had led in the early sixties to a series of radically aggressive statements and actions that had all at once reflected the confrontational strategy of the black civil rights movement and heralded the rejection of apologetics that would subsequently typify the gay movement.

CRAIG, FOSTER

One day in June 1964, Craig Rodwell was sitting at the Mattachine reception desk in New York when a man in his late thirties, sporting a crew cut, bow tie, and cigar, with a broad smile and a prematurely spreading waistline, entered the office. Craig was immediately on guard, thinking this might well be one of those fakely affable government agents rumored to be poking into "subversive" organizations of all kinds. (Though proof was not available at the time, definitive evidence has since surfaced that agents from BOSS—the Bureau of Special Services—did indeed have homophile activities in New York under surveillance as early as the 1950s. And in 1963, an agent covering Randy Wicker's speech "The Homosexual in Our Society," given at City College, revealed in his report to superiors that postal inspectors had also been "conducting an investigation" of Wicker's mail.)[2]

Craig, with a decided edge to his voice, asked the smiling man who stood above his desk just who he was and what he wanted. The man introduced himself as Foster Gunnison, Jr., said he lived in Hartford, Connecticut, had read about the existence of Mattachine in Donald Webster Cory's book, *The Homosexual in America*, and had come looking for more information. Craig was a quick study, his bullshit detector always on alert, and he decided Foster was telling the truth. He invited him to have a seat and the two men talked for some time.[3]

Foster explained that he had recently completed a second master's degree, this time in philosophy, at Trinity College; that he had known for some time that he was "not developing into a heterosexual"; and that he had read about New York Mattachine and had been thinking about doing some sort of organizational work—which, he told Craig, he thoroughly enjoyed and was rather good at.

Craig was delighted at the prospect of another volunteer, and especially one who seemed affable and prosperous. (Since Foster had not mentioned holding down a job, Craig had assumed, rightly, that he was financially independent.) Foster made it clear that he was unlikely to get much involved in New York Mattachine, other than in some distantly supportive way, since he did, after all, live in Connecticut. But he signed up for formal membership, took some Mattachine literature home with him, and agreed to Craig's suggestion that they stay in touch.

The activist seed had been planted. Foster had taken a crucial first step in aligning himself with the homophile movement (as it was increasingly calling itself)[4]—a step surprising for a man who had all his life behaved dutifully. The successful completion of his second master's degree had given Foster a new burst of confidence. He had earned the degree in half the time he had taken to complete his first master's, and had done so with real distinction: his thesis on "Soft Determinism, Responsibility and the Idea of Control" was highly praised, and he compiled an outstanding academic record.

All of which did wonders for Foster's self-esteem, and for a time he contemplated going on for a doctorate. Yet ultimately he would decide against a life in academia. Enough self-doubt remained to make him wonder whether his gifts would really prove competitive in the university world, and besides, he felt no particular affinity for either research or teaching. What he *had* always been drawn to was organizational work, preferably in a behind-the-scenes capacity, and once he had discovered the homophile movement, his involvement quickly accelerated.

The Mattachine Society was no longer national in scope. As a result of internal divisions that included charges of malfeasance and competitive bickering between the San Francisco and the New York chapters (New York having become the largest by 1960), Mattachine had dissolved as a national organization in March 1961, leaving local chapters to chart their own course. That had led, in short order, to a duplication of effort and a decrease in effectiveness. So in late 1962, Franklin Kameny, the guiding (and militant) spirit of the Mattachine Society of Washington, had suggested that East Coast homophile groups form at least some loose affiliation.

Accordingly, four organizations—New York DOB and the former Mattachine chapters of New York, Washington, and Philadelphia (the latter having renamed itself the Janus Society after the national organization disintegrated)—met in Philadelphia in January 1963 and formed the East Coast Homophile Organizations (ECHO). Craig Rodwell became an ECHO member soon after, and over the next two years he and others in the movement who were inclined toward greater militancy got to know each other and began to plan strategy for securing more aggressive homophile leadership.[5]

"Militancy" in these early years of the homophile movement was not synonymous with across-the-board defiance. Even Frank Kameny himself—though more responsible than any other individual for the newly aggressive tone in the movement—put decided boundaries on protest. He insisted that "you are not going to cure the effects of the impact upon the homosexual of society's prejudices by leading the homosexual into a rejection of society's values." He felt nonconforming students, especially, needed to be kept in line by older, wiser heads. As an individual, Kameny sympathized with nonconformity of all kinds, but he felt certain (about almost everything, Kameny felt *certain*) that homosexuals would "never gain acceptance by assuming the appearance of unacceptability."[6]

Foster Gunnison read about ECHO in the literature he had brought home with him from New York Mattachine, and began to go to their meetings. There he met, among others, Jack Nichols ("Warren D. Adkins"), a friend and ally of Kameny's, and Richard Inman, who had started Mattachine of Florida, an ECHO affiliate. Foster and Inman were both prodigious letter writers, and the two men started a lengthy correspondence, which Foster later credited with having helped him sharpen his understanding of the homophile movement and the role he might play in it. When the correspondence began, late in 1965, Foster was still feeling (as he wrote Inman) "brand new to, and not a little overwhelmed by, this movement." Within six months, he was gratefully writing Inman that "anything I am able to do eventually to assist the movement will owe a good deal of credit to you."[7]

Foster recognized that Inman was a difficult man, a "lone wolf" who chafed against organizational restraints (he would later describe Inman as "halfway between a drifter and a taxi driver"). But Foster also came to see him as "an unsung hero of the movement," an outspoken, one-man crusade in Florida, and he felt indebted to Inman for helping him to clarify a number of his own views. When Foster, for example, expressed concern to Inman over proliferating antidraft and anti–Vietnam War demonstrations that seemed to him "badly lacking in rational justification" and in danger of giving protest of all sorts "a bad name," Inman wrote back that for homosexuals to affiliate with other groups or issues was "a VERY dangerous course." Homophile goals, he insisted, should never be "contaminated" with the agenda of any other movement—be it pro-black or anti-war.

He also buttressed Foster's sense that the breakup of Mattachine as a national organization in 1961 had been a lamentable mistake and that a new, unifying central body was urgently needed. Not that either man was keen about resuscitating Mattachine itself. Foster had started to come down frequently from Hartford to attend Mattachine meetings in New York, but what he saw and heard left him with mixed feelings. "I might just as well visit a brickyard," he wrote Inman after one Mattachine meeting. "The room can be full of fifty people and no one seems to know you or anyone else or anything that's going on."

Foster was heartened to hear various people at the ECHO meetings speak of the need to form a new national coalition. But he was less pleased that much of the interest seemed to center on some sort of informal federation. That would not, in Foster's view, be adequate; he instinctively leaned toward a more centralized organization that could encourage the development of a powerful, militant movement. He believed (presciently) that the movement *would* gain in militancy ("someday this movement is going to break out into the open and hit the headlines"), would push with "reasonable aggressiveness" the view that homosexuality was "a fully acceptable and rewarding way of life."

His emphasis *was* on "reasonable." If Foster wanted to get the homophile house in order, he wanted it to be a house cleansed of "fringe elements." He deplored the possibility that the movement might get identified with "beatniks and other professional non-conformists"; their presence would prevent homosexuals from establishing a "decent" reputation and "gaining acceptance." He was therefore "strictly against" an "open door policy": in Foster's view, any emerging national organization would have to "keep as tight a rein as possible" over admissions, selecting its membership with an eye to "a certain degree of reasonable conformity."

He also believed that a new organization should take its cue from the successful West Coast group, SIR, and provide its members with social outlets (which some Mattachine old-timers frowned on); but at the same time he wanted to keep social activities to a modest level. Foster worried that too much emphasis on in-group activities might encourage the further development of the kind of gay subculture he disapproved: "affected mannerisms, special shops for the Homo tastes and styles, various other group interests and ways of life." He did not believe that homosexuals and heterosexuals were identical, but did feel "reluctant to see ourselves committing ourselves to differences that have not been thoroughly established as valid and as good. I believe that a subculture will always be readier prey for discrimination and pogroms than an integrated variation in behavior."

None of which meant that Foster blamed homosexuals themselves for aspects of a life-style he disapproved of, or for their current lack of acceptance. He did see much in homosexual life that he found "maladaptive," but he believed "any unhappiness or difficulties" were "principally due to the destructive consequences of prejudice." On the other hand, he questioned neither psychotherapeutic claims (since disproved) of successful "conversion" from gay to straight, nor even the advisability of some individuals' undergoing such "therapy." He believed that homosexuality was not always "ego-syntonic with the basic personality pattern"—just as he also believed that "a repressed homo seeking compulsive hetero adjustment might do better to come to terms with his H instincts." Individuals, according to Foster's libertarian philosophy, had the right to make those decisions for themselves, had the right to opt out of a life-style that gave so little pleasure and so much pain.

Yet Foster was firm in his belief that homosexuality was not an illness—and in those years, when the psychoanalytic equation of homosexuality with pathology was all but universally accepted, his view automatically put him in the avant-garde. In speculating about etiology, moreover, Foster daringly (for those years) suggested that "there was no reason to believe the causes [of homosexuality] are any different from heterosexuality." In both instances, he argued, "the drives behind sexual orientation are very profound and quite the opposite of simple matters of choice." Which did not mean to him, in turn, that orientation was simply a product of biological factors. On that question, he threw up his hands—as even the best informed have continued to do since.

Foster, like most people, was imprisoned by the assumptions of his time. Unlike most, he had managed to transcend at least some of them.

After Craig returned to New York from Los Angeles in January 1964, he plunged deeper than ever into movement work. And on several fronts. To try to draw younger (and, Craig assumed, more militant) people into Mattachine, he started Mattachine Young Adults. To advertise their meetings, Craig took out "Bulletin Board" ads in *The Village Voice*, and that involved a running battle with the paper, the *Voice* objecting, at various points, to the use of the words "homophile" and "homosexual" in the ads. After much arguing, Craig ultimately got the okay for both—but it would take a full-scale Gay Liberation Front action in 1969 before the *Voice* would sanction the use of the word "gay."

To further attract recruits for Mattachine Young Adults, Craig organized two-person (one male, one female whenever possible) leafleting teams in the Village. Expecting some hostile reactions, the teams developed strategy for forestalling actual physical attack: "If someone calls you a fag or a dyke, don't respond to them verbally. Be dignified. Don't get on their level. That will only encourage them to do something further, possibly worse. And it will put you in a state of mind where you can't really think about what's going on. Try to stay calm and centered."

The tactics worked most of the time. And as often as not, the teams got a positive response. On one snowy night when Craig was leafleting at the Sheridan Square subway entrance, a woman who had taken a flyer and read it came back and told Craig she didn't know anything about homosexuals, but their cause had to be good if he was willing to stand outside in such terrible weather.

He was willing to do a lot more. One of his ideas, which came to him in a fit of anger and which he never pushed, was that every time there was a gay-bashing, gays should announce that they were going to randomly beat up a straight. Something else he wanted to do—twenty-five years before the controversy over "outing"—was to place an ad announcing that all gay people would have five years to come out, and then on January 1, 1970, the name of every gay person would be published.

In Craig's mind visibility *was* the key to ending oppression, and he kept searching for ways to swell the ranks of the openly gay. To that end, he willingly appeared in the public media, doing a number of radio shows with his cohort Randy Wicker, who had already proven himself something of a genius in media manipulation. Wicker could be arch and self-aggrandizing, which grated on Craig, but he was grateful to find somebody who shared his belief that Mattachine should act as if it were a movement, not a hospital ward; and in tribute, Craig gave a featured place in the Mattachine newsletter to Randy's regular column of political tidbits, "The Wicker Basket."

When *The Alan Burke Show*—a Saturday night TV talk show that for a time rivaled David Susskind's in popularity—called Mattachine for "a homosexual" to interview, Craig volunteered to go. By that time, he had become well aware that the media were primarily interested in sensationalistic "entertainment," and he did his considerable best to forestall such exploitation. When he was told to appear a full hour before airtime to be made up for the Burke show, Craig got a straight actress friend of his who knew all about stage makeup to come with him. She stood over him while the makeup man went to work, and made sure that nothing more than a little powder and cheek coloring was used.

Craig also dressed for the occasion, donning a rare tie and jacket, looking for all the world like Joe College. And when he got the usual hostile questions from the audience about "sickness" and "child molestation," he fielded them expertly. One macho young man stood up in the audience to describe the "sick" experience he had had when staying overnight at a YMCA—how "a coupla homo-sexuals tried to come on to me, they're *always* tryin' to come on to me." Craig waited a beat, and then said quietly, "You flatter yourself." The audience broke up.

Craig's efforts to bring more young people into Mattachine, and in general to swell its membership rolls, paid off handsomely. The person actually in charge of the membership committee in 1964 was

Alfred Sawahata, a Japanese-American architect who was one of Craig's favorite people at Mattachine. Sawahata taught Craig how to color-code the membership list in order to tell at a glance who needed to renew his or her dues, and how to send out discreet reminders to mail them in.

Craig went several steps further. He printed up a membership form urging people to join Mattachine, and then aggressively distributed it throughout the Village. And to create the impression that Mattachine was awash in activity, he also made sure that the newsletter came out on time. Thanks largely to these efforts, Mattachine's monthly meeting at Freedom House was, by 1965, often playing to full houses, and the rolls showed some three hundred paid-up members. By mid-1966, the number had gone to five hundred.

Craig personally recruited some of the people who would shortly become prominent in the struggle to steer New York Mattachine into more militant waters. Through Mattachine Young Adults he brought in Renée Cafiero, Bobby Gonzalez, and Michael Belser. And through a love affair, he brought in Dick Leitsch, who would become the dominant figure in Mattachine for the next half-dozen years.[8]

Craig and Dick met in a doorway while both were cruising Greenwich Avenue one night, and they started to see each other fairly often. Leitsch was working at the time in the paint department at Gimbel's department store, and had never attended a Mattachine meeting. But it quickly became apparent to him that Mattachine was Craig's passion and that if he wanted to see more of Craig he would have to start going to meetings, since that was where Craig seemed to spend all his spare time.

Leitsch soon became interested in the proceedings and from the first, he (like Craig) eschewed the use of a pseudonym. And he soon began to think of himself and Craig as lovers—though Craig never did. Craig enjoyed sex with Leitsch, but rejected his possessive attempts to control his every breath. Growing up with an alcoholic mother, and a father who worked long hours, Leitsch from an early age had felt "in charge." He was an articulate, persuasive man, and could be an exceedingly charming one. But when he wasn't getting his way, he could become explosively dictatorial.

One night when the two men were sitting at a restaurant counter having coffee, Craig said he didn't want Dick to come back with him to his apartment on Horatio Street; he felt like being alone that night. Leitsch, without a word, threw his coffee cup to the floor with such violence that the owner of the restaurant came running—and Craig, frightened, beat a hasty retreat out the back door. But ten minutes after he got home, the doorbell rang downstairs. Knowing it was Leitsch, Craig ignored the ring. Then he heard Leitsch screaming out his name in the street. Again he ignored it. But somehow Leitsch got into the building and tried to break down Craig's door. Terrified, Craig was about to go down the fire escape, when he heard a neighbor (who knew both men) calming Leitsch down, and ultimately persuading him to leave.

Craig's affair with Leitsch, not surprisingly, lasted less than a year. But by then Leitsch was thoroughly hooked on Mattachine and he and Craig, despite residual anger at each other, became staunch political allies. In 1964–1965, New York Mattachine was still controlled by the conservatives. They believed in gradualism and quietism, in modifying *gay* comportment so that it would better coincide with middle-class notions of proper behavior, in concentrating on education, in allying with and relying on whatever sympathetic experts they could find in straight religious, legal, and psychiatric circles.

Where the conservatives emphasized the need for the homosexual to adjust to society, the militants, taking their cue from the black civil rights struggle, insisted that society had to do the adjusting, had to stop belittling and persecuting gay people. Frank Kameny summed up the militant view succinctly in a speech he gave to New York Mattachine in July 1964. Assailing the unproven assumptions and sloppy research that lay behind the psychoanalytic view of homosexuality as a disorder, Kameny threw out this challenge to the conservatives: "The entire movement is going to stand or fall upon the question of whether homosexuality is a sickness, and upon our taking a firm stand on it."

Kameny's speech helped to shift the views of Julian Hodges, another man Craig had gotten interested in Mattachine. Hodges was from a prominent North Carolina family (a close relative, Luther Hodges, was Kennedy's secretary of commerce), and after he joined New York Mattachine in 1964 he, like Leitsch, had quickly assumed a leading role in the organization. Craig, Hodges, Leitsch, and sometimes Randy Wicker took to having dinner together after Mattachine meetings to talk about how they could wrest control of the organization from the conservatives. They finally decided to run an opposing slate in the upcoming May 1965 election, with Julian Hodges standing for president against the conservatives' candidate, David Goldberger (who headed Mattachine's West Side Discussion Group).

Mattachine elections were formal and secret. Ballots went out in the mail, within a doubly sealed return envelope. Then, at the annual meeting, the ballots were opened in front of the entire membership present. In the May 1965 election, Leitsch and Hodges were entrusted with the responsibility of bringing to the annual meeting all the ballots that had been received in the mail.

Leitsch later confessed to Craig that he and Hodges had steamed open the envelopes the night before the meeting and changed some of the ballots to make sure that Hodges would be declared the winner. As indeed he was, by a three-to-two margin. Not realizing that the election may have been stolen from them, many conservatives left Mattachine immediately afterward. And their creature, the West Side Discussion Group, was cut loose from Mattachine by the Board of Directors. But despite, or—in a national climate that was increasingly confrontational—perhaps because of those conservative defections, the membership rolls of New York Mattachine continued to climb toward five hundred. "See what action does?" Leitsch wrote exultantly to Frank Kameny.[9]

New York Mattachine now joined Washington Mattachine, led by Kameny, in the militant column. Yet Leitsch and Kameny, two strong-willed, ambitious, authoritarian men, were soon at odds. Leitsch complained that Washington Mattachine was out "to dominate," presenting itself as "the conscience of the movement." In Leitsch's view, the Kameny group was in fact "a thorn in the side of the Eastern organizations," given to excommunicating individuals and groups not abiding by its own "puritanical" standards. After Kameny "chastised" the Philadelphia Janus Society and its leader, Clark Polak (known to be as testy and egocentric as most of the other East Coast leaders), for including "titillating" pictures in its magazine, DRUM, and helped to get Janus kicked out of ECHO, Leitsch scornfully pointed out that DRUM had a circulation of ten thousand whereas Washington Mattachine's Eastern Mattachine Review had a mere 2,500 readers.[10]

Not that Leitsch had much use for Polak, DRUM, Janus—or, for that matter, ECHO. When some of his associates in the movement sent him glowing reports of an ECHO conference in the fall of 1965, Leitsch sent enthusiastic congratulations even as he was expressing to other correspondents his disdain ("ECHO is a trifle silly . . . and possibly ridiculous"), and simultaneously attempting to undercut ECHO by forming a separate alliance with the New York chapter of Daughters of Bilitis. "ECHO no longer provides our two organizations," Leitsch wrote a DOB officer, "with a real means of cooperation," and he suggested dates for a get-together "to explore means and methods of working together."[11]

After he succeeded Hodges as president of Mattachine New York in November 1965, Leitsch seemed to take every criticism of MSNY as a personal affront, and to take every opportunity to vilify other movement leaders and groups. He roundly denounced Polak, Inman, Shirley Willer of DOB and Dorr Legg of Los Angeles's ONE as "obstructionists," and ascribed their motives to jealousy of MSNY's prominence and accomplishments; they were, in Leitsch's view, hankering to "get in on the headlines."[12]

What *was* unequivocally true was that Leitsch and Hodges had embarked on an aggressive series of actions and could point to an impressive set of working relationships with New York City officials. Among other moves, Leitsch had kept after the State Liquor Authority to clarify its policies regarding gay bars and, when its replies proved evasive, had denounced the SLA chairman for his "uncooperative and . . . non-committal" response. Leitsch had also held the *Suffolk County News* to point when it continued to print the names, occupations, and addresses of men arrested in police sweeps of the gay Fire Island resorts, excoriating the paper for conducting "a witch-hunt" that encouraged blackmail, crimes of violence, and police harassment.[13]

And when the New York mayoral election in 1965 was won by John Lindsay, a liberal Republican thought to be more of a genuine reformer than his Democratic predecessors, Leitsch was quick to hail his victory as marking "hope for New York City to become a free and open society in which the rights of minority groups and the rights of those who are different will be protected and respected." Yet when Lindsay, a few months later, authorized a "cleanup" of Times Square and Greenwich Village, Leitsch was equally quick to protest the infringement on civil liberties. That led to a meeting between Lindsay, Leitsch, and others which later culminated in the mayor ordering the police to end all efforts to entrap homosexuals.[14]

In San Francisco, too, the successful fight against an attempted police crackdown on the bars in 1964–1965 slowly swelled homophile ranks. Matters culminated in 1966 with three major events: the appearance of Democratic party powerhouses John Burton and Willie Brown at SIR meetings to appeal for gay votes; a series of demonstrations in several California cities (and elsewhere as well) to protest the exclusion of homosexuals from the armed forces; and a battle between gays and the police in San Francisco that lasted for three nights following a police attempt to raid Compton's Cafeteria, a gay hangout at Turk and Taylor streets.[15]

Within ECHO, the strategy of picketing produced a considerable uproar, and Craig became centrally involved in the issue. Inspired by the direct-action tactics that black college students and Freedom Riders had employed in their confrontations with segregated facilities, Craig was eager to take a comparable stand against the institutional structures that perpetuated gay oppression. Through his involvement with ECHO, he got to know Frank Kameny, Barbara Gittings, Kay "Tobin" (Lahusen), and other militants well; at Kameny's suggestion, they had started to meet together regularly to talk about organizing a series of public demonstrations. (At Craig's first encounter with Barbara and Kay, he watched them carefully, lovingly, set up tape recorders and microphones for an ECHO conference, and was moved to tears— moved at the absence of the kind of egotistical, aggressive power-tripping he had been witnessing in New York Mattachine.)

The group decided that to protest the exclusion of homosexuals from federal employment and the armed services, it would picket in front of the Pentagon, the Civil Service Commission, the State Department, and—to culminate the series—the White House. Kameny, based in Washington, did most of the legwork in getting permits and picket signs readied (and the American flags that by law had to be carried at all demonstrations). Most of the troops, a hard core of twenty to forty people, came down from New York and Philadelphia, with smaller contingents from Boston and Washington. They were joined for the climactic White House demonstration by Foster Gunnison, Jr., from Hartford.

At Kameny's insistence, a strict dress code was enforced on all participants. "If we want to be employed by the Federal Government," Kameny intoned, "we have to look employable to the Federal Government." Craig protested that the focus on federal employment was Kameny's own hobbyhorse (Kameny had been fired from government work in the late fifties when it was discovered that he had been arrested in 1956 on the catch-all charge of "lewd and indecent acts"), and was *not* the sole or even primary purpose of the demonstrations. But Kameny and his allies replied that whatever the purpose, it was important to look ordinary, to get bystanders to hear the message rather than be prematurely turned off by appearances.[16]

Refusing at first to yield, Craig stubbornly insisted that "the only thing we have in common with heterosexuals is what we do in bed" (a radical notion indeed in 1965), and he grumbled about the need to let people make their own personal statements, and about not wanting to look like a church group on a Sunday picnic. But—for the time being—he finally decided to defer to Kameny's activist record and to his authority (though he disliked the iron way Kameny wielded it). Craig joined the other men in dutifully donning suit and tie. The women wore dresses.

Dick Leitsch shared Craig's contempt for Kameny's dress code —but went beyond it to descry the demonstrations in their entirety as tactically ill-conceived. *Numbers* were what mattered, Leitsch insisted. "The difference between us," he wrote Kameny, "is that I believe we must impress authority and the power-structure with our strength; you seem to believe we must impress Everyman with our decency. (Whatever that is.)" Far better, in Leitsch's view, to mobilize two hundred people in casual, neat clothing than fifty suited and dressed to look like super-respectable citizens. Government officials *might* respond to the presence of significant numbers of demonstrators, but would remain indifferent to being picketed by a small group of "quality" folks—especially since the picketing would be focused not on one site but, consecutively, on three or four.[17]

But Kameny, who prided himself on being "practical," continued to insist that "clean-scrubbed demonstrations will get us ahead . . . FAR, FAR faster than court cases. . . . [T]he man in a suit is STILL the overwhelming norm in this country." "Hundreds of beatnik types in front of the Civil Service Commission," he wrote Leitsch, would be not only a tactical mistake but a misrepresentation of the homosexual community. "Grubbiness has never, to my knowledge," he huffily asserted, "been a stereotype of a homosexual. Do our pickets *your* way, and it will soon become so."[18]

Kameny had his way. Marching quietly in single file, carrying their signs (SEXUAL PREFERENCE IS IRRELEVANT TO FEDERAL EMPLOYMENT; CIVIL SERVICE COMMISSION IS UN-AMERICAN), wearing their "Equality for Homosexuals" buttons, kept in constant motion by the police, his intrepid group of demonstrators—no gay protest had ever been seen in the nation's capital, and precious few anywhere else— carried out their picketing without serious incident. The demonstration in front of the White House in April 1965 was to Craig the most thrilling. More than seventy marchers participated, and more media showed up than previously (though the biggest press notice came from the sensationalistic rag *Confidential*, which in its October 1965 issue ran an article under the heading "Homos on the March").

Craig thought it was "the most wonderful day of my life," and sitting afterward in a coffee shop with Kameny, Jack Nichols, and a few others, he felt too excited to eat. As people shared their sadness that the whole series of demonstrations had now wound down, with no plans for anything further, Craig suddenly had a brainstorm. "It doesn't *have* to be over!" he fairly shouted. "I couldn't bear for it to be over!" And then he presented his idea: to demonstrate every Fourth of July in front of Independence Hall in Philadelphia—"create like a gay holiday. We can call it the Annual Reminder—the Reminder that a group of Americans still don't have their basic rights to life, liberty and the pursuit of happiness."

Everybody was instantly entranced (though Kameny seemed a little annoyed that someone else had seized the initiative), and enthusiasm proved so high that the first Annual Reminder, sponsored by the New York, Washington, and Philadelphia Mattachine societies, took place that very July, only three months after Craig had come up with the idea. Thirty-nine people (including several from Midwest Mattachine) picketed in front of Independence Hall from three-thirty to five P.M., and the demonstration got mentioned on the local TV news and on the front page of *The Philadelphia Inquirer*. Kameny had taken pains to notify the appropriate authorities in advance, and he was pleased that police behavior was "proper and cordial" and the demonstrators "dignified and orderly."[19]

For the next five years, an indefatigable band of thirty to a hundred people, always including Craig, Frank Kameny, Barbara Gittings, and Kay Tobin, would appear with their placards and buttons (BILL OF RIGHTS FOR HOMOSEXUALS; 15,000,000 HOMOSEXUAL AMERICANS ASK FOR EQUALITY, OPPORTUNITY, DIGNITY) in front of Independence Hall, earnestly asserting what then seemed the far distant and possibly utopian demand for "gay rights." As Barbara Gittings later recalled, those who participated in the Annual Reminders would "smile and smile," would hand out leaflets to anyone who passed by (though many refused to take them), and would try to swallow their own discomfort at "not knowing what the consequences would be," whether their names would be printed in the paper and their jobs lost, or whether they might even be arrested.

By the time of the Second Annual Reminder, in 1966, the event had attracted enough attention to warrant the presence of agents from the Bureau of Special Services. Their reports dutifully quoted from Craig's advertisement for the picket ("this annual demonstration is held to call to the attention of the American people discriminatory

laws and regulations by the government directed against its homosexual citizens"), as if uncovering a monstrous conspiracy against the
Constitution. Following the event, moreover, BOSS agents also sat
in on New York Mattachine meetings, and earnestly reported the
momentous news that a guest speaker had "spent 30 years handling
Immigration and Deportation cases," and that a doctoral candidate in
psychology had requested volunteers to fill out a questionnaire.

More ominously, three men dressed in dark business suits
knocked on the door of Craig's apartment one night and then barged
in, flashing FBI badges. They said they were looking for Michael
Levy (a man Craig had recently had a brief affair with), who was
wanted for passing bad checks. Then they searched the apartment—
Craig was too stunned to ask to see a warrant—and left. But that was
not the end of it. One of the agents continued to call Craig every few
months for years, blandly asking him each time "if everything was
okay." Then, in 1970, the same agent relayed a suggestion from his
boss, John Caufield (as head of White House security, Caufield would
later testify at the Watergate hearings), that Craig attend Gay Liberation Front meetings and report back to them what had taken place.
Craig turned the offer down.

Instead of sating Craig's appetite for activism, the successful launching
of the Annual Reminder further stimulated it. He, Leitsch, and
Leitsch's current lover, John Timmons, decided to combine forces for
an action they dubbed "the sip-in." The point was to challenge the
State Liquor Authority regulation that prohibited bars and restaurants
from selling drinks to homosexuals, on penalty of having their licenses
revoked. Leitsch sent out press releases and telegrams announcing
their impending defiance of the regulation.[20]

On April 21, 1966, the trio, dressed immaculately in suits and
ties ("the picture of a Madison Avenue executive," the *Voice* later
reported), rendezvoused as planned and found reporters from *The New
York Times*, *The Village Voice*, and the *New York Post* waiting for
them—which promised greater media coverage than had attended any
previous movement event. Activists and reporters moved off together
to the Ukrainian-American Village Bar on St. Mark's Place, which
had long had a hand-lettered sign above the bar reading, "If you are
gay, please stay away." But the bar must have gotten wind of the
pending invasion: When the group arrived there, they found the place
locked.

They decided to shift the action to the Howard Johnson's on

Sixth Avenue and Eighth Street (which had a famously cruisy men's room in the basement, even if the restaurant supposedly didn't sell drinks to faggots). Sitting down in a booth, the trio called over the manager and handed him their pre-prepared statement: "We, the undersigned, are homosexuals. We believe that a place of public accommodation has an obligation to serve an orderly person, and that we are entitled to service as long as we are orderly. We therefore ask to be served on your premises. Should you refuse to serve us, we will be obligated to file a complaint against you with the State Liquor Authority."

"How do I know you're homosexuals?" the manager genially responded—and then, to the trio's astonishment, broke out laughing. "Why shouldn't they be served a drink?" he asked the reporters. "They look like perfect gentlemen to me. I drink. Who knows if I'm a homosexual or not?" He then went on to declare that he had problems, too, what with two children and three grandchildren, and whose business was it anyway what a person's sex life happened to be. He ordered the waiter to "bring the boys a drink"—and the reporters, too. Clearly Howard Johnson's was not going to play the part assigned it in the activist drama.

So on they went to the Waikiki, a bar on Sixth Avenue between Ninth and Tenth streets. Once again, the manager foiled the protest. "I serve anybody," he said, "so long as he doesn't annoy anybody." And once more drinks appeared for all hands. By now John Timmons was feeling a little woozy from the liquor, but the trio, still trailed by the expectant reporters, decided to press on. They next entered Julius' on West Tenth Street, confidently telling the reporters that they *would* be denied service there: Though long a gay hangout, Julius' had recently been the scene of several plainclothes-police entrapments, and Craig had himself been thrown out of there for wearing an "Equality for Homosexuals" button.

When they entered Julius', several gay men were having drinks at the bar. "We are homosexuals and we would like a drink," Dick Leitsch said to the bartender. "I don't know what you're trying to prove," the bartender answered. "You can't serve us if we are homosexuals?" Leitsch asked hopefully. "No," came the long-desired answer. John Timmons sighed contentedly. "Another bourbon and water and I would have been under the table."

The point had been made, the action completed. New York Mattachine immediately announced that it was filing a complaint with the State Liquor Authority against Julius' for unconstitutionally discriminating against homosexuals in violation of the First and Fourteenth amendments. And it announced further that it would pay any legal expenses Julius' incurred.

But it was unclear for some time longer whether a victory could be claimed. The State Liquor Authority quickly announced that it would take no action against bars that refused service to homosexuals. And there the matter might have ended, the Mattachine action thwarted, had it not been for William H. Booth, the black chairman of the Commission on Human Rights. Booth responded to the SLA statement by saying publicly that the Human Rights Commission had jurisdiction over discrimination based on sex, and he *would* try to put an end to SLA policy on serving homosexuals if a complaint against Julius was filed with his office. Mattachine immediately complied.

By then, several newspapers had run editorials against the SLA's discriminatory policies, and a committee of prominent heterosexuals, including the Episcopal bishop of New York, had formed in support of Commissioner Booth's position. Still, the case had to go to court, and it wasn't until the following year that the state's Appellate Division ruled that serving a homosexual was not (as the SLA had previously held) the equivalent of running "a disorderly house" and that a bar's license could be revoked only if "substantial evidence" of indecent behavior had been demonstrated.

The ruling was well worth having, but it hardly put an end to police harassment of gay bars or to the police practice of sending out comely young cops, carefully attired in up-to-date chinos and tennis shoes, to entrap gay men on the street. Given Commissioner Booth's stance in the Julius case, Dick Leitsch turned to him for help against entrapment. Booth discussed the issue with Chief Inspector Sanford D. Garelick, who assured him that the police department gave no official encouragement to entrapment, and solemnly promised to investigate any such incidents that came to his attention.

Needless to say, none did. Instead, Mattachine continued to get calls from desperate gay men who had been arrested for "soliciting" a police officer. Mattachine kept a list of those few lawyers willing to handle such "distasteful" cases, but the field had pretty much become the monopoly of two of them, Gertrude Gottlieb ("Dirty Gertie," to the boys) and Enid Gerling. As the mythology of the day had it, even before family or friends had heard the news, Gottlieb and Gerling would appear at the police station, apparently tipped off by the cops—for a piece of the standard two-thousand-dollar action, of course.

This double-dealing game of collusion and blackmail enraged Craig, and he helped to persuade Mattachine's officers to remove the two women's names from the referral list. Enid Gerling was not one to take that lying down. She came storming into the Mattachine office, her voice already at full volume, screaming that they couldn't do this to her, that they would rue the day they had crossed her path, that she would have the place closed down if her name wasn't put back on the referral list *at once*. But Mattachine held its ground. And Gerling never followed through on her threats.[21]

But police entrapment and bar raids continued. Indeed, in 1966, "liberal" Mayor John Lindsay (who would subsequently put an end to entrapment) endorsed a sweeping police campaign to rid both Times Square and Washington Square Park of "undesirables." On the night the police poured from their vans into Times Square, Sylvia Rivera was standing at her usual spot on Ninth Avenue and Forty-fourth Street, trying to turn just one more trick before calling it a night— but ended in jail instead.

KARLA

During Karla's first week as a Barnard freshman in 1964, she heard about the two women who had been expelled the previous year. A male student at Columbia (directly across the street from Barnard) had peered into the women's dormitory room with a pair of binoculars and seen them making love. The Peeping Tom was allowed to stay and, by some, was praised; the women were kicked out. Hearing the story, Karla "realized for the first time that there was something wrong with being a lesbian," and decided she "had better cover up."

She started dating a young man from Yale whom she had met at one of the freshman dances. He was from Louisiana and had never seen a Jew. Karla tried a joke to relieve his astonishment, saying something about how Jews nowadays clipped off the infant's horns at birth. But he took the statement at face value and solemnly replied that he "hadn't known that." The relationship was never romantic and never sexual; yet it persisted throughout Karla's undergraduate years. The two would see each other every few weeks, talk superficially about events of the day, peck each other on the lips—and make another date. Karla is convinced, in retrospect, that her Yalie was gay and that they were using each other as cover.

But Karla soon had a steady female date as well, and that relationship quickly became sexual. Not that *they* ever talked about it, either. The woman, an undergraduate at City College, had a boyfriend on the side and treated her relationship with Karla in the spirit of the rising counterculture: something she did because it felt good—no guilt, no attachments. But Karla was looking for some other kind of connection, though she had trouble defining it even to herself. It had something to do with wanting to find out more about herself by meeting women who already shared her emotional space, including its confusions.

In a subculture that could not yet claim many social or institutional structures, let alone a political voice, bars were among the few places where lesbians felt they could congregate and be themselves in relative safety. This was especially true for working-class women, who, much more than their middle-class and upper-class sisters, were given to strict "butch" and "femme" role divisions. Karla's family background was a mix of working-class status and middle-class income, and her own high educational level had un-classed her still further.

In appearance, too, Karla failed to fit neatly into either of the dichotomous butch-femme roles that the lesbian bar world encouraged in these years. She was athletic and compact in build, but her self-presentation was "muddied" (in the eyes of the bar world) by long hair and dangling earrings. All at once strong and feminine (even glamorous), Karla invited instant disapproval from those who insisted on a choice between one or the other. But Karla refused to choose. She regarded strict role divisions as destructive mimicry of rigid heterosexual norms; in her view, they narrowed and pigeonholed the wide actual range of human impulses and identifications.[22]

Not surprisingly, then, the first time Karla walked into the Sea Colony, a popular lesbian bar during the mid-sixties, her immediate reaction was that she didn't belong there. The smoke and noise confused her; she felt upset watching women consume alcohol as if it were soda pop, and annoyed at the alternatively demure or belligerent patrons. She didn't meet any women who went to college (or who admitted they did), and in fact had trouble meeting anybody at all. Her self-presentation was apparently experienced as threatening; she evoked distrust without meaning or wanting to. When asked—which always happened quickly—whether she was butch or femme, Karla wouldn't know what to say, and the other woman would soon walk away. If these women were lesbians, Karla thought, then maybe she wasn't. Far from giving Karla the feeling that she had come home at last, the Sea Colony made her think that she might have made a terrible mistake. She went back not more than three or four times during her entire undergraduate life.

Even if she had not found the bar scene uncongenial, Karla would have had little time for it. She was kept busy simply trying to make ends meet. Through a ruse, she managed to live illegally in one of the Barnard dorms. Since she had no meal card, she would simply pick up a plate and join the cafeteria line, pretending she was going back for seconds on the main course (which was allowed). Almost every night of the week she baby-sat, for $1.25 an hour *and*—this was more urgent than the money—permission to raid the refrigerator. When she and friends compared notes on clients, it wasn't about whether the child was difficult or easy but about how much and what kind of food the family had.

She picked up other kinds of work as well. During the summers, she would hold down both day and evening jobs—everything from camp counseling, to sales work in a department store, to punching and cataloging material for a Columbia professor's encyclopedia-in-progress. During the school year she was able to use her two years of Latin and five of French at Bromley to get a job at the Barnard language laboratory; it paid well (four dollars an hour) and allowed her time, in between signing out tapes and explaining how the machines worked, to get some studying done.

It was about the only time she did have for schoolwork, and as a result she got mostly B's. She gave some thought to a premed major, but realized she would never be able to afford medical school; besides, she turned off to the profession after experiencing firsthand—one of her part-time jobs was as an operating-room clerk—its routine malpractices. Karla's main interest continued to be languages. She was especially drawn to French and Russian, and ended up majoring in French.

She had as little time for a social life as for studying. In her junior year she moved into a seventy-five-dollar-a-month apartment at 107th Street and Broadway, which she shared with several roommates; they became her main social outlet. They ate spaghetti together every night (managing to find a powdered sauce that cost nine cents a serving), and her roommates introduced Karla first to pot and then to a variety of other drugs. Being poor, they tried smoking anything they heard produced a high, including peppers and banana skins, and inhaling the gas from Reddi-Wip cans (which did work). Karla believes that taking drugs "really did expand my mind and loosened me up in many ways."

But becoming more countercultural did not immediately make her more political. Nothing in her background predisposed her to activism. She describes her parents as "slightly to the right of Archie Bunker"; they had no politics but plenty of prejudices, especially about Christians and blacks. Nene, they insisted, was different from other blacks, and they treated her like one of the family. As for Nene, she understandably never spoke of the black civil rights struggle around the Jays, and simply said that she "accepted people as people." (She had left when Karla was twelve and no longer needed her, going to work as a nurse's aide in the Brooklyn Eye and Ear Hospital.) And Karla's years at the Bromley Institute, with its unbroken expanse of privileged white faces, did nothing to raise her consciousness about injustice.

Yet she did think of herself as a liberal, and ascribes that mostly to Nene, whose presence, not preachments, in her life had kept her from growing up with clearcut notions about race or gender. It never occurred to Karla as a child that her lighter skin color made her different from Nene in any significant way; the closeness and identification were complete. As to gender, when she and Nene were rooting for Pee Wee Reese at Ebbets Field, Nene never hinted that Karla couldn't duplicate his feats or that the game of baseball was reserved for boys.

Like almost everyone else at Barnard, Karla was against the war in Vietnam and for the civil rights movement. But as late as her senior year in 1968, she had not joined any of the proliferating marches or protests in support of those positions. And then came the upheaval at Columbia University in April of her senior year, an event that would change Karla irrevocably, moving her from abstract sympathy to emotional identification with the outsiders of the world.

There were two key issues during the Columbia disruptions. The first was the university's pending construction of a gym in a park used by Harlem residents—the latest of a long series of encroachments by Columbia that, with little or no concern for the wishes and well-being of poor tenants, had forced them out. The second issue concerned the university's affiliation with the Institute for Defense Analyses (IDA), an affiliation symbolic of academia's widespread involvement with government-sponsored weapons research (at Columbia the research focused on antisubmarine warfare), and on complicity with what was aptly being called the military-industrial complex. In 1968 more than two thirds of university research funds came from agencies of the federal government connected with defense matters, and about a quarter of the two hundred largest industrial corporations in the country had university officials on their boards of directors.[23]

Columbia's insensitivity to its black neighbors seemed to many on the left of a piece with its willingness to create instruments of death for use against Asians. But when student representatives tried to open up a dialogue with the Columbia administration, they were swiftly rebuffed—and on top of that, had to listen to faculty mandarins like Jacques Barzun smugly reprimand them for operating on the false assumption that the university did or should function as a democracy, for having failed to "earn" a voice in policy deliberations—and for being "mere transients," ill equipped and ill prepared to participate in the higher councils of higher education.

The student radicals thought otherwise, and on April 23, 1968, a group of them seized a building on the Columbia campus and issued a set of demands denouncing the planned gym and the university's complicity with weapons research. In the following days, more buildings were occupied. Live-in "communes" and round-the-clock speakouts were set up within them, and Columbia found itself faced with a full-scale insurrection. Karla went in and out of the buildings all week long, astounded by the audacity of her fellow students, electrified by their compelling arguments. Talking to the radicals, hearing for the first time the dismaying details of Columbia's callousness toward its black neighbors and of America's brutality toward the Vietnamese, changed her life. "I had just never had time before to think about it all," she later said, "but now I felt the injustice in a very personal and deep way."

She was also present when, in the early morning hours of April 30, the Columbia administration called in the police. She witnessed the cops dragging students out of the buildings and—though most of them offered only passive resistance—beating them indiscriminately. She also watched, terrified, as mounted police charged through the campus, striking out at any student in their path and, before the rampage was over, injuring more than two hundred. That barbarous police attack brought the faculty (though not, of course, its Jacques Barzuns) over to the side of the students, and the next day a campus-wide strike shut the university down.

Karla's education had taken a giant leap forward. She had been radicalized in several directions at once. The viciousness of entrenched authority—whether embodied in university administrators or in uniformed police—was no longer a rhetorical abstraction; nor were bleeding protesters any longer a distant image on some front page or television screen. She had now seen it all for herself.

And what she had also seen—and this was perhaps the least expected and therefore the most revelatory—was that many of the radical male students fully matched their antagonists in strident, strutting machismo. "I was appalled by the behavior of the men," Karla later said. "I could see that left-wing men were not any different." They, like their right-wing brothers, felt that women were made to be auxiliaries, secondary backups for their own frontline heroics. During the building takeover, some of them had actually told Karla and other female students to take off for the local stores to buy food supplies. They even had a little rap about it, about how everyone who wanted to help the revolution should do the job they were best qualified to do. The men didn't know how to make coffee and the women did, so the women should do it—for the "greater cause"—and should do it cheerfully.

Karla thought all that was self-justifying crap—even if she didn't say so at the moment. But she did think it. And that alone, as she would soon discover, put her straight on the road to feminism. The family trait of stubbornness was about to find a new channel.

RAY

On the day Sylvia went to jail at Rikers Island, she weighed a strapping 140 pounds. When she came out two and a half months later, she was down to 115. It wasn't jail food, bad though that was, that caused the drop. It was heroin.

Sylvia was turned on in jail by a "nice queen" named Penny—"pure peer pressure" is how Sylvia later described it. When Penny asked her one day, "Do you shoot drugs?" Sylvia answered with her customary bravado: "Well, of course I do. I love them." It was easy to get dope in jail. True to her word, Penny came up with both heroin and a needle. Afterward, Sylvia was as sick as a dog for three days. It was the start of a habit that would grip her for five years.

She had a huge tolerance for heroin. When everyone else was nodding out, kissing their toes, Sylvia would be wide awake and more than a little annoyed that she hadn't gotten off. So one night (this was later, after she got out of jail) when their connection warned Sylvia and her friends that the dope they had just bought was super-strong, Sylvia ignored him and shot up a full dose. She went out like a light and woke up in a snowbank on the street. Her friends had dragged her down three flights, afraid she was dead. But she came out of it, and within seconds was cursing them out for "fucking up my coat" by dumping her in the snowbank.

Due to the police crackdown in 1966, the cellblock in the Rikers Island prison reserved for gay-related "crimes" was filled to overflowing. Most of the queens welcomed the separate unit as a refuge from rape and harassment and as a place where, with a little ingenuity, they could recreate some semblance of their life on the outside. They saved pats of butter from meals to use as grease for sex, and they used Kool-Aid to dye the dreary blue prison garb more becoming shades. To prepare for the Christmas party, they pieced together outfits, converting work clothes into dresses and using bars of soap to press them. It was even rumored that a few of the queens got themselves rearrested in order to take part in the Christmas party.[24]

Yet conditions were harsh on the block. While other prisoners on Rikers were allowed to shower every day, the queens got to shower once a week, even during the steamy summer months. They were also denied library privileges, could receive visits only from family members, not from friends, were offered no prison jobs (like working in the bakery or the kitchen) to break the monotony of the day, and indeed were let out of their cells only for twenty minutes every evening to wash up.

Sylvia made at least one good friend while in jail, a beautiful black queen named Bambi Lamour. On their way to breakfast one morning, Bambi looked over disdainfully at the newly arrived Sylvia and demanded, "Who are you, bitch? Since when did they let dykes in the block?" Sylvia knew it was her cue to be haughty. "I'm no dyke, bitch," she sniffed back. "I'm more boy than you. But *you* can call me Sylvia." That did it. They became fast friends on the spot and for the next few months gloried in their reputation as "crazy, abnormal bitches." They'd walk down the corridor snapping their fingers and calling out "Taxi! Taxi! Take us to Forty-second and Ninth. We got to make us some money!" Or they'd refuse to sit with anyone else at meals, once upending a table and dragging it into a corner for privacy. "Nobody ever fucked with us," Sylvia recalls with satisfaction.

Soon after she got out of jail, Sylvia teamed up with a straight hooker named Kim as her hustling partner. They figured—correctly, it turned out—that they could make more money that way, play into a greater range of fantasies, open up more opportunities to steal. One standard variation went this way:

> CUSTOMER (*approaching Kim and Sylvia on the corner*): Are you two dykes?
> KIM: Yeah. (*pointing to Sylvia*) That's my butch over there. You want to party?
> CUSTOMER: How much is standard?
> SYLVIA: If you ain't spending enough money, we ain't going. You want to have a freebie trip, or you want to have a good trip?

Usually, the customer would opt for the "good trip." Once they had him back in the hotel room, Sylvia—who had started to take hormone shots—would pop off her bra and jiggle her breasts for the customer to play with. But she always kept her G-string on, and the customer at a safe distance. In another variation, Kim and Sylvia would take turns sucking on each other's breasts or feeling each other up on the bed. That usually drove the customer crazy—at which point Sylvia would announce that it was "time for him to pop his nut." According to the game plan, Kim would then screw him while Sylvia rifled his wallet. Sylvia would snap her fingers—"Time's up!"—to signal that she had secured the guy's money; they would then quickly end the scene.

They made a lot of money, enough to finance Sylvia's heroin habit—at one point she was shooting up two hundred dollars' worth a day—as well as the white fox coat she took to hustling in. And enough money to pay for her hormone treatments as well. She had started the treatments thinking she wanted to have a sex-change operation, and had trooped along with her friends to a doctor on the Lower East Side—that is, until she started to get a discharge from her right breast, and discovered that she was being given monkey hormones. She then shifted to a Dr. Stern on Fifth Avenue, who, "if you let him play with you for a little while, he'd give you anything for free." (Craig Rodwell also had his experiences with Dr. Stern when sent to him, under suspicion of having gonorrhea, by Harvey Milk. Stern told Craig to "lie down on the examination table, take out your penis and get it hard." Stern then discreetly left the room, returning to masturbate Craig while explaining that he needed the semen to test for gonorrhea. Afterward, he invited Craig into his office and showed him a photo album filled with attractive male models, every now and then exclaiming, "Oh, this one is from Chicago, too." Craig never got a bill.)

Initially, Sylvia liked what Dr. Stern's hormones did to her body, reducing facial hair and making her more curvaceous. But she soon decided to stop the injections. "I came to the conclusion," she later recalled, "that I don't want to be a woman. I just want to be me. I want to be Sylvia Rivera. I like pretending. I like to have the role. I like to dress up and pretend, and let the world think about what I am. Is he, or isn't he? That's what I enjoy. I don't want to be a woman. Why? That means I can't fuck nobody up the ass. Two holes? No, no, no. That ain't going to get it. No, no, no."

She did love drag, though. But like so many others in the life, she disliked the actual term. As one of her friends, Ivan Valentin (who later headlined the "Leading Ladies of New York" show), explained, "A drag or transvestite is somebody who always dresses as a woman. A female impersonator is somebody who claims to actually *be* a woman. I'm just a man who likes to dress up." Sylvia felt more or less the same way (less, in her hormone-taking phase). In part, Ivan and Sylvia were accepting the inescapable: they tended to look like boys or butch dykes even when dressed in full drag. (Many of Sylvia's customers would have disagreed, perhaps to avoid the realization that their cocks were getting hard in reaction to a boy.) In any case, neither Sylvia nor Ivan was interested in having cosmetic surgery to burnish the illusion.[25]

And that helps to explain why Sylvia never attempted to work as a performer, though by the mid-sixties there were many more such opportunities opening up in New York than had recently been the case. In an earlier era, the drag performer Julian Eltinge had been so hugely popular that he had had a Broadway theater named after him, and in the forties and fifties Phil Black's drag shows in Harlem, Frankie Quinn's in midtown Manhattan, and Dazee Dee's in Brooklyn—reputedly the classiest of them all—were major events.[26]

It was still possible in the 1950s for T. C. Jones to bring in a crowd for his Broadway revue, *Mask and Gown* (and to do his impersonations of Bette Davis and Tallulah in Leonard Sillman's *New Faces of 1956*). But the great drag star Minette recalls that by the late fifties only two drag clubs existed in New York City—fewer than in some small Southern cities (though those were subject to sudden closings and arrests). The opening of the 82 Club on East Fourth Street, which became something of a tourist attraction in the sixties, helped to spark a revival, and by the end of that decade, drag had been featured in several off-off-Broadway productions (including H. M. Koutoukas's *Medea in the Laundromat* at Caffè Cino).[27]

By the early seventies, drag had very nearly gone mainstream, with Jackie Curtis, Candy Darling, and Holly Woodlawn all becoming Warhol-made celebrities, though the *term* "drag" continued to be variously regarded. Individual definitions ranged from "dress-up artist" and "performer" to, in Holly Woodlawn's case, a simple "fabulous." ("It's not a man or a woman, it's *fabulous*. When men's fashions start to be more fabulous, I'll use *them* to dress up.") Holly further insisted, contradicting Ivan Valentin, that a "true" drag was not someone who "always dresses as a woman," but rather someone who "only gets it on for the stage." Since prostitution might be regarded as a form of dramatic presentation, Sylvia would have qualified under Holly Woodlawn's definition, as she surely did under Holly's more encompassing "fabulous."[28]

But Sylvia didn't care much about definitions, which was precisely why she would emerge as a radical figure. She disliked any attempt to categorize her random, sometimes contradictory impulses, to make them seem more uniform and predictable than they were. That was precisely why she decided against a sex change. She didn't want to be cast in *any* one mold. Her own description of her cross-dressing best captures the spontaneity at its core: "I like to pull some shit out of the closet, throw on some female attire, a blouse or whatever—not complete drag—paint on a little makeup—and hit the streets."

Sylvia's grandmother did not share her enthusiasm for drag. One night on Ninth Avenue, a queen who lived in Viejita's building yelled over to Sylvia that her grandmother wasn't feeling well and wanted to see her. "Oh sure," Sylvia yelled back, "she pulls that one on me all the time." But she hailed a cab immediately, though stoned and in drag—and though it was two o'clock in the morning. The first thing Viejita said when she opened the door was "Oh my God, you look just like your mother!" "Well, who am I supposed to look like?" Sylvia shot back.

The visit went downhill from there. Viejita told Sylvia that she had to change. "Change what?" Sylvia answered, as if mystified (while wondering, in her stoned state, if Viejita was encouraging her to go back on hormones). "You have to get *married*!" Viejita shouted. "Married? Married? I *am* married—you met Gary. And I ain't gettin' married again." Another ten minutes of shouting at each other and Sylvia slammed the door behind her and took a cab back to Times Square.

But Viejita wasn't finished with her. One night in the "Hostro" (as the Hispanic prostitutes called the Times Square area), Sylvia was talking on the street with one of her steady customers ("a good trick —fifty dollars just to give him a lousy blow job!") and getting ready to clinch the deal when a woman behind her shouted, "Don't you know that's a man?" Sylvia, in an instant rage, whirled around ready to pop what she assumed was a competing hooker in the face—and came flat up against Viejita. "That's a man! That's my grandson!" Viejita repeated, screaming at the potential customer. When Sylvia tried to calm her down, Viejita accused her (falsely) of no longer sending money home and (accurately) of rarely coming to see her. By this time, the potential customer had fled into the night, never to return.

The running battle with Viejita went on for years, but six months after their confrontation in Times Square, Sylvia was able to use drag to save herself from a much larger battlefront. Approaching the ripe old age of eighteen, and with the country, in 1967, exploding in militant resistance to the escalating war in Vietnam, Sylvia abruptly got notice to report to the local draft board in Jersey City (where she was living at the time).

She made an instant decision: She was not, under any circumstances, going to war. She considered herself a patriotic American, and swore that if anybody ever tried to invade this country, she would pick up a gun—"and I know how to use a gun, honey"—and "blow them away off the continent." But she was "*not* going over there to fight for something that I don't know really what we're going for." The only question was how to get out of it.

Sylvia made up her mind to appear at the draft board in full drag: high heels, miniskirt, long red nails, the works. But she nervously wondered if that would do it; she had heard rumors that even queens had been drafted, to do clerical work. When she arrived at the draft board on the scheduled morning, in full regalia, she was directed to a desk at which sat two sergeants, one male, one female. The female sergeant assumed the new arrival was in her jurisdiction: "Women who are enlisting," she said, smiling and pointing, "go to *that* side of the room."

"But I'm one of the boys," Sylvia said. "My name is Ray. Ray Rivera."

Now it was the turn of the male sergeant. Gruffly, unsmilingly, he repeated—whether because of nearsightedness or incomprehension—that Sylvia should join the ladies on *that* side of the room. And next thing Sylvia knew, she was on a bus with a bunch of women headed for the induction center in Newark. "All of these bitches got no nails and short cropped hair. They looked butcher than I do at my best." Halfway into the trip, Sylvia noticed one of the tougher-looking women giving her the eye. Sylvia wheeled on her indignantly. "I am *not* a woman!" she yelled. "I *happen* to be one of the boys!"

At the induction center they took Sylvia straight to the psychiatrist's office.

"What's your name?" the psychiatrist asked.

"Which one, darling?"

"Your male Christian name."

"Oh. That's Ray José Christian Rivera. Alias Miss Sylvia Lee Rivera."

"Is there a problem with your sexuality?"

"Is there? I don't know," said Sylvia, arching her eyebrows in feigned innocence. "I know I like men. I know I like to wear dresses. But I don't know what any *problem* is."

The psychiatrist frowned, so Sylvia knew she was on the right track and plunged ahead. "I got papers here from when I was in the hospital. A doctor signed them. The papers state that I am a homosexual. Is that what you mean by a 'problem'?"

Without another word, the psychiatrist stamped "HOMOSEXUAL" in three-inch-high red letters on Sylvia's induction notice, then told her that she could go home.

Knowing she had gotten off, Sylvia giddily opted for one last bit of grandstanding camp. "I ain't got no money to go home," she announced with maximum petulance. "You all brought me here, now you all got to get me home. Somebody's *got to take me home*!"

And damned if they didn't drive her all the way back to Jersey City.

Jim Fouratt was finding his own ways to resist the draft—to resist what he had come to view as entrenched and irresponsible American power. After his first, almost inadvertent antiwar demonstration in Times Square in 1964, he rapidly became politicized. A crucial turning point for him was getting to know Abbie Hoffman in 1966. As an offshoot of his involvement in the black civil rights struggle, Hoffman had come to New York to open Liberty House—a store devoted to selling handmade goods produced in Mississippi—on the Lower East Side. Impressed with Jim's work in helping to organize New York's first "be-in"—a gathering and display of the countercultural hippie tribes at the Sheep Meadow in Central Park—Abbie sought him out.[29]

Jim's guess is that Abbie was also drawn to him as that intriguing Other, the blond, blue-eyed and—Jim encouraging the notion—purportedly upper-class WASP. Whatever the source of the initial attraction, the two men became increasingly involved in political work together and between 1967 and 1969, Jim became one of the most prominent figures in the "Yippie!" wing of the movement. ("Yippie" was the name given to politicized hippies.) Abbie defined the Yippie group with his characteristically stylish blend of humor and high purpose: The Yippies, he wrote, represented a "blending of pot and politics into a political grass leaves movement—a cross-fertilization of the hippie and New Left philosophies." The group's aim—though in true Yippie fashion it would have disavowed so linear a goal and the planning and leadership implied—was to "tie together as much of the underground as was willing into some gigantic national get-together" whose purpose would be to develop "a model for an alternate society."[30]

Jim grew to love Abbie "in a way that one loves a comrade," even though he felt early on that Abbie, and even more, his fellow Yippie leader, Jerry Rubin, were deeply, almost reflexively homophobic—which Abbie himself acknowledged late in life. Jim remained indifferent to Rubin, dismissing him as a manipulative careerist, but emotionally, he invested heavily in Abbie—and would end up feeling that Abbie had misused and betrayed him. There were

early signs, signs that for the most part Jim chose to ignore. On a
television program he and Abbie did in the spring of 1967, Abbie
declared, with a big grin, "I'm not a hippie. Hippies are fags. Sorry
about that. I don't think they know how to love." Jim said nothing,
either during the show or after (though he would later, on the Susskind
show, come out publicly), preferring to chalk up Abbie's remarks to
his fondness for playing the macho, gay-bashing street hood in public,
even though he seemed comfortable in private with people he knew
to be gay.[31]

But the trouble with this theory was that in private Abbie *wasn't*
always comfortable. In 1968, when Jim was living with his then lover,
Howie Weinstein, in a loft on Bond Street, Abbie would frequently
drop by. But he would look through Howie as if he weren't there and
sometimes, right in front of him, make some clunky remark about a
woman he wanted to fix Jim up with. Afterward, Howie would be
angry and would berate Jim for not having spoken up. "But what was
there to say?" Jim would lamely respond, "You're here. This is our
house. You sleep in this bed with me. Everybody knows that. What
is there to say?" "But he can't even *look* at me!" Howie would howl,
"How can you trust a man like that?"

For several years Jim buried his own doubts about Abbie. He
closely identified with the values Abbie espoused, and preferred to
believe that the espousal and the practice were essentially one, give
or take the usual human discrepancies. Jim had found a political home
and didn't want to lose it, a prominent identity and didn't want to
jeopardize it. He was so immersed for a time in the Yippie cause that
he actually called himself Jimmy Digger in tribute to the parent group
in California, the Diggers, whose philosophy had centrally inspired
the Yippies.

The Diggers took their name from the seventeenth-century English revolutionaries who denounced private property and heralded the
reign of love. The Californians regarded all forms of authority (and
especially that of the state) as illegitimate, felt a romantic solidarity
with the underclasses, denied the morality of a money economy,
distributed surplus goods free for the asking, and were devoted to
spontaneous forms of expression, pleasure, and resistance. They were
more serious-minded and theoretically coherent than the Yippies, who
popularized the Digger views and won, with their bowdlerized version, far more publicity than the parent group ever had or wanted.

With his keen analytic intelligence and philosophical seriousness,
Jim probably felt more closely identified with the Diggers than did

any of the other Yippie leaders. His androgynous look, his flowing blond hair and delicate features, belied the intense, committed person within. Jim *looked* the part of a boundaryless hippie more than most of those who claimed the label, but if one was foolish enough to equate that look with a limp, passive personality, one was in for a rude shock.

For—except with Abbie—Jim rarely pulled his punches or hesitated about speaking his mind. And rather than behaving like a docile follower, he was quick to initiate a line of action. He had been impressed in San Francisco with Chester Anderson's "Communications Company," which periodically published leaflets to disseminate news of interest to the hip left community. When Jim's friend Howard Smith, a *Village Voice* writer, offered him a Gestetner duplicating machine that the *Voice* was discarding, Jim suddenly had the means to start a comparable operation in New York. He single-handedly wrote and distributed a street newspaper which, in homage to the San Francisco operation, he called *The Communications Company*. And on his travels in and out of various worlds, Jim was always careful to bring along copies of his paper to distribute.

The preeminent gathering place of the influential avant-garde in the late sixties was Max's Kansas City—or simply "Max's," to those in the know—the favorite late-night hangout for Andy Warhol and friends (and those who wanted to be). Warhol himself often occupied the corner table in the back room, the silent puppeteer, expertly working the strings, delighting in the manipulated dance—a fake Zen master who rationalized his indifference to other people's pain as a "necessary" offshoot of his artistic self-absorption. Jim first met Warhol in 1965, and found him charming, if maddeningly passive-aggressive; he also saw clearly that Warhol was a control freak who goaded people to perform for him while rejecting all responsibility for the behavior he had elicited.

Jim's friend from Caffè Cino days, Bob Heide, could personally testify to Warhol's ice-cold exploitations. Though he had given Warhol the idea (at a time when Warhol was lamenting his artistic bankruptcy) of changing around the colors and doing repetitions on his Campbell's Soup and Marilyn Monroe series, Warhol neither credited him nor subsequently showed him a tinge of gratitude. To the contrary, he mistreated him. Warhol filmed Heide's play *The Bed*, but when the film's financial backer tried to get it shown, Warhol hid it and denied its existence, and then later spliced a sequence from it into his movie *Chelsea Girls*—without crediting Heide's play as the source.[32]

Much as he sometimes found Warhol repellent, Jim was willing to put up with him. He enjoyed being part of whatever the red-hot scene of the moment was—especially if he could juggle it with several other scenes bidding for attention—and that meant hanging out in Max's. Warhol's holding court there was not a compelling reason for staying away, and Jim made a point of ending nearly every evening by dropping into Max's. He distributed the latest edition of *The Communications Company*, picked up information for the next one, and congratulated himself on being in the scene without being in Warhol's orbit.

Like Yvonne Flowers, Jim loved the simultaneous life, loved a multiplicity of actions—perhaps not least because he could never quite find the *one* channel that could maximally focus his gifts, could not stay quiet long enough to allow that channel to emerge. At the same time that he was doing a turn at personal journalism, he was continuing his acting classes with Lee Strasberg and periodically landing a part in a play. In 1967 he acted in *The Peace Creeps*, performed in the theater above the trendy nightclub Arthur's, with James Earl Jones and a shy, promising newcomer named Al Pacino (Jim thought Pacino's chief talent onstage was an ability to get believably angry).

Next came a Broadway production, *The Freaking Out of Stephanie Blake*, with Jean Arthur—a play about hippies that became legendary for its three months of previews and its failure ever to open. Jean Arthur was a notoriously difficult person to work with, a demanding perfectionist who had previously walked out on *St. Joan of the Stockyards*. But Jim developed enormous respect for her hard work and her magical abilities (though he was considerably less enamored of her lesbian lover/nurse, an ex-marine who always hovered threateningly at Jean's side). After changing directors three times, Jean walked off the stage during a preview performance of *Stephanie Blake* in the middle of her one scene with Jim, leaving him the nightmarish job of having to ad-lib until the curtain finally came down. She never returned to the play, and the producers closed it.

Soon after, Jim hooked up with Joe Chaikin's experimental group, the Open Theater. Distrustful of the theater's traditional reliance on words, Chaikin had begun to use intense physical exercises to explore nonverbal forms of communication; his brilliant production of *The Serpent* in the late sixties would make the Open Theater the most admired of all the experimental companies. But by then, Jim, typically, had already left—this time sparking off to do an electric "up-to-the-minute" column for a Hearst publication called *Eye*. Since it had a three-month lead time, Jim would make up events and then, with his friends, see to it that they came true in time for the column to appear.

His most consistent (though never singular) commitment in the mid-to-late sixties remained with Abbie Hoffman and the Yippies, and he played a central role in several of the "spontaneous" actions that all at once imaginatively protested the inequities and deformities of American life and the escalating war in Vietnam, "blew the minds" of the Yippies' straight-shooting comrades on the left, and made the Yippies media celebrities and countercultural heroes.

In June 1967 Jim, wearing purple pants, accompanied Abbie (in his now *de rigueur* beads and bell-bottoms) to the SDS "Drawing Board" conference in Michigan. The gathering had been called mostly to redefine the New Left's relationship to an emergent "black power" movement that advised whites henceforth to work in their own communities. The New York Yippies were joined in Michigan by a delegation from the San Francisco Diggers, led by Emmett Grogan, and together they managed to wreak havoc with the "rational discourse" favored by SDS.

After Tom Hayden had finished his evaluation of white organizing efforts in the black ghetto of Newark, the Digger contingent disrupted the meeting with assorted shouts and antics. Emmett Grogan told the crowd (in Grogan's recollection) "about the importance of anonymity to persons who seriously attempted to effect relevant changes in any social order," and he made fun of the fondness of Abbie Hoffman and others for the limelight. When Abbie countered that Grogan would end up on the cover of *Time* magazine, Grogan vehemently denied it, and to punctuate his point kicked over a Formica table, punched and slapped people, yelled that they were all "fags," that they didn't have "the balls to go mad" or to make a real revolution, that they would "piss in their pants" if violence ever erupted. Then he read aloud Gary Snyder's poem "Day of Judgment upon Us."[33]

The Diggers, the Yippies, and some SDSers then proceeded to get stoned (Jim was known in Yippie circles as comparatively abstemious), and talk till dawn about the need for the New Left to understand that a revolution in consciousness had to precede, or at the least accompany, any hoped-for revolution in social arrangements. According to one printed account—which Jim decries as apocryphal—he tried to make the countercultural point concrete by abruptly kissing the square-rigger SDS leader, Bob Ross, full on the lips. When the stunned Ross purportedly recoiled, Jim is said to have explained that he had always been powerfully attracted to Jewish men.[34]

Back in New York, Jim and Abbie led a series of daringly theatrical actions that employed the symbols of authority in order to discredit them. In a Flower Power demonstration, perhaps the very first dramatization of ecological concerns, they set off soot bombs at Con Edison headquarters and, to the accompaniment of a rock band playing from a nearby flatbed truck, planted a tree in front of the popular disco the Electric Circus, as a way of protesting the city's lack of greenery. But their most imaginative and best-publicized action took place at the New York Stock Exchange.

The original idea for the action had been Jim's, but Abbie, as was his disconcerting way, soon claimed it for his own. Alerting the media in advance, a group of eighteen Yippies simply joined the line of tourists and thus made their way into the gallery overlooking the trading floor. They then started throwing wads of dollar bills down onto the floor below. The ticker tape stopped; the brokers stared up at the balcony in disbelief; and then a number of them rushed to scoop up the dollar bills, as the Yippies rapturously applauded—until the guards collared and ejected them. (In 1989, apparently unaware of the earlier precedent, members of ACT UP threw thousands of fake hundred-dollar bills onto the floor of the Stock Exchange.) Back out in front of the Exchange, the Yippies, for the further edification of the gathered reporters, burned a final bundle of bills in symbolic disdain for the material life.

The Wall Street action was widely covered in the media—with the usual discrepancies. Some of the accounts had the Yippies tossing Monopoly money, others twenty-dollar bills, and still others ripped-up singles. "It was the perfect mythical event," Abbie later gloated, and he took special delight in the CBS report, which alone among the networks accurately reported his insistence that he was really Cardinal Spellman and had tossed at least a thousand dollars in small bills onto the trading floor.[35]

Jim's growing prominence as a result of his Yippie activities did not go unnoticed by the FBI. Deciding to gather additional information on him, the Bureau sent two FBI agents to his parents' home in Rhode Island. Not finding his mother in, they went to the Newport restaurant where Jim's stepfather worked as a chef and told him that Jim was wanted for a bank robbery. His stepfather begged the FBI agents not to bother Jim's mother; she had recently been hospitalized after a breakdown and was still in fragile shape. The agents promised to leave her alone, and promptly returned to her house. This time she was in, and the agents convinced the trembling woman that she could best protect her son by turning over everything that related to him—pictures, letters, whatever. Which she did.

Jim was furious when he heard about the cruel intimidation. Except for an occasional telephone call or postcard, he hadn't been in regular contact with his parents for some time. They knew nothing about his political life except that he was against the war in Vietnam—which they supported, as they supported all official acts of the government. The FBI visit put an end to their innocence. Hearing from Jim that he had never been involved in a bank robbery, and from her husband that the FBI had promised *not* to bother her, Jim's mother wrung her hands in guilty remorse over having cooperated with the agents. Jim quieted her down, but the FBI's casual disregard for the defenseless woman's well-being got emotionally linked in his mind with the fate of defenseless Vietnamese peasants. It further hardened his determination to resist the impervious, cold-hearted men in Washington.

But his next major action, on March 22, 1968, ended in disaster. The Yippies decided to stage a "celebration of the spring equinox" in the heart of the working world's bustle: Grand Central Station. The demonstration drew a large crowd of some six thousand, and soon veered from benign antics to heated confrontation. Several people—possibly provocateurs, possibly members of the anarchist East Village group Up Against the Wall Motherfuckers, who believed in confrontational tactics—scrambled on top of the information booth in the center of the huge main hall, started chanting "Burn, baby, burn!" and tore the hands off the booth's clock. Then two cherry bombs went off, and a large contingent of police charged the crowd, flailing about with their nightsticks, clubbing those already fallen. They rammed a *Village Voice* reporter headfirst into a glass door and beat Abbie (who had come dressed as an American Indian) into unconsciousness. He nonetheless hailed the event for putting Yippies "on the map."[36]

Jim was not nearly so sanguine. Having helped to announce the event on WBAI and organize it through handouts of his paper, *The Communications Company*, he felt personally responsible for the debacle. And he was deeply shaken by it as a possible harbinger of what might happen that summer at the planned "Festival of Life" demonstration during the Democratic National Convention in Chicago. Jim's politics did not encompass violence, revolutionary or otherwise. His activism, as he saw it, derived from moral imperatives and was concerned above all with the transformation of consciousness—and he even defined his work in avant-garde theater as further feeding into that "revolution in feeling." He was now worried that there would be another explosive confrontation at the Democratic convention and that it would put everything he valued in jeopardy.

Abbie reassured him that the Yippie presence in Chicago would focus (as the posters promised) on "Lights–Theater–Magic–Free Music," thereby abetting precisely the cultural renovation Jim had been working for. But Abbie's giddy talk to the press about slipping LSD into the water supply, fucking openly in the parks, and releasing greased pigs on the convention floor, struck Jim as irresponsible and heightened his anxiety. As the time for the convention drew near, he became increasingly convinced that confrontation, not celebration, would be the end result. During Yippie planning sessions, he openly predicted a "bloodbath" and insisted that if people were going to have to fight in the streets then they damn well ought to be told what was coming so they could prepare for it—instead of being encouraged to believe, as official Yippie releases had it, that some wondrously benign love-in was afoot.

Abbie later claimed that the Grand Central Station Massacre had "let the whole world know there would be blood on the streets of Chicago" and that anyone who came there knew full well in advance "that they were risking their life." It is certainly true that others besides Jim—if not Abbie himself—gave ample warning that events in the Windy City could take a violent turn. Abe Peck, editor of the underground publication *Seed*, had written, for example, "If you're coming to Chicago, be sure to wear some armor in your hair." And those warnings were ultimately heard. No more than a couple of thousand young people showed up for the Festival of Life.[37]

Abbie did finally arrange for medical and legal assistance at the planned Lincoln Park and Grant Park gathering sites, but he apparently continued to believe—such was his optimistic nature—in a peaceful outcome. If so, he hadn't reckoned on Richard J. Daley, Chicago's mayor. Many months before the Democratic delegates were due to arrive, Daley talked as if a berserk cadre of "hoodlums and Communists" was determined on a bloody takeover of the city, and he darkly hinted at assassination plots against the leading presidential candidates. To meet this wildly exaggerated threat, Daley armed his police to the teeth and set the city's nerves on edge with his doomsday rhetoric. When, just a few months before the Democrats were due to convene, Robert F. Kennedy was gunned down, the apocalyptic mood deepened.

Daley proved a self-fulfilling prophet. For the better part of a week, the police, with little or no provocation, literally assaulted antiwar demonstrators and yippies alike, spilling so much blood, and bashing onlookers, reporters, and "freaks" so indiscriminately, that TV images of their rampaging brutality produced national revulsion. A number of convention delegates expressed open horror at the police riot, but the convention nonetheless proceeded to vote down a peace plank and to nominate Hubert Humphrey, closely identified with the Vietnam War, as the Democratic presidential candidate.

As much as Jim deplored on all counts the outcome at Chicago, he recognized, with some satisfaction, that hordes of "mere" liberals had been driven leftward and that the heightened polarization of the country held out the eventual promise of its rejuvenation.

THE
LATE
SIXTIES

YVONNE

Yvonne felt that being single was a temporary state. As she put it, "I was always falling in love and there was always somebody ready to fall in love, too. And there were always women ready for sex." In retrospect she thinks of herself as having been "compulsively romantic" in the mid-sixties, "always having two or three affairs going on at the same time. . . . I was used to the insanity. Good old dyke drama."

Her intense interactions were almost entirely with other black women; over the years she became involved with only three or four women who were white. She found black women more political ("If she doesn't have any politics I'm not even interested in her"), more mature emotionally, and with greater "energy for living, for dancing, for life, for people. . . . There are so many things about me they understand, where it comes from, what it's about, so I can cut across a whole lot of stuff."[1]

After Anne left her in 1963, Yvonne still came into Manhattan often from Brooklyn; she had a passion for museums and galleries, for staring transfixed at buildings and bridges ("My eyes were hungry")—and, of course, she came to hang out in the gay clubs and to hear her beloved jazz. She heard "every musician who was anybody who passed through New York"—including, at the Five Spot, one of the last appearances by Coleman Hawkins and one of the first by Ornette Coleman. For a week, jazz aficionados showed up for every one of Ornette Coleman's sets, but true to the supercool style of the clubs would only allow as how "this dude with the plastic horn, you'd have to say, it ain't bad."

Following a midnight set, Yvonne would take off, say, for a dance given by the M.C. Social Club in the Bronx or at the Audubon Ballroom in Manhattan; and, when that party ended at three A.M. or so, would go on to an all-women's after-hours place like Snooky's, and dance, eat, and drink till daybreak. But she found more time for studying than she had when younger, and it took her no more than the usual two years to get her O.T. (occupational therapy) graduate certificate from NYU, in 1966.

But it was a close call. In her last term before graduating, Yvonne developed a huge fibroid tumor and several gynecological cysts, and had to have major surgery. Unable to attend classes for the final weeks of the semester, she nonetheless managed, with the help of classmates and friends, to complete her assignments and graduate in June.

She went straight to work at Hillside Psychiatric Hospital. She had done some of her undergraduate field work there (indeed, she had worked in psychiatric facilities, off and on, since she was eighteen), and the hospital administrators, impressed with her abilities and experience, had offered her a staff job in occupational therapy as soon as she graduated.

Hillside specialized in young adults and drug abusers—meaning, in those years, mostly acidheads and potheads. Yvonne, of course—along with others on the staff—herself qualified in both categories. When she became a supervisor a few years later, she would often, come three o'clock on a Friday afternoon, push the furniture in her office to one side, put on some music, turn the lights down low, get the booze out of the filing-cabinet drawer—and party. From that point on in the weekend, Yvonne was off and running. Her hangovers would be so intense by Monday that she made sure not to schedule anything before one o'clock. (She made up the time by working late one night a week.)

Yet her work performance remained superior, and before long she was promoted to director of vocational rehabilitation. In addition —remarkably, given the fact that undiagnosed lupus was already sapping her energy—she managed to find time, between work and partying, for participation in a variety of political actions. Those ranged from occasional antiwar protests to demonstrations for community control in the Ocean Hill–Brownsville school district to joining a lie-in at the Downstate Medical Center building site to protest the lack of black construction workers.

The 1968 Ocean Hill–Brownsville controversy particularly engaged her. The conflict was essentially between poor black parents and the mostly white, Jewish teachers who taught their children. Claiming that the teachers were doing a lousy job of it, the parents fought for control of the school board. But the conflict took on broader dimensions still: It seemed to pit the social vision of decentralization and "participatory democracy" against those who believed in centralized authority and the transmission of knowledge and services *down* to the client. Citywide battle lines were drawn accordingly.

Yvonne's sympathies were with the black parents, and she took vigorous part in the assorted marches and meetings that attempted to rally support for them. But as the strike dragged interminably on, Yvonne's activism gradually weakened. Resisting any consistent, prolonged organizational affiliation had become something of a pattern with her. And she had some good reasons for resisting (along with some unexamined private ones). Above all, she was reluctant to deal with the endemic homophobia of the left, and felt she could not pass as straight even if she had wanted to participate in that kind of subterfuge. She had heard that there were *some* out lesbians working with the Black Panthers—but had also heard that the brothers had been giving them a hard time. But if she steered clear of any sustained organizational ties, she made it a point of honor to turn the lights up at a party—often to indignant shouts—in order to pass the hat for this group or that action.

Hers was a sharply compartmentalized life, with few overlaps in her professional-partying-political activities. The closest she came to bridging the divisions, to bringing the different parts of her life together, happened almost against her will. "Ellen," a white, heterosexual woman with whom Yvonne worked, inherited a good deal of money from her parents (a well-known actress and a famous playwright), bought a house with it in Rowe, Massachusetts, and kept inviting Yvonne to come up for a weekend.

Yvonne resisted. She didn't want to spend time "with these straight white people," and especially not with Ellen's husband, a Vietnam War vet with decidedly unpredictable moods. Finally Ellen walked into Yvonne's office one day, threw the keys to the house on her desk, and said, "Look: This is a *nice* house. I love this house and I love you, and I want you to enjoy it. So you take whoever you want and you go up there."

It proved to be a nice house indeed—spacious, set on a lake, with a sun deck, a large front porch, and a huge kitchen that invited free-flowing, intimate talk. It also had a backyard filled with wildflowers in the spring, and a creek with beaver dams. Yvonne loved the house and the setting immediately, and over the years would come to think of Rowe, Massachusetts, as a cherished second home. But on her first visit, she took along Audre Lorde's ten-year-old daughter, as well as her then lover Yolanda's three-year-old child—as a kind of protection during this incursion into foreign territory.

After the initial few visits, Yvonne would go up to Rowe with various combinations of people, including even Ellen and her husband. She loved to walk in the woods, to have her own sense of solitude comfortably confirmed by the serene surroundings, and she eventually grew to love the place so much that she bought a formal share in it. The house had a piano, which Yvonne constantly played, reliving the childhood days when her mother's musicality and her own would, more or less harmoniously, blend. In Rowe, Yvonne would play, as she later put it, "this very weird music—now it would be called New Age music, but at that time it was just the music I heard in my head."

Yvonne and her friends brought their city drugs with them—including LSD. They were enchanted with the effects of seeming to see the fish at the bottom of the lake or the trees literally dancing in the breeze. But once, unexpectedly, Yvonne had a terrible trip, and it so frightened her that she thereafter swore off LSD. Ellen, on the other hand, became so entranced with her mystical experiences that in the early seventies she left on a pilgrimage to India and ultimately ended up in Oregon with Rajneesh, to whom she reportedly gave all her money.

But for the five to six years before the household in Rowe broke up, Yvonne was able to find there a needed respite from her frantic, disjunctive life in the city. The comfort of the place, in combination with the solidity of her professional life, provided ballast for a life otherwise unbalanced by late hours, too much booze and too many drugs, and a frantic sexual pace that kept any sustained emotional connection at arm's length. The balance would hold well into the seventies, and then, in a simultaneous double blow, she would lose both the house and her job.

By then she had gained a reputation at Hillside for being not only a skillful occupational therapist and supervisor, but a superb grant writer. Influenced by her own political activism in behalf of community control in Brownsville, she decided to write a grant for outpatient drug treatment that, through the device of advisory boards, would involve the local community in Queens Village in the decision-making process. She wrote the grant proposal with two male psychologists on the Hillside staff with whom she had worked earlier, and ended up liking it so much that when the National Institute of Mental Health funded it, she decided to direct the program herself.

That meant leaving her post as director of vocational rehabilitation and, though she didn't realize it at the time, putting herself in a position where she could be fired. As it turned out, the two psychologists were more interested in the funding than in the project. After Yvonne had been heading the program for nine months, and enjoying it enormously, she was called into the office of her immediate boss, the director of activities therapy, and told that she was being let go. The news took her utterly by surprise, and it was years before she could piece together what had happened. Even then, she managed only an incomplete, unsatisfying version.

The project had received funding for a full four years, and the two psychologists apparently decided that they wanted to control the funds for their own purposes, which only peripherally included the outpatient drug program. One of the woman volunteers in the program was also involved in the move to get Yvonne fired; she wanted to direct the activities-therapy program herself, and since (as Yvonne later discovered) her uncle was on the Hillside board of directors, she had the needed clout behind her ambition.

The sense of personal betrayal was the most painful part of the firing. Yvonne had gone to school at NYU with the activities director, and considered him a close friend. Her intuition had told her that he was a closeted gay, but Yvonne, figuring that it was none of her business, had never attempted an alliance on those grounds. Nor did she think that in turning on her, he was projecting outward his own unacknowledged self-hatred. More likely, she believed, he had become seriously addicted and needed to secure his own job by doing the unquestioned bidding of the higher-ups at Hillside.

As is usually the case with black lesbians, Yvonne found it difficult to tell which of the "isms"—racism, heterosexism, sexism—was most operative against her at Hillside. Though she *was* the only black person in the activities-therapy department at Hillside, she had experienced little overt racism there, and had been given regular promotions and salary increases. Because Yvonne was too scrupulous to assign blame without solid proof, and was further hamstrung by the fact that concrete evidence is always difficult to obtain in discrimination cases of any kind, the suit she finally did bring against the hospital was dismissed for lack of specificity. Yvonne was left with a festering sense of failure—she was unable to convert unease into righteous anger—coupled with the debilitating feeling that people she had trusted had turned on her for no apparent reason.

What she did have to fall back on was a substantial severance payment. That allowed her not to work for a year, and the respite, in turn, had two decidedly positive results. The day before the firing, Theo, Yvonne's widowed mother, who had been living with her, became ill (terminally, as it turned out), and not having to go to work every day gave Yvonne the precious opportunity to spend the last three months of her mother's life entirely by her side. Theo, too ill to get around much, would often watch television from her bed, exclaiming in disbelief at this or that retrograde or racist development. A born optimist, she had actually believed the whole issue of race was going to be resolved in her lifetime. Yvonne would shake her head in amazement at her mother's rosy expectations, never having believed herself in anything more than the necessity for ongoing struggle. Today, she "thanks God that Mother isn't alive to see the backwardness that's going on here now."

The severance from Hillside also led to a career change. It began with Yvonne being invited to give guest lectures at this or that college and ended with the staff at CUNY's York campus being so impressed with her presentation that she was offered a permanent faculty appointment. Becoming a teacher was about the last thing Yvonne—who had never even liked school, much as she had always loved learning—had dreamed of. Yet it would open up a new and satisfying world to her.

FOSTER

At age forty-one, Foster Gunnison was, along with Frank Kameny, the oldest delegate to the homophile planning conference. In all, some forty people (only eight of them women) from fourteen organizations gathered at the State Hotel in Kansas City, Missouri, from February 18 to 21, 1966, to discuss whether and how cooperation between local homophile groups could be increased.[2]

New York Mattachine was not among them. Dick Leitsch had acidly expressed the hope that the gathering would accomplish something "besides the breast-beating, navel-contemplating and smugness that characterized ECHO meetings"—but had then refused to pay expenses for MSNY members whose presence might have helped to make that hope a reality.

The militants associated with Kameny and Gittings came to Kansas City hoping to win approval for the formation of a national organization, and one with an activist philosophy. But it rapidly became clear that they would have to settle for an arrangement considerably short of that.

At the very first session of the conference, spokespeople for each organization gave brief descriptions of their group's activities, staking out, with pardonable pride, what they took to be their special accomplishments. Phyllis Lyon emphasized the importance of the Daughters of Bilitis in providing a place for women in what was a predominantly male homophile movement; Bill Beardemphl emphasized the success San Francisco's SIR had had in inducing homosexuals to become politically involved by first offering them an array of social activities; Chuck Thompson outlined the essential educational and research programs at ONE, Inc., of Los Angeles; Mark Forrester underscored the unique mission of San Francisco's Council on Religion and the Homosexual in acting as a bridge between homosexuals and heterosexuals; Robert Walker talked of Mattachine–San Francisco's work in counseling individuals; Guy Strait pitched his own crusade to persuade the homosexual that "salvation lay within himself and not in society's acceptance of him," while Kameny, oppositely, spoke of the importance of getting people to see that "all the problems of the homosexuals are questions of [social] prejudice and discrimination."

It was clear from the initial presentations that any movement toward merger would likely fall victim to entrenched local devotions. Indeed, only four of the fourteen organizations had authorized their representatives to commit to policies or programs that the conference might recommend; and it sometimes proved necessary, before a given matter could be brought to a vote, to state explicitly that it would be "in principle only" and would carry no mandate for action. Under that formula, such noncontroversial goals as "the right of homosexuals to equality of opportunity" could be affirmed—but not specific programs designed to make that goal a reality.

Indeed, it even proved difficult getting consensus for a resolution that declared homosexuality irrelevant for security clearance and employment by the government. When Clark Polak pressed for a statement that homosexuality "must be considered as neither a sickness, disturbance [nor] neurosis," some delegates thought the matter best left to "experts" in mental health and some wanted to go *beyond* the resolution to argue that "a more definite assertion of the nonpathological nature of homosexuality should be made." In the upshot the Polak resolution failed to carry, but the conference did issue a statement that "objective research projects undertaken thus far have indicated that findings of homosexual undesirability are based on opinion, value judgments or emotional reaction rather than on scientific evidence or fact."

When it came time for the conference to turn its attention to the possible creation of a national homophile organization, it voted, not surprisingly, "against considering the item." Yet the militants did win support in Kansas City for the establishment of a national legal fund, for a nationwide day of protest in May against the military's policy of excluding homosexuals, for a "cooperative exchange of ideas and information among homophile groups," and for another conference to be held in August in San Francisco—all of which gave the militants considerable grounds for optimism. They felt hopeful that in San Francisco five months hence, a national organization with real powers could be established.

Foster played a backseat role at the convention. Sensitive to the fact that he was still "a complete novice" in the movement, and modest by temperament, he kept out of the more heated debates. But he was eager to learn more and to meet people, and on all three nights of the conference he hosted a "hospitality suite" that went from eleven P.M. to four A.M. He had already met several movement leaders at ECHO conferences and during the 1965 White House demonstration, and came away from Kansas City admiring Frank Kameny, Barbara Gittings, and Kay Tobin all the more. ("My mind runs in the same track with Kameny's," Foster wrote; "we both instinctively lean toward formalisms.") Of those homophile movers and shakers whom he now met for the first time, he expansively decided that he "liked most everyone."

Yet within that ecumenical embrace, he allowed for some gradations. He was especially taken with twenty-two-year-old Bill Kelley of Chicago's Mattachine Midwest, who served as recording secretary of the convention, awarding him the highest Gunnison virtues: "tactful, sincere, solid reasoning, good detail man." And at first, he found a few of the more celebrated movement figures less than endearing. He thought Don Slater, the head of L.A.'s Tangents, "wispy, waspy" and temperamental; was intimidated by "butch" Shirley Willer, the president of New York DOB; considered Clark Polak, the leader of

Philadelphia's Janus Society, "brash and brassy"; and thought Guy Strait, editor of the *Citizens' News*, his "temperamental opposite"—"a rank individualist opposed to anything that smacks of discipline, order or authority . . . a living symbol of all that is wrong with the movement."

But basically Foster was thrilled with being in the thick of things and felt inspired by the presence of so many dedicated people. If a few of them had rubbed him the wrong way, and if the conference had not talked as much as he would have liked about concrete actions and the need to create a new national structure, he nonetheless came home from Kansas City convinced that "the importance of the move-ment and the happiness to millions of suffering persons that it will bring in the long run easily overshadows the pains of growing." Re-solving to devote himself to the homophile cause, he immediately began to disengage from some of his organizational work with bar-bershop quartets.

And he began to put some of his thoughts to paper. Within a few weeks after returning from Kansas City, and apparently influ-enced by the militants there, he wrote a compelling essay for *The Homosexual Citizen* (Washington Mattachine's monthly) entitled "The Agony of the Mask." In it, Foster—the least self-promoting of men —made a strong plea for ending secrecy and openly avowing one's homosexuality. It was the only way, Foster argued, that gay people could "help repair the damage done to them by others"—a phrasing that reflected the militant view that an oppressive society, and not bad genes or character, had produced whatever disabling aspects were present in the homosexual life-style.

Yet Foster's cautionary side remained. He was not advocating, he hastened to make clear in the article, any form of "disconcerting melodrama," any belligerent "exhibitionism." His goal was social ac-ceptance, not social upheaval; he wanted the homosexual to gain entry into mainstream institutional life, not, as later radicals would, to press for revamping the institutions themselves along more egalitarian lines. Indeed, Foster argued against secrecy precisely in order to win "in-stitutional support," convinced that the emergence of a legion of well-behaved, well-dressed homosexuals would contradict the view that all gay people were "far-out types and professional nonconformists." Once that stereotype was contradicted, Foster believed, experts and institutions of "caliber" would rally to the homosexual's support.[3]

This was a complex appeal, not simply a call to conformity. Foster personally found "far-out types" distasteful, but in calling on homosexuals who did not fit "the storybook caricatures" to publicly declare themselves, he was working on a track somewhat parallel to that of the psychologist Evelyn Hooker. Starting in the late fifties, Hooker had published several pathbreaking articles—which Foster had read —that used a nonclinical sample of gay men (previous studies had been drawn from patient and prison populations) to demonstrate that the psychological profile of the "healthy" gay men in her study differed in no essential way from her control group of heterosexual men.

In other words, Hooker had shown that at least *some* homosexuals existed who were not "maladjusted" or unhappy with their lives, and did not fit the dominant psychiatric view that equated their "condition" with pathology. Though Foster had thought Hooker's work "hardly immune to criticism," he, like her, was trying to increase the pool of publicly visible homosexuals whose lives were similar to those of other middle-class Americans (and thus could be validated as "normal")—even if, unlike Hooker, he was personally uncomfortable with any nonconforming behavior *other* than homosexuality.

At the "Ten Days in August" conference, which convened in San Francisco in the summer of 1966, Foster got a chance to share his views with a wider audience, having been chosen as one of five speakers scheduled to give major addresses. And he spoke to a crowd double the size of that attending the Kansas City gathering some five months before—though it had fewer than a dozen women among some eighty delegates. Indeed, the San Francisco conference proved to be the largest homophile gathering ever held in the United States, and its offerings ranged from a panel discussion of law reform (with an impressive roster that included California state legislators Willie Brown and John L. Burton), to a theatrical presentation, "Gay 90's Night," to a picnic that one gay paper claimed more than six hundred people attended.[4]

The increase in numbers produced the usual corollary: heightened tension. This was a gathering worth fighting over. There was contention, even before the convention opened, about which organizations should be accredited and how many votes should be delegated to each. And the convention itself produced such a proliferation of resolutions—and of arguments for and against them—that many delegates felt more numbed than enlightened. Perhaps because one of his own resolutions was voted down, and he was unable to get the floor as often as he wanted (which was often), Guy Strait—a flamboyant San Franciscan whose penchant for youthful partners got him in periodic trouble with the law—later wrote that "never before in the history of mankind has so much time been wasted by so few people in order that they may hear their own voices."

The disgruntled also included two of the West Coast's legendary activists, Harry Hay and Dorr Legg. Hay was the convener of that small group of gay men who had founded the Mattachine Society in 1950, but now, in 1966, his interest had veered to his newest creation, the Circle of Loving Companions, a group meant to function according to Whitmanesque principles of comradely love. The Circle did occasionally broaden out to include a few friends, but it was usually made up solely of Hay and his lover, John Burnside. The two attended the San Francisco conference as representatives of the Circle, and Hay came away from it more confirmed than ever in the splendor of his chosen isolation: No one else was evolved enough to share his vision—"conservative" Easterners, with their attraction to assimilation, least of all.[5]

Dorr Legg arrived at the conference already bruised. In the spring of 1965, the ONE, Inc. mini-empire over which he presided with an acerbic voice and iron hand, had come apart. Don Slater, a disaffected board member of ONE, simply packed up the organization's thousand-volume library one weekend and hauled it to his own quarters. "The Heist," as it became known, produced years of litigation and decades of ill feeling. Long rumored to have ice water in his veins, Dorr Legg frostily impaled almost everyone who took a prominent role at the San Francisco gathering—and especially the militants.

Legg used *ONE Confidential*, the newsletter he edited under the pseudonym "Marvin Cutler," to skewer the keynote speakers one by one. Frank Kameny, described as "somewhat fanatic and doctrinaire," had given, according to Legg, a typically "belligerent, militant paper." The speech by William Beardemphl, president of SIR, was said to contain "so many inaccuracies" as to be very nearly worthless. Shirley Willer, recently elected national president of the Daughters of Bilitis, was chastised for "a booming delivery that took some listeners aback"—a putdown that went a long way toward corroborating the central contention in Willer's speech that DOB should be wary of participating in homophile coalitions, since they were dominated by gay men patronizingly insensitive to their lesbian sisters.[6]

Not that Legg, for one, was any more sensitive to his gay male brethren. He characterized Clark Polak, president of Philadelphia's Janus Society and the fourth keynote speaker, as an "arrogant and insufferable boor," whose "conduct throughout the entire Conference . . . alienated most of the delegates." Polak had indeed spoken strong words, accusing some of the leaders in the movement of failing to "rid themselves of their own anti-homosexual sentiments" and of caring only for the welfare of the "good" homosexual—attitudes Polak had labeled "Aunt Maryism."

Of the five keynoters, only Foster escaped Dorr Legg's bitter tongue. This was the more surprising because Foster had all his life been terrified of public speaking and was a despised Easterner—and Legg had announced that "the loudest noises and most extreme behavior seem to be coming from the East Coast" (a view directly counter to Harry Hay's that the East Coast was more conservative than the West). Legg did not regard Foster's arguments in favor of a national organization as "conclusive," but did feel that "in the main" Foster had argued his case "reasonably" well—and for Dorr Legg, that was remarkably high praise.

Foster deserved it. His speech cogently argued that the homophile movement had reached a point where only a national organization could advance it to the next stage. In the name of gaining greater prestige, security, publicity, and stability, he pressed the case for ending the confused duplication of disparate local efforts. "When homosexuality finally hits No. 1 topic of the day—and I think the day may be approaching fast," Foster argued, "it would be well to be prepared. . . . If we don't define ourselves—they will. If we don't state our aims—they will."[7]

Foster went on in his speech to reiterate the view that homosexuals had to abandon secrecy—or accept the fact that their image would continue to be constructed with data taken from psychiatric patients alone. But in a spasm of conservatism that drew him away from militants like Kameny, he did call for continued reliance on well-placed, sympathetic "experts"—on the physicians, judges, legislators, clergy, et al., who Foster confidently felt, despite the experience of recent decades, would rally to the homosexuals' side once a more "substantial" image had been presented.

Foster also recoiled in his speech from any suggestion that he was advocating "flamboyant" direct action. "It won't be necessary," he predicted, "to trot down to city square, climb up on the statue of General Sheridan, and wave a banner"; such behavior, "violating the law," would not do anything "constructive" to effect change. And yet in nearly the same breath—convulsing back again to a position *beyond* anything that Kameny and other militants had suggested—Foster proceeded to champion "public displays of affection." This, he felt, could "demonstrate to the public, as in no other manner, the futility of its laws and perhaps its attitude." It could further demonstrate, he argued—perhaps with his own situation in mind—"that there is more to homosexuality than sex."

Somehow Foster felt that this could be done without crossing the line to "exhibitionism" and without becoming "intentionally pro-vocative." All that he was advocating, he insisted, "was physical expression of genuine affection under prevailing ethical norms and accepted rules of propriety and good taste that govern heterosexual behavior." But the "accepted norms" of the mid-sixties could never tolerate *any* open expression of gay affection. And for Foster to hold out hope that it would, reflected an innocent, unwarranted faith in the American way.

When it came time for the conference to set up a national orga-nization, the final product was closer to Shirley Willer's blueprint for a loosely structured federation—what Foster called "a sort of U.N.-type forum for ideas"—than to the more centralized organization he and others had argued for. Named the North American Conference of Homophile Organizations (NACHO), the new grouping was bound by an Articles of Confederation, as it were, not a Constitution. Even so, a number of prominent lesbians, led by Del Martin (the cofounder of DOB), were wary of it and insisted on the primary importance of maintaining DOB's autonomy. Martin and others had begun to shift their energies into the emerging women's movement. They distrusted the ability or willingness of their gay male associates to understand feminism, let alone the special needs and perspectives of lesbians.[8]

Though NACHO had not been given the extensive powers Foster thought necessary, he felt optimistic about the organization's future and left the conference full of high spirits. He had had "a great time" and had been delighted at being appointed chairman of the Credentials Committee—even though one disgruntled young delegate had told him that he exemplified the "pompous, midaged, overweight men" who held leadership positions in the movement. Foster good-naturedly acknowledged the need of each generation to cannibalize the preceding one and, on his return to Hartford following the conference, con-tentedly applied himself to his new duties. It would be essentially his responsibility to decide who should or should not attend the next NACHO conference, to be held in Washington, D.C., in August 1967.[9]

The month after returning home from San Francisco, Foster decided to try psychoanalysis. As part and parcel of his excitement at linking up to the homophile movement, his juices had apparently started to flow again and he wanted to see if he couldn't do something about his now entrenched pattern of celibacy. The therapist told him that treatment would require four visits a week (at twenty-five dollars per visit) for three years, and Foster nonchalantly embarked on it. But he "kept falling asleep on the couch," and after less than a year, he "gave it up as a bum deal."[10]

In the postconference period, he also turned to writing. Utilizing his academic skills, he embarked on an extended essay, "An Introduction to the Homophile Movement." Over the following year, the essay would turn into a thirty-seven-page pamphlet, which Foster published at his own expense in time to distribute at the 1967 Washington conference. Dorr Legg (under his pseudonym, Marvin Cutler) had ten years earlier published *Homosexuals Today—1956*, a comprehensive guide to the contemporary movement; but that was no longer up-to-date and, besides, it lacked the comprehensive historical overview that Foster attempted.[11]

In the first line of his preface to the pamphlet, Foster announced that "homosexuals are getting themselves organized to challenge a society that rejects them," and he went boldly on to describe the goals of the new movement as "not rehabilitation, not cure, not acceptance of homosexuals as persons in distinction from their acts, nor restriction of their acts to a special privacy." Rather, flatly rejecting such "fatuous" aims and "false distinctions," Foster characterized the emergent homophile movement as "a struggle for equal rights and, eventually, equal social status."[12]

As always with Foster, one vigorous step forward was followed by a cautious step backward. Having sounded a militant note in the opening section of his booklet, he went on to urge homosexuals—even as he acknowledged that they were rightfully angry at organized religion and the psychiatric profession for reinforcing oppressive views—*not* to abandon the hope of a beneficial rapprochement with both. In Foster's view, "many homosexuals who have associated themselves with the movement . . . if not always in actual need of psychiatric treatment could nonetheless benefit extensively from it, as they could from religious counselling."

Moving on in the pamphlet to a historical discussion, Foster drew a portrait of pre-nineteenth-century efforts at homosexual solidarity as "highly secretive and cult-like" and characterized the common purpose of these early groups as "debauchery" and their few clandestine publications as "pornographic." These early attempts were not, in Foster's view, constructive, did not appeal to homosexuals on a "high enough plane." He looked far more favorably on late-nineteenth-century and early-twentieth-century efforts, reserving special praise for Magnus Hirschfeld's Scientific Humanitarian Committee in Weimar Germany and Edward Carpenter's intellectual circle in England. Gone was the old secrecy, he exulted, and gone, too, the unfortunate previous concentration on "orgies, pornography, magic and ritual." The new groups aimed to create a unified movement with well-defined grievances and strategies for reform (in other words, a movement in Foster's own image).

When he turned in the pamphlet to the United States, Foster showed surprising awareness of some early attempts to organize that remain poorly documented even to this day: Henry Gerber's short-lived Society for Human Rights, in Chicago in the 1920s; the Veterans Benevolent Association, which formed after World War II in New York City; and two possibly apocryphal groups, the Sons of Hamidy and the Legion of the Damned, whose existence Foster accepted at face value, as have most historians since. When his chronology came to the Daughters of Bilitis and the Mattachine Society of the 1950s, Foster gave generous credit to both for their pioneering efforts, but lamented how much time they had wasted on trying to figure out the *why* of homosexuality—what its origins were in the individual.[13]

He applauded the recent shift of energy into promoting social reforms and challenging long-standing discriminatory practices. The old emphasis on "How did we get here?" was giving way to the new: "Here we are, let's take it from there." Understandably, Foster reserved his fullest enthusiasm for the contemporary movement in which he was himself active; he welcomed the emerging sense of homosexuality "as in no way inferior to its counterpart" and the growing expectation "that society will eventually come around to a similar view."

Foster was particularly proud of the determination of those (including himself) who, in gathering to plan for the 1967 Washington conference, decided that homophile organizations would be judged as qualified to participate only if they agreed to the central aim of establishing the homosexual in society as "a first class human being and a first class citizen." He was proud, too, of his call for "concrete action programs," with new initiatives for "injecting our views into the planning of sex education programs" and for a large scale fund-raising effort to finance a national legal defense fund.[14]

But as he himself realized, not everyone agreed that the organization should be strengthened. Mattachine New York continued to stand entirely aloof, with Dick Leitsch privately characterizing "the so-called 'homophile movement' [as] . . . too often an albatross around the necks of those who are trying to be effective in the cause for which we are all supposedly working." Leitsch was determined to avoid the rest of the movement "as much as possible. . . . If this means MSNY is isolationist, so be it. I believe it is better to be alone and effective than to be part of an ineffective crowd."[15]

To get a clearer sense of the divisions within the homophile movement, Foster went out to the West Coast during the summer of 1967 and had a round of talks with representatives of various groups. He concluded that there was a decided regional difference of opinion. Many on the West Coast preferred to put their energies and limited resources into a new regional network; and they tended to be *somewhat* less single-mindedly certain than were many Easterners that their way was the *only* way and that anyone disagreeing was either stupid or evil. The Western leaders were therefore inclined, for the time being anyway, to hold a national organization "to a consultative rather than a legislative level" and to confine it largely "to communications problems and projects."

Stopping off in Chicago to see Bill Kelley of Mattachine Midwest, Foster listened to the puzzlement of the "in-between" region. "What's all the controversy about?" Kelley asked. "Why all the in-fighting? Why all the legalistic technicalities?"—especially since most of the participating organizations had made it clear that no vote would be binding on them. Foster basically agreed with Kelley; he was eager to get beyond regional fears and jealousies and to set up a national organization with real teeth in it. But, a conciliator by nature, he was prepared to advise patience. "We all know," he wrote in summarizing his trip, "that cooperation amongst homophilers is going to come very hard. It's going to take time. The nationals may really be serving little more purpose at present than 'group therapy' "—a channel for venting "hostile feelings, fears, [and] individualistic . . . personalities." Besides, Foster felt, "it is perfectly natural that cooperation should be sought first in one's 'neighborhood' before taking on the country as a whole."

The 1967 homophile conference met in Washington, D.C., in mid-August and received decidedly mixed reviews. The new West Coast publication, *The Advocate*, hailed the conference as "the most productive and beneficial" of the meetings thus far, and quoted the pioneering activist Jim Kepner, among others, as pleased with the impressive presence of delegates from seventeen organizations and the improved communication that developed between East and West Coast groups.[16]

But that was putting the best face on matters. New York Mattachine had again refused to participate; indeed, Leitsch had begun to toy with the idea of forming a "meaningful" national association of his own. On the West Coast, Dorr Legg had persuaded ONE to boycott the convention (Don Slater's rival L.A. group, Tangents, did attend) out of the growing conviction that the "eastern generals" were intent on a legislative body aimed at displacing the valuable variety of Western organizations, with their diverse aims and memberships.[17]

At the root of the problem was Foster's Credentials Committee. The Westerners and Midwesterners were on the whole committed to the principle of inclusiveness and objected strenuously to Foster's "extremely meticulous nosing" (in Jim Kepner's words) into every aspect of an applicant group's structure, purpose, and membership— especially since Foster himself had no real organizational affiliation, other than his own one-person creation, the Institute of Social Ethics. Dorr Legg, among others, fumed over Foster making final judgments about which organization was or was not a legitimate part of the movement, when he himself was an unaffiliated Johnny-come-lately.

Jim Kepner was the only Westerner to remain on the Credentials Committee in the face of Foster's meddlesome ways. He thought it was important for *someone* to fight a rearguard action in favor of a diverse movement ("I favored, as many Westerners did, a conference open to anyone willing to attend") against Foster's tendency to homogenize it into respectable conformity. But even Kepner—who liked Foster personally—joined the angry protest when it was discovered that Foster, in consultation with Kameny, had peremptorily barred the critic Leslie Fiedler (an avowed heterosexual who nonetheless had wanted to "observe" the proceedings, for a possible essay). "I didn't have any idea who the hell he was," Foster confessed, "I thought he was a bum off the streets." The mistake led to a volatile general discussion of the Credential Committee's policies, and only a timely, public apology from Foster averted a vote of censure.

Fiedler was ultimately admitted to the conference, but the performance of the Credentials Committee continued to be excoriated in postconference discussions. One of the committee's own members angrily denounced its "power-hungry" ways, insisting that some organizations with what he termed little or no evidence of actual existence—such as Pursuit and Symposium (Los Angeles) or the Society Advocating Mutual Equality (Rock Island, Illinois)—had been given voting privileges, while more substantial groups (like Craig Rodwell's HYMN*) had been turned away. In the past year, the dissident committee member charged, "the movement has created an *establishment*," and in protest he resigned.[18]

In arguing against admitting the "motley hordes," Foster had been especially concerned about unaffiliated "leftwingers" who might (as one of the articles later written on the conference put it) "jeopardize the social acceptance necessary to put into constructive action the expressions of the group's needs." In 1967, few such left-wing radicals were present at the national planning conference, but by the following year, at the gathering in Chicago, Foster's annoyance at what he called "infiltrators" would increase—and at the 1969 conference in Kansas City would become pronounced.[19]

Foster also opposed the view that "prejudice against homosexuality is but one manifestation of an unhealthy attitude on the part of society toward sex in general, and that this attitude must be attacked in its totality before homosexuals can hope to improve their status." Foster called such a view "speculative" and, "from a public relations standpoint, risky." Similarly, he argued against the notion that "anything goes so long as no one else is being 'harmed,' " characterizing that attitude as "an implied rejection of the authority of convention." Such doctrines, he wrote, "have not yet received official sanction by the homophile movement," and he expressed the personal hope that "they will not."[20]

Though later a defender of the women's movement, Foster also had trouble dealing with emerging feminism. He felt in 1967 that homophile and feminist concerns should be kept separate (though within two years he *would* be able to recognize their linkage), and he saw the small group of women who had affiliated with the national planning conference as "becoming very defensive," and some of them downright "disruptive." The "problem," like that of left-wing "infiltration," would grow over the next few years, exacerbated by the—yes—"defensive" attitude of gay men like Foster.

As the activist lesbian leader Del Martin put it in specifically singling out Foster's Credentials Committee for condemnation, it was (she wrote) "a debating society, an exercise in self-aggrandizement of self-proclaimed leaders of an unrepresented minority." Del Martin did not advocate that lesbians withdraw entirely from participation in the

* About which more on p. 164.

homophile movement—"for there are many worthy mutual endeavors demanding and deserving the support of female homosexuals." But she did insist that "consuming and costly" participation should be limited to areas where there is "some semblance of cooperation, or at least some hope thereof"—and she did not see any such semblance in the national conference.[21]

But there were too few women connected with it, and too few of that limited number who thought of themselves as what would soon be called feminists, for the dominant divisions within the planning conference to take on a specifically male-female cast—just as the contentiousness during the 1967 convention cannot be ascribed to a falling-out between men sympathetic to New Left views and men to the right of them. In fact, few of the men active in the conference had—or would ever have—strong connections to Left protest movements of the day (though some did derive inspiration from those movements). Such divisions as developed seem to have been contests more for turf than for principles—though principles were assuredly involved. On both sides of a given dispute, politically centrist men— marginalized only because of their deviant sexuality, not because they were in any other sense radical—battled over which individuals, ideas, and organizations would control a movement which was itself something of a Robert's Rules replica of mainstream political groupings (just as the very idea of battling for turf was very much a mainstream male phenomenon).

The battle was comparatively muted and polite in 1967. It focused on what kind of national organization should be attempted, what degree of unity was both desirable and feasible. Not much had yet been done among affiliates to explicate, let alone resolve, existing ideological differences between local and regional homophile organizations. Nor had much been accomplished by way of joint participation in public projects designed to improve the lot of homosexuals. Of the nationally conceived activities that *had* won sanction at the two previous conventions in 1966, few had actually materialized. Only the idea of a national legal defense fund had seen any significant implementation, and even that was still in a preliminary, formative stage.

What was needed at the 1967 national convention, in Foster's view, was the adoption of at least a rudimentary constitution and statement of purpose, as well as some sort of governing council to make decisions between conventions. But Foster understood that "the extreme fear on the part of the [local] organizations to a national structuring, and jealousy of their own individual sovereignty" required that the convention proceed with "extreme caution" lest the fragile coalition be rent asunder.[22]

What came out of the convention was a good deal less than Foster had envisioned, and more caution than even he had thought necessary. The statement of purpose on which the convention finally agreed was vague enough to put it beyond dispute: The delegates merely pledged themselves to "the improvement of the status of the homosexual." To further that end, "intergroup projects and cooperation" were "encouraged," but lest that be taken as a mandate, the national conference was specifically described as merely "consultative in nature and function." At least the organization's future life had been assured: the delegates did vote that the planning conference be regarded as "a duly constituted continuing body." They even proved willing to hold out the "ultimate goal of establishing a legitimate homophile movement on a national scale."[23]

CRAIG

Craig wanted Mattachine to get out of its fifth-floor office, which was only open in the evenings, and into a location more accessible to the gay community. He thought a storefront office would be just the thing—especially if it could double as a bookstore and thereby help to augment the lack of available movement materials. The San Francisco homophile organization, SIR, put out an attractive monthly magazine called *Vector*, but *The Mattachine Review* had trailed off, and two versions of *ONE* magazine competed uncertainly in the aftermath of the punishing 1965 internecine struggle in the Los Angeles movement. Craig felt strongly that if Mattachine would open a storefront-cum-bookstore in New York, it could all at once do a public service, increase awareness of the organization's existence, and help pay the rent.

He persuaded Dick Leitsch to look at possible sites with him, and they found a place on Hudson Street that seemed ideal. Leitsch expressed interest and said he would take the matter up with the Mattachine board. But in retrospect, Craig doubts that he ever did. Leitsch had never been really enthusiastic about moving Mattachine out into the community, and he soon reported back to Craig that the board's decision had been negative.

Craig was furious at what he took to be Mattachine's endemic fear of risk-taking. The conservatives had supposedly been routed in the 1965 election, and Leitsch had himself recently led a successful protest against discriminatory practices by the New York Civil Service Commission. But Craig had increasingly come to distrust the quality of Leitsch's militancy, and to fear that he had become an accommodationist in order to maintain his control over New York Mattachine's councils. Besides, Craig had become uneasy over renewed rumors that Leitsch was involved in financial impropriety. Back in 1965—and as a direct result of Craig's suspicions and prodding—Mattachine treasurer Jack Weeden had discovered that Leitsch and Hodges had used a $5,000 gift to Mattachine to cover their own expenses, including a house rental on Fire Island. Hodges had been forced to resign from the presidency, but Leitsch had been given a second chance. Within a year, rumors of impropriety were again circulating—though it wouldn't be for another two or three years that Leitsch would be discovered diverting Mattachine funds to a secret bank account in Albany.

In April 1966, Craig decided that the time had come to resign from Mattachine and to pursue on his own the idea of opening a bookstore. But how to raise the needed money? Casting around for ideas, he hit on the notion of working summers at Fire Island Pines as a way of accumulating capital. The Pines was a relatively recent gay community, which had developed as an alternative for upscale homosexuals disenchanted with the "plebeian" atmosphere of Cherry Grove, the gay Fire Island community that dated back to the 1920s. Following a disastrous fire in the Pines, Yetta Cohen and her partner, John Whyte—both grandes dames—had built the Boatel, which sat at the Pines's harborside dock and served as a focal point for the new community.

In joining the Boatel staff in the summer of 1966, Craig knew in advance that the job would not be easy. He had heard the rumors of Mafia control and the tales of John Whyte's demanding ways (Whyte was secretly known as the Queen of Romania, or Snow—as in "Snow Whyte"). He worked his staff long hours, treated them like subjects, and played them off against each other to ensure maximum competition for his favor—just as Mr. Kilburn had back when Craig was at the Chicago Junior School. Whyte was especially fond of his "gold whale" ceremony, the Pines version of being knighted. Whyte would gather the Boatel staff to watch him award a particularly trustworthy employee with a gold pendant in the shape of a whale—which Whyte would himself place around the honoree's presumably grateful neck. Most of the staff regarded the whale as a brand and would thereafter refrain from saying or doing anything around the honoree that they were unwilling to have reported immediately to Whyte.

Each staff member was given one day off a week, and a half-hour every afternoon to go to the beach. Those breaks aside, they worked away steadily at making beds, cleaning toilets, ensuring that each room met Whyte's standards of spotlessness. "John thought he was running the Plaza" is how Craig later put it; "he would personally inspect each room." And with good reason, since rates were (for the mid-sixties) high: about $70 a weekend for a small double without private bath, and $175 for two rooms facing the ocean. The staff was housed in a long barrackslike structure referred to as Steerage.

The occupants of the Boatel rooms were almost all gay, but an occasional straight couple, devotees of the magnificent Pines beach, would arrive for a few days at a time. (The actress Monique van Vooren was a weekend regular; all Craig can recall is an "overpowering trail of perfume wherever she went.") Occasionally a high-priced female prostitute would take a room in the Boatel to service the heterosexual men from the yachts tied up in the basin. Since the "yacht people" paid high fees for dockside rights, John Whyte instructed the staff to ignore their antics.

The staff was also told to treat the police as honored guests—to give them free meals and drinks—just in case the Mafia go-betweens hadn't made their payments on time. These were the years in which gay people, even in their secluded vacation resorts, survived on sufferance. Plainclothesmen would come over from the Long Island town of Sayville, across the bay from Fire Island, and conduct spot raids at the Meat Rack (then located in front of the co-op apartments on the beach) or entrap unsuspecting singles along the cruisy boardwalks.

The cops would take the arrested men to the telephone pole that used to sit in the middle of the Pines dock and chain them together to the pole. Then the cops would return to the Meat Rack and boardwalks for another series of arrests, and repeat the process until they had some thirty to forty men chained at the dock. By now it would be two or three A.M. A special police launch would take the men over to Long Island, where a kind of kangaroo court, held in the back of a drugstore, would collect steep fines and then release the arrested men with thirty-day suspended sentences. Terrified, none of the men dared report what was in fact organized theft.

When Craig saw what was going on, he was livid. One night he tried to find a hacksaw to free the chained men from the pole while the cops were temporarily away from the dock, but he couldn't get any of the other employees to join him. He himself had to participate directly in another of the more humiliating rites that characterized the supposedly carefree Fire Island atmosphere of those years.

On Saturday nights, when the dance floor was packed with people, Boatel employees had to take turns sitting on top of a huge ladder, ten rungs high, and be ready to shine a flashlight as rudely as possible into the eyes of anyone engaging in "illegal" behavior. That was defined as two men even *facing* each other; actually dancing together was beyond the pale. All male eyes on the dance floor were supposed to be aimed exclusively at the occasional female—somebody's lesbian friend or one of the straight women from the yachts—who had been persuaded to participate. Sometimes there would be four or five circles of men on the dance floor, all facing the sole woman in the middle.

Craig only had to do ladder duty occasionally, to relieve another staffer, but even so, he had to psych himself up for it—had to keep reminding himself "that it was worth putting up with anything for the sake of the future bookstore." Some of the bolder dancers would push against the ladder, or even shake it, and Craig had to restrain himself from egging them on. He learned that marijuana was a big help in cooling himself out, and by the second summer, 1967, he had learned about "little greenies," amphetamine tablets that did wonders to replenish exhausted energy.

Hard work and humiliations aside, the two summers at Fire Island accomplished what Craig had intended. With free room and board, he had no expenses except cigarettes, and he managed to bank a fair portion of the $125 he made each week. By the fall of 1967, he had saved a little more than a thousand dollars and felt ready to make his move. The cheapest storefront he could find in the Village, at 291 Mercer Street, went for $115 a month. He also had to plunk down two months' security—which meant a third of his nest egg was gone before he could start buying stock. But he did quickly come up with a name: the Oscar Wilde Memorial Bookshop. He wanted the store named after someone who was readily identifiable as a homosexual, and Wilde seemed the most obvious candidate. (A few years later, Craig felt some regret at not having named the store after "a more militant and upfront" figure, but being "a rather sentimental person," he decided to stick with the original name.)[24]

As the day of the opening approached, and with a thousand things still undone, Craig asked his mother to fly in from Chicago to help out with last-minute preparations. He met Marion at the airport on Thanksgiving Day, 1967, and took her straight to his shop. They stayed up all night finishing the dozen bookshelves (with about twenty-five titles total), then opened up on schedule the next day for business, serving free coffee and cookies to all comers.

In those years a "gay" bookstore had meant only one thing: pornography. But Craig had a straitlaced, proper side, and he had decided early on that the Oscar Wilde Memorial Bookshop would carry only "the better titles" and no pornography of any kind. Though hardly a puritan sexually, he regarded the sex magazines as exploitative—"a ten-dollar price on something that makes sex look dirty and furtive." He was determined to have a store where gay people did not feel manipulated or used. There was no ADULT READING sign in the window, and no peep show in the back room. And the ad Craig later took out in *The Village Voice* was headlined GAY IS GOOD.

Craig was determined to carry that message to his customers. True activist that he was, he viewed the Oscar Wilde shop as a vehicle for promoting a more positive view of homosexuality. And toward that goal, he invited none other than Foster Gunnison to sit in the bookstore on opening day and autograph copies of his recently completed booklet, "An Introduction to the Homophile Movement." "There Foster sat," Craig later recalled, "in his bow tie and his crew cut and his cigar. To look at Foster physically, he'd be the last person in the world you'd think would write that booklet."

Along with books and pamphlets, the shop carried buttons and cards relating to the homophile movement, and it had a community bulletin board that listed announcements of interest. Moreover, as Craig put it in his first press release, the bookshop "will also act as a clearing house for individuals and organizations supporting homosexual law reform in New York State." He also used Oscar Wilde as the storefront headquarters for a new group he now started: the Homophile Youth Movement. (He then added "in Neighborhoods" to the name, so that the acronym could be HYMN instead of the sexist HYM.) In the first issue of the group's *The New York Hymnal*, Craig wrote a blazing article denouncing Mafia control of gay bars. During the bookshop's first year of existence, it served as a counseling agency for more than a thousand young homosexual men and women, "helping them to gain a sense of identity and pride as young homosexuals."[25]

The Oscar Wilde shop was a pioneering enterprise, and customers were happily startled to find a "real" bookstore devoted solely to gay and lesbian titles. Craig's earlier lover Harvey Milk dropped by frequently, his fascination marking (in Craig's estimate) "the beginnings of an interest on Harvey's part in the movement." Indeed, when Milk moved to San Francisco soon after, he told Craig that he intended to open a similar bookstore as a way of getting involved in community work. He settled for a camera store instead, but it did serve the same function as a community center.

Jim Fouratt also came by the bookstore often. He and Craig would stand in the crowded little store arguing each other to a standstill about political strategy. Jim was contemptuous of the Annual Reminders as misguided efforts to win acceptance from a mainstream America that was itself in desperate need of renovation, and he thought of Craig and other "earnest" reformers as "not real radicals"—not, like the Yippies, involved in any fundamental challenge to a sick society. But he admired Craig, even while discounting him, aware that he was someone who "always tried to tell the truth." Years later, Jim would come to have much more respect for the courage of those who, like Craig and Foster, had stood with their "Equality for Homosexuals" signs, unprotected, outside those symbolic citadels of American power, the White House and Independence Hall.

Though Craig put in seventy-hour weeks and for the first eighteen months ran the store entirely himself, the verdict on Oscar Wilde was not unanimously favorable. Those who missed porn on the shelves denounced Craig as an antisex puritan. And lesbian customers complained from the beginning that the store was too heavily weighted toward gay male titles. Karla Jay would occasionally drop in and was among those who felt uncomfortable there. It wasn't so much Craig himself that she objected to, but some of the other men; more intent on browsing for pickups than for books, they would give her nasty looks, as if to say "What are *you* doing in *our* store?"

Craig stiff-armed the pro-pornography crowd, but tried to be responsive to lesbian discontent. He felt that his Christian Science upbringing, which had included the teaching that God is a Father-Mother, had made him nonsexist, and he wanted to create a better balance in his store between gay male and lesbian titles. The problem was that he had no respect for what he called the "trashy" lesbian pulp novels of the day, and those aside, he felt the pickings were slim.

But he did increase his stock of lesbian titles as much as he felt he could, and Karla was able to find *The Ladder* there ("which I would have been afraid of subscribing to on my own"), as well as two books she would always cherish: Violette Leduc's *La Bâtarde* and Jane Rule's *Desert of the Heart*. To further signal his concern, Craig hired two lesbian architects to remodel the store in 1969. But even by then, no more than 30 percent of the titles in Oscar Wilde were lesbian-oriented, and it was only later, with the expansion of lesbian publishing, that he achieved the parity he had always wanted.

The straight reaction to Oscar Wilde ranged from oblivious to venomous. The *New York Post* columnist Harriet Van Horne, listing aspects of the New Permissiveness that disgusted her, included—along with see-through dresses, topless dancers, and "skin-flicks"—the Oscar Wilde Memorial Bookshop (little dreaming or, apparently, caring that Craig shared her antipathy to porn).[26] But Van Horne was politeness itself compared to the anonymous harassment that plagued Craig from the day he opened the doors. Phone threats were a constant, with the most frequent callers insisting that they would burn the store down or carve Craig up. At first the threats frightened him, and, ever the activist, he would try to reason with the callers. But— perhaps to preserve his own sanity—he soon decided that venting on the phone was itself enough to sate the callers' anger. Still, it was hard not to feel unnerved when arriving at the shop in the morning to find swastikas or "Kill Fags" scrawled on the outside.

Besides, the landlord was hardly cordial. He had asked Craig, when they were drawing up a lease, what the store was going to be, and Craig had simply said it would be a bookshop—the Oscar Wilde Memorial Bookshop. The landlord allowed as how he had heard of Oscar Wilde, said nothing beyond that—and did sign the lease. Then came opening day, with the sign in the front of the store announcing BOOKSHOP OF THE HOMOPHILE MOVEMENT, and the sign in the window reading GAY IS GOOD. Livid, the landlord threatened Craig with eviction. Craig consulted a lawyer, and learned that his lease was airtight. But the lawyer warned him never to be late with the rent and never to pay less than the full amount—never, in other words, to give the landlord an out. It was a timely warning since Craig, always more interested in helping the movement than in fattening his bank account, usually lived close to the edge.

Some years later, in 1973, when Craig decided to relocate, his old landlord came by the new store to wish Craig well and to tell him that he had "learned a lot." He had always thought gay people were a "sick bunch," he told Craig, but over the years he had seen all the "nice people" who came into the store, and had been impressed with how "well behaved" they were. Craig was not one to downplay differentness or to encourage polite behavior, but he thanked the landlord for his good wishes—and went back to plotting the revolution.

1969

As the sixties came to a close, the United States was a notably different country from what it had been a mere decade before. The image of the fifties as a period *merely* of conformity and consensus has probably been overdrawn; after all, there was *Mad* magazine, rock and roll, the Beats, and that much imitated, sloe-eyed soul of alienation, James Dean. But compared with what came after, the fifties were decidedly a time of quiescence. The Bomb did indeed cause foreboding, and the Cold War a tangible sense of pending disaster. But left-wing agitation no longer marked the national scene, and the country remained secure in its self-image as the repository of Rectitude in a world beset by (Communist) Evil.

By the close of the sixties, that smugness had come undone. Within a six-month period from late 1967 to early 1968, the maverick Eugene McCarthy announced for the presidency; the Tet offensive in Vietnam blew apart the claims of an inevitable American victory; the police in Orangeburg, South Carolina, fired on black demonstrators, killing three and wounding dozens; Martin Luther King, Jr., was assassinated, and enraged black Americans rioted in dozens of cities; college students across the country took over campus buildings to protest war-related research; and the assassination of Robert Kennedy seemed to many to spell the end of hope for peaceful domestic reform.

When the police rioted at the Democratic National Convention that summer in Chicago, the drift toward militancy became a stampede. By the fall of 1968, there were at least a third again as many SDS chapters as before the convention; black students took over administration buildings at Cornell while boldly brandishing their rifles in front of the television cameras; the Black Panthers and the Oakland police had a shoot-out; a contingent of feminists invaded the hitherto sacrosanct Miss America pageant; and incidents of arson and bombings became commonplace.

This fevered escalation gave heart to those on the left who believed that confrontation was a necessary precursor to substantive change: Out of polarization, the argument went, would come realignment; out of realignment, shifts in power—and out of widespread disruption, the first seedlings of a new and better world. The forces of repression, exemplified by the state, seemed in this scenario, to play their part to perfection. The Justice Department, as if on cue, duly indicted the "Chicago 8" on conspiracy charges. And then, in Berkeley, California, in May 1969, the whole repressive might of state power seemed epitomized when the police sealed off People's Park, bulldozed its gardens, and, in a major confrontation with protesters, wounded some hundred people.

Governor Ronald Reagan promptly sent in the National Guard —and growing legions of the young promptly decided that all the rules were off, their allegiance to established institutions severed, the cement of loyalty dissolved. By early 1969, circulation figures for the counterculture press shot upward; the readership of the weekly *Berkeley Barb* rose from a mere five thousand four years earlier to nearly 100,000, while New York's *East Village Other* soared to 65,000. And a Yankelovich poll found that 20 percent of American college students identified more with Che Guevara than with presidential candidates Nixon and Humphrey.[1]

Arbitrary authority, in all areas of national life, was now decidedly under siege. (Indeed, not only in the United States: Rebellions were spreading throughout Western Europe as well.) The Black Panthers demanded "Power to the People," and the students in SDS insisted on "participatory democracy," the right of those affected by a decision to set its parameters. Over and over, the question was being raised: "Who makes the rules—and by what right?"

In this confrontational context of anger and defiance, the assimilationist civil rights goals of NACHO, the national homophile planning conference, and NACHO's characteristic tactic of petitioning for the redress of grievances, seemed old-fashioned—just as their longstanding insistence that homosexuals *were* an oppressed minority and

ABOVE: Craig Rodwell on the Riis Park beach, New York, 1960. (COURTESY OF CRAIG RODWELL) BELOW: Yvonne Flowers and her mother Theo at the World's Fair Exposition in New York, 1964. (COURTESY OF YVONNE [MAUA] FLOWERS)

Police raid on the Artists' Exotic Carnival and Ball at the Manhattan Center, Halloween, 1962. (UPI/BETTMANN NEWSPHOTOS)

RIGHT: Foster Gunnison, Jr., 1958. (COURTESY OF FOSTER GUNNISON, JR.) BELOW: ECHO Convention, 1965. Kneeling at far left: Julian Hodges next to Dick Leitsch; kneeling at far right: Dick Gayer. Standing: second from left, Clark Polak; fourth from left, Shirley Willer; fifth from left, Jack Nichols; on Nichols' right, Bill Beardemphl; second from right, Franklin Kameny; fourth from right, Bob Basker ("Bob Sloane," founder of Mattachine Midwest). (I.G.I.C. COLLECTION, NEW YORK PUBLIC LIBRARY)

ABOVE: Picketing for gay right in front of the White House May 29, 1965. First in line is Jack Nichols, second is Franklin Kameny, third is Lilli Vincenz (UPI/BETTMANN NEWSPHOTOS) LEFT Sylvia Ray Rivera and two un identified drag queens, 1969-70 (GAY FLAMES #5; I.G.I.C. COLLECTION NEW YORK PUBLIC LIBRARY OPPOSITE: Jim Fouratt, in the mid-sixties. (COURTESY OF JIM FOURATT)

OPPOSITE, TOP: Gay Activists Alliance meeting in the Firehouse, 1970. (I.G.I.C. COLLECTION, NEW YORK PUBLIC LIBRARY) OPPOSITE, CENTER: The Firehouse, home of the Gay Activists Alliance. (UPI/BETTMANN NEWSPHOTOS) OPPOSITE, BOTTOM AND THIS PAGE: Various "zaps" by the Gay Activists Alliance, in New York City. (UPI/BETTMANN NEWSPHOTOS)

COME OUT!!

JOIN
HE SISTERS & BROTHERS OF THE
GAY LIBERATION FRONT

ABOVE: Gay Liberation Front poster. (PHOTO BY PETER HUJAR) OPPOSITE, TOP: Karla Jay and friends, Los Angeles, 1970. (PHOTO BY LEE MASON) OPPOSITE, BOTTOM: The Stonewall Inn on Christopher Street, post-riots and vacant. (PHOTO BY GEORGE DESANTIS, "GAY FREEDOM 1970," QQ MAGAZINE)

ABOVE: Craig Rodwell negotiating with the police before the first gay pride march. (PHOTO BY GEORGE DESANTIS, "GAY FREEDOM 1970," QQ MAGAZINE) BELOW AND RIGHT: The first gay pride march, Sixth Avenue, New York City, 1970. (THE NEW YORK TIMES)

Conclusion of the first gay pride march, the Sheep Meadow in Central Park, New York, 1970. (UPI/BETTMANN NEWSPHOTOS)

ABOVE: Sylvia Rivera and Bebe Scarpi at the GLF Bellevue demonstration, fall 1970.
BELOW: Yvonne (Maua) Flowers at a political meeting in 1988 at the Lesbian and Gay
Community Services Center in New York City. The black glove on her right hand was
being worn prior to her first surgery for Lupus. (COURTESY OF YVONNE [MAUA]
FLOWERS)

ABOVE, LEFT: Foster Gunnison, Jr., 1991. (COURTESY OF THE HARTFORD COURANT; PHOTO BY PAULA BRONSTEIN) ABOVE, RIGHT: Karla Jay, 1992. (PHOTO BY YEMAYA KAURI-ALETO) BELOW: Craig Rodwell in front of the Oscar Wilde Memorial Bookshop, 1992.

Gay pride march, New York City, 1991. Left to right: Ivan Valentin, Nori Nke Aka, Sylvia Ray Rivera, Jim Fouratt, Marsha P. Johnson. (PHOTO BY JOE CAPUTO)

had legitimate grievances suddenly seemed in harmony with the newly widespread resistance to traditional authority. Most younger gays and lesbians who sympathized with the New Left's broad agenda for ending inequality at home and interventionism abroad, joined not NACHO—which struck them as hopelessly bourgeois—but Students for a Democratic Society, or one of several organizations enlisted in the struggle for black empowerment.

But that is not the whole story, either. A fair percentage of the radical young who were gay or lesbian had not yet come to terms with their own sexuality. Some of them steered clear of NACHO not—or not simply—because of its centrist political views, but because they felt unready and threatened in the one area where NACHO did take a radical stance: namely, in its insistence that homosexuality was neither abnormal nor unnatural. Here was irony aplenty. The members of NACHO, centrist in all else, were raising one radical standard under which the nonconforming young did not dare to rally.

Leo Laurence, a reporter for radio station KGO in San Francisco, covered the confrontations between antiwar demonstrators and the police at the 1968 Chicago Democratic Convention, and the experience changed his life. A thirty-six-year-old gay man who had previously toed the polite homophile line, Laurence now decided that gays, too, needed to adopt a militant posture. He began to write articles for the *Berkeley Barb* and for SIR's *Vector*, calling for an alliance with Black Panthers and antiwar radicals. After he became editor of *Vector*, Laurence denounced the guilty, apologetic style that he felt was favored by "timid" homophile leaders—whom he characterized as "a bunch of middle-class, uptight, bitchy old queens"—and called for the same "proud" affirmation that characterized other radical groups.[2]

Laurence and his lover, Gale Whittington, posed together bare-chested for a picture accompanying a *Berkeley Barb* article in which Whittington openly proclaimed his homosexuality, saying it was time for gays to declare themselves. When, as a result, he lost his job as an accounting clerk with the States Steamship Company, he, Laurence, and a half-dozen other gay men demonstrated, in early April 1969, in front of the company's offices in San Francisco's financial district. They carried signs reading FREEDOM FOR HOMOS NOW and LET GAYS LIVE, Laurence wore a button proclaiming "Gay Is Good," and he and Whittington told reporters that they were beginning a "vigorous and public" progay campaign that was being opposed by the gay world's own "square" establishment. "They are scared," Laurence asserted. But, as he soon found out, not *that* scared. In May, Laurence was fired from *Vector* and kicked out of SIR—perhaps for his belligerence as much as his militance.

A similar scenario developed within the Daughters of Bilitis. When Rita Laporte and Barbara Grier tried to convert the organization and its publication, *The Ladder*, to a feminist perspective, urging DOB to leave NACHO and join forces instead with heterosexual feminists, a serious split developed among lesbian activists. The ensuing fight for control would end, by 1970, in both the demise of *The Ladder* and the dissolution of DOB's national structure.[3]

New York City was also astir. The Student Homophile League at Columbia had come into being in 1967 on a campus where, only two years before, the famous classicist Gilbert Highet had canceled a lecture in protest over a representative of New York Mattachine having been allowed to speak in Ferris Booth Hall. The foundation of the League led to a deluge of outraged letters, but the handful of courageous students who signed up as members proceeded with their work of education and counseling. (They also formed a largely figurehead alumni committee, headed by Foster Gunnison, Jr.) By the fall of 1967 several other New York campuses had followed Columbia's example and had formed Student Homophile League chapters (Rita Mae Brown was a member of the New York University group).

In 1968, the Columbia Student Homophile League initiated a notable assault on the psychiatric establishment. When the medical school staffed a panel discussion on homosexuality with a group of "experts" known (except for the Kinsey Institute's Paul Gebhard) to regard it as a pathological adjustment, SHL representatives invaded the meeting and publicly demanded that in the future the discussion of homosexuality be placed "in its proper setting as a sociological problem of deeply entrenched prejudice and discrimination against a minority group."[4] That very evening, the Columbia campus exploded in student protests over U.S. incursions overseas and the university's incursions against its black neighbors—and many members of the Student Homophile League joined in the occupation of campus buildings that accompanied the protests.

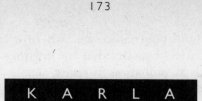

KARLA

Karla had gone to a few NOW meetings, but had quickly decided they weren't for her; she found the organization too oriented toward winning legislative changes, and overall too tame, too focused on asking to be "let in." Working to achieve equality in an unjust society was pointless to Karla. She also disliked the then common notion that feminism should take a backseat to the "main" struggles against capitalism, racism, and imperialism. She saw that argument as a convenient one for men, as a long-standing rationale for deferring women's liberation by insisting that its time had not *yet* come, while arguing that it would *automatically* come once the "larger" struggle had been won.

Karla had less trouble pulling away from the male left than some women did, for the simple reason that she had never been closely identified with it. For her, the upheaval at Columbia University had been the starting point, not the culmination, of struggle. And during the Columbia fracas, she had been appalled at the macho behavior of the left-wing male students. Unlike some radical feminists, Karla became convinced early on that male-supremacist behavior was not simply the result of men being the agents of an oppressive capitalist system, and would not automatically disappear with the destruction of that system. She was in favor of changing the country's economic structure, but was skeptical that such change alone would liberate women—or, for that matter, free blacks either.

These views drew Karla to Redstockings, a radical feminist group founded by Ellen Willis and Shulamith Firestone in February 1969. Her membership in the group, in turn, further clarified her views. Without being rigidly Marxist, the Redstockings selectively employed Marxist analysis, and particularly in insisting that women's behavior resulted from the material circumstances in which they found themselves; they married, for example, not because they had been conditioned to believe they should (as many feminists argued) but because they consciously realized that women's low-paying, alienating work made the single life too difficult.[5]

Karla was not among the original organizers of Redstockings, but did join the group within a few months of its founding. By then, the dominant faction (and one had to be part of a faction to feel fully alive in the late sixties) had decided to downplay activism in favor of establishing and participating in consciousness-raising groups. In Marxist style, Redstockings created those groups along the lines of semi-independent cells. Each group was assigned a single letter of the alphabet as a name, and each sent a single delegate to the meetings of a central committee. Karla was often chosen as her group's representative, and she also went out often on speaking engagements to explain to other women how they could form their own consciousness-raising groups.

Unlike some other feminist groups—for example, the celibacy-advocating Boston-based Cell 16—the dominant faction in Redstockings did not denounce heterosexuality as an institution that perpetuated male dominance; women, they argued, should confront, not abandon men. The charismatic Rita Mae Brown was among those who felt that Redstockings was not merely pro-heterosexual, but downright heterosexist. When she decided to come out as a lesbian to her consciousness-raising group (not the one Karla was in), she found maximum discomfort and minimal support—and left Redstockings soon after.

Rita Mae Brown was at first alone in her daring. Karla had picked up early, in her own group, the same hesitant, uncomfortable reaction to any hint of lesbianism, but for a while she chose to be silent about it. She had finally found women with whom she felt comfortable personally and politically—more comfortable, certainly, than she had felt with the butch/femme women she met in the lesbian bars. They had insisted, because of her flowered dresses and long hair, that she was a femme, but she had resented the attempt to lock her into a role that constricted the actual range of her impulses. Knowing her own aggressive strength, she hated being stereotyped on the basis of outer appearances alone.

She felt differently typecast, but typecast nonetheless, on the few occasions when she went to a Daughters of Bilitis meeting. She looked much younger than her actual age—hitchhiking at the age of twenty-three, she was mistaken for a fifteen-year-old runaway and arrested—and the conservative women in DOB reacted to her in terror. She tried to convince them that she was not jailbait, but they kept nervously insisting that DOB was not in the business of bringing out teenage girls. Angry and disgruntled, Karla would afterwards refer to them as "the Daughters of Bursitis."

By comparison with being pigeonholed as a femme and fled from as a juvenile, Karla felt herself well treated—respected as a many-faceted adult—in Redstockings. And the group's reluctance to discuss lesbianism did not especially faze her because she was not, in 1969, at all eager to label herself a lesbian. While an undergraduate at Barnard, both she and her steady girlfriend from CUNY thought of themselves as bisexuals. Though that particular relationship ended at about the time Karla graduated, and though it was followed by a series of casual affairs with women, she had several prolonged affairs with men during the same period.

Her boyfriends ranged from an upstairs neighbor, to a Swiss body builder (who also self-identified as bisexual), to a countercultural printer. What she liked about these men was not their conversation —"I didn't like men's patriarchal heads," she later said—but their ability to give her physical pleasure. The men she chose seemed turned on by her aggressiveness, and she got them to do what *she* wanted to do sexually. Which didn't mean that she always controlled the relationships and got to end them whenever they stopped working for her. Her most satisfying lover, the printer, walked out abruptly on her after finding her in bed one day with a woman.

Karla was juggling several kinds of lives simultaneously—much like Jim and Yvonne. Along with her bisexual affairs and her political involvement with Redstockings, she was taking graduate courses in comparative literature at night and holding down a full-time job during the day. Her first choice for graduate school had been U.C. Berkeley, where her high board scores, offsetting her B average, had won her a scholarship. But she felt unable to accept it. She had so little money that it seemed less risky to stay in familiar New York, get a daytime job, and work on her doctorate at night. She decided on New York University, though the school didn't make it easy for her: two of her male friends, with lower grades and board scores, got scholarships there, but she was turned down.

The first summer following graduation from Barnard, Karla found a temporary job—thanks to her excellent French—with the prestigious literary agent Georges Borchardt. Impressed with her work, Borchardt, at the end of the summer, got her a full-time, ninety-five-dollar-a-week position as an assistant editor with the David McKay Corporation. Kennett and Eleanor Rawson, the owners of the McKay publishing house, were in the process of editing David Reuben's *Everything You Ever Wanted To Know About Sex but Were Afraid to Ask*—a book that would become a runaway best-seller.

Asked if she wanted to have a look at the manuscript, Karla was horrified to find it filled with racist and homophobic remarks—like the question-and-answer colloquy in which the query "How could the Mayor's daughter get VD?" was answered by "Sleeping with a guy who slept with a black prostitute." Karla brought the material to the Rawsons' attention, and found them sympathetic to her complaints. But in the end they were unable to persuade Reuben to remove most of the offending remarks.

Soon after starting work with McKay, Karla was riding her bike one day when several teenagers appeared out of nowhere. She tried to speed away but they grabbed her, threw her down a nearby flight of cellar stairs, and ran off with her bike. When she got up, she was unable to straighten out her leg and the pain was excruciating. X-rays revealed that her back was broken in three places. When the doctor saw the plates, he was incredulous and asked Karla how she had managed to get to his office. Who had carried her in? When she said she had walked in by herself, the doctor gasped, "Impossible!" He wanted to put her in a hospital, but she refused to go, so she was given a steel brace and put in traction in her own apartment.

Her roommate and friends took care of her. The doctor had told her that she would *probably* be able to walk again but would never be able to straighten her leg. With typical spunk, Karla set out to prove him wrong. Among the friends ministering to her were the novelist Joel Lieber (later a suicide) and his wife, Sylvia, who lived around the corner. The couple was involved with Zen Buddhism and gradually got Karla interested too.

She started doing meditation in which she visualized herself whole and well, and every day she would try to straighten out her leg a little more, painful though the exercise was. She also became a vegetarian. She had already been leaning in that direction because of the war in Vietnam: "I considered myself a pacifist," she said later. "I was really into Gandhi. I didn't approve of killing and I didn't want other people killing in my place. And that included killing a cow for me. I haven't eaten red meat since 1968."

She had to wear a corsetlike brace for about a year, and limped badly for several more years after that. But her leg did gradually straighten, and later X-rays revealed that her back had regenerated. She had to give up bowling, because the jerking motion was inadvisable, but apart from that had no residual problems of any kind. Did meditation and vegetarianism do the trick? Karla doesn't pretend to know, saying simply, "I have no explanation." But once well, she vowed never again to feel so defenseless, and took up judo. That, in turn, helped her quickly lose the fifty pounds she had gained from lying around in bed.

And, limp and all, she also returned to politics. In September 1969, she took part in the second feminist protest at the Miss America contest in Atlantic City. (The first protest, a year earlier, had involved day-long picketing and guerrilla-theater skits but not—as the massive coverage claimed—bra-burning.⁶) At the second demonstration, Karla and the other feminists passed out roses on the boardwalk and told each woman they gave one to that *she* was the real Miss America.

Karla was beginning to notice strange things about her telephone. If she hung up and then quickly lifted the receiver again to make a second call, there was a little space before she could get a dial tone. And then came the time when she picked the phone back up and heard one man asking another, "What do you think she meant by that?" Karla had previously assumed that her phone was being tapped, but the actual discovery still proved a shock.

It later turned out that the New York City "Red Squad" was not only listening in on the conversations of various women in Redstockings, but had planted someone at meetings—in much the way the FBI had long had socialists and Communists under surveillance and was currently doing its best to subvert the black civil rights struggle. Karla later became one of the plaintiffs in the famed *Handschu* case against the Red Squad, which dragged on for years; in the process she saw full reports of the Redstockings' central committee meetings, complete down to descriptions of objects in the room. Though Karla was one of only seven or eight women who sat on that committee, they were never able to find out who the plant was.

The day finally came in Karla's consciousness-raising group when Micela Griffo—who had been brought out sexually by Rita Mae Brown, and who would be active in the Gay Liberation Front just a short while later—finally spoke openly of her lesbianism. Some of the straight women in the group, especially Alix Kates Shulman, were supportive, and Karla felt encouraged to speak out herself. She still disliked labels, but since she *was* sleeping with women she felt the responsibility of sharing the burden of whatever negative consequences might follow.

But what she discovered was that "there were quite a number of lesbians in quite a number of closets in Redstockings," and instead of opprobrium she got "a whole new supply of lovers"—though, in many cases, not very good ones. As a "gesture of solidarity" with their lesbian sisters, some straight women had started to take on the lesbian label and to do some experimenting in bed. These "political lesbians," as they were known, tended to be lousy sex partners. Despite themselves, they brought their homophobic leftist baggage with them to bed, and were likely to find their sexual experiences with women disappointing. "They were really boring in bed," Karla said later. "It was like eating matzoh." It didn't take her long to decide that if any more straight women wanted to experiment sexually, they could do it with somebody else. Then, if they decided they liked lesbianism, Karla would be there.

J I M

Jim Fouratt regarded Abbie Hoffman as his brother. They had been through a lot together—from the action on the floor of the stock exchange to the confrontation at the Democratic convention in Chicago. And in 1969 they managed to bring the David Susskind television show to a dead stop by unveiling a live duck that promptly shat all over the stage. (Jim had already stunned Susskind by appearing dressed all in white; an apparition, complete with flowing blond hair, that seemed a miraculous reincarnation of Jesus Christ himself.)

Through all the high jinks and the serious politicking, Jim had swallowed his doubts about Abbie—about his self-celebration, his drug-taking, his (in Jim's view) "irresponsible" tendency to lead people into more trouble than they had bargained for. But an incident finally occurred that crystallized Jim's doubts and led to a definitive break between the two men. In order to do his political work—to notify and mobilize people for actions through his fly sheet, *The Communications Company*—Jim had long relied on his trusty Gestetner duplicating machine. One night he returned to his apartment to find the machine gone, apparently stolen. His suspicion immediately focused on Abbie, because of the disagreements the two had recently had over the 1968 Chicago confrontations and Abbie's dismissive comment that Jim "didn't really understand politics."

Jim went straight over to Abbie's place and confronted him. Abbie didn't even bother to deny the theft. Instead he acted as if the Gestetner was legitimately his by right of his superior understanding of the requirements of political organizing. Deeply wounded—"I would have died for Abbie"—Jim gave up the contest in despair, reluctantly concluding that he could never again trust Abbie, could never believe in his ability to put loyalty to a friend above the presumed exigencies of politics.

Ever the moralist, Jim decided there was a lesson to be learned: "not to endow people with what I want them to be, but to try to see them as they are so that I'm not set up to be disappointed or destroyed." But like anyone with a good heart and a large capacity for trust, Jim would have to learn that lesson over and over. Fortunately, he never learned it for long—fortunately, because an optimistic sense of the "goodness" of human nature is always the essential fuel for activism.

But for the moment, hurt and confused, Jim retreated from the movement. He went out to San Francisco for three months with his lover, Howie, and took up weaving—the hippie alternative to confrontational politics. But weaving turned out not to be "it" after all —"I was bored out of my mind"—and early in 1969 Jim was back in New York, where he dabbled for a time in that other hippie alternative, drugs. Give or take an occasional puff, Jim had previously avoided drugs, but now he started going regularly to the Sutton Place office of "Dr. Feelgood" (John Bishop). There, assorted celebrities crowded the waiting room for their "vitamin" shots ("Amphetamines? Well, of course not!" Dr. Feelgood would reassure those patients determined to be gullible). But after overdosing one day—and being peremptorily put out on the street by Dr. Feelgood—Jim at first cut down on and then kicked the shots.

Within a few months, Jim landed a paying job in the music world. Music had always been an important ingredient in his life, and his contacts with musicians had proliferated over the years. One day his friend Al Kooper, who had started the group Blood, Sweat & Tears, asked him if he was interested in a job with CBS as a staff producer. Jim grabbed it. Not only had his life lost its political focus, but his bills had mounted, and the notion of steady, well-paying work seemed the perfect simultaneous cure for ennui and indebtedness.

CBS hired Jim as the "house freak" with its corporate eyes wide open. Its recent "hip" ad campaign—"The Man Can't Bust Our Music"—had backfired. *Rolling Stone* had made fun of CBS's sudden countercultural conversion, and the underground press had reacted indignantly to what it branded a slick, commercial exploitation of the reality of police brutality. Jim Fouratt was hired to repair all that damage, to serve as liaison among the music executives, the cutting-edge artists CBS represented—Joplin, Chicago, Santana—and the radical communities from which they had emerged.[7]

Jim took to his job with gusto and proved a superlative liaison (the personal dividends included a weeklong affair with Jim Morrison). Before long, he had worked himself up to be an assistant to CBS president Clive Davis, who was not then known to be gay. And he had also discovered an unexpected knack for writing advertising copy. Developing a whole new campaign of his own around the slogan "Know Who Your Friends Are," he featured countercultural images of long-haired hippies, blacks, and Native Americans. And he deflected any negative reaction from the underground press for this latest appropriation of its imagery by persuading CBS to invest hefty advertising sums in left-wing and hippie publications. The infusion of revenue helped to keep the underground newspaper consortium, Liberation News Service, alive, and it gave Jim enormous satisfaction to know that he was making a significant political contribution through his job.

But if criticism from the underground press was defused, the response from elsewhere was inflamed. An FBI memo sent from San Francisco to Washington in January 1969 assailed CBS's infusion of money into left-wing publications as "giving active aid and comfort to enemies of the United States," and "suggested that the FBI should use its contacts to persuade" CBS to stop. Within three months, that wish had come to pass: CBS withdrew all advertising from the underground press. Jim blamed the turnabout on the avalanche of negative mail, apparently orchestrated by right-wing groups, that had poured into the network. At the least, the mail confirmed a shift in policy that conservative CBS bigwigs Frank Stanton and William S. Paley, who had their own cherished network of ties to D.C. bigwigs and the CIA, had already determined on. Whatever the reasons, CBS ceased to place ads in any but mainstream publications, even as they cynically began a new campaign—which Jim opposed and argued against—featuring the proclamation that "the Revolutionaries" were on the CBS label.[8]

STONEWALL

Craig Rodwell—like Leo Laurence in San Francisco—wanted militant activism to be the touchstone of New York's homophile movement. He was thoroughly fed up with Dick Leitsch's controlling influence over Mattachine, for if Leitsch had once been a militant, he was now, in Craig's view, interested solely in the advancement of Leitsch. He had become a mere politician, concerned more with protecting and inflating his own role as the broker between gays and the city administration than with empowering gays themselves, through confrontational action, to build a proud, assertive movement.[9]

Craig was also fed up with the gay bar scene in New York—with Mafia control over the only public space most gays could claim, with the contempt shown the gay clientele, with the speakeasy, clandestine atmosphere, the watered, overpriced drinks, the police payoffs and raids. His anger was compounded by tales he heard from his friend Dawn Hampton, a torch singer who, between engagements, worked the hatcheck at a Greenwich Village gay bar called the Stonewall Inn. Because Dawn was straight, the Mafia men who ran Stonewall talked freely in front of her—talked about their hatred for the "faggot scumbags" who made their fortunes.

Indeed, the Stonewall Inn, at 53 Christopher Street, epitomized for Craig everything that was wrong with the bar scene. When a hepatitis epidemic broke out among gay men early in 1969, Craig printed an angry article in his newsletter, *New York Hymnal*, blaming the epidemic on the unsterile drinking glasses at the Stonewall Inn. And he was probably right. Stonewall had no running water behind the bar; a returned glass was simply run through one of two stagnant vats of water kept underneath the bar, refilled, and then served to the next customer. By the end of an evening the water was murky and multicolored.[10]

Craig also thought Stonewall was a haven for "chicken hawks" —adult males who coveted underage boys. Jim Fouratt shared that view. He characterized Stonewall as "a real dive, an awful, sleazy place set up by the Mob for hustlers, chickens to be bought by older people." But this was, at most, a partial view. One segment of Stonewall's varied clientele did consist of street queens who hustled; but even for that contingent, Stonewall was primarily a social, not a business place. Some sixteen- and seventeen-year-olds did frequent Stonewall, and were admitted with the friendly complicity of somebody at the door (the drinking age was then eighteen)—but not for purposes of prostitution. As in any club, of course, the occasional cash transaction undoubtedly took place.

Figuring prominently in Craig and Jim's scenario is the figure of Ed Murphy, one of the bouncer-doormen at the Stonewall Inn, whom they accuse of purveying drugs and young flesh there. The indictment, though overdrawn, has some substance. Murphy did deal drugs, did lech after teenagers, did make "introductions" (for which he accepted "tips"), and was involved in corruption, simultaneously taking payoffs from the Mafia and the New York Police Department. (That is, until the police badly beat him up one night, and he stopped informing for them.)[11]

Sascha L., who in 1969 briefly worked the door at Stonewall alongside Murphy, began by thinking of him as a father figure— posing as a cop, Murphy had once rescued Sascha from an angry john wanting more than Sascha had been willing to give—but finally decided that Murphy was a run-of-the-mill crook. Sascha was eyewitness one night to an underage boy named Tommy turning over to Murphy, in the Stonewall basement, a bag of wallets stolen during the evening.[12]

But Murphy and the Stonewall Inn had many defenders. Murphy had been employed in gay bars and after-hours places since 1946 and in the course of that long career had made—along with detractors and enemies—some staunch friends. (Indeed, in later years the Christopher Street Heritage of Pride Committee would canonize Murphy as an originating saint of the gay movement.) And as for the Stonewall Inn, it had, in the course of its two-and-a-half-year existence, become the most popular gay bar in Greenwich Village. Many saw it as an oasis, a safe retreat from the harassment of everyday life, a place less susceptible to police raids than other gay bars and one that drew a magical mix of patrons ranging from tweedy East Siders to street queens. It was also the only gay male bar in New York where dancing was permitted.[13]

Sylvia Rivera was among the staunchest defenders of Stonewall, and of its omnipresent bouncer Ed Murphy. When down on their luck, which was often, Sylvia and her street-queen friends always knew they could turn to Murphy for a handout. Some of them called him Papa Murphy, and Sylvia's friend Ivan Valentin seems to have been his special favorite. "To me," Ivan says, "Ed Murphy never did anything wrong." Murphy had a soft spot in general for Hispanics like Ivan, and also for blacks; indeed, later gay bar owners who employed Murphy would worry that he would "turn the club black" and—since racism has always been alive and well in the gay world —frighten off the white clientele.[14]

But though Sylvia and her friends enjoyed going to Stonewall, their bars of choice were in fact Washington Square, on Broadway and Third Street and, to a lesser extent, the Gold Bug and the Tenth of Always (an after-after-hours place that catered to all possible variations of illicit life and stayed open so late it converted by nine A.M. into a regular working-class bar). The Washington Square was owned by the Joe Gallo family, which also controlled Tony Pastor's and the Purple Onion (whereas the Genovese family operated Stonewall, Tele-Star, the Tenth of Always, the Bon Soir on Eighth Street, and—run by Anna Genovese—the Eighty-Two Club in the East Village, which featured drag shows for an audience largely composed of straight tourists). Washington Square was Sylvia's special favorite. It *opened* at three in the morning and catered primarily (rather than incidentally, as was the case with Stonewall) to transvestites; the more upscale ones would arrive in limos with their wealthy johns and spend the evening ostentatiously drinking champagne. But others, like Sylvia, went there for relaxing nightcaps and gossip after a hard evening of hustling on the streets.[15]

The Mob usually provided only a limited amount of money to Family members interested in opening a club; it thereafter became the individual's responsibility to turn a profit. That meant, among other things, not investing too heavily in liquor. When Washington Square first opened, the Mafia members who ran the place lost twelve cases of liquor and fifty cases of beer during the first police raid. Thereafter, only a few bottles were kept in the club and the rest of the liquor was stored in a nearby car; when the bartender was about to run out, someone would go around the corner to the parked car, put a few bottles under his arm, and return to the club. (Other bars had different strategies, such as keeping the liquor hidden behind a panel in the wall.) By thus preventing the police from confiscating large amounts of liquor during any one of their commonplace raids, it was possible—and also commonplace—to open up again for business the next day.[16]

The Stonewall Inn had, in its varied incarnations during the fifties, been a straight restaurant and a straight nightclub. In 1966 it was taken over by three Mafia figures who had grown up together on

Mulberry Street in Little Italy: "Mario" (the best-liked of the three), Zucchi, who also dealt in firecrackers, and "Fat Tony" Lauria, who weighed in at 420 pounds. Together they put up $3,500 to reopen the Stonewall as a gay club; Fat Tony put up $2,000, which made him the controlling partner, but Mario served as Stonewall's manager and ran the place on a day-to-day basis.[17]

Tony Lauria was the best-connected of the three. He had gotten a B.A. at Xavier, had married and divorced, and lived at 136 Waverly Place, a Mob-owned apartment building. It was home to a host of related Mafia figures involved in assorted rackets: vending machines, carting companies, and sanitation. Tony's two uncles and his father also lived in the building; the latter (whose other son was a stockbroker) was high up in Mob circles and sat on the board of the Bank of Commerce on Delancey Street, a bank that laundered a fair share of Mafia money. Lauria Senior did not approve of his wayward son's penchant for hanging around street mobsters and getting involved in the "fag bar" scene.[18]

Fat Tony lived from 1966 to 1971 with Chuck Shaheen, an openly gay man in his mid-twenties of Italian descent. The relationship was secretarial, not erotic. Shaheen acted as a man Friday, serving at different times as everything from a Stonewall bartender to the trusted go-between who "picked up the banks"—the accumulated cash—at the bar several times a night and carried the money home to his boss. According to Shaheen, Tony developed a heavy methamphetamine habit, shooting the crystal several times a day into his veins. Under the drug's influence, Tony lost about two hundred pounds, stayed up all night at clubs (at Stonewall, his favorite hangout, he would embarrass his partners by insistently doing parlor tricks, like twirling cigarettes in the air), and began, for the first time in his life, to go to bed with men—though, to Shaheen's relief, not with him. Tony's father stopped speaking to him altogether and Shaheen had to carry messages between them. Increasingly shunned, Tony, so the rumor mill had it, was later killed by the Family.[19]

Tony and his partners, Mario and Zucchi, had opened Stonewall as a private "bottle club." That was a common ruse for getting around the lack of a liquor license; bottles would be labeled with fictitious names and the bar would then—contrary to a law forbidding bottle clubs from selling drinks—proceed to do a cash business just like any other bar. The three partners spent less than a thousand dollars in fixing up the club's interior. They settled for a third-rate sound system, hired a local electrician and his assistant to build a bar and raise

the dance-floor stage, and got their jukebox and cigarette machines—
had to get them—from the local don, Matty "the Horse" Iannello.[20]

As the man who controlled the district in which Stonewall was
located, Iannello was automatically entitled to a cut in the operation.
Shaheen never once saw Iannello in Stonewall, nor did he ever meet
him, but Matty the Horse got his percentage like clockwork. The
Stonewall partners also had to pay off the notoriously corrupt Sixth
Precinct. A patrolman would stop by Stonewall once a week to pick
up the envelopes filled with cash—including those for the captains
and desk sergeants, who never collected their payoffs in person. The
total cash dispensed to the police each week came to about two thousand dollars.[21]

Despite the assorted payoffs, Stonewall turned a huge weekly
profit for its owners. With rent at only three hundred dollars a month,
and with the take (all in cash) typically running to five thousand dollars
on a Friday night and sixty-five hundred on a Saturday, Stonewall
quickly became a money machine. Some of the profit was made
through side gigs for which Stonewall as a place was merely the
occasion. In Shaheen's words, "all kinds of mobsters used to come
in. There were all kinds of deals going on. All kinds of hot merchan-
dise. They would deal the stuff out of the trunks of cars parked in
front of the bar. You could buy all kinds of things at Stonewall."
Shaheen recalls vividly the time a Cuban couple was swindled out of
a clay plate with multicarat diamonds hidden under the glaze; they
had taken the plate with them when fleeing Castro. Fat Tony had a
ring made from one of the bigger (five-carat) stones and, when he later
fell on hard times, had Shaheen negotiate its sale to Cartier.

Some of the Mob members who worked gay clubs were themselves gay—and terrified of being found out. "Big Bobby," who was
on the door at Tony Pastor's, a Mafia-run place at Sixth Avenue and
MacDougal Street, almost blew his cover when he became indiscreet
about his passion for a Chinese drag queen named Tony Lee (who,
though going lamentably to fat, was famed for her ballerina act). The
Stonewall Inn seems to have had more than the usual number of gay
mobsters. "Petey," who hung out at Stonewall as a kind of free-lance,
circulating bouncer, had a thick Italian street accent, acted "dumb,"
and favored black shirts and ties; he was the very picture of a Mafia
mobster—except for his habit of falling for patrons and coworkers.

He took a shine to Sascha L., but they would have sex only when
Petey was drunk, and no mention could be made of it afterward.
Some of the other mobsters would take Sascha aside and question

him—Sascha was openly gay—about whether Petey "didn't seem a little funny." Sascha would dutifully answer no, and as a reward—and perhaps, too, because his presence made Petey nervous—Petey got Sascha a better-paying job at Washington Square.[22]

Petey turned his attentions to a drag queen named Désirée, apparently figuring that if he were caught, getting a blow job from a drag queen would be far more forgivable than giving a blow job to a stocky male doorman. Besides, Désirée was Italian. A beautiful boy with shoulder-length hair and huge amber eyes, she had a figure so stunningly "feminine" that she passed as a woman—as a gorgeous woman—in broad daylight.

But even the beautiful Désirée was outclassed by blond Harlow. (Petey had developed a huge lech for Harlow, too, but he couldn't get near her.) Harlow rarely came to Stonewall, preferring a tonier, straight uptown scene, but when she did, her chic black dresses and real jewelry set the standard for aspiring queens on the Washington Square–Stonewall circuit. Harlow never had the luck to catch Andy Warhol's eye, and so never achieved the widespread notoriety of Holly Woodlawn, Jackie Curtis, and Candy Darling, who made it into Warhol's movies and were thereby elevated into mainstream New York stardom. But Harlow—at least according to drag-queen mythology—later achieved her own kind of stardom, purportedly marrying a congressman, getting a sex-change operation at his expense, and buying (again courtesy of the congressman) a club in Philadelphia.

As for Désirée, she and Petey eventually ran off together to live outside of New York as a heterosexual couple. But—again according to the rumor mill—theirs was not a storybook ending: Petey subsequently turned "bad" and, in a fit of jealousy, shot and killed Désirée.

Most of the employees at Stonewall, and some of the customers, did drugs, primarily "uppers." Desbutal—a mix of Desoxyn and Nembutal—was a great favorite (though later banned by the FDA), and the bar was also known as a good place to buy acid. The chief supplier was Maggie Jiggs, a famous queen who worked the main bar at Stonewall, along with her partner, Tommy Long. (Tommy kept a toy duck on the bar that quacked whenever someone left a tip.) They were a well-known team with a big following. Maggie, blonde, chubby, and loud, knew everybody's business and would think nothing of yelling out in the middle of the crowded bar, "Hey, girl, I hear you got a whole new plate of false teeth from that fabulous dentist you been fucking!" But Maggie loved people, had good drugs, was always surrounded by gorgeous men, and arranged wonderful three-ways, so her outspokenness, and even her occasional thievery, were usually forgiven.

Maggie and Tommy were stationed behind the main bar, one of two bars in the Stonewall. But before you could get to it, you had to pass muster at the door (a ritual some of the customers welcomed as a relief from the lax security that characterized most gay bars). That usually meant inspection, through a peephole in the heavy front door by Ed Murphy, "Bobby Shades," or muscular Frank Esselourne. "Blond Frankie," as he was known, was gay, but in those years not advertising it, and was famous for being able to spot straights or undercover cops with a single glance.[23]

If you got the okay at the door—and for underage street kids that was always problematic—you moved a few steps to a table, usually covered by members of what one wag called the Junior Achievement Mafia team. That could mean, on different nights, Zucchi; Mario; Ernie Sgroi, who always wore a suit and tie and whose father had started the famed Bon Soir on Eighth Street; "Vito," who was on salary directly from Fat Tony, was hugely proud of his personal collection of S.S. uniforms and Nazi flags, and made bombs on the side; or "Tony the Sniff" Verra, who had a legendary nose for no-goods and kept a baseball bat behind the door to deal with them. At the table, you had to plunk down three dollars (one dollar on weekdays), for which you got two tickets that could be exchanged for two watered-down drinks. (According to Chuck Shaheen, *all* drinks were watered, even those carrying the fanciest labels.) You then signed your name in a book kept to prove, should the question arise in court, that Stonewall was indeed a private "bottle club." People rarely signed their real names. "Judy Garland," "Donald Duck," and "Elizabeth Taylor" were the popular favorites.[24]

Once inside Stonewall, you took a step down and straight in front of you was the main bar where Maggie held court. Behind the bar some pulsating gel lights went on and off—later exaggeratedly claimed by some to be the precursor of the innovative light shows at the Sanctuary and other gay discos that followed. On weekends, a scantily clad go-go boy with a pin spot on him danced in a gilded cage on top of the bar. Straight ahead, beyond the bar, was a spacious dancing area, at one point in the bar's history lit only with black lights. That in itself became a subject for camp, because the queens, with Murine in their eyes, all looked as if they had white streaks running down their faces. Should the police (known as Lily Law, Alice Blue Gown—Alice for short—or Betty Badge) or a suspected plainclothesman unexpectedly arrive, white bulbs instantly came on in the dance area, signaling everyone to stop dancing or touching.[25]

The queens rarely hung out at the main bar. There was another, smaller room off to one side, with a stone wishing well in the middle, its own jukebox and service bar, and booths. That became head-quarters for the more flamboyant contingent in Stonewall's melting pot of customers. There were the "scare drag queens" like Tommy Lanigan-Schmidt, Birdie Rivera, and Martin Boyce—"boys who looked like girls but who you knew were boys." And there were the "flame" (not drag) queens who wore eye makeup and teased hair, but essentially dressed in male clothes—if an effeminate version with fluffy sweaters and Tom Jones shirts.

Only a few favored full-time transvestites, like Tiffany, Spanola Jerry, a hairdresser from Sheepshead Bay, and Tammy Novak, who performed at the Eighty-Two Club, were allowed to enter Stonewall in drag (Tammy sometimes transgressed by dressing as a boy). Not even "Tish" (Joe Tish) would be admitted, though he had been a well-known drag performer since the early fifties, when he had worked at the Moroccan Village on Eighth Street, and though in the late sixties he had a long-running show at the Crazy Horse, a nearby café on Bleecker Street. Tish *was* admitted into some uptown straight clubs in full drag; there, as he sniffily put it, his "artistry" was recognized.[26]

Some of the younger queens were homeless and more or less camped out in the small park directly opposite the Stonewall bar. Bob Kohler, a gay man in his early forties who lived nearby, became something of a protector. (Kohler would later be prominent in the Gay Liberation Front, but had long since developed empathy for outsiders: In the early sixties, his talent agency on West Fifty-seventh Street represented a number of black artists no one else would take on.) Kohler would give the young queens clothing and change, or sometimes pay for a room in a local fleabag hotel; and when out walking his dog, he would often sit on a park bench with them and listen to their troubles and dreams. He was able to hear their pain even as he chuckled at their antics. Once, when he went down to bail out Sylvia Rivera's good friend, Marsha P. Johnson, he heard Judge Bruce Wright ask Marsha what the "P" was for. "Pay it no mind," Marsha snapped back; Judge Wright broke up laughing and told Koh-ler to "get her out of here."[27]

Yet for all their wit and style, Kohler never glamorized street queens as heroic deviants pushing against rigid gender categories, self-conscious pioneers of a boundary-free existence. He knew too much about the misery of their lives. He knew a drugged-out queen who fell asleep on a rooftop and lay in the sun so long that she ended up near death with a third-degree burn. He knew "cross-eyed Cynthia," killed when she was pushed out of a window of the St. George Hotel in Brooklyn—and another "Sylvia," who jumped off its roof. He knew Dusty, "ugly as sin, never out of drag, very funny, big mouth," who made the mistake of calling the wrong person "nigger" and was stabbed to death. And he knew several queens who had themselves stabbed a recalcitrant customer—or a competitive sister.

The queens considered Stonewall and Washington Square the most congenial downtown bars. If they passed muster at the Stonewall door, they could buy or cajole drinks, exchange cosmetics and the favored Tabu or Ambush perfume, admire or deplore somebody's latest Kanecalon wig, make fun of six-foot transsexual Lynn's size-12 women's shoes (while admiring her fishnet stockings and miniskirts and giggling over her tales of servicing the firemen around the corner at their Tenth Street station), move constantly in and out of the ladies room (where they deplored the fact that a single red light bulb made the application of makeup difficult), and dance in a feverish sweat till closing time at four A.M.

The jukebox on the dance floor played a variety of songs, even an occasional "Smoke Gets in Your Eyes" to appease the romantics. The Motown label was still top of the heap in the summer of 1969; three of the five hit singles for the week of June 28—by Marvin Gaye, Junior Walker, and the Temptations—carried its imprint. On the pop side, the Stonewall jukebox played the love theme from the movie version of *Romeo and Juliet* over and over, the record's saccharine periodically cut by the Beatles' "Get Back" or Elvis Presley's "In the Ghetto." And all the new dances—the Boston Jerk, the Monkey, the Spider—were tried out with relish. If the crowd was in a particularly campy mood (and the management was feeling loose enough), ten or fifteen dancers would line up to learn the latest ritual steps, beginning with a shouted "Hit it, girls!"[28]

The chino-and-penny-loafer crowd pretty much stayed near the main bar, fraternizing with the queens mostly on the dance floor, if at all. ("Two queens can't bump pussy," one of them explained. "And I don't care how beefy and brawny the pussy is. And certainly not for a relationship.") The age range at Stonewall was mostly late teens to early thirties; the over-thirty-five crowd hung out at Julius', and the leather crowd (then in its infancy) at Keller's. There could also be seen at Stonewall just a sprinkling of the new kind of gay man beginning to emerge: the hippie, long-haired, bell-bottomed, laid-back, and likely to have "weird," radical views.

Very few women ever appeared in Stonewall. Sascha L. flatly declares that he can't remember *any*, except for the occasional "fag hag" (like Blond Frankie's straight friend Lucille, who lived with the doorman at One-Two-Three and hung out at Stonewall), or "one or two dykes who looked almost like boys." But Chuck Shaheen, who spent much more time at Stonewall, remembers—while acknowledging that the bar was "98 percent male"—a few more lesbian customers than Sascha does, and, of those, a number who were decidedly femme. One of the lesbians who did go to Stonewall "a few times," tagging along with some of her gay male friends, recalls that she "felt like a visitor." It wasn't as if the male patrons went out of their way to make her feel uncomfortable, but rather that the territory was theirs, not hers: "There didn't seem to be hostility, but there didn't seem to be camaraderie."29

SYLVIA, JIM, CRAIG

Sylvia Rivera had been invited to Marsha P. Johnson's party on the night of June 27, but she decided not to go. It wasn't that she was mad at Marsha; she simply felt strung out. She had been working as an accounting clerk in a Jersey City chain-store warehouse, keeping tally sheets of what the truckers took out—a good job with a good boss who let her wear makeup whenever she felt like it. But it was an eleven-to-seven shift, Sundays through Thursdays, all-night stints that kept her away from her friends on the street and decidedly short of the cash she had made from hustling.

Yes, she wanted to clean up her act and start leading a "normal" life. But she hadn't counted on missing the money so much, or on her drug habit persisting—and sixty-seven dollars a week in take-home pay just wasn't doing it. So she and her lover, Gary, decided to piece out their income with a side gig—passing bad checks—and on June 27, a Friday, they had just gotten back from papering Washington, D.C. The first news they heard on returning was about Judy

Garland's funeral that very day, how twenty thousand people had waited up to four hours in the blistering heat to view her body at Frank E. Campbell's funeral home on Madison Avenue and Eighty-first Street. The news sent a melodramatic shiver up Sylvia's spine, and she decided to become "completely hysterical." "It's the end of an era," she tearfully announced. "The greatest singer, the greatest actress of my childhood is no more. Never again 'Over the Rainbow' "—here Sylvia sobbed loudly—"no one left to look up to."

No, she was not going to Marsha's party. She would stay home, light her consoling religious candles (Viejita had taught her *that* much), and say a few prayers for Judy. But then the phone rang and her buddy Tammy Novak—who sounded more stoned than usual—*insisted* that Sylvia and Gary join her later that night at Stonewall. Sylvia hesitated. If she was going out at all—"Was it all right to dance with the martyred Judy not cold in her grave?"—she would go to Washington Square. She had never been crazy about Stonewall, she reminded Tammy: Men in makeup were tolerated there, but not exactly cherished. And if she was going to go out, she wanted to *vent*—to be just as outrageous, as grief-stricken, as makeup would allow. But Tammy absolutely *refused* to take no for an answer and so Sylvia, moaning theatrically, gave in. She popped a black beauty and she and Gary headed downtown.

Jim's job at CBS required long hours, and he often got back to his apartment (after a stopover at Max's Kansas City) in the early morning. On the night of June 27 he had worked in the office until midnight, had gone for a nightcap at Max's, and about one A.M. had headed back to his apartment in the Village. Passing by the Stonewall Inn —a bar he despised, insistent it was a haven for marauding chicken hawks—Jim noticed a cluster of cops in front of the bar, looking as if they were about to enter. He shrugged it off as just another routine raid, and even found himself hoping that *this* time (Stonewall had been raided just two weeks before) the police would succeed in closing the joint.

But as Jim got closer, he could see that a small group of onlookers had gathered. That was somewhat surprising, since the first sign of a raid usually led to an immediate scattering; typically, gays fled rather than loitered, and fled as quietly and as quickly as possible, grateful not to be implicated at the scene of the "crime." Jim spotted Craig Rodwell at the top of the row of steps leading up to a brownstone adjacent to the Stonewall Inn. Craig looked agitated, expectant. Something was decidedly in the air.

Craig had taken up his position only moments before. Like Jim, he had been on his way home—from playing cards at a friend's—and had stumbled on the gathering crowd in front of the Stonewall. He was with Fred Sargeant, his current lover, and the two of them had scrambled up the brownstone steps to get a better view. The crowd was decidedly small, but what was riveting was its strangely quiet, expectant air, as if awaiting the next development. Just then, the police pushed open the front door of the Stonewall and marched in. Craig looked at his watch: It was one-twenty A.M.

Sylvia was feeling *very* little pain. The black beauty had hopped her up and the scotch had smoothed her out. Her lover, Gary, had come along; Tammy, Bambi, and Ivan were there; and rumor had it that Marsha Johnson, disgusted at all the no-shows for her party, was also headed downtown to Stonewall, determined to dance *somewhere*. It looked like a good night. Sylvia expansively decided she did like Stonewall after all, and was just saying that to Tammy, who looked as if she was about to keel over—"that chile [Tammy was seventeen, Sylvia eighteen] could not control her intake"—when the cops came barreling through the front door. (The white warning lights had earlier started flashing on the dance floor, but Sylvia and her friends had been oblivious.)

The next thing she knew, the cops, with their usual arrogance, were stomping through, ordering the patrons to line up and get their IDs ready for examination. "Oh my God!" Sylvia shouted at Gary, "I didn't bring my ID!" Before she could panic, Gary reached in his pocket and produced her card; he had brought it along. "Praise be to Saint Barbara!" Sylvia shrieked, snatching the precious ID. If the raid went according to the usual pattern, the only people who would be arrested would be those without IDs, those dressed in the clothes of the opposite gender, and some or all of the employees. Everyone else would be let go with a few shoves and a few contemptuous words. The bar would soon reopen and they would all be back dancing. It was annoying to have one's Friday night screwed up, but hardly unprecedented.

Sylvia tried to take it in stride; she'd been through lots worse, and with her ID in hand and nothing more than face makeup on, she knew the hassling would be minimal. But she was pissed; the good high she had was gone, and her nerve ends felt as raw as when she had been crying over Judy earlier in the evening. She wished she'd gone to the Washington Square, a place she preferred anyway. She was sick of being treated like scum; "I was just not in the mood" was how she later put it. "It had got to the point where I didn't want to be bothered anymore." When one of the cops grabbed the ID out of her hand and asked her with a smirk if she was a boy or a girl, she almost swung at him, but Gary grabbed her hand in time. The cop gave her a shove toward the door, and told her to get the hell out.

Not all of the two hundred or so people who were inside Stonewall fared that well. Chico, a forty-five-year-old patron who looked sixty, was arrested for not having an ID proving he was over 18. Another patron, asked for "some kind of ID, like a birth certificate," said to the cop, "I don't happen to carry mine around with me. Do you have yours, Officer?"; the cop arrested him. Eighteen-year-old Joey Dey had been dancing for a while with a guy in a suit, but had decided he wasn't interested and had tried to get away; the man had insisted they go on dancing and then, just as the police came through the door, pulled out a badge and told him he was under arrest.[30]

Harry Beard, one of the dance-floor waiters, had been coming off a ten-day amphetamine run and was crashed out in one of the side-room booths when the police arrived. He knew that the only way to avoid arrest was to pretend he was a customer, so he grabbed a drink off the bar, crossed his legs provocatively, and tried to act unconcerned. Fortunately for him, he had gone into one of the new unisex shops that very day and was wearing a soft pink blouse with ruffles around the wrist and down the front. One of the cops looked at him quizzically and said, "I know you. You work here." Harry was on welfare at the time, so, adopting his nelliest tone, he thrust his welfare card at the cop and replied, "Work here? Oh, don't be silly! I'm just a poor girl on welfare. Here's my welfare card. Besides, I wouldn't work in a toilet like this!" The cop looked skeptical but told Harry he could leave.[31]

The Stonewall management had always been tipped off by the police before a raid took place—this happened, on average, once a month—and the raid itself was usually staged early enough in the evening to produce minimal commotion and allow for a quick reopening. Indeed, sometimes the "raid" consisted of little more than the police striding arrogantly through the bar and then leaving, with no arrests made. Given the size of the weekly payoff, the police had an understandable stake in keeping the golden calf alive.

But this raid was different. It was carried out by eight detectives from the First Division (only one of them in uniform), and the Sixth Precinct had been asked to participate only at the last possible second. Moreover, the raid had occurred at one-twenty A.M.—the height of the merriment—and with no advance warning to the Stonewall management. (Chuck Shaheen recalls some vague tip-off that a raid *might* happen, but since the early-evening hours had passed without incident, the management had dismissed the tip as inaccurate.)[32]

There have been an abundance of theories as to why the Sixth Precinct failed on this occasion to alert Stonewall's owners. One centers on the possibility that a payment had not been made on time or made at all. Another suggests that the extent of Stonewall's profits had recently become known to the police, and the Sixth Precinct brass had decided, as a prelude to its demand for a larger cut, to flex a little muscle. Yet a third explanation points to the possibility that the new commanding officer at the precinct was out of sympathy with payoffs, or hadn't yet learned how profitable they could be.

But evidence has surfaced to suggest that the machinations of the Sixth Precinct were in fact incidental to the raid. Ryder Fitzgerald, a sometime carpenter who had helped remodel the Stonewall interior and whose friends Willis and Elf (a straight hippie couple) lived rent-free in the apartment above the Stonewall in exchange for performing caretaker chores, was privy the day after the raid to a revealing conversation. Ernie, one of Stonewall's Mafia team, stormed around Willis and Elf's apartment, cursing out (in Ryder's presence) the Sixth Precinct for having failed to provide warning in time. And in the course of his tirade, Ernie revealed that the raid had been inspired by federal agents. The Bureau of Alcohol, Tobacco and Firearms (BATF) had apparently discovered that the liquor bottles used at Stonewall had no federal stamps on them—which meant they had been hijacked or bootlegged straight out of the distillery. Putting Stonewall under surveillance, BATF had then discovered the bar's corrupt alliance with the Sixth Precinct. Thus when the feds decided to launch a raid on Stonewall, they deliberately kept the local police in the dark until the unavoidable last minute.[33]

When the raid, contrary to expectations, did get going, the previous systems put in place by the Mafia owners stood them in good stead. The strong front door bought needed time until the white lights had a chance to do their warning work: Patrons instantly stopped dancing and touching; and the bartenders quickly took the money from the cigar boxes that served as cash registers, jumped from behind the bar, and mingled inconspicuously with the customers. Maggie Jiggs, already known for her "two for the bar, one for myself" approach to cash, disappeared into the crowd with a cigar box full of money; when a cop asked to see the contents, Maggie said it contained her tips as a "cigarette girl," and they let her go. When questioned by her employers later, Maggie claimed that the cop had taken the box *and* the money. She got away with the lie.[34]

The standard Mafia policy of putting gay employees on the door so they could take the heat while everyone else got their act together, also paid off for the owners. Eddie Murphy managed to get out ("Of course," his detractors add, "he was on the police payroll"), but Blond Frankie was arrested. There was already a warrant outstanding for Frankie's arrest (purportedly for homicide; he was known for "acting first and not bothering to think even later"). Realizing that this was no ordinary raid, that this time an arrest might not merely mean detention for a few hours at Centre Street, followed by a quick release, Frankie was determined not to be taken in. Owners Zucchi and Mario, through a back door connected to the office, were soon safely out on the street in front of the Stonewall. So, too, were almost all of the bar's customers, released after their IDs had been checked and their attire deemed "appropriate" to their gender—a process accompanied, as in Sylvia's case, by derisive, ugly police banter.[35]

As for "Fat Tony," at the time the raid took place he had still not left his apartment on Waverly Place, a few blocks from the Stonewall. Under the spell of methamphetamine, he had already spent three hours combing and recombing his beard and agitatedly changing from one outfit to another, acting for all the world like one of those "demented queens" he vilified. He and Chuck Shaheen could see the commotion from their apartment window, but only after an emergency call from Zucchi could Tony be persuaded to leave the apartment for the bar.[36]

Some of the campier patrons, emerging one by one from the Stonewall to find an unexpected crowd, took the opportunity to strike instant poses, starlet style, while the onlookers whistled and shouted their applause-meter ratings. But when a paddy wagon pulled up, the mood turned more somber. And it turned sullen when the police officers started to emerge from Stonewall with prisoners in tow and moved with them toward the waiting van. Jim Fouratt at the back of the crowd, Sylvia standing with Gary near the small park across the street from Stonewall, and Craig perched on top of the brownstone stairs near the front of the crowd—all sensed something unusual in the air, all felt a kind of tensed expectancy.

The police (two of whom were women) were oblivious to it initially. Everything up to that point had gone so routinely that they expected to see the crowd quickly disperse. Instead, a few people started to boo; others pressed against the waiting van, while the cops standing near it yelled angrily for the crowd to move back. According to Sylvia, "You could feel the electricity going through people. You could actually feel it. People were getting really, really pissed and uptight." A guy in a dark red T-shirt danced in and out of the crowd, shouting "Nobody's gonna fuck with me!" and "Ain't gonna take this shit!"[37]

As the cops started loading their prisoners into the van—among them, Blond Frankie, the doorman—more people joined in the shouting. Sylvia spotted Tammy Novak among the three queens lined up for the paddy wagon, and along with others in the crowd started yelling "Tammy! Tammy!," Sylvia's shriek rising above the rest. But Tammy apparently didn't hear, and Sylvia guessed that she was too stoned to know what was going on. Yet when a cop shoved Tammy and told her to "keep moving! keep moving!," poking her with his club, Tammy told him to stop pushing and when he didn't, she started swinging. From that point on, so much happened so quickly as to seem simultaneous.[38]

Jim Fouratt insists that *the* explosive moment came when "a dyke dressed in men's clothing," who had been visiting a male employee inside the bar, started to act up as the cops moved her toward the paddy wagon. According to Jim, "the queens were acting like queens, throwing their change and giving lots of attitude and lip. But the dyke had to be more butch than the queens. So when the police moved her into the wagon, she got out the other side and started to rock it."

Harry Beard, the Stonewall waiter who had been inside the bar, partly corroborates Jim's account, though differing on the moment of explosion. According to Beard, the cops had arrested the cross-dressed lesbian inside the bar for not wearing the requisite (as mandated by a New York statute) three pieces of clothing "appropriate to one's gender." As they led her out of the bar, so Beard's version goes, she complained that the handcuffs they had put on her were too tight; in response, one of the cops slapped her in the head with his nightstick. Seeing the cops hit her, people standing immediately outside the door started throwing coins at the police.[39]

But Craig Rodwell and a number of other eyewitnesses sharply contest the view that the arrest of a lesbian was *the* precipitating incident, or even that a lesbian had been present in the bar. And they skeptically ask why, if she did exist, she has never stepped forward to claim the credit; to the answer that she may long since have died, they sardonically reply, "And she never told another soul? And if she did, why haven't *they* stepped forward to claim credit for her?" As if all that isn't muddle enough, those eyewitnesses who deny the lesbian claimant, themselves divide over whether to give the palm to a queen—Tammy Novak being the leading candidate—or to one of the many ordinary gay male patrons of the bar. Craig Rodwell's view probably comes as close as we are likely to get to the truth: "A number of incidents were happening simultaneously. There was no one thing that happened or one person, there was just . . . a flash of group— of mass—anger."[40]

As the police, amid a growing crowd and mounting anger, continued to load prisoners into the van, Martin Boyce, an eighteen-year-old scare drag queen, saw a leg in nylons and sporting a high heel shoot out of the back of the paddy wagon into the chest of a cop, throwing him backward. Another queen then opened the door on the side of the wagon and jumped out. The cops chased and caught her, but Blond Frankie quickly managed to engineer another escape from the van; several queens successfully made their way out with him and were swallowed up in the crowd. Tammy Novak was one of them; she ran all the way to Joe Tish's apartment, where she holed up throughout the weekend. The police handcuffed subsequent prisoners to the inside of the van, and succeeded in driving away from the scene to book them at the precinct house. Deputy Inspector Seymour Pine, the ranking officer, nervously told the departing police to "just drop them off at the Sixth Precinct and hurry back."[41]

From this point on, the mêlée broke out in several directions and swiftly mounted in intensity. The crowd, now in full cry, started screaming epithets at the police—"Pigs!" "Faggot cops!" Sylvia and Craig enthusiastically joined in, Sylvia shouting her lungs out, Craig letting go with a full-throated "Gay power!" One young gay Puerto Rican went fearlessly up to a policeman and yelled in his face, "What you got against faggots? We don't do you nuthin'!" Another teenager started kicking at a cop, frequently missing as the cop held him at arm's length. One queen mashed an officer with her heel, knocked him down, grabbed his handcuff keys, freed herself, and passed the keys to another queen behind her.[42]

By now, the crowd had swelled to a mob, and people were picking up and throwing whatever loose objects came to hand—coins, bottles, cans, bricks from a nearby construction site. Someone even picked up dog shit from the street and threw it in the cops' direction. As the fever mounted, Zucchi was overheard nervously asking Mario what the hell the crowd was upset about: the Mafia or the police? The *police*, Mario reassured him. Zucchi gave a big grin of relief and decided to vent some stored-up anger of his own: He egged on bystanders in their effort to rip up a damaged fire hydrant and he persuaded a young kid named Timmy to throw the wire-mesh garbage can nearby. Timmy was not much bigger than the can (and had just come out the week before), but he gave it his all—the can went sailing into the plate-glass window (painted black and reinforced from behind by plywood) that stretched across the front of the Stonewall.[43]

Stunned and frightened by the crowd's unexpected fury, the police, at the order of Deputy Inspector Pine, retreated inside the bar. Pine had been accustomed to two or three cops being able to handle with ease any number of cowering gays, but here the crowd wasn't cowering; it had routed eight cops and made them run for cover. As Pine later said, "I had been in combat situations, [but] there was never any time that I felt more scared than then." With the cops holed up inside Stonewall, the crowd was now in control of the street, and it bellowed in triumph and pent-up rage.[44]

Craig dashed to a nearby phone booth. Ever conscious of the need for publicity—for visibility—and realizing that a critical moment had arrived, he called all three daily papers, the *Times*, the *Post*, and the *News*, and alerted them that "a major news story was breaking." Then he ran to his apartment a few blocks away to get his camera.

Jim Fouratt also dashed to the phones—to call his straight radical-left friends, to tell them "people were fighting the cops—it was just like Newark!" He urged them to rush down and lend their support (just as he had long done for *their* causes). Then he went into the nearby Ninth Circle and Julius', to try to get the patrons to come out into the street. But none of them would. Nor did any of his straight radical friends show up. It taught Jim a bitter lesson about how low on the scale of priorities his erstwhile comrades ranked "faggot" concerns.

Gary tried to persuade Sylvia to go home with him to get a change of clothes. "Are you nuts?" she yelled. "I'm not missing a minute of this—it's the *revolution*!" So Gary left to get clothes for both of them. Blond Frankie, meanwhile—perhaps taking his cue from Zucchi—

uprooted a loose parking meter and offered it for use as a battering ram against the Stonewall's door. At nearly the same moment somebody started squirting lighter fluid through the shattered glass window on the bar's façade, tossing in matches after it. Inspector Pine later referred to this as "throwing Molotov cocktails into the place," but the only reality *that* described was the inflamed state of Pine's nerves.[45]

Still, the danger was very real, and the police were badly frightened. The shock to self-esteem had been stunning enough; now came an actual threat to physical safety. Dodging flying glass and missiles, Patrolman Gil Weisman, the one cop in uniform, was hit near the eye with a shard, and blood spurted out. With that, the fear turned abruptly to fury. Three of the cops, led by Pine, ran out the front door, which had crashed in from the battering, and started screaming threats at the crowd, thinking to cow it. But instead a rain of coins and bottles came down, and a beer can glanced off Deputy Inspector Charles Smyth's head. Pine lunged into the crowd, grabbed somebody around the waist, pulled him back into the doorway, and then dragged him by the hair, inside.[46]

Ironically, the prisoner was the well-known—and heterosexual —folk singer Dave Van Ronk. Earlier that night Van Ronk had been in and out of the Lion's Head, a bar a few doors down from Stonewall that catered to a noisy, macho journalist crowd scornful of the "faggots" down the block. Once the riot got going, the Lion's Head locked its doors; the management didn't want faggots moaning and bleeding over the paying customers. As soon as Pine got Van Ronk back into the Stonewall, he angrily accused him of throwing dangerous objects—a cue to Patrolman Weisman to shout that Van Ronk was the one who had cut his eye, and then to start punching the singer hard while several other cops held him down. When Van Ronk looked as if he was going to pass out, the police handcuffed him, and Pine snapped, "All right, we book him for assault."[47]

The cops then found a fire hose, wedged it into a crack in the door, and directed the spray out at the crowd, thinking that would certainly scatter it. But the stream was weak and the crowd howled derisively, while inside the cops started slipping on the wet floor. A reporter from *The Village Voice*, Howard Smith, had retreated inside the bar when the police did; he later wrote that by that point in the evening "the sound filtering in [didn't] suggest dancing faggots any more; it sound[ed] like a powerful rage bent on vendetta." By now the Stonewall's front door was hanging wide open, the plywood brace behind the windows was splintered, and it seemed only a matter of

minutes before the howling mob would break in and wreak its venge-
ance. One cop armed himself with Tony the Sniff's baseball bat; the
others drew their guns, and Pine stationed several officers on either
side of the corridor leading to the front door. One of them growled,
"We'll shoot the first motherfucker that comes through the door."[48]

At that moment, an arm reached in through the shattered window, squirted more lighter fluid into the room, and then threw in
another lit match. This time the match caught, and there was a whoosh
of flame. Standing only ten feet away, Pine aimed his gun at the
receding arm and (he later said) was preparing to shoot when he heard
the sound of sirens coming down Christopher Street. At two-fifty-
five A.M. Pine had sent out emergency signal 10-41—a call for help
to the fearsome Tactical Patrol Force—and relief was now rounding
the corner.[49]

The TPF was a highly trained, crack riot-control unit that had
been set up to respond to the proliferation of protests against the
Vietnam War. Wearing helmets with visors, carrying assorted weapons, including billy clubs and tear gas, its two dozen members all
seemed massively proportioned. They were a formidable sight as,
linked arm in arm, they came up Christopher Street in a wedge formation that resembled (by design) a Roman legion. In their path, the
rioters slowly retreated, but—contrary to police expectations—did
not break and run. Craig, for one, knelt down in the middle of the
street with the camera he'd retrieved from his apartment and, determined to capture the moment, snapped photo after photo of the on-
coming TPF minions.[50]

As the troopers bore down on him, he scampered up and joined
the hundreds of others who scattered to avoid the billy clubs but then
raced around the block, doubled back behind the troopers, and pelted
them with debris. When the cops realized that a considerable crowd
had simply re-formed to their rear, they flailed out angrily at anyone
who came within striking distance. But the protesters would not be
cowed. The pattern repeated itself several times: The TPF would
disperse the jeering mob only to have it re-form behind them, yelling
taunts, tossing bottles and bricks, setting fires in trash cans. When
the police whirled around to reverse direction at one point, they found
themselves face to face with their worst nightmare: a chorus line of
mocking queens, their arms clasped around each other, kicking their
heels in the air Rockettes-style and singing at the tops of their sardonic
voices:

"We are the Stonewall girls
We wear our hair in curls
We wear no underwear
We show our pubic hair . . .
We wear our dungarees
Above our nelly knees!"

It was a deliciously witty, contemptuous counterpoint to the TPF's brute force, a tactic that transformed an otherwise traditionally macho eye-for-an-eye combat and that provided at least the glimpse of a different and revelatory kind of consciousness. Perhaps that was exactly the moment Sylvia had in mind when she later said, "Something lifted off my shoulders."[51]

But the tactic incited the TPF to yet further violence. As they were badly beating up on one effeminate-looking boy, a portion of the angry crowd surged in, snatched the boy away, and prevented the cops from reclaiming him. Elsewhere, a cop grabbed "a wild Puerto Rican queen" and lifted his arm as if to club him. Instead of cowering, the queen yelled, "How'd you like a big Spanish dick up your little Irish ass?" The nonplussed cop hesitated just long enough to give the queen time to run off into the crowd.[52]

The cops themselves hardly escaped scot-free. Somebody managed to drop a concrete block on one parked police car; nobody was injured, but the cops inside were shaken up. At another point, a gold-braided police officer being driven around to survey the action got a sack of wet garbage thrown at him through the open window of his car; a direct hit was scored, and soggy coffee grounds dripped down the officer's face as he tried to maintain a stoic expression. Still later, as some hundred people were being chased down Waverly Place by two cops, someone in the crowd suddenly realized the unequal odds and started yelling, "There are only two of 'em! Catch 'em! Rip their clothes off! Fuck 'em!" As the crowd took up the cry, the two officers fled.

Before the police finally succeeded in clearing the streets—for that evening only, it would turn out—a considerable amount of blood had been shed. Among the undetermined number of people injured was Sylvia's friend Ivan Valentin; hit in the knee by a policeman's billy club, he had ten stitches taken at St. Vincent's Hospital. A teenager named Lenny had his hand slammed in a car door and lost two fingers. Four big cops beat up a young queen so badly—there is evidence that the cops singled out "feminine boys"—that she bled simultaneously from her mouth, nose, and ears. Craig and Sylvia both escaped injury (as did Jim, who had hung back on the fringe of the crowd), but so much blood splattered over Sylvia's blouse that at one point she had to go down to the piers and change into the clean clothes Gary had brought back for her.[53]

Four police officers were also hurt. Most of them sustained minor abrasions from kicks and bites, but Officer Scheu, after being hit with a rolled-up newspaper, had fallen to the cement sidewalk and broken his wrist. When Craig heard that news, he couldn't resist chuckling over what he called the "symbolic justice" of the injury. Thirteen people (including Dave Van Ronk) were booked at the Sixth Precinct, seven of them Stonewall employees, on charges ranging from harassment to resisting arrest to disorderly conduct. At three-thirty-five A.M., signal 10-41 was canceled and an uneasy calm settled over the area. It was not to last.[54]

Word of the confrontation spread through the gay grapevine all day Saturday. Moreover, all three of the dailies wrote about the riot (the *News* put the story on page one), and local television and radio reported it as well. The extensive coverage brought out the crowds, just as Craig had predicted (and had worked to achieve). All day Saturday, curious knots of people gathered outside the bar to gape at the damage and warily celebrate the implausible fact that, for once, cops, not gays, had been routed.

The police had left the Stonewall a shambles. Jukeboxes, mirrors, and cigarette machines lay smashed; phones were ripped out; toilets were plugged up and overflowing; and shards of glass and debris littered the floors. (According to at least one account, moreover, the police had simply pocketed all the money from the jukeboxes, cigarette machines, cash register, and safe.) On the boarded-up front window that faced the street, anonymous protesters had scrawled signs and slogans—THEY INVADED OUR RIGHTS, THERE IS ALL COLLEGE BOYS AND GIRLS IN HERE, LEGALIZE GAY BARS, SUPPORT GAY POWER—and newly emboldened same-gender couples were seen holding hands as they anxiously conferred about the meaning of these uncommon new assertions.[55]

True to her determination not to miss *anything*, Sylvia hadn't slept all night. Even after the crowd had dispersed and gone home, she kept walking the streets, setting garbage cans on fire, venting her pent-up anger, the black beauty still working in her, further feeding

her agitation. Later she put it this way: "I wanted to do every destructive thing I could think of to get back at those who had hurt us
over the years. Letting loose, fighting back, was the only way to get
across to straight society and the cops that we weren't going to take
their fucking bullshit any more."

Craig finally got to sleep at six A.M., but was up again within a
few hours. Like Sylvia, he could hardly contain his excitement, but
channeled it according to his own temperament—by jump-starting
organizational work. What was needed, Craig quickly decided, was
a leaflet, some crystallizing statement of what had happened and why,
complete with a set of demands for the future. And to distribute it,
he hit upon the idea of two-person teams, one man and one woman
on each, just like those he had earlier organized at Mattachine. He
hoped to have the leaflet and the teams in place by nightfall. But
events overtook him.

Something like a carnival, an outsized block party, had gotten
going by early evening in front of the Stonewall. While older, conservative chinos-and-sweater gays watched warily, and some disap-
provingly, from the sidelines, "stars" from the previous night's
confrontation reappeared to pose campily for photographs; hand-
holding and kissing became endemic; cheerleaders led the crowd in
shouts of "Gay power"; and chorus lines repeatedly belted out refrains
of "We are the girls from Stonewall."

But the cops, including Tactical Patrol Force units, were out in
force, were not amused at the antics, and seemed grim-facedly determined not to have a repeat of Friday night's humiliation. The TPF
lined up across the street from the Stonewall, visors in place, batons
and shields at the ready. When the fearless chorus line of queens
insisted on yet another refrain, kicking their heels high in the air, as
if in direct defiance, the TPF moved forward, ferociously pushing
their nightsticks into the ribs of anyone who didn't jump immediately
out of their path.

But the crowd had grown too large to be easily cowed or controlled. Thousands of people were by now spilling over the sidewalks,
including an indeterminate but sizable number of curious straights
and a sprinkling of street people gleefully poised to join any kind of
developing rampage. When the TPF tried to sweep people away from
the front of the Stonewall, the crowd simply repeated the previous
night's strategy of temporarily retreating down a side street and then
doubling back on the police. In Craig's part of the crowd, the idea
took hold of blocking off Christopher Street, preventing any vehicular

traffic from coming through. When an occasional car did try to bull-doze its way in, the crowd quickly surrounded it, rocking it back and forth so vigorously that the occupants soon proved more than happy to be allowed to retreat.

Craig was enjoying this all hugely until a taxicab edged around the corner from Greenwich Avenue. As the crowd gave the cab a vigorous rocking, and a frenzied queen jumped on top of it and started beating on the hood, Craig caught a glimpse inside and saw two terrified passengers and a driver who looked as if he was having a heart attack. Sylvia came on that same scene and gleefully cheered the queen on. But Craig realized that the cab held innocent people, not fag-hating cops, and he worked with others to free it from the crowd's grip so it could back out.

From that point on, and in several parts of the crowd simulta-neously, all hell broke loose. Sylvia's friend Marsha P. Johnson climbed to the top of a lamppost and dropped a bag with something heavy in it on a squad car parked directly below, shattering its wind-shield. Craig was only six feet away and saw the cops jump out of the car, grab some luckless soul who happened to be close at hand, and beat him badly. On nearby Gay Street, three or four cars filled with a wedding party were stopped in their tracks for a while; some-body in the crowd shouted, "We have the right to marry, too!" The unintimidated and decidedly unamused passengers screamed back, angrily threatening to call the police. That produced some laughter ("The police are already here!") and more shouts, until finally the wedding party was allowed to proceed.[56]

From the park side of Sheridan Square, a barrage of bottles and bricks—seemingly hundreds of them, apparently aimed at the police lines—rained down across the square, injuring several onlookers but no officers. Jim had returned to the Stonewall scene in the early evening; when the bottle-throwing started, he raced to the area in the back where it seemed to be coming from, and—using his experience from previous street actions—tried to persuade the bottle-tossers that they were playing a dangerous game, threatening the lives of the protesters more than those of the police.

They didn't seem to care. Jim identified them as "straight an-archist types, Weathermen types," determined "to be really butch about their anger" (unlike those "frightened sissies"), to foment as large-scale and gory a riot as possible. He thought they were possibly "crazies"—or police provocateurs—and he realized it would be inef-fective simply to say, "Stop doing this!" So, as he tells it, he tried to temper their behavior by appealing to their macho instincts, suggesting that it would be *even* braver of them to throw their bottles from the front of the line; that way, if the police, taunted by the flying glass, charged the crowd, they could bear the brunt of the attack themselves. The argument didn't wash; the bottle-throwing continued.

If Jim didn't want people actually getting hurt, he did want to feed the riot. Still smoldering from the failure of his straight friends to show up the previous night (some of his closeted left-wing gay friends, particularly the crowd at Liberation News Service, had also done nothing in response to his calls), he wanted this gay riot "to be as good as any riot" his straight onetime comrades had ever put together or participated in. And to that end, he carried with him the tools of the guerrilla trade: marbles (to throw under the contingent of mounted police that had by now arrived) and pins (to stick into the horses' flanks).

But the cops needed no additional provocation; they had been determined from the beginning to quell the demonstration, and at whatever cost in bashed heads and shattered bones. Twice the police broke ranks and charged into the crowd, flailing wildly with their nightsticks; at least two men were clubbed to the ground. The sporadic skirmishing went on until four A.M., when the police finally withdrew their units from the area. The next day, *The New York Times* insisted that Saturday night was "less violent" than Friday (even while describing the crowd as "angrier"). Sylvia, too, considered the first night "the worst." But a number of others, including Craig, thought the second night was the more violent one; that it marked "a public assertion of real anger by gay people that was just electric."[57]

When he got back to his apartment early Sunday morning, his anger and excitement still bubbling, Craig sat down and composed a one-page flyer. Speaking in the name of the Homophile Youth Movement (HYMN) that he had founded, Craig headlined the flyer GET THE MAFIA AND THE COPS OUT OF GAY BARS—a rallying cry that would have chilled Zucchi (who had earlier been reassured by co-owner Mario that the gays *only* had it in for the cops). Craig went on in the flyer to predict that the events of the previous two nights "will go down in history"; to accuse the police of colluding with the Mafia to prevent gay businesspeople from opening "decent gay bars with a healthy social atmosphere (as opposed to the hell-hole atmosphere of places typified by the Stonewall)"; to call on gay people to boycott places like the Stonewall ("The only way . . . we can get criminal elements out of the gay bars is simply to make it unprofitable for them"); and to urge them to "write to Mayor Lindsay demanding a thorough investigation and effective action to correct this intolerable situation."[58]

Using his own money, Craig printed up thousands of the flyers and then set about organizing his two-person teams. He had them out on the streets leafleting passersby by midday on Sunday. They weren't alone. After the second night of rioting, it had become clear to many that a major upheaval, a kind of seismic shift, was at hand, and brisk activity was developing in several quarters.

But not all gays were pleased about the eruption at Stonewall. Those satisfied by, or at least habituated to, the status quo preferred to minimize or dismiss what was happening. Many wealthier gays, sunning at Fire Island or in the Hamptons for the weekend, either heard about the rioting and ignored it (as one of them later put it: "No one [at Fire Island Pines] mentioned Stonewall"), or caught up with the news belatedly. When they did, they tended to characterize the events at Stonewall as "regrettable," as the demented carryings-on of "stoned, tacky queens"—precisely those elements in the gay world from whom they had long since dissociated themselves. Coming back into the city on Sunday night, the beach set might have hastened off to see the nude stage show *Oh, Calcutta!* or the film *Midnight Cowboy* (in which Jon Voight played a Forty-second Street hustler)—titillated by such mainstream daring, while oblivious or scornful of the real-life counterparts being acted out before their averted eyes.[59]

Indeed some older gays, and not just the wealthy ones, even sided with the police, praising them for the "restraint" they had shown in not employing more violence against the protesters. As one of the leaders of the West Side Discussion Group reportedly said, "How can we expect the police to allow us to congregate? Let's face it, we're criminals. You can't allow criminals to congregate." Others applauded what they called the "long-overdue" closing of what for years had been an unsightly "sleaze joint." There have even been tales that some of the customers at Julius', the bar down the street from Stonewall that had long been favored by older gays ("the good girls from the fifties," as one queen put it), actually held three of the rioters for the police.[60]

Along with Craig's teams, there were others on the streets of the Village that Sunday who had been galvanized into action and were trying to organize demonstrations or meetings. Left-wing radicals like Jim Fouratt, thrilled with the *lack* of leadership in evidence during the two nights of rioting, saw the chance for a new kind of egalitarian gay organization to emerge. He hoped it would incorporate ideas about gender parity and "rotating leadership" from the bourgeoning feminist movement and build, as well, on the long-standing struggle of the black movement against racism. At the same time, Jim and his fellow gay radicals were not interested in being subsumed any longer under anyone else's banner. They had long fought for every worthy cause other than their own, and—as the events at Stonewall had proven—without any hope of reciprocity. They felt it was time to refocus their energies on themselves.

The Mattachine Society had still another view. With its head-quarters right down the street from the Stonewall Inn, Mattachine was in 1969 pretty much the creature of Dick Leitsch, who had considerable sympathy for New Left causes but none for challenges to his leadership. Randy Wicker, himself a pioneer activist and lately a critic of Leitsch, now joined forces with him to pronounce the events at Stonewall "horrible." Wicker's earlier activism had been fueled by the notion that gays were "jes' folks"—just like straights except for their sexual orientation—and the sight (in his words) "of screaming queens forming chorus lines and kicking went against everything that I wanted people to think about homosexuals . . . that we were a bunch of drag queens in the Village acting disorderly and tacky and cheap." On Sunday those wandering by Stonewall saw a new sign on its boarded-up façade, this one printed in neat block letters:[61]

> WE HOMOSEXUALS PLEAD WITH
> OUR PEOPLE TO PLEASE HELP
> MAINTAIN PEACEFUL AND QUIET
> CONDUCT ON THE STREETS OF
> THE VILLAGE—MATTACHINE

The streets that Sunday evening stayed comparatively quiet, dominated by what one observer called a "tense watchfulness." Knots of the curious continued to congregate in front of Stonewall, and some of the primping and posing of the previous two nights was still in evidence. By Sunday, Karla Jay had heard about the riots, and she tried to get Redstockings to issue some sort of sympathetic statement. But just as Jim had failed to rally his left-wing male friends, so Karla was unable to get any gesture of support from straight radical feminists.

She went down to the Village herself for a quick look at the riot scene. But she didn't linger. She had learned during the Columbia upheaval that uninvolved bystanders could be routinely arrested and, headed for a career in academia, she didn't want that on her record. She would wait to see where the riots would lead. She had never been taken with the bar crowd, gay or lesbian, and this unsavory bunch seemed to have inadvertently *stumbled* into rebellion. She wanted to save herself for the *big* arrest, for the *real* revolution. She was sure that was coming, but not at all sure the Stonewall riots represented its imminent arrival.

The police on Sunday night seemed spoiling for trouble. "Start something, faggot, just start something," one cop repeated over and over. "I'd like to break your ass wide open." (A brave young man purportedly yelled, "What a Freudian comment, officer!"—and then scampered to safety.) Two other cops, cruising in a police car, kept yelling obscenities at passersby, trying to start a fight, and a third, standing on the corner of Christopher Street and Waverly Place, kept swinging his nightstick and making nasty remarks about "faggots."

At one A.M. the TPF made a largely uncontested sweep of the area and the crowds melted away. Allen Ginsberg strolled by, flashed the peace sign and, after seeing "Gay Power!" scratched on the front of the Stonewall, expressed satisfaction to a *Village Voice* reporter: "We're one of the largest minorities in the country—10 percent, you know. It's about time we did something to assert ourselves."[62]

By Sunday some of the wreckage inside the bar had been cleaned up, and employees had been stationed out on the street to coax patrons back in: "We're honest businessmen here. We're American-born boys. We run a legitimate joint here. There ain't nuttin' bein' done wrong in dis place. Everybody come and see." Never having been inside the Stonewall, Ginsberg went in and briefly joined the handful of dancers. After emerging, he described the patrons as "beautiful—they've lost that wounded look that fags all had 10 years ago." Deputy Inspector Pine later echoed Ginsberg: "For those of us in public morals, things were completely changed . . . suddenly they were not submissive anymore."[63]

In part because of rain, Monday and Tuesday nights continued quiet, with only occasional, random confrontations; the most notable probably came when a queen stuck a lit firecracker under a strutting, wisecracking cop, the impact causing him to land on what the queen called his "moneymaker." But Wednesday evening saw a return to something like the large-scale protest of the previous weekend. Perhaps as a result of the appearance that day of two front-page *Village Voice* articles about the initial rioting, a crowd of some thousand people gathered in the area. Trash baskets were again set on fire, and bottles and beer cans were tossed in the direction of the cops (sometimes hitting protesters instead); the action was accompanied by militant shouts of "Pig motherfuckers!" "Fag rapists!" and "Gestapo!" The TPF wielded their nightsticks indiscriminately, openly beat people up, left them bleeding on the street, and carted off four to jail on the usual charge of "harassment."[64]

That proved the last of the Stonewall riots, but when it came time only two days later for the fifth annual picket of Independence Hall, the repercussions could be clearly measured. As the originator of the Annual Reminder, Craig was again centrally involved in organizing it. But when he placed ads in *The Village Voice* to drum up interest, he got, along with some fifty recruits (half of whom were women, including two who brought along their young children), a series of ugly, threatening phone calls. The callers warned Craig that the bus he had rented to go to Philadelphia would be followed and capsized, and its occupants beaten to a pulp.

Sure enough, when the participants gathered at eight A.M. on July 4 to board the bus in front of Craig's bookstore on Mercer Street, a convertible with four "white rednecks in it brandishing baseball bats" pulled up and parked across the street. The four men simply sat there, glaring at the group in front of Craig's shop, apparently waiting for them to set off. But Craig was a step ahead of them. After he had gotten three or four of the threatening calls, he had contacted the police and had somehow convinced them to put an officer on the bus with them up to the Holland Tunnel. Then, on the other side of the tunnel, Craig managed to arrange for a New Jersey state trooper to board the bus and accompany it halfway down to Philadelphia.

The men in the convertible never followed the bus beyond Craig's bookstore. This was not, in Craig's view, because the sight of a policeman frightened them off, but because the presence of women and children took them by surprise; they had expected to see "just faggots," and as well-indoctrinated macho men felt they had to desist from a physical attack on "innocents." In any case, the bus arrived in Philadelphia without incident.

The demonstration in front of Independence Hall began in much the way it had in previous years: the group of some seventy-five people—men in suits and ties, women in dresses, despite the ninety-five-degree heat—walked silently in a circle, radiating respectability, eschewing any outward sign of anger. (Craig even kept his temper when a mean-looking man on the sidelines hissed "Suck!" in his face every time he passed by.) But the events at Stonewall had had their effect. After a half hour of marching quietly in single file, two of the women suddenly broke ranks and started to walk together, holding hands. Seeing them, Craig thought elatedly, "O-oh—that's *wonderful!*"

But Frank Kameny, the Washington, D.C., leader who had long considered himself to be in charge of the demonstration, had a quite different reaction. Back in 1966 Kameny hadn't hesitated in pulling a man from the line who had dared to appear without a jacket and wearing sneakers, and Kameny was not about to tolerate this latest infraction of his rule that the demonstration be "lawful, orderly, dignified." His face puffy with indignation and yelling, "None of that! None of that!" Kameny came up behind the two women and angrily broke their hands apart.[65]

Craig instantly hit the ceiling. When Kameny went over to talk to the two reporters who had turned up for the event (one from a Philadelphia paper and one from Reuters), Craig barged up to them and blurted out, "I've got a few things to say!" And what he said—in his own description, "ranting and raving"—was that the events in New York the previous week had shown that the current gay leadership was bankrupt, that gays were entitled to do whatever straights did in public—yes, wearing cool clothes in the heat, and, if they felt like it, holding hands too.

Kameny was furious at this unprecedented challenge to his authority, and, on different grounds, the veteran activists Barbara Gittings and Kay Tobin chided Craig for calling so much "personal attention" to himself. But, as had not been the case in previous years, many of those who had come down on the bus from New York were young people personally recruited by Craig at his bookstore. Some of them were students at NYU and, being much younger than Kameny or Gittings, had no prior movement affiliation (and no respect for what the homophile movement had accomplished). They had been energized by Stonewall, were impatient for further direct confrontation with oppressive traditions and habits—and vigorously applauded Craig's initiative.

All the way back on the bus, they argued with their recalcitrant elders for a new impetus, a new departure that would embody the defiant spirit of Stonewall. As the contention continued, it became clear to Craig that this would be the final Reminder—that a new day had dawned, which required different tactics, a different format. Yet it saddened him to think that a common enterprise of five years standing would pass from the scene without any immediate replacement in sight. And then it came to him. Why shouldn't there be an immediate replacement? Didn't the events at Stonewall themselves require commemoration? Maybe the Annual Reminder simply ought to be moved to New York—but, unlike the Reminder, be designed not as a silent plea for rights but as an overt demand for them. Craig thought of a name right then and there: Christopher Street Liberation Day.

That same July Fourth evening, New York Mattachine called a public meeting at St. John's Church on Waverly Place, designed to derail precisely the kind of rumored plans for new demonstrations and organizations that Craig had in mind. Dick Leitsch, described by one reporter as wearing a "staid brown suit" and looking like "a dependable fortyish Cartier salesclerk," told the packed crowd of two hundred (mostly male, mostly young) that it was indeed important to protest police brutality, but it was also important to remember that "the gay world must retain the favor of the Establishment, especially those who make and change the laws." Acceptance, Leitsch cautioned, "would come slowly by educating the straight community with grace and good humor and—"[66]

Leitsch was interrupted by an angry young man who stood up and yelled, "We don't want acceptance, goddamn it! We want respect!"—and he was seconded by shouts from others. Leitsch's loyal lieutenant at Mattachine, Madolin Cervantes (who was heterosexual) took the mike to call for a candlelight vigil, saying, "We should be firm, but just as amicable and sweet as—" She, too, was interrupted—this time by Jim Fouratt, who had been sitting agitatedly in the audience and had held his peace up to that point.

"*Sweet?*" Jim hollered, "Sweet! *Bullshit!* There's the stereotype homo again . . . soft, weak, sensitive! . . . That's the role society has been forcing these queens to play. . . . We have got to radicalize. . . . Be proud of what you are. . . . And if it takes riots or even guns to show them what we are, well, that's the only language that the pigs understand!"

His impassioned speech led to a wild burst of applause. Leitsch tried to reply, but Jim shouted him down: "All the oppressed have got to unite! . . . Not one straight radical group showed up at Stonewall! If it'd been a black demonstration they'd have been there. . . . We've got to work together with *all* the New Left!" By then a dozen people were on their feet, shouting encouragement. Leitsch tried to regain control of the meeting, but to no avail. "This meeting is over!"

Jim yelled, and invited all those who shared his views to follow him over to Alternate University, a loft space on Fourteenth Street and Sixth Avenue that was home to a variety of radical enterprises. (It was known to the cognoscenti as "Alternate U.") By Jim's recollection, some thirty-five or forty people followed him out of St. John's. In the reconstituted meeting at Alternate U., they began to talk about forming a new activist gay organization—talk that would soon culminate in the Gay Liberation Front.

As for "Fat Tony" Lauria, he was quick to see the handwriting on the wall. He and his partners, Mario and Zucchi, decided that with the pending investigation of corruption within the police department by a special commission, and with Stonewall now notorious, the bar could never again operate profitably. Fat Tony soon sold the Stonewall lease to Nicky de Martino, the owner of the Tenth of Always, and had the satisfaction of watching him fail quickly—even though, with the help of Ed Murphy, de Martino got some street queens to parade around in front of Stonewall with balloons for a week or two.[67]

POST-STONEWALL: 1969–70

CRAIG, JIM

Jim and Craig were not the only ones with new ideas. True, in the immediate aftermath of Stonewall, *Time* magazine went right on referring to homosexuality as "a serious and sometimes crippling maladjustment" and to the homosexual subculture as "without question shallow and unstable." And U.S. attorney Thomas Foran (who had prosecuted the Chicago Seven) gravely announced that "We've lost our kids to the freaking fag revolution."[1]

But homosexuals themselves, in a rush of suddenly released energy, and in unprecedented numbers, were newly determined to challenge those hoary stereotypes. Two days after Craig returned from the Annual Reminder, a meeting was called at the Electric Circus, the popular (and straight) night spot on Eighth Street in Greenwich Village. "If you are tired of raids, Mafia control, and checks at the front door," the flyer advertising the meeting read, "join us for a beautiful evening on Sunday night, July 6th."[2]

The organizers asked Randy Wicker to speak at the meeting in his capacity as a "premature" gay militant. Bounding to the mike in an American flag shirt and striped blue-and-white bell-bottoms, he looked for all the world like the gay equivalent of a militant Yippie. But what he said to the packed crowd of long-haired, mustachioed, hip young men and blue-jeaned, tie-dyed young women, was in a far different vein. He told them that he was appalled at what had happened at Stonewall, that "rocks through windows don't open doors," that the way to find public acceptance was not to "behave disorderly" in the streets.

But he had barely begun his windup when a heterosexual customer—apparently realizing for the first time that the Electric Circus had inexplicably been overrun by queers—began swinging wildly at anyone within reach, yelling "Faggots! Goddamn faggots!" He was subdued long enough for Wicker to say a few more words and for Dick Leitsch to get up and ask for donations from homosexuals to help replant the trees recently uprooted in a Queens public park by vigilantes trying to discourage gay cruising there. But fighting soon erupted again, and the meeting—along with the experiment in gay-straight nightlife integration—was adjourned.[3]

Dick Leitsch had no intention of ceding the foreground either to straight rowdies or to gay lefties. He blamed Craig above all others (as perhaps only an ex-lover can) for the rioting at Stonewall, and yet he wanted to harness the youthful energies of the emergent gay radicals to Mattachine's own cart. When a twenty-eight-year-old New Left gay man named Michael Brown came to see him one day, Leitsch hit upon what he felt was the ideal plan. Brown was one of those numerous radicals who were gay but had remained in the closet while working in left-wing organizations. Once a staff member in Hubert Humphrey's 1968 presidential campaign, Brown now considered himself countercultural and socialist in sympathies.[4]

He told Leitsch that the events at Stonewall had opened up the opportunity for an alliance between gays, blacks, and antiwar activists that could work to restructure American society. Leitsch told him that such expectations were unrealistic, that the maintenance of good relations—as pioneered and exemplified by Mattachine—between the homosexual community and the powers-that-be had to take priority above all other considerations. As an individual, Leitsch argued, he might feel sympathy for, say, the Black Panthers, but any overt association with them could "endanger the liaisons we have made with civil-rights organizations who disagree" with the Panthers' philosophy. In the privacy of a letter, Leitsch was blunter still: "Panthers . . . are none of our damned business, as homosexuals."[5]

But as a compromise to accommodate the young gay radicals, Leitsch set up the Mattachine Action Committee and offered Michael Brown the job of heading it. Brown warily accepted, and for a brief period did try to work within the Mattachine traces. He brought in some of his activist friends, including "Stephen Donaldson" (Bob Martin) and Martha Shelley (née Altman; she had legally changed her last name to Shelley, the nickname her first lover had given her because of the romantic poetry she wrote). Donaldson had been one of the founders in 1967 of the Student Homophile League at Columbia University and was currently involved in organizing a youth caucus bent on radicalizing NACHO—Foster Gunnison's chief base of operations—at its forthcoming August meeting.[6]

Martha Shelley had had an affair with Donaldson, had already, at age twenty-six, been president for a brief period (she decided she wasn't good at organizational work) of New York Daughters of Bilitis, and on the second night of rioting at Stonewall had stumbled on the uproar while giving two women from Boston DOB a tour of the Village. Shelley had also taken part in the antiwar protests at the 1968 Democratic National Convention in Chicago, had represented DOB at NACHO conferences, and had just come back from participating in the Annual Reminder in Philadelphia on July 4 (where the injunction to wear a skirt and be "ladylike" had seemed to her annoying and absurd).[7]

The Mattachine Action Committee sponsored two open meetings to discuss the implications of the Stonewall riots. The first, on July 9 at Freedom House at 20 West Fortieth Street, where Mattachine held its monthly lecture series, was attended by some 125 people (as well as by two police informers). Leitsch chaired the meeting, made a few introductory remarks acknowledging "the importance" of the riots, and then opened up the floor for general discussion. It proved much too tame for Brown and his friends, focusing as it did on future plans for a silent vigil in Washington Square Park—*with* the permission of the proper authorities.[8]

In the interim before the second meeting, Brown, Shelley, Jim Fouratt, and others posted notices for a demonstration in support of the Black Panther party members currently jailed in the Women's House of Detention (the huge stone prison in the heart of the West Village). Leitsch had been insistent that Mattachine *not* be associated with any action that might prove offensive to the authorities, so in order to be able to list a sponsor for the demonstration, Brown and his friends came up—in what Jim remembers as "a spontaneous eruption"—with the name Gay Liberation Front, as a way of paying homage to the liberation struggles in Algeria and Vietnam.[9]

At the Mattachine Action Committee's second meeting, Leitsch spoke against the planned rally at the Women's House of Detention, arguing instead for his own earlier suggestion of a silent vigil in Washington Square to protest continuing police harassment. Still keyed up from his earlier confrontation with Leitsch at the Mattachine gathering of June 29, Jim was in no mood for further counsels of moderation. He again jumped to his feet, heatedly insisted that gays ought to stop asking and start demanding, and challenged Leitsch to "get with the revolution." But Leitsch was unmoved, and young radicals like Jim, Michael Brown, and Martha Shelley realized that it was time to give up on Mattachine and put their energies into the nascent Gay Liberation Front.[10]

Leitsch's concern with continuing police harassment may have been narrowly conceived, but was nonetheless warranted. In the aftermath of the Stonewall riots, the police had instituted a widespread, sometimes savage crackdown. Sascha L., who had once worked briefly at Stonewall and was now on the door at the Washington Square bar, remembers walking by the Tele-Star bar about a week after the riots and telling Ed Murphy, who had gone to work there, about rumors of a pending series of raids. Murphy told him not to worry; those rumors were always in the air (perhaps secretly confident that if they had any real substance, his police buddies would tip him off in advance).[11]

Sascha shrugged and went off to work at Washington Square—not failing, on his way inside the bar, to smile coquettishly at the handsome Con Edison workers who had been digging up the street all week. (On one recent hot day, he had even jokingly plopped on the lap of another employee seated in a chair out front, and nervily waved to the Con Ed boys.)

Early that same evening, with no more than a dozen customers on the premises, Sascha spotted some forty men dressed in suits and ties coming down Third Street toward the Washington Square bar. He dashed back inside to warn the others; they barely had time to pick up the liquor and throw it into the yard behind the bar when the federal agents marched in. Brisk and businesslike, the feds used a bullhorn to tell the customers that they would all be let go, that no one would be harmed, that they were interested only in arresting employees of the bar. They then read a list of the employees' names and brandished photographs—taken, Sascha later learned, by those cute "Con Edison" boys working in the street.

A queen named Michelle saved Sascha by hugging him close and yelling at the cops, "No one—*no one!*—is going to separate me and my husband! My husband *has* to come with me!" When a cop asked Sascha his name, he gave a false one, and since he had quickly disposed of his trademark cap and eyeglasses, he got through the gauntlet without being recognized as the campy employee who had waved seductively at the Con Edison crew. Sascha hid out for the weekend and then on Monday decided to turn himself in, figuring he had to be able to work and couldn't spend his life hiding. Enid Gerling, the well-paid specialist in "springing" entrapped gay men, took Sascha's case.

When he arrived in court, he ran smack into Ed Murphy, who was covered with cuts and welts; he had bandages all over his face, his arm was fractured, and he seemed barely able to walk. It turned out Murphy had refused to let the cops into Tele-Star and they had beaten him up badly—at the instigation, Sascha later heard, of Deputy Inspector Seymour Pine, the same officer who had led the raid against Stonewall. In jail, Murphy was subsequently (so he later told Sascha) raped by a black man—again, perhaps, at the behest of the police, who had heard that he "liked niggers" and that he hung out with and protected black teenagers. When Murphy was released, he forswore (again, according to Sascha) any further cooperation with the police, and never again gave them tips or did their bidding.[12]

YVONNE, KARLA

Yvonne had been upstate at the country house she shared in Rowe, Massachusetts, when the events at Stonewall began to unfold, and it was two days before she had any news of the rioting. Her initial reaction was a mix of exhilaration and fear. "Uh-oh," she thought, "here comes the Gestapo, beating people up. And winning. Being able to just crush people . . ." Her style, as always, was to stay aloof, to warily reconnoiter just a little longer—not primarily out of fear of the police, but from uncertainty about whether and where, in the ranks of the protesters, a hard-drinking black lesbian would find a genuine welcome.

Karla had been initially disdainful of the "little penny-ante thing" going on at Stonewall; to her it was just another all-male squabble with the prize nothing more than the right to lead an unhampered bar life—a life she scorned. But then she got wind of the effort afoot to form a Gay Liberation Front—men *and* women working together to produce broad social change. Now that *did* interest her. When she heard that a series of open meetings were scheduled for late July at

Alternate U.—with which she was already familiar from her radical-feminist work—she decided to attend.

What she found were a number of suddenly visible young gays and lesbians who, like herself, had had experience in prior radical struggles. Martha Shelley, Jim Fouratt, and Michael Brown had marched for black rights and against the Vietnam War; Susan "Silverwoman" had been active in various feminist groups; Lois Hart had been involved with Timothy Leary and was a follower of the mystic Meher Baba; Ron Ballard was an avowed Marxist, John O'Brien a sometime member of the Young Socialist Alliance, and Pete Wilson an adherent of the League for Sexual Freedom. Though they had come out for all these causes, few of these radical gays had revealed their sexuality to their co-activists.[13]

Jim Fouratt, it is true, had made his way in the political left without ever explicitly *denying* that he was a gay man. But he had never explicitly affirmed it, either; and so the possibility could be ignored or disbelieved. And Jim, if anything, had gained his left-wing credentials *less* anonymously than most radical young gays, who had often made a point of dating the opposite gender and had steered carefully clear of tipping their actual sexual preference. They had had little choice—that is, if they wanted to join forces with others who shared their passionate concern for social change. The straight men who dominated the antiwar and black civil rights struggles had persistently condescended to heterosexual women, treating them essentially as bed partners or coffee-makers. Gay men and lesbians had been beyond the pale.

When these young gay and lesbian radicals now flocked to join the Gay Liberation Front, they brought with them a rich set of insights from their prior involvements: from the black civil rights movement came an awareness of the inequities of American life; from the women's movement, consciousness of sexism and the profoundly important idea that the personal is the political, that one's experience *mattered*; from the antiwar struggle, the revelation that the government operated as a bulwark of conformity and privilege; from the countercultural revolution, the injunction to reject all received authority, to "do it now, to be what you want to be." They had learned much in making everybody else's revolution; now they would apply that learning to making their own.

Karla responded to the Gay Liberation Front with immediate enthusiasm. The message articulated in the first issue of *Come Out!*, the GLF paper, that "we are going to transform the society at large through the open realization of our own consciousness," was something she had learned in her Redstockings group—but this time around, the message was devoid of any overtones of homophobia. Consciousness-raising was, from nearly the beginning, a central feature of GLF, and Karla, familiar with the process, joined with Lois Hart and others in explaining—for not everyone in GLF had been a left-wing activist—that the process of self-realization that would emerge from speaking freely and honestly to other gays in the protected atmosphere of a consciousness-raising session would ramify outward, that speaking truth would end by cleansing and reconstituting the society at large.

Karla felt "like the religious fanatic who constantly searches for just the 'right' spiritual base—and is astounded to actually find it." Redstockings had come close, but GLF seemed to have the same devotion to substantive social change, and without any attendant nervousness over lesbianism. The women who turned up for the early GLF meetings—only some half dozen in a sea of fifty men—were no more into butch or femme self-presentations (which Karla deplored) than had been the women in Redstockings; but Karla had never been a separatist, had never felt the need for women to struggle apart from men—and in GLF radical women and men seemed determined on struggling *together*.

GLF appealed to Karla's millenarian side. She could be hardheadedly practical, but she was also strongly committed to the notion that the corrupt world should—and *could*—be cleansed. She shared with GLF the optimism essential for sustained political work: the bedrock, magical belief that if one took an action, consequences, *good* consequences, would follow, and the conditions of life would be transformed.

Karla felt she had finally come home, and she plunged into GLF with all of her formidable energy.

FOSTER, CRAIG, JIM

As GLF plunged ebulliently ahead in the early summer of 1969, Foster Gunnison was toiling away at the yeoman work of preparing for the August 1969 national conference. If GLF's natural habitat was heady abstraction, Foster was never happier than when dealing with the minutia of organizational work. As head of the Credentials Committee, he had a thousand matters to attend to and he fluttered over them with chipper, efficient enthusiasm. "It's one hell of a job running this operation," he wrote Bill Kelley of Mattachine Midwest. "I enjoy it . . . [but] hate to think of what it will be when we get up to 100 or 150 organizations (which of course we all nonetheless want)."[14]

In the wake of the Stonewall riots, it was clear that the conference could not proceed with business as usual. For a time, it was not entirely clear that it could proceed at all. The previous year's meeting in Chicago had not gone well. Some progress could be claimed for the 1968 convention: the name North American Conference of Homophile Organizations (NACHO), frequently used informally, had been officially adopted as a replacement for North American Planning Conference; an executive committee had been created to carry out business between conventions; a Homosexual Bill of Rights had been passed and—in a resolution proposed by Kameny and Gittings—the motto "Gay is good" had been adopted as NACHO's official slogan in an effort "to replace a wishy-washy negativism toward homosexuality with a firm no-nonsense positivism."[15]

These were genuine accomplishments, yet the close of the 1968 conference had seen a torrent of complaint: DOB (too "hidebound" in the view of Shirley Willer, its ex-president, to agree to demonstrations and the like) announced that it was pulling out of NACHO for good; Bill Beardemphl and Larry Littlejohn from San Francisco's SIR (the country's largest homophile organization) had grumbled that "no action program had been discussed" and had implied that their further participation was in doubt; others had complained about the protracted speechifying, the continuing rigidity of Foster's Credentials Committee in screening applicant organizations, the scant progress in creating genuine unity, and the continuing absence of Mattachine New York. "We must be doing something wrong," Arthur Warner, an ally of Dick Leitsch's, had groused, "if SIR, the largest organization, was unhappy and Mattachine New York, the second largest, was not even present."[16]

In March 1969, William Wynne ("Marc Jeffers"), the NACHO chair (and founding member of Kansas City's Phoenix Society), felt it necessary to assert in his interim report that "NACHO is not dead but very much alive and kicking." But no funds were available to cover travel expenses, and at the last minute, the meeting place had to be shifted from Houston to Kansas City because the Promethean

Society, the small homophile group in Houston, had been unable to make the needed arrangements.[17]

Some forty delegates—all of them white and only half a dozen women—representing some twenty homophile groups gathered at the Bellerive Hotel in Kansas City from August 23 through August 31. Each organization had an equal number of votes (five), despite the fact that some of them—including Foster's own Institute of Social Ethics—were essentially one-person organizations. This alone led to anger and conflict—to charges that a small number of "Kamenyites" were unfairly perpetuating their control over NACHO.[18]

But far more pronounced conflict came from what Foster and others would call GLF "infiltration." Initially, the dispute centered on Stephen Donaldson. He had earlier helped to form within NACHO a "Young Turks" group, which had been active in the 1967 and 1968 conferences. Foster had gotten to know and like Donaldson during those two prior conferences, even while being "continually irritated with him," and even though he acknowledged that Donaldson's general reputation for being "devious" and "manipulative" was well deserved.[19]

Donaldson chaired the NACHO "Committee on Youth," which at its meeting of August 28—right at the midpoint of the conference—unanimously adopted "A Radical Manifesto." The twelve-point document closely reflected the views of the GLF chapters proliferating across the country. It linked the homophile struggle to that of other minorities, declaring support for "the black, the feminist, the Spanish-American, the Indian, the hippie, the young, the student, the worker, and other victims of oppression and prejudice." It identified the "enemy" as "an implacable, repressive governmental system," along with "much of organized religion, business and medicine," and declared that these negative forces would never be moved by appeals to reason and justice, "but only by power and force." The manifesto further insisted that homosexuals develop a life-style and aesthetic that were independent of and made no reference to, heterosexual mores. And it specifically rejected "the insane war in Vietnam," refusing all complicity with it and opposing any attempt by the gay movement to work for security clearances for homosexuals—which had been a long-standing homophile project.[20]

In both tone and content, the manifesto represented a significant departure from NACHO's earlier posture. The Stonewall riots had indeed sparked a new mood. Yet they had not—as GLF radicals sometimes insisted—invented either gay pride or gay protest. Part of what outraged homophile old-timers like Foster Gunnison about GLF *was* its political platform; but antagonism also resulted from the seeming presumption of the militant young that nothing significant or worthy had preceded their own efforts.

As a man of scholarly instincts, Foster knew (and had so written in his pamphlet, "An Introduction to the Homophile Movement") that the homosexual liberation movement had roots deep in the nineteenth century—in the pioneering publications of the German scholar Karl Heinrich Ulrichs and the German-Hungarian writer Karoly Maria Kertbeny—and had continued in the early twentieth, with Magnus Hirschfeld's Scientific Humanitarian Committee in Berlin. Not even militant rhetoric and confrontational tactics were entirely new; Frank Kameny, among others, had been spitting bullets for half a dozen years.

East Coast parochialism further fanned the generational flames. It had been on the West Coast, after all, that the Mattachine Society had been formed, and where—for more than a decade before Stonewall—a score of publications, organizations, legal challenges, and militant actions had taken place. (And, beginning with the mid-sixties, Chicago and a few other midwestern cities had seen comparable developments.)

But if the Stonewall riots did not *begin* the gay revolution (as East Coasters, younger gays, and the national media have been wont to claim), it remains true that those riots became a symbolic event of international importance—a symbol of such potency as to serve, ever since 1969, as a motivating force and rallying cry. There was enough glory for both coasts, the hinterland, and several generations—though not many could see it in 1969.

But if Foster was outraged at the radical agenda and attitude, he was also soft-hearted. He could not bear to reject young Donaldson (who, among other things, had interrupted Foster's decades-old celibacy when the two shared a room at a NACHO conference). As dislike of Donaldson's arrogance mounted, Foster continued to plead his case with detractors like Barbara Gittings, characterizing him as "a sort of diamond in the rough" despite his "tendencies toward arbitrariness and manipulation." Indeed, after the 1969 conference elected Foster treasurer of NACHO, leading him to decline to continue as chair of the Credentials Committee, he successfully pushed Donaldson for the job—even while declaring that "it would crush me if Steve used his committee to promote the radical views that he holds."[21]

In the postconference period, Foster did try to remain scrupulously fair about those "radical views"; it was his nature to be fair. At one point he even suggested that GLF "could be an asset" to the older homophile movement, could inject it with "heavy doses of militancy" that might profitably "shake things up a bit . . . maybe substitute a demonstration or two, or even an occasional riot, in place of paper resolutions and positions on this or that." In the months following the NACHO conference, Foster even traveled down from his home in Hartford to sit in on several GLF meetings in New York City in order to form a firsthand opinion of the group.[22]

But that was Foster stretching to the outer limit of his open-mindedness—and the stretch soon slackened. Too much, temperamentally and philosophically, weighed against his ability to accommodate himself to the GLF agenda. Once his feelings against GLF solidified, he summed up his objections in three parts: "rudeness in personal behavior; resentment against authority and systematic procedure"; and involvement with other minority groups and their "alien issues." The most dangerous of the three, Foster felt, was the feeling that "if the homosexual is going to make any progress he must ally his groups with every other minority group in the country" (or rather, every minority group "with a strong leftist bent"), and the corollary view that if the homosexual is to make any progress, "the entire existing social/political/economic establishment must be overthrown —possibly with force."[23]

But it was not a matter of the homophile veterans simply wanting to confine their goals to civil rights and being unable to conceive of any strategy other than apologetics or earnest appeals for acceptance. In the month before the NACHO convention, for example, Foster had drawn up a proposed set of "aims and purposes" for the organization that did include "the firm establishment in society of the homosexual as a first class citizen," but went considerably beyond civil rights in asserting that "the unqualified acceptance by society of homosexuality as a wholly natural personal trait, and a highly valued expression of human love" was "the chief over-all long-range aim of the movement."[24]

Moreover, Foster opposed the notion that heterosexuality was somehow the norm "by which all other relationships must be judged." He urged homosexuals "to expose themselves for what they are, and to refrain from withdrawing from heterosexual society"—to aim instead at the "free and open public expression of homosexual affections." And in the name of these goals, Foster declared himself in favor of "radical-militant tactics," including confrontations, street demonstrations, "blatant and open hard-hitting assaults on social institutions practicing or fomenting discrimination," and even welcomed, "where called for," riots and violence.[25]

Foster's antagonism was to "disorderly" procedures and "alien" (nonhomophile) goals. The dangers (as he saw them) of anarchistic methods and "extraneous" involvement in other causes were made manifest at the November 1–2, 1969, meeting of ERCHO, the Eastern Regional Conference of Homophile Organizations. ERCHO was one of three regional divisions of NACHO, and far more active than the two others, the Midwest and Far West conferences. Craig Rodwell and Jim Fouratt were both centrally involved with what happened at the November ERCHO meeting, and although Foster would soon work closely and affectionately with Craig, he would never forgive Jim Fouratt for *his* behavior at the conference.[26]

Craig had some hope of utilizing ERCHO as the conduit for the planned Christopher Street Liberation Day March in June, on which he had already been working. At the same time, he was deeply sympathetic with GLF's championing of other minority causes (and would himself soon march in a Black Panther demonstration), and he happily stocked GLF flyers in his bookstore. Yet his sympathy was ambivalent. When he went to GLF meetings he felt "thrilled at the energy level, at the numbers of women present, and at the obvious dignity and pride at being lesbians and gay men—something which hadn't ever been seen before."

Yet he never developed any strong allegiance to GLF. The lengthy discussions, in which everyone was encouraged to vent at length, turned him off—especially since the sought-for consensus often proved elusive and the meetings failed to produce the kind of clear-cut decisions Craig temperamentally required. Besides, the "rhetorical stuff" bored him, especially the "dialectical arguments," the private "terminology and language" spouted by committed socialists like John Lauritsen and John O'Brien (who with a few others soon withdrew into the Red Butterfly, a gay Marxist study group). Craig, in turn, despite his passion and his extraordinary record for radicalism within Mattachine, tended to be viewed in GLF as that most unhip of creatures—a Midwestern Christian Scientist, the essential square.[27]

Due to attend the November 1969 ERCHO conference as head

of his own organization, HYMN, Craig obligingly made it possible
for half a dozen staunch GLF partisans (including Lois Hart and Jim
Fouratt) to attend as well. Craig and Jim had put their heads together
and found a loophole in the ERCHO procedural rules that allowed
any member organization to bring representatives of other organizations as guests. On behalf of HYMN, Craig forthwith invited the
GLFers, furnishing them with HYMN badges for accreditation.

The November ERCHO conference took place in the immediate
aftermath of the October 15 Moratorium, when millions of Americans
had stopped business as usual to register their disapproval of American
policy in Vietnam, and just before the gigantic November 15 Mobi-
lization would convene in Washington, D.C., to protest the war's
continuation. It was an apocalyptic time. President Nixon had been
secretly and mercilessly bombing the neutral country of Cambodia
for more than six months, Vice President Agnew had been denouncing
the "effete snobs" and "small cadres of professional protesters" who
had refused to hail the massacre of hundreds of thousands as a triumph
for democracy, and in early December, the Chicago police would
invade Black Panther headquarters and kill its state chairman, Fred
Hampton, in his bed.

The student left had recently divided into antagonistic splinter
groups, and the 1969 SDS national convention would be its last.
Several of the new factions employed revolutionary rhetoric and talked
increasingly of armed struggle, and the Weatherman faction had, just
three weeks before the ERCHO convention, embarked on its Days
of Rage action in Chicago, smashing through the streets of the Loop
and the Gold Coast and confronting the police, who shot six, beat
dozens and arrested 250. Less than five months later, a Weatherman
cell in Greenwich Village would blow itself sky-high in its Eleventh
Street townhouse bomb factory.

It was in this riven, overheated national climate that the ERCHO
convention opened on November 1, 1969. The GLF contingent was
in no mood for moderation, convinced more than ever that to compromise with evil was to collaborate with it. On their side, many of
the older homophile delegates were more inclined than ever to view
anything other than moderation as destructive extremism. The confrontation between the two began when some of the conference participants decided to question the legitimacy of the GLF accreditation,
and to pose a few pointed questions to their delegation. Did they
regard themselves as revolutionaries? Were they prepared to work for
their ideas within the frame of parliamentary procedures? Did they

consider themselves Good Americans, or were they bent on destroying the country's basic institutions? Jim Fouratt, experienced in politics and trained as an actor, took on the role of chief spokesperson for the group. He characterized the questions as "too insulting" to merit a direct response, and substituted instead a forceful argument in behalf of the GLF agenda. His antagonists promptly dubbed him "Goldilocks," yet to his critics' surprise—and Jim's—his remarks generated considerable applause.[28]

Indeed, Jim and the other GLFers managed to dominate the ERCHO convention to an unexpected degree. They did so with the help of Student Homophile League delegates from Columbia, Cornell, and NYU, and a scattering of radicals (like Martha Shelley of DOB) who were serving as representatives from older homophile organizations. Together they convened a "radical caucus," drew up a set of resolutions calling, among other things, for support of the Black Panthers, the striking West Coast grape pickers, and the Chicago Eight (one of whom was Abbie Hoffman), then under indictment for conspiracy. Debate on those resolutions took up so much convention time that Arthur Warner of New York Mattachine, one of many outraged old-guarders, accused the GLF delegates of foisting "by questionable parliamentary tactics" a platform involving matters "not even remotely pertinent to the homophile movement."

Warner focused his anger as much on Craig as on Jim, characterizing Craig as the owner of a bookstore which "already serves as general field headquarters for every revolutionary gay in the New York area," and denouncing his proposal for a demonstration on the last Sunday in June to commemorate the Stonewall riots as itself "revolutionary," as little more than a call for *new* riots. Yet Warner and the other delegates from New York Mattachine found themselves in a minority in their opposition to the commemorative march; and to their horror, several other resolutions presented by Jim and his friends (including a call to homosexuals to participate in protests against the Vietnam War, and a denial of the right of educational, religious, and governmental institutions to "define and limit sexuality") found, in diluted form, some favor with the convention—leading a majority of the delegates to dissociate themselves from the resolutions.[29]

Foster was if anything even more horrified than Arthur Warner at the "unbelievable crudeness, rudeness, and vulgarity" of the GLF delegates. A few days after the convention, he wrote Bill Kelley, the

NACHO activist in Chicago, that the ERCHO meeting had been a "disaster"; it had been "invaded," he wrote, by "radical, revolutionary, anarchistic (& I think communist) GLF." He thought Lois Hart "was the most insidious of the lot" ("an intellectual shyster if I ever saw one"), but he also condemned as a "brawl" ("Wild. Chaotic. Awful") Jim Fouratt's "up in your face" confrontation with Madolin Cervantes (during which Jim had yelled that she, a heterosexual MSNY delegate, was not qualified to comment in any way on homosexuality).[30]

Jim acknowledges that he and the other GLFers were so strident that the old-timers felt as if they had been literally assaulted. He and his friends had no patience with counsels of moderation and no appreciation for the work previously done, against great odds, to bring the gay movement to its current level of visibility. "We wanted to *end* the homophile movement" is how Jim later put it. "We wanted *them* to join *us* in making a gay revolution." And he adds, with retrospective compassion, that "we were a nightmare to them. They were committed to being nice, acceptable status quo Americans, and we were not; we had no interest at all in being acceptable."

Bill Kelley, himself sympathetic to at least part of the GLF agenda, apparently admonished Foster for his vehemence against the young radicals. In reply, Foster reassured Kelley that he was not "a 'reactionary.' . . . I fear you may suspect I'm something of a fascist. NO—I'm just as liberal as you are on most of these social issues. A few (like the Vietnam war) I am 'on the fence' about (i.e. undecided). But I do object strongly to injection of these other issues (eg. Black Panthers . . . grape pickers . . . and so on into our homophile cause —especially when I know that they are being injected less for a sincere belief in them than for an attempt to overthrow the establishment & the government lock-stock-&-barrel, as well as for ulterior purposes such as anarchy & communism. But even without these ulterior motives I still object to involving us in external issues. We have *enough* problems just finding agreement among ourselves on strictly homosexual issues."[31]

In claiming to "know" that the motives of Jim and the other GLFers were "insincere," Foster was substituting personal distrust for proof—even though Jim would have agreed with Foster's contention that he and his friends were intent on doing away with current institutional arrangements and their established inequities. But Foster, too, felt misunderstood. He insisted that he was not the knee-jerk reactionary GLF claimed he was, and he tried to salvage his middle-of-the-road credentials by drawing a distinction between militancy, which he said he favored, and "subversion," which he declared he would "forever oppose." He had been "thrilled," he asserted, with the Stonewall "uprising," but that didn't mean he felt the social order was so rotted with inequities that it deserved the wholesale attack GLF and other "revolutionary" groups had launched on it.[32]

After attending a few GLF meetings at the Church of the Holy Apostles in New York City, Foster was honest enough to admit that GLF members were *not* united behind a single revolutionary program. This discovery, he subsequently wrote in a report on GLF to various homophile leaders, was "a pleasant surprise"—but not pleasant enough to negate his fears.[33]

He continued to disapprove of GLF's lack of structure, continued to conspiratorially suspect that behind the loose leadership arrangements lay "a cohesive manipulating force," a subversive, not merely militant, direction. And (like Craig) he found the free-flowing discussion during the GLF meetings "chaotic," an obstacle to making unified decisions. So if Foster had discovered "some normal people" in GLF whose presence held out "some faint hope for the group as a worthy addition to ERCHO or NACHO," on the whole he thought the odds were stacked against such a positive outcome. For one thing, he had heard ERCHO denounced during GLF meetings as "a meaningless, non-existent, non-entity . . . where people got together and did nothing." For another, he simply saw what in his mind were too many "Marxian theorists, assorted crackpots and obvious headcases."[34]

Foster's "report" somehow got leaked to GLF, and he got two blistering letters from Bob Kohler (a GLF mainstay, and the friend and protector of Sylvia Rivera and other street queens). In reply, Foster retreated somewhat, claiming that his hostility had really been aimed at the "shocking" behavior of the GLF contingent at the recent ERCHO conference. He insisted to Kohler that he and other homophile leaders did feel sympathy for many of the causes GLF championed ("though I may not be actively involved in them"), but didn't like "being told what causes I am going to support," and felt strongly, moreover, that the homophile movement needed to focus exclusively on homophile issues. (Which was precisely the ground on which a significant number of members would themselves defect from GLF a few months later in order to found the Gay Activists Alliance, an organization devoted solely to achieving gay rights.)[35] Bending over backwards to be (or to appear) fair, Foster concluded his letter to Kohler by "urging that there is no one right road to heaven—let a hundred flowers bloom. . . . Only time will tell" whether the ERCHO or the GLF strategy was the more valuable.

Unlike most of his adversaries, Foster could indeed be open-minded on many subjects. But in fact he had long since concluded that the emergence of GLF would prove destructive to the moderate homophile organizations to which he had devoted his energies. And in the months following the 1969 ERCHO conference, signs began to proliferate that the homophile movement was indeed succumbing to a combination of attack from without and discontent within. Arthur Warner, for one, continued to wage his longstanding war against Frank Kameny's leadership in NACHO and ERCHO. Foster characterized Warner's attacks as a "personal vendetta," but a serious disagreement about how to change the law did underlie the antipathy. Kameny wanted to bring discrimination suits at every level and to pursue them all with utmost vigor, whereas Warner argued that "bad cases make bad law"—insisting that *his* legal committee had to pass on the viability of all pending suits. Though Kameny, especially in the heat of argument, outstripped Warner in abrasive omniscience, Warner's outsized tantrums were legendary.[36]

Warner, in the past, had often denounced ERCHO for "wallowing" in "sterile mediocrity," but now he found others echoing that view—if not for his reasons. A number of ERCHO delegates had, after all, supported the GLF resolutions presented at the recent convention (albeit in modified form), and homophile activists like Scoop Phillips of Kansas City raised their voices in the postconvention period to insist that NACHO "does need some radicalization" and that it was "better to die swiftly in the quicksand than starve to death in the bush."

But attrition was in fact to be NACHO and ERCHO's fate. And as the homophile movement began to fall apart, Foster's own health declined in tandem. It started with a series of episodes in which his heart pounded and his body spasmed; then one night he felt suddenly short of breath, started to tremble, and went to the Hartford hospital, convinced he was having a heart attack. But the doctors' verdict was "cumulative nervous tension." They put Foster on medication and advised him to reduce stress in his life.

That was easier said than done. Foster felt his "heart was breaking." Here were these "wild-eyed kids" in GLF thinking "they are going to take over America and the world," when in fact, Foster was convinced, they "will trigger a right-wing reaction in this country that will sink all of our ships together."[37]

On December 21, 1969, nineteen people gathered in writer Arthur Bell's Greenwich Village apartment to put the finishing touches on the constitution for a new organization, the Gay Activists Alliance. Dissent from GLF's philosophy and tactics had been present almost from that group's inception, but now, with the birth of GAA, it took on institutional form. In the constitution GAA drew up that day, it declared itself "completely and solely dedicated"—unlike GLF, with its concern for minority oppression of all kinds—to securing basic rights for homosexuals. To achieve those rights, GAA would prove entirely willing to take to the streets and employ militant, confrontational tactics, but would do so in order to win acceptance for gays within the country's institutional structure—not to topple or transform that structure, as was GLF's intent.[38]

Jim Fouratt thought GAA mistaken in its one-issue politics, Karla Jay denounced it as "a cop-out—as much too interested in mainstream establishment stuff," and Craig Rodwell saw the organization—at least in comparison with GLF—as "rather conservative." But Foster Gunnison, not surprisingly, thought better of GAA than he had of GLF. And as GAA grew in strength over the next two years, he expressed pleasure that it (and not GLF) was "top dog"; in Foster's view GAA had "earned its position—and well deserves it." The new organization, after all, did share the older homophile view, which Foster exemplified, that gay groups must focus on gay rights to the exclusion of all else, and must conduct their affairs in orderly, Robert's-Rules fashion. But that is not to say that the reformers of GAA merely continued the policies of the homophile movement, elbowing to the sidelines, to their mutual relief, the "dangerous" radicals of GLF.[39]

GAA was much more assertive than NACHO or ERCHO had been in affirming the validity (and health) of the gay life-style, even as it denied that homosexuals were, except for the little matter of sexual orientation, carbon-copy heterosexuals. Where the homophile movement had stressed the importance of gays acting "responsibly" in order to win mainstream acceptance, GAA emphasized building pride in subcultural *difference* and organizing a political bloc to *demand* equal rights.[40]

The demands were imaginatively packaged in the form of "zaps"—lightning-quick confrontations with offending institutions, organizations or individuals. Mayor Lindsay got his at a Metropolitan Museum of Art reception; dressed in appropriate dinner jackets, GAA members joined the reception line to greet the mayor and when he extended his hand, grasped—and held—it long enough to insistently ask, "What are you going to do about civil rights for homosexuals, Mr. Mayor?" Within the year, GAA had, among other actions, in-filtrated the *Dick Cavett Show*; carried off a series of disruptions at the various branch offices of Household Finance for refusing loans to known homosexuals; demonstrated at the county clerk's office to de-mand the right to marry; and traveled to Long Island, Hartford, and Albany to protest gay-bashing and employment discrimination and to lobby for a statewide gay-rights bill.[41]

A little more than a year after its inception, GAA decided to lease an abandoned firehouse in the SoHo district of Manhattan, south of Greenwich Village. The Firehouse quickly became the political and cultural headquarters for the gay movement in New York, its spacious quarters a beehive of assorted activities. On Saturday nights, the large meeting hall would be converted into a dance floor and the packed revels (an average crowd of fifteen hundred per dance) become a cherished alternative to the bar scene, drawing the apolitical as well as the committed, and attracting both men and women (though men were always in a decided majority).

YVONNE

Yvonne Flowers was among the many venturing down to the Fire-house who had never previously belonged to a liberationist organi-zation (though she had participated in any number of black and left-oriented demonstrations). For her, the experience proved both confirmatory and surprising. The absence of black faces confirmed her earlier sense that the gay movement had not succeeded in drawing—or perhaps had not even tried to draw—people of color. Yet at the same time, she was surprised to see at least a scattering of blacks present.

The numbers were small, yet marked some advance over the homophile movement. With the exception of "Ernestine Eppinger," who had participated in the Washington, D.C., picketing during the mid-sixties, no black person had played a prominent role in Mattachine, DOB, NACHO, or ERCHO, though many white members of those groups had been sympathetic to the black civil rights struggle, and Frank Kameny, for one, had always credited it with centrally shaping his own ideas. Ernestine Eppinger herself believed that "the homophile movement [was] more open to Negroes than, say, a lot of churches," but she acknowledged that few blacks had felt comfortable enough actually to join. Once, in the early sixties, Yvonne had gone with another black woman to a DOB meeting on Manhattan's Lower East Side, and had been repelled by it. The white women reacted to the black women's presence first with shock, then with a supercilious casualness that was at least as offensive. Yvonne never returned; "I can't be here," she decided, "with all these white girls."[42]

With the advent of GLF and GAA, the gay world became *somewhat* more integrated (sexually, gay men had long crossed racial and class lines). Even so, gay blacks within the movement felt sufficiently at odds with it—perceiving their needs to be distinct enough, their perspectives ignored enough—to form their own Third World Caucus. Of course, in the feminist movement in these years as well, women of color were few and the issue of racism was muted. Yvonne Flowers was hardly alone in the late sixties or early seventies in feeling caught between the endemic sexism and homophobia of the black struggle and the pervasive racism in the feminist and gay ones.[43]

Yvonne found just enough black faces to keep her coming back to the Firehouse with some frequency. Before long, she and a few other black lesbians, including Luvinia Pinson (whom she had known before) and Donna Allegra, were getting together every Sunday as the Black Lesbian Caucus. "There were never enough people to really get a structure," Yvonne recalls, "to have officers or dues, but it was good in that we could at least talk to each other without being in a bar scene, and talk about racism within the gay community." None of them, it turned out, felt comfortable being in the Firehouse—which they called "a white boy's playhouse"—and since few of the women showed up on a regular basis, the group soon stopped meeting. Still, they *had* formed a loose network and within a year, they would again try to form an organization.

S Y L V I A

Given how fully Sylvia had involved herself in the Stonewall riots, she was by comparison detached in the months following. The reasons were mostly circumstantial, the result of living and working in New Jersey. Cut off from her usual contacts, she had heard nothing about the sudden emergence of GLF, or the subsequent formation of GAA. Bumping into Marsha P. Johnson on the street one day, she listened in amazement to Marsha's excited talk of the GLF meetings she had started to attend. Then, soon after, Sylvia spotted a copy of *Gay Power* on a newsstand (the biweekly had started publishing on September 15, 1969, about six weeks before *Gay* and GLF's *Come Out!* also hit the stands), and realized something really *had* happened following the riots, and that she had to find out exactly what.

Sylvia and another queen, Josie, both of them in full face makeup, descended on a GAA meeting. Sylvia was given some static at the door, but managed to get inside, where she and Josie decided to sit in the back of the meeting on the unlikely chance they would be inconspicuous. Looking around the room, Sylvia "didn't see a queen in there," and she and Josie started talking loudly in Spanish about how this didn't seem like exactly the place for them. A head turned around in the row directly in front: "I understand some of what you girls are saying, because I'm Italian." "Ooh my," thought Sylvia to herself, "I do think this chile is one of ours." She was. Her name was Bebe Scarpi, she was an undergraduate at Queens College (which she denied choosing for its name), and she assured Sylvia and Josie that they *were* in the right place, that "the sisters were welcome." Bebe was to become a fast friend of Sylvia's (and later, as a transvestite, would sit on the first board of the National Gay Task Force).[44]

But Bebe wasn't entirely right about "the sisters being welcome." They were and they weren't, depending on whom you asked and which night you asked them. Arthur Bell, one of the founders of GAA, observed that "the general membership is frightened of Sylvia and thinks she's a troublemaker. They're frightened by street people." A Hispanic street queen's transgressive being produced automatic alarm: Sylvia was from the wrong ethnic group, from the wrong side of the tracks, wearing the wrong clothes—managing single-handedly and simultaneously to embody several frightening, overlapping categories of Otherness. By her mere presence, she was likely to trespass against *some* encoded middle-class white script, and could count on being constantly patronized when not being summarily excluded. If someone was not shunning her darker skin or sniggering at her passionate, fractured English, they were deploring her rude anarchism as inimical to order or denouncing her sashaying ways as offensive to womanhood. Sylvia's ability to represent herself in unconventional form had enabled her to have a life, but it had also made her a haunting affront to those inhabiting standardized shapes.[45]

In the years ahead, Sylvia would often feel rejected and only occasionally welcome. But she stuck it out. Taking immediately to confrontational politics, she jumped into "actions" full blast, feeling hurt when the chino set tried to shunt her to the sidelines, but rarely feeling discouraged. *No one*, she quickly decided, was going to prevent her from fighting for her own cause.

And just like Yvonne Flowers, Sylvia found enough friends and allies to keep her coming back, at least for a few years. In GAA Arthur Evans could always be counted on to defend her ("many times Arthur and me sat down and talked heart-to-heart"), and in both GLF and GAA she met some lesbians (like Kay Tobin and Judy Rathill) who accepted and respected her. Never known for being tactful, Sylvia told Judy Rathill on their first meeting, "You look like one of those tough old dykes I used to hang out with up at the Hilltop in Harlem." Judy laughed, assured her that she was "not a dyke, but a woman," and opened up her apartment to Sylvia and her friends whenever they had no other place to stay. Sylvia affectionately remembers how she and Judy "raised each other's consciousness."

But the angry denunciation of Sylvia by GAA's Jean O'Leary (subsequently cochair of the National Gay Task Force) for "parodying" womanhood was more typical of how movement women responded to her. Later, at the 1973 Gay Pride Rally, O'Leary would attempt to keep Sylvia from speaking, and the angry public confrontation that resulted would lead Sylvia, as an aftermath, to attempt suicide and to drop out of the movement. And many years after that, O'Leary would express deep regret at her attitude: "Looking back, I find this so embarrassing because my views have changed so much since then. I would never pick on a transvestite now."[46]

O'Leary's denunciation of Sylvia was atypically heated. A more standard exchange between Sylvia and a GLF woman went (according to Sylvia) something like this:

WOMAN: Why do you like to wear women's clothing?

SYLVIA: Because I feel very comfortable. Do you like wearing pants?

WOMAN: Yeah.

SYLVIA: Well, I like wearing a skirt. What can I tell you? I like to feel flowing. You like to be confined. That's your problem.

Karla Jay was one of the GLF women who liked Sylvia personally. But even Karla felt ambivalent about her. She, Sylvia, and Marsha often had fun together; they would be part of a group that piled into a car after a GLF meeting to go "liberate" an all–gay male or all-lesbian bar. And in transit, Sylvia and Marsha would feel Karla up in the backseat; it wasn't sexual—it was comparative shopping. They would feel themselves up at the same time, judging how they measured up against "the real thing." Karla remembers that after Marsha had felt her breasts one time, she distractedly lamented, "I've worked really hard and all's I got is lemons; she's got watermelons."

Despite the fun they had together, Karla would tell Sylvia and Marsha that their jewelry, makeup, and tight clothes were exactly what women were trying to get rid of; she resented the way they were "copying and flaunting some of the worst aspects of female oppression." Besides, Karla would say, "you are *not* really women, you are biological men and can reclaim that privilege at any time. *We* are females forever." Sylvia, more than Marsha, would sometimes get offended, and Sylvia offended was not some trifle. "She was as tough as nails," Karla remembers, "I could see her getting a crew cut and going out and joining the marines."

In GLF, Bob Kohler often made a pitch for the queens: "These people started the riot, they're starving, *do* something for them!" That would usually be greeted by more boos than applause—heavy role-playing, whether by effeminate queens or by bulldykes, was viewed by many as a residue of the bad old days of trying to win acceptance from heterosexuals by mimicking their dichotomous role-playing. But the influential Lois Hart strongly supported Kohler's position, and indeed urged him to try to get more queens to attend the GLF meetings. Kohler at various times brought along Li'l Orphan Annie (red curls and big eyes), Lola Montez, Hormona, Boom-Boom Santiago, Black Bambi, Nova, and a host of other queens. But only a few had Sylvia's commitment and staying power—were willing, as Kohler puts it, to "tough it through."[47]

Kohler was a member of the Aquarius Cell, the GLF affinity group that organized the dances. He put Sylvia on door duty, where she would sit, usually stoned on speed and brandishing a large butcher knife, fiercely collecting and guarding the money. "Fierce" became the operative word in describing Sylvia. She would throw herself into every meeting, party, or action with such passion that those who insisted on remaining her detractors had to shift their vocabularies: She was no longer Sylvia, the flighty, unreliable queen, but rather Sylvia, the fierce harridan, ready to run any risk and run through any obstacle in order to achieve her frequently shrieked goal of FREEDOM.

Jim Fouratt was one of Sylvia's defenders. In his view, "her instincts were always correct." Even when she was screwed up on drugs or booze and being abrasively loud, Sylvia had, to Jim's mind, a gut-level understanding of oppression and a willingness to speak her mind that more than made up for her "incorrect" vocabulary, her brazen, bullhorn voice, her inability to shut up. Jim, in general, saw himself as favoring "a revolution that transformed not only society, but roles," and he could witheringly enunciate a position not far from Jean O'Leary's: "Men dressing up as women to play out roles that men have created to entice and seduce men, has nothing to do with being female." Yet he felt he understood Sylvia's need for "narcissistic visibility," for flamboyantly asserting, over and over, a right to exist that she herself had trouble accepting.

Jim was especially impressed with the way Sylvia handled her critics. When attacked by a GLF woman for "showing off" or for "denying her male privilege by pretending to be a woman," Sylvia would only rarely attack back, would not (like some of the other GLF queens) try stridently to put the woman down as "a jealous bitch." Instead, Sylvia would try to explain that she was simply being "Sylvia," a man with a penis who liked to dress up as a woman—it was as untheoretical as that.

When attacked by a GAA man—who, in trying to liberate himself from traditional ridicule about being a surrogate woman, could be impatiently moralistic about cross-dressing "stereotypes"—Sylvia *would* attack back; she would remind him how tough you had to be to survive as a street queen, how you had to fight, cheat, and steal to get from one day to the next. Most impressive of all to Jim was that Sylvia never stole from or physically attacked anyone within the movement; she treated people in GAA and GLF as comrades, exempt from the treacheries of the street. Jim may have been romanticizing what he chose to call Sylvia's "lumpen morality," but if so, not by much. Like so many others in the movement, Sylvia felt she had found a home. And she would defend it with ferocious loyalty.

JIM

Jim was himself strongly committed to a movement that welcomed diversity. He had long identified with countercultural hippies and Third World revolutionaries, and he believed passionately in the need for multi-issue—not simply gay—politics. He also had an impressive track record of putting his beliefs into practice, of "making revolution in our lifetime" (as the New Left liked to put it). And so, during 1969–1970, he went to live for a time in the GLF Seventeenth Street commune—three white and two black men—out of which came a collective that traveled around the country trying to organize Gay Liberation Fronts.[48]

Their first stop was Minnesota, where one of their group, Richard, invited them to stay on his family farm. Having grown up there, Richard knew how to handle a gun and he offered to teach the others. To heighten the experience, they got high on LSD before trooping off to the nearby woods to shoot at cans and trees and bull's-eyes. The acid didn't fully kick in until they had returned to the farm, where Richard's mother had prepared a huge meal for them. As Jim, a vegetarian, later described it, "there was all this red meat which she had cooked for us. And I'm tripping my brains out and I'm seeing this meat looming on the table and talking to me and crying. And also we're trying not to let his parents know that we're gay, and not to let his parents know that we're on acid. And I'm taking this meat, putting it into my mouth, chewing it a little bit, taking a napkin and surreptitiously spitting into it, and holding it under the table while in my hand the meat is crying out."

Following that epiphany, the group went south for another. The two black men in their commune had lived (just like Sylvia, whom they knew) as transvestite hookers, and (again like Sylvia) were not afraid to speak their minds to whites, not afraid to express their anger at *and* their attraction to the oppressor. A great deal of consciousness-raising—always an emblematic activity for GLFers—got done on that trip south; and also a fair amount of organizational work. "A correct idea," Jim believed, "catches the imagination of people everywhere," and "even in a small town in Alabama, we would find people who wanted what we had. And it wasn't about one supergroup in New York leading everybody else; it was about forming a network together, dealing with the needs of the local communities."

In late 1969, Jim also helped organize the first Venceremos Brigade, a group of some two hundred volunteers who went to Cuba by way of Mexico—in open defiance of a State Department ban on travel to Cuba—to cut sugar cane in support of Castro's revolution. Jim fully intended to go with the Brigade and, expecting to be in Cuba for two months, went ahead and sublet his apartment. But then he was told that he had not been accepted. Why? Because it was felt that his chief purpose in going to Cuba would be to organize gays and lesbians there, and that would not sit well with the revolutionary comrades. Furious that straight radicals were once again refusing to take his own cause (and his nature) seriously, Jim tried arguing against the decision. He pointed out that he didn't speak Spanish and added, with acid sarcasm, that it would be exceedingly difficult to organize Cuban gays on the basis of blow jobs alone. But the decision held.

Bitter at being rejected, and with no apartment to return to, Jim took his savings (and his sublet money), bought himself a VW van, and drove down to Texas to visit his friend Kit Carson, a screenwriter, and to attend a gay liberation conference in Austin. On the way back, he ran into some serious trouble. Dressed in black leather pants, a cowboy hat, and a brightly colored shirt, and with his long blond hair flowing loosely down his back, he was "a rather startling sight." So, at least, thought the police officers who stopped him. It seemed his license plates were out of date, and he had failed to get a new sticker. But that was the least of it: After searching his van, the police charged him with possession of heroin and dynamite.

Neither was in the van, but a hefty collection of New Left, Black Panther, and gay liberation literature was—and Jim was arrested and put in the Dallas County jail. He managed to get a call out to Kit Carson, who arranged for a lawyer and worked to get Jim released on bail. It took three months. In the interim, Jim sent a letter to his friend Howard Smith, the *Village Voice* columnist, asking him to raise some money for him, and Smith put a notice in the *Voice* announcing the Jim Fouratt Defense Fund.

The three-month wait was hellish. On first arriving in the Dallas jail, Jim was paraded in front of the holding tanks while a loudspeaker blared, "Who wants her? Who wants her?" He was then given a uniform and put in an overcrowded cell. Remarkably, he was not raped. As he remembers it—though his actor's attraction to dramatic emphasis sometimes heightens that memory—he had read enough books about jail to come up with a successful strategy for avoiding rape. When another prisoner threatened him with a knife, Jim, though "scared to death," grabbed the man's wrist—and the cell broke up with laughter: The "pussy" had proven himself. But just to be sure, Jim later found a protector. Not a "husband," but a friend—"a huge, tough, redneck hippie," arrested for drug smuggling, who took Jim under his wing when he found out he was in jail for political reasons.

Possibly the worst moment came with the arrival of another gay man, a porn-theater projectionist in his forties. He acted—so Jim saw it—"flamboyantly, as if arriving in heaven," and, with no complaint on his part, "proceeded to get fucked by anybody who wanted to fuck him." Jim felt he should reach out to the man, "felt a comradeship on some level, even though really disgusted by his behavior"; but he didn't know how to do it without blowing his own cover. In the end he did nothing, preferring to believe that the man "was having a great time."

Kit Carson's lawyer finally got the charges against Jim reduced to possession of marijuana—though Jim rarely smoked pot and swears none was in the car. To pay the legal fees and have money to eventually get back to New York, Jim intended to sell his car. But he emerged from jail to discover that—in accordance with Texas law, which allowed the property of a drug dealer to be auctioned off—his car had been sold for fifty dollars to a police officer's wife. And there was nothing he could do about it; if he had gotten the car on credit, instead of paying cash for it, he could have relied on the finance company to contest the seizure.

Out on bail, Jim was restricted to the Fort Worth area and, as he tells it, an interlude of surreal luxury followed. Jim Meeker, a friend of Carson's and a well-known art patron, took him under his wing. He stayed at Meeker's Fort Worth mansion and did his bit as "the interesting hippie kid from New York" to entertain the likes of Kris Kristofferson and Samantha Eggar at dinner parties; as Jim put it years later, "it was more like my Warhol than my gay liberation phase."

After Jim went back into court, he was allowed to shift his residence to Dallas, where he lived with June Josie, a friend of Meeker's. She was "a Tennessee Williams lady," complete with flaming red hair, five Cadillac convertibles (to match her changing outfits), and a dead gay husband who had been killed by her father when he found him in bed with another man—all of which appealed hugely to Jim's penchant for dramatic amplitude. For further amplitude still, he helped form the Dallas Purple Star Tribe collective, headquartered in Gene Leggett's house. Leggett was a pompous, charming Methodist minister who had left his wife and three children and founded a mission for homosexuals, drug addicts, and the homeless. Through him, Jim managed to get connected as well to the Dallas Theater Center, for which he quickly developed a New York actor's predictable disdain.[49]

Put on four years' probation at a third court hearing and finally allowed to leave Texas, Jim was in short order rearrested on his way to a New Left meeting. His probation officer, it turned out, had sent word ahead of his "gay liberationist" activities and, since homosexuality was against the law in Texas, he was picked up by marshals and once again remanded to jail. All that was bad enough—he was soon released again—but what was worse, what he could *not* shake and what bothered him infinitely more than his assorted jail stays, were the rumors he began to hear that he was himself a federal agent.

Those rumors pursued him for the next twenty years, and have persisted down to the present day. From the outside, Jim's glamorous life (or rather, his multiple lives)—his travels, his expensive wardrobe, his fancy friends—invited both envious speculation and, among political purists, considerable disapproval. How did a self-declared radical become personal assistant to Clive Davis, president of CBS? What was a Yippie leader doing consorting with the likes of Andy Warhol? How could someone who never seemed to have much money or, until the CBS job, any visible means of support, manage to fly off, at the drop of a hat, for mysterious meetings in distant parts?

If Jim had not been so articulate and opinionated for so long, had not so persistently engaged during political meetings in "disruptive shenanigans" (as one GAA member put it), had not sometimes acted holier(more Left)-than-thou (jumping over the subway turnstile, he once mocked an activist friend for paying his token, for "playing the capitalist game")—had he not done and been all these things, Jim might have made fewer enemies and created less resentment. But his detractors were—and remain—legion, and they proved determined to believe the worst about him.

In Jim's view, the rumors of his FBI/CIA connections arose when they did—in the period immediately following the November 1969 ERCHO meeting—because he had deeply offended many of the old-line homophile leaders there. Several of them had noisily speculated about his being a provocateur of one kind or another; in Jim's scenario, Foster Gunnison became so convinced that he was a Communist, that he actually reported Jim to the FBI—which Foster, however, denies.

It was generally accepted in both GLF and GAA that one or several undercover agents *had* infiltrated the organizations. And those suspicions were well founded. The FBI had been attending gay political meetings in New York since the heyday of Mattachine, and would continue to cover movement events right through the seventies ("Wendy Wonderful," for example, was drummed out of the feminist *RAT* collective in 1970 for being an agent—though Karla, for one, was never convinced of Wendy's guilt). The FBI didn't always get their facts right: Initially they rendered "gay" as "gaye," and "Alternate U." as "Ultimate You"; they defined the Transvestites as "a militant group of women," and characterized the GLF Marxist study group, Red Butterfly, as prototypically anarchist (they "do not recognize authority of any kind"). But usually the FBI got it right, and no wonder, since the Bureau could rely (as one of its agent reports puts it) on "highly placed, sensitive source[s]" serving as informers from within the gay movement. Those sources have never been identified.[50]

Jim thinks it's possible that the FBI might itself have deliberately planted the false rumor that he was one of them in order to destroy his credibility within the New Left—just as it had done earlier in the case of the Communist party leader Bill Albertson. Years before, the FBI had floated the false rumor that Albertson was one of its agents; he had been expelled from the party—and broken in spirit. Only after his premature death was it revealed that the FBI had wholly invented the purported evidence of Albertson's connection to them.[51]

Jim wanted more immediate vindication and, as the rumors mounted, he finally demanded a formal hearing at GAA, where an ex-lover, Marty Robinson, had, in Jim's view, been leading the effort to discredit him. Jim relished the prospect of rising dramatically to his own defense, and at the GAA gathering he did eloquently represent himself, telling the assembled group how, as an actor and a hippie, he had learned to live resourcefully, with little money, and how angry and deeply hurt he was at the false accusation that he was a paid FBI informant. The proceeding may have been exhilarating theater, but Jim also found it "incredibly painful." In the upshot, the GAA meeting did exonerate him of all charges. That was a sweet victory indeed, but as it turned out, an incomplete one. Not even a formal vote in GAA proved capable of laying the rumors permanently to rest.

In January 1970, the feminist staff members of the countercultural paper *RAT*, dissatisfied with the lack of space devoted to women's issues, physically seized the Fourteenth Street premises and sent out a call to other feminists to join them. Karla Jay was one of those who responded. She had remained a committed feminist after leaving Redstockings, and had recently begun to write. To her multiple other activities, she now added attendance at *RAT* editorial meetings and writing up movement-oriented material for publication in it.

One of her major efforts was a participant-observer piece about the March 1970 occupation of the *Ladies' Home Journal*. To Karla, that action was "the most successful ever done in the early women's movement"—though not many other feminists agreed with her estimate.

The move against the *Journal* resulted from months of planning by women from various New York liberation groups (including Redstockings). On the day of the action, between a hundred and two hundred women invaded the *Journal* and "liberated" the office of its editor-in-chief, John Mack Carter. They denounced a magazine purportedly for women that was run and written by men and that catered to consumerism; instead of selling detergent, as Karla put it in her subsequent *RAT* article, "the magazine should in fact be telling their consumers how detergents pollute water." The protestors also pointed out that the few women who did work for the *Journal* were underpaid and that black women were notable by their absence. They then read Carter a set of demands that included his own resignation in favor of a woman editor.

When the reading was over, Carter, known to be imperious, said flatly, "I will not negotiate under siege!" Karla yelled, "You have no choice!" But Carter thought he did, and the stalemated sit-in went on for a number of hours. Tempers began to fray and at one point Karla, thinking Shulamith Firestone was about to lunge at Carter and wanting to save her from injury or jail, grabbed Firestone's arm and restrained her. Carter finally deigned to negotiate with the women's demands, but announced that he would do so not with the group as a whole, but with a delegation—to be no larger than twelve.

The offer produced considerable dissension among the women, some of whom were fearful that it was a divisive tactic designed to appeal to some of the more prominent, career-minded among them. After another lengthy stalemate, a delegation was chosen and did meet with Carter—but emerged with only a single demand met: The *Journal* agreed to put up ten thousand dollars for a separate issue of the magazine devoted solely to the women's movement; the issue would be written collectively by the protestors themselves (though with Carter maintaining final editorial control). The women were ultimately able to use the bulk of the money to support feminist work—providing bail money, for example, for women in prison—but the compromise was angrily denounced both at the time, and later in print, by some of the protesters.

Karla was herself at first inclined to view the result as "elitist." As she wrote in *RAT*, "What good had we done? Aside from the publicity, which might awaken Middle Amerika [a spelling commonplace among 1970 radicals] to its hypocrisy and lies, we had succeeded only in getting Vassar girls higher paying jobs in publishing." But on reconsideration, Karla decided the action had succeeded in several important ways. Five of the largest—and in the past, squabbling—women's groups had managed to work together with reasonable harmony. The number of women participating in the action had sent "a firm warning" to the media to mend their ways in reporting on women's lives. And finally, the protesters had gotten an issue of the *Journal* all to themselves, and that promised to reach large numbers of women across the country with the message of liberation.

Other feminists thought the negatives outweighed—some thought *far* outweighed—the positives. The special "women's-liberation issue" of the *Journal*, they argued, would probably prove a commercial bonanza for its male owners. (The "issue" became a centerfold insert and appeared a year later.) And what of all the other demands which had been shunted to the side? The same issue of *RAT* that carried Karla's description of the protest carried a second article (by "Verna Tomasson") lamenting that nothing had been done about the just call for child-care facilities, for more black employees, for a training program to enable secretaries to move into editorial work, for an end to insulting ads, and for an increase in wages. "Somewhere in the night," Tomasson wrote, "the action came down with a severe case of anemia." It may have produced some effective publicity, but measured by the standards of a *radical* action—"one which effects changes in the existing structure"—it had in Tomasson's view proven a failure.[52]

SYLVIA, JIM, KARLA

Sylvia was worried about her sisters. Worrying about something other than survival was one of the wondrous new luxuries attendant on the birth of GLF and GAA. Suddenly new possibilities and expectations were in the air. People began to dream about something other than getting from one day to the next with a minimum of discomfort. Sylvia's new dream was to have a place that underage street queens could call home.

At first she thought that place might be the new gay organizations themselves: "I thought that night in 1969 was going to be our unity for the rest of our lives." But as Sylvia and everyone else in GLF and GAA soon learned, the diversity of gay and lesbian life would require multiple, sometimes conflicting, expression, just as the traditional dominance of educated, middle-class white men would require constant challenge.

It did not seem, initially, that diversity had to generate disagreement, or disagreement, in turn, division. Many besides Sylvia harbored a vision of unbroken, harmonious solidarity, a determined linking of arms to march into a mistily tender-hearted future. And in the hope of containing differences, GLF had from the first organized around affinity cells, encouraging people, in accord with good anarchist tradition, to congregate around work of mutual interest. It had also opted for one large weekly meeting every Sunday night, run without the formal structure of permanent leaders or parliamentary procedures. Anyone who wanted to could attend and vote, though consensus was considered the ideal—and achievable—form of reaching resolution.

It wasn't long before the Sunday night meetings became forums of excited antagonism—revolutionaries advocated armed struggle, socialists called for an end to capitalism, moderates defended the reliability of American institutions and the basic decency of American life. Debates often became protracted, resolution difficult, bedlam the norm. Some of the men, newly alive to the possibility that although gay they could reclaim their male prerogatives, did what their socialization had trained them to do—interrupt, monopolize discussion, insist on the correctness of their own views, belittle and denounce those who disagreed. And some of the women, true to *their* socialization, deferred to male authority and kept a low profile. But certainly not all of the women.

Rita Mae Brown, for one, had worked hard to raise consciousness within the feminist movement about lesbianism; in GLF, she, Lois Hart, Martha Shelley, and others encouraged lesbians to form feminist consciousness-raising groups—not solely to resist "male chauvinism," but also to end personal feelings of alienation. Lois Hart argued that the women in GLF were better off than heterosexual women "on the outside" because many gay men in the organization *did* believe in feminist principles of gender parity and did applaud all-women consciousness-raising groups that would further encourage independence and equality. "We are in a really tough situation," Hart wrote. "We want to be able to call each other brother and sister, yet we are still in some ways in the roles of oppressor and oppressed. Women are going to feel anger and men will feel fear and resentment."[53]

Many of those feelings surfaced over the issue of separate women's dances. GLF women, including Karla, had worked hard (even chopping ice and sweeping floors) to make the GLF dances at Alternate U. a success. But they grew to resent the "pack 'em in" attitude of the GLF men. Outnumbered by at least five to one, the women had trouble even finding each other at the overwhelmingly male dances, which to them seemed increasingly to resemble nothing so much as a standard gay male bar, overcrowded and dimly lit, with human contact "limited to groping and dryfucking."[54]

Deciding that they wanted a space of their own for dances, the GLF women (never more than ten to twenty percent of the organization) demanded that one of the large rooms at Alternate U. be declared off-limits to men and that a portion of the GLF treasury be set aside to finance separate women's dances. Some of the GLF men denounced the plan as divisive, others denied that there was a male-female problem significant enough to require so "drastic" a solution, and still others instantly supported the women's demands. After a great deal of discussion, which was the GLF way, funds for the separate dances were somewhat reluctantly voted.

The GLF women wanted a social space that would not only be

free of male domination, but would also serve as an alternative to the lesbian bars then in existence. The famous Sea Colony having closed in 1968, there were only two lesbian bars in Manhattan in 1970: Kooky's, on West Fourteenth Street, and Gianni's, on West Nineteenth; both served watered-down, overpriced drinks in an atmosphere less than congenial. Kooky's was named after the fearsome woman who was herself always on the premises. A heterosexual, and purportedly an ex-prostitute, Kooky had dyed, lacquered blond hair and was given to wearing pink crinoline dresses. Karla has described Kooky as looking "more like a poorly put-together transvestite than a woman."[55]

And she ran her bar like a tyrannical man, ordering the lesbian patrons around as if they were scum, beneath contempt. She would think nothing of coming up to a woman sitting at the bar, grabbing her glass, and shoving it up to her mouth. "Drink up, drink up," she would growl in her Brooklynese accent. "This ain't a church, y'know. You wanna spend all your time talkin', go to a church and talk in the pew." Then Kooky would turn to the bartender and bark, "She's buying another drink." The women were afraid of her, sensing her violence, guessing at her Mafia connections. The occasional patron who resisted Kooky's commands could be sure that Kooky would take the lit cigarette always dangling from her mouth, put it right under the woman's chin, and then signal the two bouncers to throw her out.[56]

When Karla and some other GLF women tried to leaflet Kooky's one night with announcements of the forthcoming lesbian dance at Alternate U., Kooky had her male bouncers toss them outside into the snow. It was clear Kooky would not look kindly on the prospect of business being taken away by "some goddamned liberation group." The women then tried leafleting near the bar, but when Kooky saw the flyers in some of her customers' hands, she sent her bouncers outside to threaten retaliation.

Karla and the other GLF women were understandably on edge when the night of the first lesbian dance, April 3, 1970, arrived. Would Kooky try something to disrupt the evening? Would enough women show up to justify all the planning effort? The answer on both counts proved to be a decided yes. A number of straight women showed up in response to a plea from their lesbian friends for support (though one woman Karla phoned—a woman who came out a year later— accused Karla of trying to force her into lesbianism). Even without straight sympathizers, the dance was mobbed and was declared by all hands a huge success; from then on, it became a regular event. But at three A.M., as a group of GLF women, including Karla, were cleaning up, the expected trouble finally arrived.

According to Karla, several large men wearing unholstered guns in their belts suddenly appeared in the Alternate U. doorway. They claimed to be police and said they were investigating charges that liquor was being sold without a license (the dance had adopted the legal ruse of requesting a "donation" at the door). The women were pretty sure at a glance that these men were not cops, but just in case, some of them ran in panic to flush their drugs down the toilet or to stash them under a couch.

It wasn't long before the goons started to push some of the women around; at that, Karla and a friend of hers ran out the back exit. Having expected trouble, they had earlier gotten the black lesbian lawyer Flo Kennedy (who was also a friend of Yvonne's) to promise to stay by her phone, and they now ran to a booth a block away—and directly in front of Kooky's—to call her. Kennedy advised them to notify the police (that is, the real police) and the media immediately, which they did. But just as Karla hung up from making the last call, two drunken men reeled out of Kooky's, where they had apparently wandered inadvertently and been thrown out. Furious, and seeing the two women in the phone booth, they started harassing them, calling them "pussy suckers" and threatening to kill them. Karla insisted she had not been in Kooky's, as the men claimed. "So then what the fuck are you doing here?" one of the men demanded. Thinking fast, Karla said, "Fixing the phone. We're from the phone company"—and to make her point, she ripped out the receiver. "See. It's broken." Grumbling, the men staggered off.

When the two women got back to Alternate U., the police and press had arrived and the goons had fled. The GLF women felt certain that Kooky had sent them, but couldn't prove it, even though the police confirmed that the men had not been officers. As for Kooky (and many of the other bar owners as well), she continued to denounce and harass the gay liberationists—that is, until it eventually became clear that the GLF dances, despite their ongoing success, did not present any significant threat to her own bar business.

Karla shared the view that gay male sexism was an impediment to gender equality and cooperation within GLF. And she thought Jim

Fouratt was among the occasional offenders—though hardly the worst. On the whole she liked and admired Jim. And she was fascinated by the disparity between the way he looked and the way he sometimes sounded. (And fascinated, too, by the same pair of tight black leather pants that he seemed always to wear; she secretly wondered how—or if—he washed them.) In looks Jim seemed androgynous, ethereal, fragile—yet as soon as he opened his mouth he became one more powerfully assured male.

Karla and some of the other GLF women complained about the aggressive way Jim and other GLF men simply stood up, interrupted, and talked whenever they felt like it. Jim took the complaints to heart. Priding himself on having a feminist consciousness, he didn't want his own aggressive behavior to become part of the problem. And so he *tried* to modulate his tone and monitor his interruptions, realizing that among other things, he had to learn the difference between standing up at a GLF meeting and shouting, "Let the women speak!" and simply saying nothing, letting a space develop in which women *could* speak—and without his patronizing intervention in their behalf.

But though gender issues were real in GLF, Jim and Karla shared the view that the organization was honest in its determination to confront sexism *and* racism, that the consciousness-raising groups which were a GLF feature provided the mechanism for doing so, and that to dilute GLF's strength through separatism would be to weaken one of the few organizations willing to challenge the basic sexist and racist assumptions of American life. For both of them, unity was the key, keeping all disparate elements under one political umbrella.

But on the issue of allying with other oppressed minorities, Karla was more ambivalent than Jim, and though she believed a revolution was coming, she recoiled from any glib talk of armed struggle. She agreed completely with Jim that GAA was misguided in its emphasis on single-issue politics, but she also felt strongly that groups like the Panthers, whom Jim tended to champion uncritically, were uncertain allies. She deeply sympathized with the Panthers' militancy but worried about their blatant chauvinism; they may have been the "vanguard," but they were "incredible pigs about women." She thought the group's politics had to be supported, but resisted the wholehearted embrace endorsed by Jim and others. And she resisted, too, the call to get behind Fidel's revolution in Cuba, to excuse Cuban homophobia by citing their Catholic heritage—since politically, after all, they were "way ahead of the rest of us." Karla wasn't buying it. She refused to dissolve her conflicted feelings about the Panthers or the Cubans into *self*-denying apologetics.

As a Hispanic, Sylvia strongly identified with those righteous revolutionaries of the Third World, the Black Panthers and their Hispanic counterpart, the Young Lords. She marched occasionally with both groups, though often in a stoned-out state, and later, in 1971, she would attend the People's Revolutionary Convention, and would count her five-minute meeting with Panther leader Huey Newton among the highlights of her life. Though Sylvia concluded that GAA wasn't "radical enough," she never left the organization, and her friend Bebe Scarpi always made sure that Sylvia's dues were paid up. But her primary allegiance, like Karla's and Jim's, came to center on GLF.

And it was primarily to GLF that she turned for help when her dream of creating a refuge for underage street queens began to stir. Sylvia was still only nineteen herself, yet she had begun to worry about "the youngsters," the kids who started to hustle on the streets, as she had, at age ten or eleven and, within a few years, were dead from a stabbing or an overdose or were locked into dead-end lives. She wanted to somehow set up a place where these young queens not only could find emotional comfort but could maybe even learn enough skills to start another kind of life.

The first person she talked all this over with was her old street-hustling buddy, Marsha P. Johnson. Marsha always had a problem staying focused in conversation; she would wander, start off talking about one thing and end up miles away; people said that drugs had ruined her mind, that she was a permanent space cadet. But when Sylvia started talking to her about "getting a place" for the young sisters, Marsha's mind concentrated wonderfully. She was instantly excited, eager to help. Sylvia had decided that she would make Marsha president of any group they formed, but Marsha, wisely, wouldn't hear of it. "You stay on one thought when you speak," she told Sylvia. "I go off in all directions. You'll be president. I'll be vice president."

They quickly hit on a name for their as-yet-nonexistent group: Street Transvestites Actual Revolutionaries (STAR), then changed "Actual" to "Action." Their first home was the back of a trailer truck seemingly abandoned in a Greenwich Village outdoor parking area; it was primitive, but a step up from sleeping in doorways, and Sylvia and Marsha were quickly able to gather together some two dozen young street transvestites. The ground rule in the trailer was that nobody *had* to go out and hustle her body, but that when they did, they had to kick back a percentage to help keep "STAR House" going. Marsha and Sylvia took it upon themselves to hustle on a regular basis and to return to the truck each morning with breakfast food for everybody.

Rounding Christopher Street on the way back to the trailer at daybreak one morning, their arms loaded with groceries, Sylvia and Marsha stopped dead in their tracks. The trailer was moving! Apparently somebody had reclaimed it and was driving it off—not realizing that some twenty queens were asleep inside. As Sylvia and Marsha watched, dumbstruck, the young queens, apparently awakened by the start-up noise, started to jump out of the back of the truck. But was anyone still inside? "We're standing there like two *yentas*," Sylvia later recalled. "I mean, we're talking about two crazy women: 'Oh, my God, the kids, the kids! Oh Lord Jesus, please don't take the children!' Two crazy women, hysterical. And in full drag." As it turned out, only one queen was still in the van. Stoned out on downers, she woke up several days later—on her way to California.

It was time for a new plan. Bubbles Rose Marie, one of the queens who had lived in the truck, airily suggested that she go talk to her "friend" Michael Umbers, a well-known Mafia figure in the Village. (The following year Umbers opened the gay after-hours club Christopher's End on the ground floor of the Christopher Street Hotel; still later, he employed Dick Leitsch as a bartender.) "He's got a building on Second Street," Bubbles added casually. Sylvia and Marsha looked at each other and shrugged, as if to say, "Why not let the crazy bitch do it? If anything goes wrong, they'll kill *her*." For a small amount of money up front, and a firm deadline on payments, Umbers let Bubbles have the building at 213 East Second Street. And why not? It was standing empty, little more than a shell.

Elated, Sylvia and Marsha sent all the queens out to panhandle and to "hustle their asses off" to raise the needed money, while they, Bambi Lamour (whom Sylvia had first met in jail at Rikers) and Andorra ("a heavyset, high-yaller black queen") set about making the building livable. There was no electricity or plumbing, and not even the boiler worked; there they sat, "four queens that don't know shit about nothing, we're looking at the tools, we're looking at each other. We just started taking things apart, putting them back together, and the next thing we knew, the motherfucker was working!" Grateful that they hadn't blown each other sky-high, they celebrated by shooting up.

People in both GLF and GAA had promised Sylvia that they

would come by and help fix up STAR House. And she had gotten some of the gay teachers in GAA to swear they would turn the top floor of the building into a kind of school, teaching some of the illiterate young runaways how to read and write. But in fact few showed up, and only Bob Kohler of GLF came by with any regularity, helping them to paint, clean up the yard, and get some primitive plumbing installed. When Sylvia decided to throw a benefit dance for STAR House at Alternate U., GLF did front her enough money to buy beer and setups. But when she went to GAA and asked that she be allowed to rent their stereo equipment, she was turned down. Arthur Bell and a few others spoke out in favor of the rental, but the dominant view was that "when we started GAA, we hadn't a thing either. . . . We're not in the rental business."[57]

The experience further embittered Sylvia toward GAA, but the benefit dance did come off in style. Sylvia and what she called her "STAR House Kids" decorated the hall with flashing Christmas bulbs and necklaces of spangled reflectors; and the costumes were extravagant—Bob Kohler appeared in a white T-shirt covered with thousands of beads and with an Indian sash draped across one hip. But Sylvia herself was not a pretty sight. Not having slept or washed for days, she settled for a simple outfit of pants and blouse and, giving off a decided odor and a lot of attitude, sat resolutely at the door collecting money. Shortly after midnight she stopped the gyrating dancers and gave a little speech: "This dance is for the people of the streets who are part of our gay community. Let's give them a better chance than I had when I came out. I don't know if any of you ever lived on the streets. Many transvestites who make up STAR do. We are asking you for money tonight. Winter is coming and we need money for clothes and rent. Please dig into your pockets and help STAR. . . ." Then some of the queens surprised Sylvia by presenting her with a huge bouquet of red roses. She wept buckets.[58]

The dance did bring in a fair amount of money, and STAR House seemed to have gotten a foothold. Sylvia started to cook big dinners at night, sternly telling "the children" that they "don't have to live off that candy shit." And before everyone went out in the evening, she "worked with the saints." Devoted from childhood to Santería, and convinced that St. Barbara was the patron saint of gay Hispanics, Sylvia set up an altar, complete with incense and candles, around which everyone would gather and "pay tribute" before they left the house.

Nobody was forced to participate, but Sylvia made it clear that they would be better protected on the streets if they showed a little respect for the saints, and especially for St. Michael. To him, her prayer would be, "I know we're doing wrong, but we gotta survive, so please help us." And she believed he did: "We *were* watched over—though Marsha came close to getting killed by tricks a number of times, and I looked down the barrel of many a gun and would say, 'Shoot me. You'll be doin' me a favor. I won't have to pay no rent.' But my saints protected me."

Then one day on Christopher Street, Sylvia found Mike Umbers blocking her path. He glowered at her and said he hadn't gotten rent money for three months and wanted the nine hundred bucks *now*. Sylvia raced home and confronted Bubbles, who had been handling the payments. Bubbles mumbled something about the cost of repairs, and Sylvia was about to light into her when Umbers himself showed up. He told Bubbles that unless he got his money, she was as good as dead. At that, Sylvia changed sides. If anything happened to Bubbles, she screamed at Umbers, she would go to the police and tell them she had heard Umbers threaten her.

"For chrissake," she yelled, "it's only money! Don't kill somebody over it! The bitch fucked up. Fine. So kick her ass. But don't kill her. You can take her outside right now and I won't stop you. Or make the bitch get out on the corner." "That bitch can't make no money," Umbers grunted. "That bitch is fat." "Well," Sylvia shot back, "if you kill her, I'll be the first one to speak up." Umbers told Sylvia she'd always been "a fucking bitch" and left.

The next thing Sylvia knew, Bubbles had skipped town ("like she always does when she gets in hot water"). Sylvia decided to make a last-ditch appeal to GAA for a loan, but her request was turned down on the grounds that it would be a dangerous precedent for GAA to get into the business of lending money. But if Sylvia wanted to, they added, she could leave a box at the front table soliciting donations. Desperate, Sylvia left the box, but the donations amounted to only a few dollars. She wasn't close to paying off what she owed Umbers.

And there were other problems. Bambi and Andorra had taken to beating each other up when they got high, and though they were soon kissing again, the dream of sisterhood was getting a little frayed. Then Marsha had a serious attack of "nerves." Her fifth husband, Candy, who was heavily into drugs, got his head blown off right on Second Street and First Avenue when he made the mistake of trying to rob a plainclothesman. Sylvia went with Marsha to the funeral in New Jersey, but no sooner had they gotten back than Marsha's beloved dog died. Marsha said she "couldn't hardly stand it," two deaths in a row, and she had to consult a doctor for her "bad nerves."[59]

Before things could get back on an even keel at STAR House, Mike Umbers evicted them. Apparently deciding against violence, he simply called the city marshals and had Sylvia and her brood put out on the street for nonpayment of rent. Knowing that they were "in no position to mess with Umbers," Sylvia threw in the towel. But before she and her "kids" left STAR House, they destroyed all the work they had put into the place and threw the refrigerator out the back window. "That's the type of people we are: You fuck us over, we fuck you over right back."

FOSTER, JIM, SYLVIA

Foster was by temperament an optimist. In the early months of 1970, as ERCHO and NACHO faltered and the future of the old homophile movement seemed in doubt, Foster preferred to emphasize its ongoing activities and potential staying power. Yet simultaneously, this complex man was able, in some moods, not only to accept that the homophile movement might have had its day, but even to urge his old comrades to jettison the past and "get with it." And Foster was impressively capable of following his own advice: Even as he worked hard to preserve the older homophile organizations, he joined hands with Craig Rodwell and others in the new gay liberation movement to prepare for the Stonewall commemorative march, scheduled for June 27, 1970.[60]

There was reason to believe that ERCHO and NACHO might survive into the new era. Some of NACHO's committees continued to show vitality, even if most of their work was being done by lone individuals. Louis Crompton, a professor of English at the University of Nebraska, kept the Religious Committee going largely through his own diligence, and in late December 1969 single-handedly produced a survey of religious attitudes toward homosexuality. And both Arthur Warner, head of NACHO's Legal Committee, and Frank Kameny, guiding force behind the effort to change federal policies toward homosexuals, continued to produce significant bodies of work.[61]

Foster himself kept up a steady bombardment of exhortatory memos and letters, quick to encourage and praise any signs of life in the old organizations. He rushed to congratulate a NACHO member for starting a newsletter early in 1970 (it lasted for exactly two issues), rejoiced when the NACHO clearinghouse for publications seemed back in regular operation (it quickly became irregular again), and continued to put an enormous amount of time and energy into drawing up agendas and sending out "bulletins" in preparation for the forthcoming NACHO convention (as it would turn out, the last). Even as he worked at maximum pitch, Foster sensed, as he wrote NACHO chair Bill Wynne, that "we may be fighting a losing battle even under the best of circumstances."[62]

ERCHO was the first of the two organizations to disintegrate. It had never really recovered from the disruptive 1969 convention, voting soon afterward to "suspend" itself for a year—"a curious move," Foster had written at the time, "akin to shooting yourself in the head before the next guy does it for you." All that he could think to say in defense of the suspension was that it probably "prevented a take-over by the extremists" and sped the day when "the homophile cause can be resurrected as a sane and rational movement."[63]

For a few months in early 1970, Forster refused to accept that ERCHO was no more. He feared (along with losing his own ballast) that the East would "be in the same boat with the Midwest and the Far West—with no effective regional conference," and for a time he struggled "with all my heart to try and save our ERCHO." He even rebuked Steve Donaldson for describing the organization as "defunct," admonishing him to remember that "the proper way to refer to the ERCHO at present is to say that 'most of the ERCHO administrative machinery has been suspended for a period of one year.' "[64]

But the ERCHO game was decidedly up, and Foster soon faced that fact. He of course couldn't resist, in a few postmortems, putting most of the blame ("75%") squarely on GLF, on what he called "the insurgency of leftist and communist oriented new radical elements." But he didn't let the older homophile leadership entirely off the hook. He chastised Frank Kameny and others for "lack of will" in putting the radicals down and, even more, blamed the corrosive jealousies that had developed among some of the old-timers themselves—above all, the long-standing, venomous rivalry between Kameny and Arthur Warner of New York Mattachine (for which Foster mostly blamed Warner's "indiscretions" of speech, even while acknowledging that Kameny could be "curt and abrasive").[65]

But NACHO seemed a much more viable and necessary organization, and Foster still hoped that hard work might save it. He described himself as "incurably an optimist, so I'll be the last to drop out or throw in the sponge." And in that spirit, he sent off a mound of proposals to various correspondents in the spring of 1970 outlining the direction that he felt the upcoming NACHO conference in San Francisco should take. He advocated doing *less* in terms of setting up committees and projects that in the past had ended up undone or half done, and concentrating instead on doing a few things well. He urged that communications—"not good throughout the movement"—be improved, starting with a functioning newsletter, and that most business matters be kept off the floor of the convention and delegated to a separate, representative body.[66]

He felt strongly that NACHO's integrity as an organization could be preserved only if the new gay liberation groups which had proliferated over the past year were kept from "inundating" the convention. Foster regarded himself "as militant in the movement as anyone you will find," but rejected what he called "a fawning and demeaning effort to suck ass with every other minority cause." He insisted that the left-wing slogans of GLF—"Power to the People!" and so on— were the essence not of liberation but of doctrinaire conformity. "Indeed," he wrote, "I have encountered few more rigid examples of conformity—in dress, thought, and action, than in some of these professional non-conformists."[67]

Foster's vehemence reflected his long-standing views, but also some very recent experience. In late April 1970, he witnessed a rally for the Black Panthers—and the police reaction to it—at Yale University. During 1968–1969, the police had raided Panther offices across the nation thirty-one times, culminating in the slaying of Chicago leader Fred Hampton; the New Haven rally was in support of the jailed "Panther Twenty-one." Foster, in his conscientious way, had gone to Yale as part of his continuing education. And he got one. The tear gas and pepper gas used by the police to break up a demonstration were so thick that he had to vacate his eighth-floor hotel room for several hours.

Later that same evening, he went to a meeting called by all the New York political groups to plan campus strikes in protest against the continued bombing of Cambodia. Foster managed to last an hour, even though it was only a matter of minutes before "inquisitive eyes" began staring at his three-piece Brooks Brothers suit. A student finally came up to him and asked him point-blank to leave—apparently on the suspicion that he was an FBI agent. Foster quickly obliged. Writing about the episode soon after to NACHO chair Bill Wynne, he played it deadpan: "I don't think these people trust me." This was Foster's version of playfulness, which never failed to startle people who preferred to see him as a one-dimensional, pontificating heavy.[68]

While in New Haven, Foster did not get to hear the speech Jim Fouratt gave at the Panther rally. If he had, it might have softened Foster's attitude toward his old antagonist. Though still a staunch supporter of the Panthers, Jim had decided that the time had come to publicly criticize their negative, patronizing view of homosexuality. "The homosexual sisters and brothers who are in this crowd," Jim told the New Haven rally, "have a complaint to make." He went on to say that the very oppression that had made so many gay people identify with the Panthers was being reproduced within the Panther movement. He called upon "every radical here today to Off the word faggot," and also "to Off the sexism which pervades this place and to begin to deal" with their hostility to "the homosexual brothers and sisters." It took considerable courage for Jim to stand up before a crowd uncritically adoring of the Panthers and bring it a message that few were yet ready to hear.[69]

Jim's own attitude had undergone considerable evolution. When Eldridge Cleaver had published his best-selling *Soul on Ice* in 1968, in which he had expressed the view that "homosexuality is a sickness, just as are baby-rape or wanting to be head of General Motors,"[70] Jim had defended Cleaver, and by implication all heterosexual left-wing men who casually disparaged "faggots." The term "faggot," Jim tried artfully to explain, had emerged from prison jargon, where it had been a metaphor for "any castrated male made impotent by society."

As he himself later said, he would "rue the day" that he leaped to Cleaver's defense, pretending to a knowledge of ghetto language he didn't have and letting his enthusiasm for the black struggle blot out the realities of black homophobia. In the two years after the publication of *Soul on Ice*, the Panthers' unwillingness to open any kind of dialogue with GLF had produced some raucous debates within GLF between those wanting to commit money to the Panthers' bail fund and those enraged at the Panthers' knee-jerk homophobia. Jim always argued for giving the bail money, but over those two years he also came to conclude that the Panthers had to be publicly confronted on their homophobia. And it was at the New Haven rally on May 1, 1970, that he chose to issue his challenge to them.[71]

It was one of "the greatest thrills" of Jim's life when Huey Newton, a short time later, published a statement in the *Black Panther* that admonished militant blacks to face up to their "insecurities" about homosexuality and expressed the view that "we should try to unite with them in revolutionary fashion," welcoming them to all future conferences and rallies. In accordance with Huey Newton's advice, the Panthers soon after extended an invitation to GLF to send a delegation to the Revolutionary People's Constitutional Convention at Temple University in Philadelphia. Not only was Jim Fouratt part of that delegation, but so was Sylvia Rivera.[72]

The Philadelphia convention—which drew upwards of ten thousand people—had been called to draft a new constitution, one that would "represent all oppressed people." Each participating group was to have its own workshop, from which would issue statements of needed rights. But the only workshop the female delegates were allowed to have was one controlled by committed Panther women—with the result that most of the female delegates, and almost all of the two dozen lesbians present, angrily bolted the convention.[73]

But for Sylvia, it was "a great moving moment to be there." When she first got off the bus and saw that she was surrounded by straights, she "panicked," sure that she wouldn't be accepted. She resolved—"completely stoned out" and carrying a knife—that "if anybody fucks with me, I'm going to cut their dick off or cut their throat." But everything came miraculously right for her when she ran into Huey Newton himself coming down a corridor and he said that he remembered meeting her ("Yeah—you're the queen from New York") at one of the earlier Panther demonstrations she'd been at. Sylvia's soaring spirits came back to earth only after she returned to New York and an angry Marsha P. Johnson accused her of having stolen STAR funds to make the trip to Philadelphia. Well yes, Sylvia acknowledged, she *had* "borrowed" the money—"and why the fuck not? I wanted to see Huey, and I'll pay the money back!" And she did—by putting in a few more hours each week hustling on the street.

Unlike the women, the gay men did get to present their statement to the convention, and consequently had a more positive reaction to the proceedings. "The Statement of the Male Homosexual Workshop" was greeted with some snickering, but it also got some applause. If it was clear that the Panthers had not been converted overnight to a more positive view of homosexuality, Jim and most of the other GLF men felt that it was only a matter of time before additional Panther leaders—probably David Hilliard and Erika Huggins—followed Huey's lead in advocating a stronger alliance with gay liberation.[74]

But Jim remained uncomfortable with Panther attitudes, and his ambivalence was captured in a single incident during the convention.

He had on a sterling silver bracelet that was not only very beautiful, but had been given to him by someone he had deeply cared about. At one point during the convention, while sitting outside on the grass talking to some of the Panthers and trying to explain why gay liberation was a legitimate movement, Jim heard one of the Panther women ask if she could try his bracelet on. "Of course," he said, nervously sensing some potential unpleasantness.

After she had worn the bracelet for a while, the woman, looking him straight in the eye, abruptly asked, "Can I have this?" Jim felt "caught in my white guilt. I knew that I didn't want to give it to her and I knew it would be inappropriate to say no." Wanting to be a "good gay," he resolved his ambivalence with an offhanded "sure." Later he berated himself both for having been taken in by "a revolutionary con" *and* for not being "truly egoless and nonmaterial." Jim was not so liberated that—like most gay people at most times—he was ever at a loss in finding multiple ways to berate himself.

As the 1970 NACHO conference approached, Foster's excitement mounted. He chose to see the preregistration figures (some twenty organizations and nearly a hundred individuals) as "amazing" proof that NACHO had a viable future. But as it turned out, the conference proved more a nightmare than a triumph for him. The very first motion from the floor after the convention had been called to order was in support of the Black Panther party. It narrowly squeaked by in an initial ballot and then was sustained when a later motion to reconsider was soundly defeated. Capitalizing on that victory, the Radical Caucus, claiming to speak in the name of "the entire West Coast," next objected to the conference's "restrictive membership policy" (Foster had sweated over the elaborate formula for long hours) and successfully pushed through the principle of one person, one vote.[75]

A second humiliation soon followed. The delegates decided to hold another NACHO convention in 1971 and proceeded to elect a Conference Committee to prepare for it. Foster was one of sixteen people nominated, but he got the third-lowest number of votes and failed to be elected. On the other hand, Dick Leitsch—who was attending a NACHO convention for the first time (outflanked by the rising tide of Gay Power, he had become interested in NACHO as a possible countervailing force)—*was* elected to the committee. And when the 1971 convention failed to come off, Foster would directly blame Leitsch's "eratic, unreliable" behavior, rightly seeing that

Leitsch, at bottom, was "anti-NACHO"—or rather, "anti-anything that he's not top dog in."[76]

Not only did NACHO never again hold a convention, but by 1972 the organization would cease to exist. The times had changed. Radical young lesbians and gays were in the saddle; they generally considered the older homophile generation irrelevant, and their accomplishments nil. Yet homophile accomplishments had been real, however necessary it may have been for a newly assertive generation to scorn them in order to establish its own hegemony. When Bill Wynne, chair of the 1970 NACHO convention, rose to address the delegates, he gave a succinct valedictory accounting of those accomplishments.

Wynne began by acknowledging that the goals NACHO had originally set at its founding in 1966 may have been "mostly grandiose and naive," and that the proliferating committees set up to accomplish those goals in the years since had mostly been nonfunctional. But nonetheless "some things of a positive nature," as Wynne put it, *had* been done and deserved enumeration. Above all, communication had been opened up between individuals and groups previously isolated from each other. That, in turn, had served to stimulate local organizing, even as it had clarified the fact that "our problems" were not merely local but national in scope. And NACHO gatherings over the years had helped to develop confidence among those attending them that a national gay response could become a reality. "Develop[ing] confidence"—that was probably the subsuming accomplishment. In Wynne's words, the homophile movement had "given courage to people to open up the whole subject."[77]

Fortunately for Foster's peace of mind, he had already, by the time of NACHO's final convention in 1970, become deeply involved in several new projects that would amply fill the vacuum in his life. Earlier on, in Foster's hometown of Hartford, Connecticut, Canon Clinton R. Jones of Christ Church Cathedral had started a counseling group for gays that by mid-1968 had helped give birth to an activist organization called the Kalos Society. Foster had been involved with Kalos from the beginning, though in early 1970 it still had only fifteen or twenty members and in Foster's view hadn't really " 'gelled' yet." But he had hopes it might eventually become "a high-powered organization for New England." It never did; but it lasted well into the seventies and left behind a news bulletin, *The Griffin*, later transformed into *Metroline*, a regional gay publication that in 1993 continues to publish.[78]

Through his own one-man organization, the Institute of Social Ethics, Foster also started work in 1970 on some elaborate publishing ventures. In order to "promote and facilitate communication," he planned to put out a "comprehensive directory of organizations, publications, events, and projects associated with the homophile movement." Initially, he entitled the pending publication *Homophile Organizations of the World*, but later chose the shorter *The Directory*. Setting to work with his usual enthusiasm and zeal, Foster tossed off memos, mailed out press releases, gathered far-flung data. After nearly a decade of work, he would ultimately abandon the project, convinced that the emergence by then of the New York City–based *Gayellow Pages*, with its national coverage, had made *The Directory* redundant. But over the years he gathered a remarkable body of material, creating an archive that is today an indispensable resource on the homophile movement.[79]

Foster was also, by 1970, deeply involved in helping Craig Rodwell plan a commemorative celebration of the first anniversary of the Stonewall riots. Long since convinced that "the main problem holding us back from where we want to get to is that of secrecy or fear, and the failure of homosexuals to get out of the closet," Foster hoped that Craig's Christopher Street Liberation Day Committee might prove an ideal vehicle for encouraging greater openness and broader movement participation.[80]

SYLVIA

Carol Greitzer of the New York City Council represented a district that included Greenwich Village and its large gay and lesbian population. Yet in the past Greitzer had more than once worked against the needs of that constituency. In 1964 she had joined Councilman Ed Koch in calling for more plainclothesmen to control the "perverts" in Washington Square Park and, in 1966, had urged that the Village be included in Operation New Broom, a police campaign to get rid of "undesirables." Nor did Greitzer's attitude seem to change after the emergence of gay liberation; when GAA leaders Jim Owles and Marty Robinson asked her in 1970 to support a fair-employment-practices bill, she tartly replied that it wasn't a proper area for legislation. GAA decided it was time to increase the pressure on Greitzer and started circulating a petition that demanded she introduce a City Council bill barring antigay discrimination and repealing existing sodomy laws.[81]

Sylvia Rivera had previously taken part in several GAA "zaps," including one against Mayor John V. Lindsay for refusing to speak out on gay rights, but somehow the petition drive caught her fancy and she decided to give it her full, formidable energy. Since she was still working Forty-second Street on a part-time basis, Sylvia decided to do her petition work right there. She parked herself in the middle of Forty-second between Seventh and Eighth Avenues and, dressed in partial drag, her auburn hair flying, raucously called out to passersby, "Sign this petition! Please sign this petition to help change the laws against homosexuals!" Some people did stop and sign. Others moved nervously on, eyes straight ahead. A few asked questions in a friendly way, but wouldn't sign. And a few others shouted slurs about "faggots."[82]

Sylvia's street-hustling friends stood around and gaped with amazement at the sister's audacity ("This be the butchest thing you ever done, girl!"), and several warned her that she was asking for trouble. But for several nights in a row Sylvia managed to gather her signatures with no interference. Then, at about seven-thirty on the night of April 15, she suddenly saw a crowd of people running toward her. She was startled and frightened—until someone explained that the Tactical Patrol Force had just broken up an antiwar demonstration in nearby Bryant Park. And right behind the fleeing crowd, of course, came a number of TPF police dressed in full riot gear.

"Move on," one of them yelled at Sylvia, "and make it snappy." Sylvia held her ground. "I'm only getting signatures to stop the discrimination against homosexuals," she said. "You have to move," the cop repeated. "Well, I'm not moving," said Sylvia, a little surprised and more than a little alarmed at her own firmness. "I got my constitutional rights, just like everybody else. I got the right to stand here and petition to change the laws just like anybody else."

"Not without an American flag, you don't," the cop said, surprisingly patient. "You can't set up a stand without an American flag—that's the law." Sylvia still wouldn't budge. "Now don't give me that," she said, her voice rising. "Number one, I'm not out here preaching the gospel like Rosy down the street. I been to jail with Rosy many a time because you don't let her preach even though she *has* the American flag." By now a police cruiser had pulled up behind Sylvia and she started to feel "a little shaky," afraid they would beat her up. Instead they arrested her on charges of "disorderly conduct" and "incitement to riot," threw her into the cruiser, and took her to the Fourteenth Precinct station.

Now she was worried she might lose her job at the A & P warehouse in Jersey if she didn't show up for the start of her eleven P.M. shift. She wanted to call her boss, but a Legal Aid lawyer told her she would have to plead guilty before they'd let her use the phone. Sylvia refused: "I'm not pleading guilty to nothing! I'm not pleading guilty to a charge that's unjust!" The lawyer finally got her out on fifty dollars bail. Fortunately she had just been paid from her warehouse job and was able to put up the money.

By now it was midnight. She called her sympathetic boss, who told her it was too late to bother to come to work, so she decided to head back up to Forty-second Street and try for a few more signatures—"and I wasn't even high on black beauties." This time nobody bothered her, and later she went to her friend Josie's apartment to sleep. The next evening she and Josie went down to the GAA meeting in the Village, and the reporter Arthur Bell overheard her tearfully telling someone about her escapade the previous night. Knowing a good story when he heard one, Bell took Sylvia and Josie back to his own apartment to get the full account. Soon after, he published it as an article in *Gay Power*, and Sylvia was made as a movement celebrity. Thereafter, as she puts it, "I could just snap my fingers and everyone would come running." A couple of people in GAA wanted to nominate her for office, but Sylvia said she "couldn't be bothered"—she wanted to "argue with the hierarchy, not be the hierarchy."[83]

But she did have to go back to court. Again accompanied by Josie (who died the following year of a drug overdose), Sylvia arrived at 100 Centre Street in a lavender pantsuit she had sewn herself; it had wide bell-bottoms and a tunic top, and across the blouse she had embroidered "GAA." She didn't have a lawyer and was scared to death, but when she pushed open the door into the courtroom, she let out a gasp. Dozens of gay men and lesbians from both GAA and GLF filled the seats, and they jumped to their feet and started to applaud as soon as Sylvia appeared. The case dragged on over a four-month period, and was eventually thrown out of court when the arresting officer failed to show up. In all likelihood, his superiors had told him not to, since the incident had already gotten more publicity than they wanted. But Sylvia, in a twist of illogic, prefers to believe that the no-show cop was the same one—"a Jewish cop, very good-looking, from Ocean Avenue in Brooklyn"—who she later discovered had signed her petition.[84]

Sylvia was part of the thirty-five-person gay activist delegation that went to the May 13 meeting of the Village Independent Democrats in order to confront Greitzer with the accumulated petition signatures. Jim Owles stood up at the meeting and declared it an outrage that homosexuals could not petition their own representative for a redress of grievances. Greitzer tried to get the VID chairman to explain that she had a bad cold and couldn't talk, but he insisted that she state her views. So she reluctantly took the microphone and said that the state attorney general was the person to introduce gay rights legislation, that she wouldn't be able to get such a measure through the City Council. And then she bumblingly added that she had no room to store the petitions in her desk.[85]

Owles asked her at least to make a public statement declaring herself on the side of gay rights—just as she had made statements in favor of women's rights and black rights. Greitzer responded obliquely, suggesting that the activists gather documentation for their claims of job discrimination. Asked point-blank by Marty Robinson if she would cosponsor an antidiscrimination bill, Greitzer said yes —in a tone Arthur Bell later described as one of "exasperated defeat." She also agreed in the end to accept the petitions—though when a GAA member later asked her to affix her own signature, Greitzer purportedly answered, "I really don't have your problem," and walked away.

Sylvia claims—though the incident is not reported in any of the other existing accounts—that at some point in the proceedings, she lost patience with Greitzer, rolled up the petitions she had herself collected and "bopped Greitzer upside the head" with them, yelling "Well, you're going to take them now, bitch!" A few weeks later, again according to Sylvia, she spotted Greitzer walking with two men on Forty-second Street, rushed up to her, called her "a fucking whore," and screamed, "Whatsa matter? You don't make enough money in the City Council, you have to come up here and steal the money from your queens, huh? You fuckin' bitch!" Greitzer, as Sylvia tells it, looked terrified, told one of the men to get the car and, pointing at Sylvia, said to the other man, "That's the one. The mean one. Because he's out." "You betcha life, bitch!" Sylvia purportedly shouted at Greitzer as she got in the car, "Don't forget—the name is Ray Sylvia Rivera, honey. And I will bop you upside your head again!"[86]

Yvonne and her black lesbian friends decided to try again. Their earlier attempts to meet together on a regular basis had dissolved after a few months, and they thought that might have been because they had held their meetings at the Firehouse, headquarters of the overwhelmingly white GAA. So this time around they started meeting in the gym of a church, a space gotten for them by one of their own group, a minister. A few Hispanic women joined them, and occasionally an Asian woman would show up as well.

By early 1970, the feeling was well advanced that it was necessary for like-categorized people to meet apart from others (however dissimilar the individuals thus categorized might turn out to be). The "Black Power" concept had by then weakened integrationist civil rights organizations, and within the gay movement not only were women of color separating themselves from white women, but also the feeling that lesbians should meet separately from gay men had become common.

Many men in GLF supported the women's movement, and some of them gave it a good deal more than lip service. Still, they had been socialized as men and despite good intentions and vigorous efforts at self-examination in consciousness-raising groups, many proved unable to rid themselves of the assumption that their male insights were superior, their male leadership essential, their male issues paramount. Nor did the lesbians in GLF feel any greater understanding from their straight sisters in the women's movement. Lesbians were tolerated rather than welcomed even in most of the radical feminist groups, and had frequently felt misunderstood and patronized.[87]

And so GLF lesbians inaugurated a Women's Caucus, which met every Wednesday night and, in April of 1970, held the first all-women's dance. Though Karla Jay continued to feel some uneasiness that the separation of women from men might sap the overall strength of the gay movement, she helped to organize the lesbian GLF action that marked the opening session of the second Congress to Unite Women on May 1, 1970. While three hundred women were sitting quietly in the auditorium waiting for the Congress to come to order, the lights suddenly went out. When they came back on, thirty or so women wearing LAVENDER MENACE T-shirts had taken over the stage. They held the convention floor for two hours, trying to explain to their straight sisters what it was like to be lesbian in a heterosexist culture, and succeeded in getting a set of pro-lesbian resolutions passed.

Dramatic as that action was (and huge fun for those who planned and executed it), lesbianism hardly swept the feminist field. Betty Friedan, for one, was furious at the "Lavender Menace" action and continued to do her considerable best to keep lesbians from holding office in NOW's New York chapter. Running into Karla at a meeting more than a decade later, Friedan *still* seemed to be fuming over what had happened in 1970. Pointing an angry finger at Karla, she hissed, "*You* caused me a lot of trouble." Karla told her to lighten up, that that had been a long time ago.[88]

The separation of women from men in gay organizations was paralleled by the separation of women of color from white women in the feminist movement. Indeed, with a few exceptions, most black women had never participated in the women's movement, dismissing it as irrelevant to their primary needs and preferring to put their energies into black causes—a situation that was not to change significantly until the 1980s. But in Yvonne's case, the black movement had proven no solution either. Whenever she had joined a black-oriented march, demonstration, or sit-in, she had come away angry and disappointed at the black male's macho insistence on running the show and on relegating women to an "appropriately" subordinate role.

Yvonne *was* black *and* lesbian, but the black movement recoiled from both her strength and her sexuality, while the white gay movement had an incomplete understanding of issues relating to her color (and gay men, of issues relating to gender). She rejected the bifurcations that her committed membership in either movement would have demanded of her; sanity—wholeness—seemed to dictate that she confine her allegiance to those who would accept all aspects of her being: namely, her own black lesbian sisters.

Despite the abortive effort to form an organization at the Firehouse, and then a second brief attempt at cohesion that also failed to survive, the black lesbian women were determined on a third try. Most of those who attended the new round of meetings came in couples (including Yvonne, who brought Yolanda, a black–Puerto Rican woman she had been seeing a lot of). As they had in their previous attempts, the women opted for an unstructured organization based on the principle of rotating leadership and devoted to grass-roots initiatives. They named the new group The Black Lesbian Counseling Collective.

But despite the name, the women were not in agreement about the group's purpose. Many of them were looking for a support group and a social alternative to the bars. But a minority, Yvonne among them, wanted to do "more outreach, more direct service to other lesbians, more political stuff." The division was between those who felt they had to get *themselves* together before they could do work in the world, and those, like Yvonne, who felt that doing work in the world was *how* people got themselves together.

Establishing a stable core of members also became a problem. The number present at each meeting varied widely. Sometimes only three or four people would show up; sometimes there would be forty. The Reverend Delores Berry, the minister who had earlier found church space for the group, was herself soon reassigned to Washington, D.C. Some of the Hispanic sisters, moreover, seemed restive in a setting dominated by black women (and indeed would later form the separate organization Las Buenas Amigas). And finally, what Yvonne calls "intrigue and seduction" also began to take a toll. Even in so self-selected and marginal an enterprise, struggles for control developed—bids to be powerful *somewhere*. Romantic infatuations, moreover, began to wreak havoc with the stability of the couples involved—people "started messing with each other's friends and whatnot."

Yvonne herself began to resent the special aura that, in the broader community of black lesbians, had begun to settle over the writers and artists among them. To her mind, there should be no special status among equals, no elite group that was somehow considered better than everyone else. She would argue angrily that lesbians were inventing "a new class"—a phenomenon she considered absurd, since they were already "on the bottom rung—as women, as people of color, and as lesbians." To elevate a few women in their midst, to suggest that those few were worthy of special privilege or had a special place, seemed to Yvonne a contradiction of the group's egalitarian, grass-roots orientation.

And she put special blame for this development on some of the artists themselves. She felt they "were there on an ego trip"; they would do a reading from their work, enjoy the attention and adulation—but then not come back on any regular basis, "were not really committed to the women there or to the organization." Yvonne herself wrote poetry now and then, good poetry:

. . . Now you can't always tell a black goddess
by how she looks.
She may laugh too loud or
stand in the middle of a silence
like my Grandma at the kitchen table
mixing cornmeal and egg.
But you can't always tell a black goddess
by what she cooks.
She may not,
or burns it,
or cooks only your flesh. . . .[89]

And a few years later, she would join the black lesbian Jamima Collective, started by Georgia Brooks. But Yvonne was determined not to let her literary efforts overshadow her political ones. And she did feel that a choice between them was necessary: "Was I going to write or was I going to do?" She made a fierce resolution that henceforth she would write maybe one piece a year, and for the rest of the time, "would live my politics rather than write about them."

Her chief work, Yvonne decided, was "to empower black lesbians to come out and to organize." A few years hence, when her long-standing physical problems had finally been diagnosed as lupus, she added health issues to her political agenda. She wanted to share with others what that disease—what any serious illness—can do to a woman's sense of herself. "So this is the work," she concluded. "I'd rather do that than write a *piece* about the poor women who are suffering from lupus. Or my personal suffering with lupus."

The third effort to form a black and Hispanic lesbian organization, beset by tensions, also failed to sustain itself. But many of the women had not only made contact, but had formed lasting bonds with each other. From those bonds, Salsa Soul Sisters would soon emerge. And this fourth time around, the glue would hold. Though Salsa Soul, too, would go through many transformations and some disaffection, it continues down to the present day; it is now called African Ancestral Lesbians United for Societal Change. And Yvonne, the last of the original founders, is still consistently active in its councils.

CRAIG, FOSTER, JIM, SYLVIA, KARLA, YVONNE

The first thing Craig did, after the final ERCHO convention in November 1969 gave its blessing to the formation of a Christopher Street Liberation Day Committee, was to diplomatically send out notices to all of ERCHO's constituent groups that such a committee had indeed come into existence. The niceties performed, Craig then had to find people to do the actual work. He began by notifying all the New York gay groups of the committee's formation and—making clear (more niceties) that the planned celebration was not owned by any one organization—asked that they send representatives.

GAA delayed until some six weeks before the celebration, and Mattachine was overtly negative until the last minute, when DOB also decided to join in. But GLF responded immediately, and from that group Brenda Howard, Marty Nixon, and Michael Brown became mainstays. To fill out the committee, Craig buttonholed some of his regular customers at the Oscar Wilde Bookshop, and managed to bag Judy Miller, recently arrived in New York from Denver, and a pair of lovers, Jack Waluska and Steve Gerrie. All three turned out to be hard workers, and stayed the course.

Foster Gunnison was part of the organizing committee from the beginning. He and Craig were in some ways at opposite ends of the political spectrum—"conservative" and "radical," in common usage. Yet those ends do meet ideologically in conservatives and radicals who identify as "libertarians" ("anarchists" is the preferred term on the left); what they share is a distrust of authority, a distrust that on the right (Foster) focuses primarily on the state, and on the left (Craig) becomes a more encompassing rejection of all established pieties handed down by church, state, law, and family.

The two men came from sharply different class backgrounds, yet took to each other as human beings, recognizing, beneath their contrasting styles, the same basic warmth and decency—which both were too modest to acknowledge about themselves. Craig was fascinated by the anomalous Foster, the only dedicated gay activist he had ever met who smoked cigars, wore three-piece Brooks Brothers suits, sported a crew cut, and spoke in an accent vaguely redolent of some upper-crust private school—"the house dick," Craig used to call him.

Foster was well aware that in both appearance and opinion he "stood out like a sore thumb" in the countercultural sixties, and that made him grateful for Craig's recognition that beneath the starchy exterior, Foster was in fact "a puppy." He, in turn, thought Craig was "a swell fellow," honest, reliable, and, by Foster's lights, also something of an anomaly—the hardworking, no-nonsense type, willing day after day to do laborious detail work, that Foster thought did not exist among the radical young. Craig was now thirty, considerably older than most of the new activists, and not closely identified either with GLF or GAA—but he was still a "kid" to forty-five-year-old Foster.[90]

Foster sometimes lamented Craig's "dislike of structure," his individualistic insistence on "doing his own thing," and his determination that the CSLDC (Christopher Street Liberation Day Committee) be a grass-roots project uncontaminated by any connection to commercial interests (such as gay bars) and uncorrupted by prior organizational loyalties (Foster confessed to harboring some hope that ERCHO could be rebuilt on CSLDC's activities). But despite these minor disagreements and annoyances—inevitable in any ongoing, close-quarters organizational work—Foster fully credited Craig with being the heartbeat of the committee: He was "like a guru," Foster later said, "everything revolved around him, and yet he was very unassuming. It was almost like a spirit sitting in the room."[91]

In February 1970, the small group of eight or so people began to meet monthly in Craig's apartment on Bleecker Street; in April, as deadlines approached, they met weekly. Foster came down faithfully from Hartford for every meeting, serving as the group's official treasurer and helping Marty Nixon keep track of assorted financial transactions. The group had hoped to add a two-day block festival in Greenwich Village to the planned march, but that fell by the wayside when they discovered that city ordinances required the posting of a million dollars worth of bonds to "protect against damage." By April 1970, the committee had firmly focused on a "march for freedom" through midtown Manhattan up to Central Park, where "a variety of activities and events, planned or spontaneous," would follow in Sheep Meadow. In its bulletins and press releases, the committee continuously announced its hope that other gay and lesbian organizations across the land would sponsor comparable efforts in their own localities.[92]

The first anniversary of the onset of the Stonewall riots would have fallen on June 27, 1970, but the committee decided to hold the celebration on Sunday, June 28. They believed that more people would be free to participate on a Sunday and that it would be easier to obtain permits and in general to cut through red tape. To raise operating funds for the planned event, the committee tried various strategies. Foster sent out notices to "All East Coast Homophile Organizations" asking for $10 donations, and he also sent an "appeal" to individuals, along with a rather peremptory pitch: "I have often thought," Foster wrote, "that the least a homosexual can do—if he doesn't want to get involved in public demonstrations or action-oriented programs—is to contribute cash to enable programs to be conducted by others on his behalf. Will you agree with that?" Not much resulted from either effort. Two months before the scheduled march, seven organizations had sent in a measly total of a hundred dollars—and Dick Leitsch, speaking for the New York Mattachine Society, had declared himself against the notion of a march entirely.[93]

But in 1970 it took only about a thousand dollars to put on the Christopher Street Liberation Day March, and Craig brought in additional money by asking his bookstore customers for donations. (He also found a twenty-dollar bill on the street and, deciding that "God has sent it for the march," added it to the treasury.) It helped, in making ends meet, that Michael Sabanosh, a graphic designer, did all of CSLDC's announcements, posters, and buttons free of charge, and that Marty Nixon, who had a job with the Arthritis Foundation, stayed late after work to surreptitiously grind out thousands of pages of CSLDC material on the Foundation's photocopy machine.[94]

In the spring of 1970, Karla was thrown so hard to the mat during a judo match that she broke several ribs. Stoic about physical pain, she hobbled along for a week. But then, when she was on her way to a GLF meeting one night, the pain grew so severe that her friend Alan Sample finally persuaded her to go to nearby St. Vincent's Hospital in Greenwich Village. The doctors there were convinced that she had been battered and they called in the police. Feeling mischievous, Karla gave Alan—who had long blond hair and looked like Greta Garbo—a glance as if to say, "What if I tell them you did it? Wouldn't that be a hoot, the idea of *you* beating up *me*?" Knowing Karla's penchant for practical jokes, Alan gave her a beseeching look back, as if to say "Don't do this to me!" So Karla bit her lip in restraint, and the police let them go.

It was clear she wouldn't be able to work for a while, which was no great blow to her. She hated the new job she had taken at Collier's

Encyclopedia: "It was very right-wing. We all hated it there. It was like the Gestapo. They had dress rules and I was in constant battles with them to wear pants." Besides, her boss had seen her picture in the paper as part of the *Ladies' Home Journal* action, and Karla was sure the reaction would be "So *that's* what she does with her day off—she seizes magazines." She thought maybe she ought to quit before being fired.

The urge was part and parcel of her growing ambivalence about graduate school. She had made some good gay male and lesbian friends at NYU, including Rita Mae Brown and Alan Sample, and she enjoyed reading for her courses. But she had been increasingly treated in class as The Feminist, and being mechanically turned to ("And what does Karla, The Feminist, think?") had angered her. She had told the professors to try finding out what some of the other women in class felt, but they had gone right on patronizing her as their token revolutionary.

Karla decided the time had come for a break from a hateful job and a conflicted academic career. It seemed an ideal time to take disability and to go sit in California for a while. She waited until early June so that she could participate in a big antiwar march. And then she headed out to the West Coast.

Jim Fouratt's lover in 1970 was Peter Hujar, who had been one of Richard Avedon's prize pupils and was in his own right already a well-known fashion photographer. Jim thought Hujar was "the most handsome man I had ever seen in my life; he looked exactly like Gary Cooper." But Hujar was notoriously difficult, too—which was perhaps understandable for a man whose mother had twice tried to kill him after discovering that he was gay.

Hujar was interested in Jim's political activities but, after going along to a few GLF meetings, had decided he wasn't *that* interested. Still, he wanted to do "something." About a month before the Christopher Street March was due to take place, Jim came up with a "something" that caught Hujar's fancy: take a photograph of a group of gay liberationists running joyously through the streets, fists clenched on high, à la the Paris Commune, that could be used as a poster to advertise the coming march.

Hujar took to the idea immediately. But bringing it to fruition proved difficult. Jim set up a telephone chain call asking all GLF members willing to be photographed to show up for the shoot at the designated time, day, and street (a semi-deserted area in the West

Twenties). The response was less than overwhelming. Appearing on the poster would be tantamount to publicly coming out, and in 1970 that was still a terrifying prospect for most people. Many of the phone messages went unanswered, and many others called back to stammer invented regrets or to express real fears.

Ultimately, some fifteen people showed up to be photographed. Hujar had them run back and forth, back and forth, down the deserted street, shouting and laughing in triumph. Dressed in the pseudo-shabby workers' drag then fashionable, they looked as if they had been recently liberated from the Bastille—and had somehow emerged singing.

In the final poster, the fifteen marchers crowd the center, and it only gradually becomes clear that the sidewalks behind them are empty; these ebullient troops seem to have no backup forces. What also becomes apparent is the nearly equal number of women and men—though in GLF itself the women were far outnumbered. That ratio seemed proud confirmation to some that the women were more willing to put up than the men were to shut up.[95]

Some of the participants had nervously hoped that the photo would take its place in the revolutionary pantheon alongside Black Panther posters and those from the 1968 French student uprising. They had expected to see it on every wall of every building—a rallying cry to come out and march in the Liberation Day Parade. But the poster was a good deal less omnipresent than that. Its real visibility came only later, when it was widely and continuously displayed on the walls of movement organizations, bookstores, and offices. Still, enough people saw it at the time to give those who had participated some strange turns. Being recognized from the poster meant being subjected to strained, worried looks from friends and even strangers, looks that seemed to say "You realize, of course, that your life is finished."

That could make the participants momentarily catch their breath, fear suddenly surging back. And they had to quickly remind themselves that their lives felt much more like they were just beginning.

The night before the march, GLF held an open house at the Washington Square Methodist Church on West Fourth Street in the Village; they offered food, housing information, literature, and around-the-clock talk. At the Church of the Holy Apostles, at Twenty-eighth Street and Ninth Avenue, a comparable set of events for women featured a bring-your-own communal supper, a "dance–party–rap session," and the promise that for the entire weekend, "there will always be sisters around with literature or time to talk. Women with no place to go or no spirit to get there can crash at the church."[96]

And over at Alternate U., a two-person team from the Quaker Project on Community Conflict was giving a crash course on crowd control to a hundred hastily gathered marshals. Many of them were still feeling skittish about having decided to march, to say nothing of taking on the responsibility of a marshal's role. As one of them later put it, "I decided I would march, but I left little clauses in my mind. . . . If I didn't feel good, I wouldn't go. If there was any violence, I would drop out. . . . If the march was going to include too many effeminate men or butch women, I would drop out. . . ."[97]

The Quaker team warned the marshals about what everybody already knew: No one had any idea how many people would show up in the morning or how much violence to expect. Nor could anyone predict whether the cops would contain or abet hostility among the spectators toward the marchers. "Be prepared for anything," the Quakers warned. Then, for several hours, they helped the novice marshals simulate pugnacious situations of all sorts. "Cocksucker!" one man was told to shout angrily at another as he lunged toward him, while the others were shown how to surround and "smother" the two combatants.[98]

Karla had arrived in Los Angeles some three weeks before the scheduled march and, though ostensibly resting, had quickly gotten involved with the local GLF. She found the same divisions that had characterized the New York group: The women and men had begun to tangle and some of the more radical men, like Sandy Blixton, were at odds strategically with moderates like Morris Kight. But the worst of the antagonisms were put on (temporary) hold in order to plan the first Christopher Street West Parade.

As it was, arrangements were begun belatedly; the request for a parade permit was submitted just four days before the deadline—and then the Police Commission insisted on security bonds totaling a million and a quarter dollars. Police Chief Ed Davis said publicly that giving the marchers a permit would be like "discommoding the citizens by permitting a parade of thieves and burglars"; he further predicted that should such a march take place, it would be mobbed by hard hats. The ACLU brought suit on behalf of Christopher Street West

—and in a photo finish, the presiding judge ruled, just hours before the march was due to begin, that the amount of money demanded in bonds was unprecedented and therefore excessive.

In New York, Sunday, June 28, dawned cloudless and cool—"An omen, an omen! *She's* on our side!" was the nervous chorus in a thousand apartments across the city. Craig had barely slept, and Foster, arriving the night before from Hartford, had been up late talking with friends and reviewing his chronometer calculations for measuring crowd size.

Sylvia was itching to get going; after facing the random violence of the streets for most of her life, she viewed a daytime march up Sixth Avenue, surrounded by friends, as a piece of cake. One of her street-queen buddies announced she would be wearing her hair in a bun—"suffragette-serious"—out of respect for the solemnity of the occasion, and would do her best not to "pluck people's nerves."

Jim, uncharacteristically, had recently taken something of a backseat; in the last weeks, as GAA had rapidly accelerated its involvement in the march, leafleting the Village, hosting a big dance at NYU, he had grown concerned that the GAA "reformers" would somehow dull the cutting edge. Jim would march, of course, but would stay close to the GLF banner.

As for Yvonne, so long on the organizational sidelines, she thought she just *might* join the march; she set her alarm, anyway, putting off a final decision until the morning.

Craig anxiously paced his apartment early Sunday. Half a dozen meetings over the preceding months with the Sixth Precinct had—just as in Los Angeles—failed to win a permit, and though the promise of one had finally been made, the permit had *still* not arrived. He was determined to go ahead regardless, especially since a second permit, to congregate in Central Park's Sheep Meadow after the march, *had* been obtained (though, again, only after half a dozen meetings). Just as Craig was about to give up and leave his apartment, the Sixth Precinct permit was delivered.

He raced up to the assembly point, on Washington Place between Sixth and Seventh Avenues. The police were already there—lots of them. They had set up sawhorses for crowd control, and dozens of cops lined the march perimeter. Most of them looked indifferent, even bored, as if this were just another parade, water off a duck's back. No more than a handful of cops seemed openly hostile, and even they, unwilling to acknowledge that such a gathering was *worth* their anger, opted for the snickering, offhanded joke. All of which was expected. The one real surprise was when a couple of the cops accepted leaflets being passed out—and when one or two were seen actually reading them.

The march wasn't scheduled to kick off until two P.M., but by late morning the marshals, with their orange armbands, were already in place, and knots of people had begun to mill around. It was impossible to tell how many had come to gape and how many to march, and Craig, now joined by Foster, nervously agreed that "not that many were going to end up marching"; Craig thought *maybe* a thousand. Had they overestimated political awareness in the community? Were people too frightened to show up—or too lazy to get out of bed on Sunday? By one P.M., an hour before the official starting time, there were still only enough apparent marchers to spread out for about two thirds of a block.

Craig held down any feelings of disappointment, reminding himself that he had successfully argued for making the march a reasonably long one, from the Village up Sixth Avenue into Central Park, on the assumption that many of the older or less committed gays and lesbians would be afraid to start out with the marchers, but might later yield to impulse and fall in somewhere along the line. He cheered up still more when balloons and signs began to appear. BETTER BLATANT THAN LATENT made him laugh out loud.

At two-ten, the march was still being held in place; some of the organizers apparently felt that a short delay might help to swell the ranks with latecomers. But the day had grown considerably warmer, and as people anxiously waited for the kickoff signal, with marchers and onlookers eyeing each other warily, with members of the news media dashing in and out of the crowd in search of the still-more-flamboyant queen, the still-angrier militant, and with marshals warning people to remove their glasses and loose jewelry "just in case," discomfort steadily grew. Word of an incident that had happened the previous night snaked its way insidiously through the crowd: At one A.M. five young gay men had been set upon in the Village by a group of toughs and beaten up; a cruising police car had finally rescued them, but at the station house the gay men had been urged to walk away from the incident and warned that if they pressed charges they would in all likelihood themselves be found guilty of "disorderly conduct."

By the time the kickoff came, at about two-fifteen, everyone, as

Foster put it, was "scared to death." As they fell in under their organizational banners—the GAAers notably resplendent in blue T-shirts with gold lambda crests, the GLFers crowded under a banner adorned with same-sex symbols—they shouted encouragement at each other, hugged their neighbors fiercely, raised clenched fists in the air, and spread their fingers wide in the V sign—for many, less a gesture of absolute defiance than a cover for embarrassment, an antidote for fear.

Confined to the far left lane of Sixth Avenue, they hoisted their signs high (HOMOSEXUAL IS NOT A FOUR–LETTER WORD; SAPPHO WAS A RIGHT–ON WOMAN), shouted their transgressive slogans—"Two, four, six, eight / Gay is just as good as straight"; "Ho-ho-homosexual / The ruling class is ineffectual." And right up front, leading the cheers all along the sixty-block route, was Sylvia. "Gimme a G!" she screamed over and over. "Gimme an A . . . a Y . . . a P . . . an O . . . a W . . . an E . . . an R . . . Whadda we want? *Gay Power!* When do we want it? *Now!*"

The kickoff in Los Angeles was just as fervent, a splash of color and sound down Hollywood Boulevard that had all the panache of what one reporter called "a political Mardi Gras." Some thirty organizations were represented, with GLF/LA and Troy Perry's Metropolitan Community Church among the largest. GLF members took turns portraying Jesus tied to a cross, being continuously prodded by a cop—with a nearby sign reading KILLED BY LAPD and listing the names of four homosexuals purportedly beaten to death by the L.A. police.

Transsexual Connie Vaughan, over six feet tall, rode proudly in an open convertible, and underground gay porn stars from Pat Rocco's films rode in other cars. Lesbian separatists did an intermittent group can-can. Banners and signs (some of which had caused controversy within the organizing committee) declared that FUCKING IS BETTER THAN KILLING and advocated MAKE LOVE, NOT BABIES. And a pickup truck exhibited an eight-foot-tall plaster-of-Paris Vaseline jar with "Gay Petroleum Jelly" on the label and an accompanying sign declaring AIN'T NOTHIN' NO GOOD WITHOUT THE GREASE. New Yorker Karla Jay found it all "*so* Hollywood!"

Karla had donned a lavender T-shirt for the march; she laughed out loud at her sartorial modesty when she ran into two male gender-fuck friends, Mother Boats and Jefferson Fuck Poland: Jeff was wearing a woman's bikini bottom, long hair—and nothing else. As in New York, a lot of closeted gays and lesbians watched from the sidewalk, but unlike New York, L.A. seems to have had a fair number of hecklers. Though the L.A. newspapers reported a relatively noncommittal crowd—without outbursts of either violence or spontaneous applause—veteran activist Jim Kepner heard a lot more cheers than that, and Karla ran into a fair amount of hostility. Whenever she tried to rest—her ribs still bothering her—people would gather around and shout nasty remarks. And at several different points, she saw bystanders angrily throwing things at the marchers.

Yvonne had awakened late with a hangover and had taken additional hours to make up her mind. It was nearly two when she finally got disgusted with her own ambivalence, jumped in her car, and headed in from Brooklyn to the Village. By the time she got to Washington Place a half hour later, the marchers had already set off. Now determined to take part, Yvonne hurried uptown to find and join them. Just as she rounded the corner approaching Macy's department store at Thirty-fourth Street, there they were—placards and banners waving bravely in the sun, voices raised on high.

She fell into the march—was *pulled* in by the sounds and sights, like so many others who had initially watched from the sidewalks, nervously calculating the risks. The exhilaration of the moment overwhelmed most calculations, just as Craig had hoped. Joining in was a major turning point for Yvonne: "It was clear to me from then on that it could no longer be just about partying. I had to save and protect myself by committing to my own liberation. It was like work time. . . ."

Foster, running back and forth through the line of marchers with his chronometer, sampling the numbers, realized with a thrill that the size of the march had more than doubled, that at least two thousand people were now taking part. Though later estimates would go as high as five thousand to ten thousand, the two FBI agents present at the march sent a teletype to J. Edgar Hoover that agreed with Foster's count: "approximately two thousand individuals." That made it twice the size of the four or five other Stonewall commemorative marches that came off across the country. Chicago managed to put fewer than a hundred people on the streets, while Los Angeles, with twelve hundred marchers, had the second-biggest turnout. By the following year, there were public celebrations in London and Paris.[99]

The marshals, fearing hostility from the onlookers and prodded by the cops, had kept the march moving at a rapid clip. But little overt anger was seen along the route. Many of those watching from the sidelines seemed to be gay; sometimes silently, and sometimes noisily, they urged the marchers on. "You're doing it for us" seemed to be their message, even as they themselves ricocheted between exhilaration and fear.

Aside from a few predictable SODOM AND GOMORRAH signs, and a Black Panther newspaper hawker shouting, "Get the Panther paper and stop all this foolishness!" the reaction of the spectators ranged from frozen to benign to overtly encouraging. The only persistent pests were tourists snapping photographs. They would rush up—"Oh look, Jane, that lesbian is eating *an ice cream cone!*"—and stick a camera in the startled lesbian's face, determined to immortalize the sight of one of the depraved licking away like the innocent child she wasn't.

It took only a little more than an hour to reach Central Park. Foster, forty-five years old and overweight, staggered in, huffing and puffing, but elated. Craig was so excited he could hardly stop smiling—at the size of the crowd, the good feeling and courage everywhere manifest. Karla, in L.A., let out a whoop when she crossed the finish line, her back killing her, her spirit soaring. Sylvia arrived yelling, Yvonne in exhausted tears. Jim, too, had tears pouring down his face as he stood on a rise in the ground and looked back at the line of people stretching some fifteen blocks into the distance: "I saw what we had done. It was remarkable. There we were in all of our diversity."

They were all, in their own ways, euphoric, just as, in their own ways, they had all somehow come through, had managed to arrive at this unimaginable coming together, this testimony to a difficult past surmounted and a potentially better future in view.

E P I L O G U E :   1 9 9 3

YVONNE FLOWERS continues to teach occupational therapy at York College, CUNY. During the seventies she was politically active with a wide variety of groups, including Black Women for Wages for Housework, the National Black Feminist Organization, and the Center for Women's Development at Medgar Evers College. She also founded "Sweet Sensations," a group that organized erotic "Tupperware parties as a means for increasing women's right to sexuality." In the mid-seventies, she got a second master's degree and, as part of an ongoing process of reclaiming her African-American heritage, changed her first name to Maua ("Flowers" in Swahili). She has long since given up drugs and alcohol, but is still afflicted with lupus.

JIM FOURATT has never ceased to be a political activist, of recent years dividing his time between New York City and Los Angeles. He was a founding board member of the Lesbian and Gay Community Services Center in New York and of Wipe Out AIDS (now known as H.E.A.L.), as well as a cofounder of ACT UP. In addition, he has been a contributing editor of *SPIN* magazine and writes a cultural column, "Ear Candy," syndicated in the gay press. He recently worked as the director of national publicity for Rhino Records.

FOSTER GUNNISON remained active in the CSLDC through 1973, but by the mid-seventies had phased himself out of the gay liberation movement—except for his archival work, which continues to this day.

Thereafter, he spent a decade cofounding several conservative political organizations in Connecticut, wrote for business magazines, and did research for the *National Conservative Digest*. In recent years he has taken growing offense (as a devoted cigar smoker) at what he calls "the neo-prohibitionary" antismoking crusade, and has helped to found a national smokers' liberation movement, which occupies most of his time today.

KARLA JAY spent the early seventies doing movement work and wandering between New York and California. She preferred the latter, but could never find any literary work there; so she lived on food stamps, hung out at Venice Beach, and wrote. She finally got a teaching assistantship in the French department at NYU (Bronx campus) and returned East for good. She began teaching English at Pace University in 1974, completed her doctorate in Comparative Literature in 1984 and then rose to the rank of full professor at Pace. She has published a number of books, including (with Allen Young) the pathbreaking *Out of the Closets*, and is currently the editor of NYU Press's series *The Cutting Edge: Lesbian Life and Literature*.

SYLVIA RIVERA quit the gay movement in 1973. Her departure was precipitated by the bruising struggle on Gay Pride Day that year over her right to speak; the more encompassing reason was the general lack of visibility and acceptance in the movement of transvestites. But in honor of her own past, she has continued to march in the yearly Christopher Street Liberation Day Parade, missing only twice in twenty years. After a close friend died from an overdose, Sylvia decided to kick drugs (but not alcohol) cold turkey. Some ten years ago, she moved to Tarrytown, New York, where she has held a variety of jobs in food services.

CRAIG RODWELL is still the proprietor of the Oscar Wilde Memorial Bookshop in Greenwich Village, and still maintains deep respect for the teachings of Mary Baker Eddy. He has begun an autobiographical and theoretical work based on his experiences in the gay movement. Of recent years he has been particularly concerned with the lack of outreach and services for gay and lesbian youth.

NOTES

(Pages 3–40)

GROWING UP

1. The description in the following pages of Foster Gunnison, Sr.'s career and marriage is drawn from material in the Gunnison Papers, kindly made available to me by Foster Gunnison, Jr. The following items have been of particular importance: Foster Gunnison, Sr., to William Adams Delano, Dec. 14, 1954; *St. Petersburg* (Florida) *Independent*, Oct. 20, 1961 (Gunnison obit); "A Keystone for a Nickel," *Forbes*, April 15, 1940; *The Prefabricated House*, #1: "A Movement Emerges," *Architectural Forum*, Dec. 1942; "Where Is Prefabrication?" *Fortune*, April 1946; "The Viceroys," *Life*, Nov. 11, 1946. Three towns in the United States—in Colorado, Utah, and Mississippi—carry the name Gunnison. For more information on the Gunnison family, see Russ Gammon, "Who Was John Gunnison?" *The Gunnison Country Times*, Dec. 28, 1988; George W. Gunnison, *A Genealogy of the Descendants of Hugh Gunnison . . . 1610–1876* (George A. Foxcroft, 1880); Foster N. Gunnison and Herbert Foster Gunnison, eds., *An Autobiography of the Reverend Nathaniel Gunnison* (Herbert Foster Gunnison, publisher, 1910); and Dwayne Vandenbusche, *The Gunnison Country* (B & B Printers, 1980).
2. The following letters in the Gunnison Papers have been the sources for reconstructing Foster Gunnison, Jr.'s college career: Gunnison Sr. to Gunnison Jr., Feb. 8, 21, 1945, Oct. 29, 1946; Thomas C. Gibb (Acting Dean) to Gunnison Sr., Feb. 6, 1945; Gunnison Jr. to Gunnison Sr., Feb. 1945; Evans to Gunnison Sr., June 14, 1945.

YOUNG ADULTHOOD

1. John D'Emilio, *Sexual Politics, Sexual Communities* (University of Chicago Press, 1983), pp. 98–99; Lillian Faderman, *Odd Girls and Twilight Lovers* (Columbia University Press, 1991), pp. 107–108, 127, 164–66.

(Pages 42–62)

2. For the information in this and the following paragraph: Eric Garber, "A Spectacle in Color: The Lesbian and Gay Subculture of Jazz Age Harlem," in Martin Duberman, Martha Vicinus, and George Chauncey, Jr., *Hidden From History: Reclaiming the Gay and Lesbian Past* (NAL, 1989; Meridian, 1990), pp. 318–31; and Lillian Faderman, *Odd Girls*, pp. 72–79.

3. The following description of lesbian life in the fifties and sixties draws especially on: Audre Lorde, *Zami: A New Spelling of My Name* (The Crossing Press, 1982), pp. 177–78 ("our rarity," the quotation in the next paragraph), 220–21, 224; "Audre Lorde & Maua Adele Ajanaku [Yvonne Flowers]: An Interview," in Andrea Weiss and Greta Schiller, *Before Stonewall: The Making of a Gay and Lesbian Community* (Naiad Press, 1988), pp. 54–55; Lillian Faderman, *Odd Girls*, chapter 7 (for "bluff," see p. 168).

4. For appreciations, however qualified, of lesbian pulp fiction, see Fran Koski and Maida Tilchen, "Some Pulp Sappho," in Karla Jay and Allen Young, eds., *Lavender Culture* (Jove/HBJ, 1978), pp. 262–74; Kate Brandt, "The Lifelines Still Hold," *Visibilities*, Jan.–Feb. 1991; Roberta Yusba, "Strange Sister: Literature of the Lurid," *Windy City Times*, June 22, 1989; and Diane Hamer, " 'I am a Woman': Ann Bannon and the Writing of Lesbian Identity in the 1950s," in Mark Lilly, ed., *Lesbian and Gay Writing: An Anthology of Critical Essays* (Temple University Press, 1990), pp. 47–75.

    For Claire Morgan, see Barbara Grier, *The Lesbian in Literature*, 3rd ed. (Naiad Press, 1981). Grier awards *The Price of Salt* an A***, which she gives only to "those few titles that stand out above all the rest and must properly belong in any collection of Lesbian literature." Bonnie Zimmerman's comprehensive study of lesbian fiction from 1969 to 1989, *The Safe Sea of Women* (Beacon, 1990), has a chapter dealing with pre-1969 work. There, Zimmerman agrees that most of the pulp fiction of the fifties contained "dreary portrayals of self-hating 'inverts' " (p. xi). But she singles out *The Price of Salt*, along with Jane Rule's *Desert of the Heart* (1964), as "sensitive and dignified . . . freed from stereotypes . . . [and containing characters] who make choices . . ." (p. 10) and who project "a positive and empowering image of lesbians" (p. xi).

5. This section draws on the following material in the Gunnison Papers, as well as on my interviews with Foster Gunnison, Jr.: press release by U.S. Steel, May 2, 1944; a "Confidential Report" on Gunnison Junior's test scores; Robert M. Vogel to Gunnison Sr., Oct. 29, 1954 ("such excellence"), Gunnison Jr. to Langhorn, May 23, 1960 (mathematical formula).

6. Little has been written about Joe Cino and his theater, but two articles do contain much useful detail: Michael Feingold, "Caffè Cino, 20 Years After Magic Time," *The Village Voice*, May 14, 1985; and Robert Heide, "Magic Time at the Caffè Cino," *New York Native*, May 6–19, 1985.

7. Arthur Bell, "The Sixties," in *The Christopher Street Reader*, eds. Michael Denneny, Charles Ortleb, and Thomas Steele (Coward-McCann, 1983), p. 28.

8. Much of the information and all of the quotes in this section come from my three interviews with Heide in 1990 and 1991.

    Heide had become connected with the Caffè Cino when Joe Cino offered him encouragement, and a home, after the critics had brutalized Heide's 1961 play, *West of the Moon*, one of the very first gay-themed plays ever done in New

York. (It had been preceded by Edward Albee's *The Zoo Story*, but the sexuality of the characters in that play was far more disguised than in Heide's; during the late fifties and early sixties, Albee and Heide were . . . good friends.)

Heide subsequently had two gay-themed plays produced at the Cino: *The Bed* (with sets and lights by Ron Link, and directed by Robert Dahdah), which ran for 150 performances in 1965; and *Moon*, which opened in 1967 and was performed widely in the late sixties. But in 1967, even so avant-garde a figure as Ellen Stewart, whose Café La Mama was an offshoot of Caffè Cino, was not cordial—though she later did provide a refuge for gay plays and playwrights (including Harvey Fierstein). In 1967, she told Heide, after seeing *The Bed*, that he should stop writing plays about homosexuals.

9. Interviews with Heide, 1990 and 1991. John Dodd had a distinguished later career in lighting; see Michael Smith's obituary in *The Village Voice*, Aug. 6, 1991. The Warhol quote is from Victor Bockris, *The Life and Death of Andy Warhol* (Bantam, 1990), p. 157.

10. The *Salute* article is reprinted in Martin Duberman, *About Time: Exploring the Gay Past*, 2nd ed. (Meridian, 1991), pp. 163–68. For the scene in the mid-sixties, see James Miller, "The Detective," *Life*, Dec. 3, 1965. Though the information and quotations in this section come almost entirely from my series of interviews with Sylvia Rivera in 1990 and 1991, I am indebted to Steven Watson's 1979 interview with her (tapes courtesy Watson) for some of the material relating to the Rivera-Johnson relationship.

THE EARLY SIXTIES

1. I am indebted to Jim Kepner (Kepner to Duberman, April 29, 1992) for some of the details in this paragraph. For more on Gerber, see Jonathan Katz, *Gay American History* (Meridian, 1992), and Jonathan Ned Katz, *Gay/Lesbian Almanac* (Harper & Row, 1983). Gerber's essay, "In Defense of Homosexuality," written under the pseudonym "Parisex," is reprinted in Martin Duberman, *About Time*, 2nd ed. (Meridian, 1991), pp. 145–48.

For more detail on the other subjects in these introductory pages, see: on the World War II experience, Allan Bérubé, *Coming Out Under Fire: The History of Gay Men and Women in World War Two* (Plume, 1991); on the founding of Mattachine, John D'Emilio, *Sexual Politics, Sexual Communities: The Making of a Homosexual Minority in the United States, 1940–1970* (University of Chicago Press, 1983), pp. 57–74, and Stuart Timmons, *The Trouble with Harry Hay* (Alyson, 1990), pp. 139–72; on the origins and early years of DOB, D'Emilio, *Sexual Politics*, pp. 101–107.

2. I am grateful to Jim Kepner (Kepner to Duberman, April 29, 1992) for the analogy to Freemasons (which is more accurate than the Communist-party analogy often made).

3. According to Jim Kepner (Kepner to Duberman, April 29, 1992), *ONE*, which was led until 1960 (when Kepner left) by Kepner, Dorr Legg, and Don Slater, continued to adhere to the notion that gays were a legitimate minority. Another West Coast group, SIR, organized in 1964, took up that same view "in practical

ways," though the "minority" theory was "stridently opposed by [Franklin] Kameny & most Eastern leaders." As to the reference in the next paragraph to *ONE*, Kepner has pointed out that philosophically the magazine stood in much the same relation to Mattachine as the NAACP did to the Urban League: "Mattachine and DOB leaders accepted that comparison, regarding *ONE* & the NAACP as too pushy or strident."

4. Jim Kepner, *Our Movement Before Stonewall* (International Gay and Lesbian Archives [IGLA], 1989).

5. Hal Call, one of the conservative leaders of Mattachine San Francisco, inflated that city's membership rolls by soliciting small donations in bars and making the donors "members"; he then got them to sign over proxies to him, which he used to maintain control of the organization. According to Kepner, *ONE* magazine had twelve hundred subscribers by 1960, about four hundred of them classified as "members" because they gave donations beyond the magazine's subscription price. By the mid-sixties, *ONE* was averaging 2,300 copies sold per issue, far outdistancing *Mattachine Review* or *The Ladder*. ONE also began to expand organizationally, setting up chapters in other cities. Today ONE of Long Beach, now an independent group, is larger than the parent organization, which is today called ONE Incorporated (Kepner to Duberman, April 29, 1992).

6. For this section, the following sources were especially useful: Barry Miles, *Ginsberg: A Biography* (Simon and Schuster, 1989), pp. 252–53 (Monk); Eric Garber, "A Spectacle in Color: The Lesbian and Gay Subculture of Jazz Age Harlem," in Duberman, et al., *Hidden from History*, pp. 318–31 (Harlem rent parties); Ira L. Jeffries, "Strange Fruit of the Purple Manor," *NYQ*, Feb. 23, 1992 (house parties); Audre Lorde, *Zami*, pp. 217–18 (food).

7. George Chauncey, Jr., and Lisa Kennedy, "Time on Two Crosses: An Interview with Bayard Rustin," *The Village Voice*, June 30, 1987.

THE MID-SIXTIES

1. For this section, the following sources (along with my interviews with Foster Gunnison, Jr.) have been central: *The New York Times*, Dec. 17, 1963, reprinted in its entirety in Duberman, *About Time*, 2nd ed. (Meridian, 1991), pp. 238–42. (For my own public quarrels with Bieber and Socarides, see Duberman, *Cures: A Gay Man's Odyssey* (Plume, 1992), pp. 64–66, 267–69; D'Emilio, *Sexual Politics*, especially, chapter 8 (1962–65 growth), pp. 150–160 (Kameny; Wicker), pp. 190–92 (SIR); Todd Gitlin, *The Sixties: Years of Hope, Days of Rage* (Bantam, 1987), p. 129 (Connor); Beth Hughes, "San Francisco's Own Stonewall," *San Francisco Sunday Examiner and Chronicle*, June 4, 1989 (Wolden; McIlvenna).

2. For examples of surveillance by government agents of homophile activities, see this book, *passim*. *Observation Post* (CCNY campus paper), Oct. 16, 1963 (for Wicker speech).

3. Cory's pioneering book, published in 1951, pleaded for an end to persecution and described gays as a legitimate minority group; it became something of a bible for the homophile movement. "Donald Webster Cory" was in fact a pseudonym for Edward Sagarin, who later became a professor of sociology and whose views

(Pages 101–103)

shifted so decisively over the years that he ended up as a defender of the psychiatric model of homosexuality as sickness, an antagonist to any kind of gay militancy, and a purported convert to heterosexuality.

4. Kameny to Hodges, March 15, 1964, International Gay Information Center Papers (henceforth IGIC Papers), NYPL: "the word *homophile* is coming into increasing currency." "Homophile" was preferred to "homosexual" because it deemphasized the stereotypical association of homosexuality with sex. (Toby Marotta, *The Politics of Homosexuality* [Houghton Mifflin, 1981], pp. 11–12.)

5. By 1965 New York Mattachine had become disaffected from ECHO, its president, Dick Leitsch, furious at (among other things) never having been reimbursed for the cost of transcribing the 1965 ECHO conference proceedings. In trying to coax the transcripts out of Leitsch (to no avail), Foster personally pledged a hundred dollars toward a total cost of some three hundred dollars. But by then Leitsch was saying that "ECHO is almost a dirty word around here," and when ERCHO (the Eastern Regional Conference, an offshoot of The North American Conference of Homophile Organizations, known as NACHO) failed in 1968 to pass resolutions of thanks to MSNY for its accomplishments (having thanked just about every other group), Leitsch was made angrier still. (Gunnison to Leitsch, Jan. 22, 26, 1967 [misdated 1968]; Leitsch to Gunnison, Jan. 23, Feb. 6, 1968—all in IGIC Papers, NYPL.)

6. Kameny to Leitsch, July 12 (students), 17, 1965. IGIC Papers, NYPL.

7. Inman to Robert Q. Achzehner, June 8, 1967; Gunnison to Inman, March 22, 1966—both in Gunnison Papers; see also D'Emilio, *Sexual Politics*, pp. 123, 152, 161–62. Inman initially called the Florida group The Atheneum Society. He "abolished" Florida Mattachine in early 1967.

The account that follows of Foster's initial involvement and his friendship with Inman derives from my interviews and from material in the Gunnison Papers, especially: Gunnison to Inman, Oct. 11, 19, Nov. 18, Dec. 21, 1965; March 9, 22, April 5, 1966; *Viewpoint* (Florida Mattachine), March, April, 1966; Inman to Kameny, Dec. 21, 1965; Inman to Clark Polak, April 7, 1966.

As an example of Inman's outspokenness, he admonished Frank Kameny, whom he hugely admired, "When pinned down, you either lash out at those who disagree, or you attempt to totally subjugate those who do agree" (Inman to Kameny, Dec. 21, 1965). Nichols and Inman, like Kameny, were, in the context of the homophile movement, militants; in the context of our own day, that militancy seems circumscribed. As late as 1965, for example, Jack Nichols was writing *against* those "who are unbalanced enough to have demonstrations —before the question of sickness had been laid to rest. . . . [The] experts can tell us whether or not we are sick. Let them decide. . . ." ("Warren Adkins" [Jack Nichols] to Dick Leitsch, April 1, 1965. IGIC Papers, NYPL.) Nichols insists, however, that this letter was meant as "a joke"—as evinced by its April 1 date. In support of that contention, see D'Emilio, *Sexual Politics*, p. 163 for a 1963 statement by Nichols in which he clearly rejects the medical model. Richard Inman, for his part, helped in 1965 to organize, in conjunction with the South Florida Psychiatric Society, a program of free counseling for teenagers who "want to get out of the gay life." (Elver A. Barker to Adkins and Inman, May 23, 1966. IGIC Papers, NYPL.)

(Pages 107–111)

8. Leitsch himself credits Craig with bringing him into Mattachine (interview with Leitsch in the gay paper *Equal Time*, Oct. 12–26, 1990).

     For the following account of developments within the New York and San Francisco homophile movements, I have relied heavily on the extensive Leitsch correspondence in the IGIC Papers, NYPL; see also D'Emilio, *Sexual Politics*, pp. 163–64, 168–73, 185–86; Beth Hughes, "San Francisco's Own Stonewall" *San Francisco Sunday Examiner and Chronicle*, June 4, 1989; Stuart Timmons, *The Trouble with Harry Hay* (Alyson, 1990), pp. 214–20 (L.A. rift).

9. Leitsch to Kameny, "Sunday" (July 1965), IGIC Papers, NYPL; Wicker to Duberman, Oct. 10, 1993.

10. Leitsch to Robert S. Walker (treasurer, Council on Religion and the Homosexual), Jan. 6, 1965; Leitsch to Elver Barker, May 27, 1966 (IGIC Papers, NYPL); Kepner to Duberman, April 29, 1992. Whereas much of the male pornography of the mid-sixties was on the order of muscular, toga-clad, ill-at-ease "Roman soldiers," the models in *DRUM* were more straightforwardly erotic.

11. Inman to Leitsch, Oct. 2, 1965; Beardemphl to Leitsch, Oct. 11, 1965; Leitsch to Wiesbauer, Oct. 21, 1965; Leitsch to Kameny, July 25, 1965 ("silly"); Leitsch to Emma Van Cott (DOB "cooperation")—all in IGIC Papers, NYPL.

12. No doubt they [the other leaders] "mean well," Leitsch acidly wrote one supporter, but "so, undoubtedly, did Adolf Hitler . . . their effectiveness is eliminated by massive egos" (meant in contrast, apparently, to Leitsch's own). He quoted with satisfaction Craig's characterization of Polak as "the homosexual's Adam Clayton Powell," scorned Shirley Willer's "constant reactionary tactics," and described his opponents within MSNY and the breakaway West Side Discussion Group as a bunch of "old aunties." (Leitsch to Elver Barker, aka Karl B. Harding, May 27, 1966. [Barker was the effective, modest leader of Denver Mattachine]); Leitsch to *CLEARING HOUSE Newsletter*, Nov. 3, 1967; Robert Hinton to Inman, March 7, 1966; Leitsch to Polak, March 23, 1965 ("old aunties"); Polak to Leitsch, June 4, 1965—all in IGIC Papers, NYPL. The following year, Leitsch insisted that *Playboy* separate MSNY clearly from Polak's Janus Society. (Leitsch to Carol Rubel, Oct. 23, 1967.)

13. Leitsch to Elver Barker, May 27, 1966; Leitsch to Donald S. Hostetter (SLA chairman), July 6, 1965; Leitsch to the editor, *Suffolk County News*, Nov. 8, 1965; Leitsch to Henry diSuvero (New York Civil Liberties Union), Sept. 12, 1966; Leitsch to Sanford D. Garelik (chief inspector, N.Y. Police Dept.), Oct. 11, 1966—all in IGIC Papers, NYPL.

14. Leitsch to John V. Lindsay, May 13, 1966; Leitsch to Evander Smith, May 13, 1966. IGIC Papers, NYPL.

15. Kepner to Duberman, April 29, 1992; Beth Hughes, "San Francisco's Own Stonewall." *San Francisco Sunday Examiner and Chronicle*, June 4, 1989. Kepner's letter includes information on several small-scale demonstrations in regard to inclusion in the armed forces; he opposed the demonstrations, "feeling that it was time for us to join the growing peace movement instead of asking for a fair share of the killing—even though I wasn't a committed dove." Mattachine in San Francisco had by this time pretty much become a front for the varied commercial operations of longtime activist Hal Call, including an "adult" bookstore that served as an entryway to a sex club where porn films, many of them

(Pages 111–117)

also made by Call, were shown. In Los Angeles, a bitter battle for internal control of ONE, Inc., had resulted by April 1965 in two separate organizations, both claiming to be the true church, with the insurgents' magazine, *Tangents*, quickly outstripping the earlier *ONE* magazine. In both cities, the older homophile organizations were being bypassed by newer, more militant groups: the Southern California Council on Religion and the Homosexual, and PRIDE, whose newsletter had evolved, by September 1967, into *The Advocate*. As for Daughters of Bilitis, it remained, on *both* coasts, wedded to polite quietism. The most vocal dissenter from that policy was Barbara Gittings, who had become editor of *The Ladder* in late 1962, and who, along with her lover, Kay "Tobin" (Lahusen), became active allies of Kameny's in ECHO.

16. *Viewpoint* (Florida Mattachine), June 1966. Richard Inman, too, had been arrested—twice in 1954—for "simply being in a gay bar"; both times he put up a $250 bond and was not prosecuted (Inman to Hodges, March 12, 1965. IGIC Papers, NYPL). For the account of the 1965 demonstrations and, subsequently, of the 1965–1968 Reminders, the following (along with my interviews) were most important: the Mattachine Society Papers in IGIC Papers, NYPL; Vito Russo interview with Barbara Gittings, Channel L (TV, NYC), Feb. 27, 1983 (tape courtesy of Russo); advertisement for Second Annual Reminder, courtesy Rodwell; Bureau of Special Services agents' reports, May 25 (twice), Aug. 17, 1966 (courtesy Scherker Estate). An agent was also present when Craig helped to organize a demonstration in front of the United Nations in response to press reports that the Cuban government had put homosexuals in labor camps. The agent reported placards that read, among others, SEX IN ANY FORM IS GOOD, and SEX IS A FUNDAMENTAL HUMAN RIGHT, and he added that he had overheard several bystanders say that the demonstration was "a disgrace" (agent's report, dated April 18, 1965 [courtesy Scherker Estate]).

17. Leitsch to Kameny, "Sunday" (July 1965). IGIC Papers, NYPL.

18. Kameny to Leitsch, July 12, 1965. IGIC Papers, NYPL.

19. *The Insider* (Mattachine Society, Washington, D.C.), July 1965. As a sample of Kameny's advance planning: Kameny to Colbert (Pennsylvania Department of Forests and Waters), June 11, 1966; Kameny to Rodwell, June 20, 1966. IGIC Papers, NYPL.

20. The account of the sip-in that follows derives from *New York Post*, April 17, 1966; *Village Voice*, May 5, 1966; *New York Times*, May 5, June 5, 1966; and Leitsch to Sheila Paine, April 29, 1966, Leitsch to Evander Smith, May 13, 1966, both in IGIC Papers, NYPL.

21. For a particularly graphic account of entrapment, see Andrew Velez, "Looking Back in Anger," *NYQ*, Nov. 3, 1991. Sascha L., who briefly worked the door at Stonewall (see p. 182), describes Gerling in those years as "looking like a drag queen—pumps and wigs." She was admired, even beloved, Sascha L. says, for cursing out the cops (and occasionally even the judge) in open court for having entrapped and arrested homosexuals. "Don't you have a girlfriend?" she would bellow. "Don't you want to get laid or something? Why are you bothering these people?" The secret to Gerling's success in getting so many gay men sprung from jail was, according to Sascha L., not simply payoffs, but her willingness—"she used to be very hot"—to put out for several of the judges. She would postpone

a case if the "right" judge—i.e., one she had slept with—wasn't sitting. (Interview with Sascha L., Aug. 26, 1991.) Chuck Shaheen (interview, Nov. 20, 1991) also heard rumors that Gerling slept with some of the judges, and adds that she was also used by the Mafia as a lawyer.

Like many gay men of my generation, I carried Enid Gerling's phone number with me when I went out for a night's cruising. And like many others, too, I (though never arrested) came to regard her as something of a heroine for having gotten so many gay men out of jail. I said as much in the speech I gave dedicating Stonewall Place in 1989—and was promptly set right by Craig Rodwell (see Duberman, *About Time*, pp. 424–27). As recently as 1990, Gerling was employed as defense counsel for fourteen men arrested on drug charges in the West Village gay bar, the Ninth Circle (*Outweek*, Oct. 24, 1990). For a one-sided whitewashing of Gerling, making her into a selfless patron saint of liberation, see *NYQ*, Feb. 16, 1992.

22. A substantial debate has opened up as to whether butch-femme categorization in the lesbian world of the forties and fifties *was* role-playing, and if so to what degree. The debate has been further enkindled by what has become known in the nineties as "the return of butch-femme." For an introduction to the large literature relating to both the historical and contemporary debate, see especially Joan Nestle, *The Persistent Desire: A Femme-Butch Reader* (Alyson, 1992); Madeline Davis and Elizabeth Kennedy, *Boots of Leather*, *Slippers of Gold* (Routledge, 1993); the Karen Kahn interview with Nestle, "Constructing the Lesbian Self," *Sojourner*, June 1992; and Lillian Faderman, "The Return of Butch and Femme: A Phenomenon in Lesbian Sexuality of the 1980s and 1990s," *Journal of the History of Sexuality*, vol. 2, no. 4 (1992), pp. 578–96.

23. The material on the Columbia strike is mostly taken from my essay, "On Misunderstanding Student Rebels," *The Atlantic Monthly*, November 1968 (reprinted in Duberman, *The Uncompleted Past* [Random House, 1969], pp. 309–31). But a large literature exists on the strike; see, for example, Ronald Fraser, *1968* (Pantheon, 1988).

24. Most of the details on life at Rikers are from my interview with Gregory Terry, August 29, 1990. Terry was also in the queens' cellblock in 1966, having been given a four-month sentence for "solicitation of a police officer." Two years later, the same plainclothesman, not recognizing Terry, tried to entrap him again. Terry simply walked up to him and said, "Excuse me, *Officer*, do you have the time?" In 1974, by then employed as an investigator for the Legal Aid Society, Terry had the satisfaction of returning to Rikers to work on cases involving prisoners' rights.

25. Interview with Ivan Valentin, July 5, 1991. Later, Ivan helped to win a major legal decision. In 1975, a moribund Connecticut state law barring female impersonators was resurrected to close Ivan's "Leading Ladies of New York" show. He took his case to the University of Connecticut School of Law, and the matter ended in more permissive legislation. (The story is told in Eric Gordon, "An Imitation of Images," *The Hartford Advocate*, Oct. 27, 1976, Feb. 9, 1977.)

26. Interview with Joe Tish, Nov. 15, 1991. Both Tish, in his late sixties, and Frankie Quinn, in his late seventies, continue to do drag shows—mostly at senior-citizen centers.

(Pages 126–146)

27. Steven Watson interview with Minette, 1979 (transcript courtesy Watson); Robert Heide, "Drag Queens," *Other Stages*, vol. 2, no. 16 (April 17–30, 1980).

28. Steven Watson interview with Holly Woodlawn, n.d. (transcript courtesy Watson). See also Holly Woodlawn's *A Low Life in High Heels* (St. Martin's, 1991).

29. Free [Abbie Hoffman], *Revolution for the Hell of It* (Dial, 1968), p. 29.

30. Hoffman, *Revolution*, p. 102.

31. The TV clip is from the PBS show *Making Sense of the Sixties* (tape courtesy Marty Jezer, to whom I'm also grateful for letting me see the page proofs of his book, *Abbie Hoffman: American Rebel* (Rutgers University Press, 1992).

   In *Do It!* (Ballantine, 1970, p. 129), Jerry Rubin wrote: "Look at the criminal record of a political activist. It reads like the record of a sex deviant—public nuisance, loitering, disorderly conduct, trespassing, disturbing the peace."

32. Interviews with Robert Heide, 1990 and 1991.

33. Hoffman, *Revolution*, pp. 33–37; Jezer, *Hoffman*, 109–110; Emmett Grogan, *Ringolevio: A Life Played for Keeps* (Little, Brown, 1972), pp. 399–401.

34. The account is in Todd Gitlin, *The Sixties: Years of Hope, Days of Rage* (Bantam, 1987), p. 231. The fabrication, in Jim's mind, is the more egregious in a book that—except for this trivializing incident—entirely lacks any treatment of gay oppression or liberation.

35. Hoffman, *Revolution*, pp. 32–33.

36. This account is largely drawn from my interviews with Fouratt, but the "on the map" quote is from Hoffman, *Revolution* p. 91.

37. Hoffman, *Revolution*, pp. 91–92; Jezer, *Hoffman*, 146, 149–50.

THE LATE SIXTIES

1. As quoted (in both paragraphs) in Clare Coss, "Single Lesbians Speak Out," *Lesbians at Midlife: The Creative Transition*, Barbara Sang, Joyce Warshow, and Adrienne J. Smith, eds. (Spinsters Book Company: 1991), pp. 137–38.

2. The following account of the Kansas City conference, and the events surrounding it, largely derives from the IGIC Papers, NYPL, and two privately held manuscript collections: the Gunnison Papers and the William B. Kelley Papers. The two private collections are storehouses of previously unresearched material on the homophile movements, and I am indebted to both Gunnison and Kelley for giving me access.

   The essential items used for describing the first planning conference are as follows: Gunnison to Leitsch, Jan. 22, 1967 (formalisms); William Kelley to Leitsch, Feb. 26, 1966; Leitsch to Kelley, Feb. 28, 1966—all in IGIC Papers, NYPL; "Persons in Attendance," Feb. 18–21, 1966, Gunnison Papers, gives a complete roster of individuals and organizations; William B. Kelley, "Minutes of the National Planning Conference of Homophile Organizations, Kansas City, Mo.," 21 typed pages, Kelley Papers. Kelley was recording secretary for the conference. The full "Statement of Purposes," drawn up by Clark Polak, is in the Gunnison Papers; it includes the resolution about "objective research." For Gunnison's reactions to individuals: Gunnison to Inman, March 9, 22, Sept. 18,

1966, Gunnison Papers. For his retreat from barbershop work: Gunnison to Inman, Oct. 11, 1965, Gunnison Papers.

3. *The Homosexual Citizen*, April 1966. Foster repeated his argument on the importance of "upgrading our image" in *Mattachine Midwest Newsletter*, vol. II, no. 1 (January 1966).

4. "Ten Days in August" was actually three consecutive conferences rolled into one: the Fourth National Convention of the DOB; the Consultation on Theology and the Homosexual; and, from August 25 to August 27, the National Planning Conference of Homophile Organizations (a name Del Martin had suggested during the Kansas City meeting). The roster at San Francisco, compiled by Gunnison, is in his papers. Most of the leaders present in Kansas City returned for the San Francisco conference (but not Nichols, Gittings, Grier, Inman or Tobin); and Dorr Legg, Harry Hay, and Jim Kepner were present for the first time. For the range of events: *Viewpoint* (Florida Mattachine), October 1966, and *Citizens' News*, vol. V, no. 10 (October 1966).

    The account of the San Francisco conference that follows, is again drawn largely from materials in the Gunnison and Kelley manuscript collections. For the argument over accreditation: Dorr Legg to Kelley, March 16, 1966, and Clarence A. Colwell to "Dear Friends," Aug. 5, 1966, both in Kelley Papers. For the proliferation of resolutions: William B. Kelley, "Preliminary Summary of Substantive Actions Approved by the National Planning Conference of Homophile Organizations . . ." Kelley Papers. For Strait's remark: *Citizens' News*, vol. V, no. 10 (October 1966). Another negative assessment ("National Conference Made Few Advances") is in *The ARC News* (Sacramento), vol. 1, no. 8 (Sept. 1966).

5. Stuart Timmons, *The Trouble with Harry Hay* (Alyson, 1990), pp. 214, 223.

6. *ONE Confidential*, vol. XI, no. 9 (September 1966). Polak's remarks, which follow in the next paragraph, are excerpted in *Citizens' News*, vol. V, no. 10 (October 1966).

7. The quotes in this and the following two paragraphs are from the typescript of Foster Gunnison, Jr., "Three Concrete Steps to Further the Homophile Movement," Gunnison Papers.

8. Del Martin, "The Lesbian's Majority Status," *The Ladder*, June 1967. The name "NACHO" was not formally adopted until the 1968 convention.

9. Jerome Stevens to Richard Inman, Sept. 12, 1966, Gunnison Papers. Gunnison had been appointed by the Rev. Clay Colwell, who was "Moderator" of the August 1966 conference. Colwell, a heterosexual, was chosen to preside because he was "independent" of the organizations involved and could be "trusted" (Gunnison to Duberman, Dec. 22, 1991)—less a shrewd calculation, perhaps, than a measure of homosexual self-distrust. Gunnison thought Colwell "the best non-homo homo that ever was," and adduced as proof that when Colwell had been " 'groped' at the Saturday evening SIR dance," he "didn't do anything about it. That's the acid test of dedication as far as I am concerned" (Gunnison to Inman, Sept. 18, 1966, Gunnison Papers). When Colwell resigned in 1967 due to ill health, he was replaced by another heterosexual, Robert W. Cromey, of St. Aidan's Episcopal Church in San Francisco (Inman to Colwell, Sept. 5, 1966, and May 25, 1967; Inman to Cromey, June 24, 1967—all in Gunnison Papers).

(Pages 154–155)

One of Foster's most enjoyable times during the convention was the evening he took Doris Hanson and Virginia Bruce out to San Francisco's famed nightclub Finocchio's, to see the female-impersonator floor show. Hanson, a close friend of Barbara Gittings, "took a crush" on him (that is, according to Foster) and "was in a most unlesbianlike frame of mind whenever I was around." Virginia Bruce was a well-known transsexual who wrote and lectured on the subject. Foster "admired her. She's really no kook," he wrote Inman, "quite sincere, a real tough problem she has to deal with, and a wry sense of humor." (Gunnison to Inman, Sept. 18, 1966—Gunnison Papers.) A few years later, Foster was asked to escort a transsexual named Charlayne to a meeting in New York of the West Side Discussion Group, and though he found her "kind of cute," he added (in a letter to Barbara Gittings, Jan. 12, 1970—Gunnison Papers), "Why can't people just stay with what God gave them? I didn't know whether to offer her a cigar on the train, or what to do."

10. Gunnison to Inman, Sept. 18, 1966, Gunnison Papers; attached note to Duberman describes the course of the therapy.

11. Marvin Cutler, *Homosexuals Today—1956: A Handbook of Organizations and Publications* (ONE, Inc., 1956). "Warren D. Adkins" (Jack Nichols) published a brief (seven-page) "The Homophile Movement: A Historical Perspective," in *The Homosexual Citizen* (Washington Mattachine's monthly), April 1967.

12. The quotations in this and the following paragraphs are all from Foster Gunnison, Jr., "An Introduction to the Homophile Movement" (The Institute of Social Ethics, Sept. 1967), Gunnison Papers.

Foster's bolder side can also be seen in two other pieces he wrote in 1966–1967. In an extended review of Ronald Atkinson's *Sexual Morality* in *The Homosexual Citizen* (December 1966), he chastised Atkinson for failing to demolish the psychoanalytic view of homosexuality as "illness"; argued that homosexuality was "an unchosen condition, resistant to change"; and even made an oblique case for homosexual marriage. In another piece for *The Homosexual Citizen* ("The Hidden Bias: The Homophile Movement and Law Reform," March 1967), Foster argued against a pending British bill that would place the age of consent for heterosexuals at sixteen, but for homosexuals at twenty-one, as a double standard that would compromise the effort to win acceptance "under the same rules that apply to everyone else."

13. For more on the Society for Human Rights and the Veterans Benevolent Association, see Jonathan Katz, *Gay American History* (2nd ed., Meridian, 1992), and (for the Society) Jonathan Ned Katz, *Gay/Lesbian Almanac* (Harper & Row, 1983).

According to Jim Kepner, whose encyclopedic knowledge is unparalleled, the Sons of Hamidy was "a *projected* organization in 1942–44, starting in Rhinelander, Wisc. . . . My Rhinelander pen pal, Wally Jordan, wrote to me & others that SOH had previous incarnations in the 1880's & 1930's, each time falling victim to 'bitch fights.' He said the organization was led by important people like 'Senators and Generals,' but there is no evidence for these earlier incarnations. . . . Years later, he wrote me that SOH, like the Legion of the Damned, was simply a wish of his—LOD being his camp term for a few gay servicemen he met at bars in Cooledge & Holbrook, AZ. . . . It was never an organization. I

(Pages 155–159)

wrote the original of the account of SOH which appeared in [Dorr] Legg's *Homosexuals Today, 1956*—but Dorr, with no personal knowledge of SOH, altered what I wrote to make it seem that SOH had real existence." (Kepner to Duberman, April 29, 1992.)

14. Jim Skaggs, "Committee on Unity Reports," *Vector*, March 1968.

15. The quotes in this and the following two paragraphs are from Leitsch to Elver Barker, May 27, 1966, IGIC Papers, NYPL; Kepner to Duberman, April 29, 1992; Gunnison, "REPORT—July 20, 1967," Gunnison Papers; and Kelley and Roland Keith to "Members of the Conference" [NACHO San Francisco, Aug. 25–27, 1966], Kelley Papers.

16. *The Advocate*, vol. 1, no. 1 (September 1967). Stephen Donaldson also referred to "a miraculous spirit of good will" at the Washington conference, though he acknowledged as well a certain amount of "acidity" (Donaldson, "The Fine Art of Compromise," Kelley Papers). Gunnison's official tally of accredited organizations came to twenty-eight (from twelve cities), but not all those accredited actually sent delegates (Gunnison, "ACCREDITED ORGANIZATIONS— June 22, 1967." Gunnison Papers).

17. Arthur Warner ("Austen Wade") to Leitsch, July 26, 1967; Leitsch to Warner, Aug. 1, 1967; Leitsch to Homophile Clearinghouse, Feb. 7, 1968; Leitsch to Randy Wicker, Feb. 20, 1968—all in IGIC Papers, NYPL; Kepner to Duberman, April 29, 1992. Leitsch leaned at one point toward forming an association with new homophile groups in Cincinnati and Phoenix, at another toward forming a statewide Mattachine Society of New York. What he was aiming for, he wrote his loyal lieutenant, Arthur Warner, was to ensure that participants be "carefully screened and selected to sift out social clubs, profiteers, vanity groups and the like." By 1970, Leitsch was trying to enlist the wealthy gay businessman Jack Campbell in his ongoing efforts to form an "affiliation of like-minded groups who can work together in harmony." He assured Campbell that the groups would be handpicked, and would avoid the "fighting and jockeying for power, and . . . back-stabbing"—"Some of us are too mature and too serious for that crap"— characteristic of other regional and national associations (Leitsch to Campbell, March 2, 1970, IGIC Papers, NYPL).

18. Typed minutes of the Aug. 16–18, 1967, NACHO conference, Kelley Papers; Kelley was not the secretary—he had been ill and unable to attend. Jerome Stevens, "A Model Program?" n.d., Gunnison Papers. Jim Kepner has listed some of the other groups denied admission: "Vancouver's ASK because they got an application in late (months before the conference); the National League for Social Understanding because they dabbled in occultism (which would bring us all into disrepute); the National Legal Defense Fund because it was initially a conference committee, later separately incorporated . . . etc" (Kepner to Duberman, April 29, 1992).

19. Virginia O. Roak, "Report on the Third North American Homophile Conference 17–19 August 1967," *The Ladder*, January 1968.

20. Gunnison, "An Introduction to the Homophile Movement," Gunnison Papers.

21. Del Martin, "The Lesbian's Majority Status," *The Ladder*, June 1967; Gunnison to Donn Teal, n.d., Kelley Papers. According to Jim Kepner, Martin "did make

(Pages 160–172)

a loud withdrawal later, insisting that lesbians had little to gain in the homophile movement" (Kepner to Duberman, April 29, 1992).

22. Gunnison to Jim Skaggs (SIR chair), Nov. 5, 1967. Kelley Papers.

23. Typed minutes of the Aug. 16–18, 1967, NACHO Conference, Kelley Papers. A "Unity Committee" was also established, with seven members each from the Eastern, Western, and Midwestern regions (Craig Rodwell was one of the Eastern representatives). The committee was empowered "to study the question of stronger national cooperation and influence through a possible federation of all interested homophile organizations." It functioned, sporadically and inefficiently, over the next two years. ("Committee on Unity Reports," n.d. IGIC Papers, NYPL.)

24. The "militant-sentimental" quote is from *The Gay Crusaders*, Kay Tobin and Randy Wicker, eds. (Paperback Library, 1972), p. 66.

25. The press release and ads are courtesy of Rodwell. Some of the meeting notes, and a statement of purpose, are in the IGIC Papers, NYPL. Craig's sensitivity to sexism was apparent in 1966 when he became vice president of MSNY. The nominating committee (of which Craig was a member) had originally presented Renée Cafiero for the post. But when a conservative opposition slate developed, it was thought unwise to present a ticket of three women and two men, and so Cafiero withdrew in favor of Craig. He told her at the time that he would later resign the position and recommend her appointment—and he did so, effective January 1, 1967 (Rodwell to Board of Directors, MSNY, Dec. 7, 1966. IGIC Papers, NYPL).

26. Harriet Van Horne, "Enough of All This," *New York Post*, April 9, 1969.

1969

1. Gitlin, *The Sixties* (Bantam, 1987), pp. 343–44. See Gitlin, *passim*, for more details on all of the developments and incidents described in this section.

2. For Laurence and Whittington: D'Emilio, *Sexual Politics*, pp. 230–31; *San Francisco Chronicle*, April 10, 1969. For comparable confrontations in L.A., especially around the police action in Wilmington against a bar called PATCH II, see John Hammond's interview with Morris Kight, "A Quarter Century of Liberation—Plus," *New York Native*, Feb. 18, 1991; and Jim Kepner, *Our Movement Before Stonewall* (IGLA, 1989), p. 14. Kepner reports that when patrons of PATCH II protested against being fag-bashed, the police response was "We aren't interested in protecting cocksuckers!" In response, Lee Glaze and forty other gay men (including Troy Perry) protested in front of the Harbor Police Station.

3. D'Emilio, *Sexual Politics*, pp. 229–30; interviews with Gunnison. (A curious sidelight: Rita Laporte had grown up with Foster Gunnison at Gypsy Trail; the two had lost track of each other as adults until they met again years later at a NACHO national planning conference.)

4. This account of the league and its action against the Columbia Medical School panel is from D'Emilio, *Sexual Politics*, pp. 209–210, 216; and Robert A. Martin ("Stephen Donaldson"), "Student Homophile League: Founder's

(Pages 173–182)

Retrospect," *Gay Books Bulletin*, no. 9, Spring/Summer 1983, pp. 30–33.

5. Alice Echols, *Daring to Be Bad: Radical Feminism in America, 1967–1975* (University of Minnesota Press, 1989), p. 60. I have relied heavily on Echols, along with my interviews with Jay, for the discussion of radical feminism and the Red-stockings.

6. Echols, *Daring to Be Bad*, pp. 92–96.

7. Interviews with Fouratt; also, Abe Peck, *Uncovering the Sixties: The Life and Times of the Underground Press* (Pantheon, 1985), pp. 169–70.

8. Peck, *Uncovering the Sixties*, pp. 176–77.

9. Randy Wicker was also fed up with Leitsch's leadership. He accused Leitsch of "spending the major part of your time writing a book [never completed] & entertaining your new lover," and withdrew from any further financial support of MSNY (Wicker to Leitsch, Feb. 11, 1968. IGIC Papers, NYPL). In response, Leitsch asked, "When, and if, I leave who else will you find who will work night and day, live and sleep Mattachine, and put up with all of the shit one has to take around here?" (Leitsch to Wicker, Feb. 20, 1969. IGIC Papers, NYPL.)

10. Interview with Chuck Shaheen, Nov. 20, 1991. Nor did Stonewall even have an ice machine; the staff used to buy huge quantities, several times a night, from Smiler's Deli.

11. Shaheen (interview, Nov. 20, 1991) confirms that Murphy was "very involved with the procurement of young boys" (though *not* at Stonewall), and that, as part of his job as bouncer and doorman, he would be told to beat up certain people. Tommy Lanigan-Schmidt (interview May 2, 1992) remembers seeing a young Puerto Rican, regarded as one of Murphy's lovers, being whisked off the sidewalk into a waiting car and never being seen again; the rumor was that he had cheated on Murphy or stolen from him. Yet Shaheen liked Murphy, and thought of him as a "perfect gentleman." And Lanigan-Schmidt talked compassionately of how the need to survive drove Murphy to reprehensible behavior.

Bob Kohler (who at the time owned a talent agency and hung out at Stonewall) confirms that Murphy "was a police informer" (interview with Kohler, Aug. 20, 1990). In an interview given on the tenth anniversary of the Stonewall riot, Murphy additionally identified himself as having until recently (1979) been "an undercover agent, specializing in gay bars and corruption, for the New York State Select Committee on Crime" (Harold Pickett, "I Like to Call It an Uprising," *Gay Community News*, June 23, 1979). Bebe Scarpi confirms that Murphy "set people up to be mugged and robbed" (phone interview with Scarpi, Aug. 22, 1990). For the police beating later administered to Murphy, see p. 219.

12. Interview with Sascha L., August 26, 1991. Sascha is currently (1992) the doorman at a popular gay bar in Greenwich Village.

13. Chris Davis interview with Murphy, n.d. (1987?), tape courtesy Davis. My Nov. 15, 1991 interview with Joe Tish (the drag performer) and my Nov. 20, 1991 interview with Chuck Shaheen, confirm Murphy's saint/sinner reputation. Murphy died, aged sixty-three, on Feb. 28, 1989, and New York City's Heritage of Pride designated him the honorary grand marshal for the twentieth-anniversary march that June. The printed 1989 Heritage program led off with "A Tribute to the 'Mayor of Christopher Street.' " Later in life, Murphy did do outstanding charitable work on behalf of the retarded.

(Pages 183–187)

Among the many positive comments on the Stonewall are Dick Kanon's "It was the best place we ever had" (*New York Post*, July 8, 1969); and Thomas Lanigan-Schmidt's "Here the consciousness of knowing you 'belonged' nestled into that warm feeling of finally being *HOME*. . . . We loved the Stonewall." ("Mother Stonewall and the Golden Rats," courtesy Lanigan-Schmidt.)

14. Interview with Ivan Valentin, July 5, 1991; interview with Sascha L., Aug. 26, 1991. It should be added, however, that Ivan, too, has been described as having been sometimes involved in "shady dealings."

15. Interviews with Sascha L. (Aug. 26, 1991) and Shaheen (Nov. 20, 1991). Shaheen and Sascha disagree in part on the ownership of some of the bars. I have accepted Shaheen on the Stonewall (Sascha has it owned by the Gambino family) because he knew its operations intimately; and I have accepted Sascha on Washington Square (Shaheen has both it and the Gold Bug owned by the Gambino family) because he knew the operations of those two establishments far better than Shaheen did.

Tommy Lanigan-Schmidt (interview May 2, 1992) went frequently to the Tenth of Always and said that so many young kids hung out there (partly because of Murphy's presence), that from his own perspective as a Catholic kid from New Jersey, it had the air of nothing so much as "a surreal Catholic Youth dance."

16. Interviews with Sascha L. (Aug. 26, 1991) and Shaheen (Nov. 20, 1991).

17. Interview with Chuck Shaheen, Nov. 20, 1991. Some details, though irregularly reliable, about the Stonewall Inn's history prior to its incarnation as a gay bar, can be found in Larry Boxx, "Remembering Stonewall," *Bay Area Reporter*, June 22, 1989 (also printed, with some slight variations, in *Long Beach/Stonewall 20— 1989*), and Mark Haile, "The Truth about Stonewall," *BLK*, June 1989.

18. Interview with Shaheen, Nov. 20, 1991.

19. The details in this and the next four paragraphs are from my interview with Shaheen, Nov. 20, 1991. Before he met Tony, Shaheen had worked in the coat-check room at the One-Two-Three, an after-hours club on University Place between Thirteenth and Fourteenth Streets.

20. Interview with Ryder Fitzgerald (assistant to "T.L.R.," the electrician), May 5, 1992.

21. Not every police precinct in New York was corrupt. It was part of Mafia lore never to open a gay club on the East Side above Fifty-ninth Street, because the police there couldn't be bought. And when Fat Tony, disregarding that advice, later opened an East Side gay club, it lasted exactly one night; the police not only raided and closed the place but, atypically, arrested everyone on the premises.

22. The information in this and the next four paragraphs is from my interview with Sascha L., Aug. 26, 1991. Many of the Mafia figures described in this section are still alive, and wherever that is the case, Sascha L. and Chuck Shaheen have asked me—for their protection and mine—to use pseudonyms.

23. Frank Esselourne, "Doorman Remembers," *Gay Community News*, June 23, 1979. "Bobby Shades" also slept with men, and dated Chuck Shaheen at one point (interview, Nov. 20, 1991).

24. Interview with Ryder Fitzgerald, May 5, 1992 (Ernie and Vito); *New York Sunday*

(Pages 188–193)

News, June 29, 1969 (Verra); Shaheen interview, Nov. 20, 1991. According to Shaheen, it was Ernie, somewhat older than the others, who dealt with Matty the Horse. In regard to the watered drinks, Shaheen puts it this way: "We didn't throw the bottles away. We reused those bottles all the time. We kept *a* real bottle of Dewar's and *a* real bottle of Smirnoff—for special customers."

25. Interviews with Tommy Lanigan-Schmidt, May 2, 1992, and Martin Boyce, May 19, 1992; Scherker interview with Danny Garvin, Dec. 15, 1988 (courtesy Scherker Estate). Lanigan-Schmidt added that the police cars, which then had one large light on top of the hood, were known as "bubble-gum machines." According to Shaheen (interview Nov. 20, 1991), there was bad blood between Fat Tony and the owners of the Sanctuary; when they took him on a tour of the about-to-open Sanctuary, Tony had Shaheen accompany him with firebombs strapped to his body. He distributed them strategically during the tour, but they failed to detonate.

26. Interview with Joe Tish, Nov. 15, 1991. Tiffany, who had silicon breast implants, lived for a while with Fat Tony and Chuck Shaheen. She once tried suicide and had to be taken out by ambulance; Tony's father "went through the roof" (Shaheen interview, Nov. 20, 1991).

27. The material in this and the following paragraph comes from an interview with Kohler, August 20, 1990.

28. Will Hermes, "Summer '69: Sweet Stone(wall) Soul Music," *Windy City Times*, June 22, 1989. Tommy Lanigan-Schmidt, at the time a dirt-poor street queen (in 1992, a well-known artist), described in our interview of May 2 the various hurdles he had to get over during a given night at Stonewall: getting admitted at the door; hurrying by the coat check to avoid paying the twenty-five-cent charge; evading the waiters' constant pressure to buy drinks. Many of the queens had a set routine for not having to buy drinks they couldn't afford: They would find discarded cans of beer, or glasses, and hold them; a beer can was preferable, because then you could go into the bathroom and fill it up halfway with water so that when one of the meaner waiters ("one of the vicious queens looking to throw his power around") checked the weight of the can, it would feel half full; "Then they'd leave you alone and wouldn't throw you out." Those with no money at all would sit along the wall, try to fade into the crowd, and when they saw one of the waiters bearing down on them, would quickly get up and dance.

29. Interviews with Sascha L. (Aug. 26, 1991) and Shaheen (Nov. 20, 1991). Bebe Scarpi (phone interview, Aug. 22, 1990) also confirms that "a few lesbians did go to Stonewall." The quote about "territory" is from an unidentified lesbian, one of the many "testimonies" about Stonewall recorded by Michael Scherker at the Lesbian and Gay Community Services Center on May 13, 1989 (tape courtesy Scherker Estate).

30. Testimony of Jerry [?] and an unidentified man on "Stonewall Reunion" tape made by Scherker at the Lesbian and Gay Community Services Center on June 13, 1989; Scherker with Joseph Dey, June 6, 1989 (tapes courtesy Scherker Estate).

31. Scherker interview with Harry Beard, Aug. 3, 1988; see also the reminiscences

of Beard, Gene Huss, and Don Knapp in Mike Long, "The Night the Girls Said No!" *San Francisco Sentinel*, June 22, 1989.

32. Howard Smith, "Full Moon over Stonewall," *The Village Voice*, July 3, 1969 (First Division); interview with Chuck Shaheen, Nov. 20, 1991; Scherker interview with Beard, Aug. 3, 1988; the time is established by the Sixth Precinct police records, obtained by Michael Scherker (courtesy Scherker Estate).

33. Interview with Ryder Fitzgerald, May 5, 1992. Fitzgerald also heard Ernie swear that he would reopen Stonewall the very next night as an expression of "displeasure" with the local police; in his determination, he borrowed stools and glasses from other bars to replace what the police had smashed.

34. Chris Davis interview with Ed Murphy, 1987 [?], tape courtesy Davis; interview with Sascha L., August 26, 1991.

35. Interview with Ryder Fitzgerald, May 5, 1992. Frankie later died in a bomb "accident."

36. Interview with Shaheen, Nov. 20, 1991.

37. "Queen Power: Fags Against Police in Stonewall Bust," *RAT*, July 1969 (for guy in T-shirt); *New York Times*, June 29, 1969; Lucian Truscott IV, "Gay Power Comes to Sheridan Square," *The Village Voice*, July 3, 1969.

38. Bebe Scarpi (phone interview, Aug. 22, 1990) confirms Sylvia's description: "Tammy hit the cop and was so stoned she didn't know what she was doing— or didn't care."

39. Though Harry Beard seems in general to be a reliable witness with a precise memory, there are some small discrepancies between his interview version (with Michael Scherker, Aug. 3, 1988; tape courtesy Scherker Estate) and his printed version (Mike Long, "The Night the Girls Said No!" *San Francisco Sentinel*, June 22, 1989). In the printed version, for example, Beard says the cop "slapped her upside the head with something—I can't recall if it was a blackjack or a nightstick or what it was"; in the interview version he describes the cop as "hitting her over the head with his billy club."

   Section 887 (7) of the New York State Criminal Code was the one traditionally invoked by the police against transvestites. The law was supposedly ignored on Halloween, though the police department handbook specified that even then, someone dressed in costume had to be wearing a certain number of garments "appropriate" to their sex. Mattachine received a number of reports of people being arrested on Halloween (Leitsch to Chief Inspector Garelik, Oct. 11, 1966—IGIC Papers, NYPL).

40. Bob Kohler (interview Aug. 20, 1990) is another who denies the involvement of a lesbian, but Kohler does add that Tony Lightfoot, "a lesbian who people thought was a drag queen," used to hang out with the queens in the small park opposite the Stonewall bar.

   Of the printed sources that give the credit to a lesbian, see *Gay Community News*, June 23, 1979; *Windy City Times*, June 22, 1989; *BLK*, June 1989; and the *San Francisco Sentinel*, June 22, 1989. But these offer no concrete evidence and seem to be merely repeating the assertions by Howard Smith and Lucian Truscott IV in their firsthand accounts in *The Village Voice*, July 3, 1969 (Truscott: "A dyke . . . put up a struggle—from car to door to car again"). But the Truscott

(Pages 197–198)

article, especially, is hardly incontrovertible: It contains a number of disputed points and is in places markedly homophobic in tone. Moreover, except for Truscott's and Smith's, no contemporary newspaper accounts of the riot mention the involvement of a woman (*New York Times*, June 28, 1969; *New York Post*, June 28, July 6, *Sunday News*, June 29, 1969). The eyewitness account in *RAT* (July 1969) specifically credits "one guy" (not a lesbian *or* a queen) for precipitating a scuffle by refusing to be put into the paddy wagon.

Of the accounts that specifically credit a queen with initiating the riot, the most important are unprinted sources: Chris Davis's interview with Ed Murphy (1988?, tape courtesy Davis); my interview with Sascha L. (Aug. 26, 1991) and the testimonies of Robert "Birdie" Rivera and Deputy Inspector Seymour Pine, recorded for David Isay's 1989 NPR show *Remembering Stonewall*.

In his interview with Chris Davis (1988?, tape courtesy Davis), Murphy claimed that he stepped between the cop and the queen being pushed and said to the cop, "Why don't you leave us alone. Didn't you do enough fucking damage, asshole?" But there is no corroboration for Murphy's claim, and other accounts (for example, Ivan Valentin, interview July 5, 1991) have him quickly leaving the scene.

At least two people credit Sylvia herself with provoking the riot: Jeremiah Newton (*New York Native*, June 25, 1990) has her throwing an empty gin bottle that smashed in front of the Stonewall door; and Ivan Valentin (interview, July 5, 1991) insists that Sylvia actually jumped a cop and thereby "started the Gay Liberation movement." But I've found no corroboration for either account and Sylvia herself, with a keener regard for the historical record, denies the accuracy of both versions. She does remember "throwing bricks and rocks and things" *after* the mêlée began, but takes no credit for initiating the confrontation.

41. Interviews with Joe Tish, Nov. 15, 1991, and Martin Boyce, May 19, 1992; Rivera and Pine testimonies on Isay's show *Remembering Stonewall*. The Pine quote is from Howard Smith, "Full Moon," *Village Voice*, July 3, 1969. Seymour Pine had been assigned in 1968 as deputy inspector in charge of enforcing public morals (that is, enforcing all laws relating to vice, gambling, prostitution, narcotics, and homosexuality) in the police department's First Division, which ran from Thirty-eighth Street in Manhattan to the Battery. According to Sascha L., Pine "worked both ways . . . he used to have his friend pick up money [from gay bars] in a patrol car" (interview, Aug. 26, 1991).

Once again, there are confusions and contradictions in the evidence. For example, in Blond Frankie's printed account (Frank Esselourne, "Doorman Remembers," *Gay Community News*, June 23, 1979), he credits only himself with engineering the escape from the van, and has the arrested queens *following* him out.

42. Scherker interview with "D.D.," Dec. 24, 1988 (Puerto Rican), and Robert Rivera, June 10, 1989 (mashed cop); Isay show, *Remembering Stonewall*.

43. Interviews with Shaheen, Nov. 20, 1991 (Zucchi) and Sascha L., Aug. 26, 1991 (dog shit); Scherker interviews, courtesy Scherker Estate, with "D.D.," Dec. 24, 1988 (dog shit), and Beard, Aug. 3, 1988 (overheard Zucchi); my phone interview with Marty Robinson, Oct. 10, 1990 (Timmy).

(Pages 198–206)

44. Frank Esselourne, "Doorman Remembers"; Pine's testimony on Isay show, *Remembering Stonewall*.

45. Mike Long, "The Night the Girls Said No!"; Pine testimony on Isay show, *Remembering Stonewall*. Martin Boyce (interview May 19, 1992) credits "the demented" "Miss New Orleans" and two other queens with tearing up the parking meter.

46. Howard Smith, "Full Moon over the Stonewall"; *Sunday News*, June 29, 1991; *New York Times*, June 28, 1969.

47. Phone interviews with Jim Slaven (*sous-chef* at the Lion's Head), Sept. 3, 1990, and Nick Browne (bartender at the Lion's Head), Sept. 12, 1990; Smith, "Full Moon over the Stonewall."

48. Smith, "Full Moon over the Stonewall."

49. Smith, "Full Moon over the Stonewall"; police records, June 28, 1969 (time; signal; courtesy Scherker Estate).

50. Police records (courtesy Scherker Estate) give the names of the TPF squad members. They came from three different precincts, the Fourth, Fifth, and Tenth. Sad to report, none of Craig Rodwell's photos came out.

51. Marty Robinson, "I Remember Stonewall," *San Francisco Examiner*, June 4, 1989; Maida Tilchen, "Mythologizing Stonewall," *Gay Community News*, June 23, 1979.

52. The incidents described in this and the following paragraph are from Dick Leitsch, "Police Raid on New York Club Sets Off First Gay Riot," *The Advocate*, Sept. 1969, p. 3. According to Ryder Fitzgerald (interview, May 5, 1992), Blond Frankie told him that he had himself smashed the windshield of a police car.

53. Interview with Ivan Valentin, July 5, 1991; Scherker interview with Rivera, June 10, 1989 (Lenny); "Stonewall Reunion" tape made by Scherker at Gay and Lesbian Community Center, June 13, 1989 ("feminine boys").

54. *New York Times*, July 29, 1969. The injuries are detailed in the police records, June 28, 1969 (courtesy Scherker Estate).

55. Interview with Ryder Fitzgerald, May 5, 1992; Truscott, "Gay Power"; Donn Teal, *The Gay Militants* (Stein & Day, 1971), p. 20; Leitsch, "Police Raid," *The Advocate*, Sept. 1969 (pocketed money).

56. Scherker interview with Lorenzo Rodriguez, June 3, 1989 (tape courtesy Scherker Estate).

57. *New York Times*, June 30, 1969. Truscott, in his *Voice* article (July 3, 1969), agreed with the *Times*'s view.

58. Copy of the HYMN flyer courtesy Rodwell.

59. Mel Horne, "20 Years of Changing Clothes," *Gay Community News*, June 23, 1979; Scherker interviews with "D.D.," Dec. 24, 1988 (courtesy Scherker Estate).

60. Scherker interview with Wicker, Aug. 8, 1988; John Wilben to Scherker, July 4, 1989 (sleaze joint—courtesy Scherker Estate); interviews with Thomas Lanigan-Schmidt, May 2, 1992 ("good girls"; Julius') and Martin Boyce, May 19, 1992 (Julius'); Rex Wockner, "It Was a Hot Night in June," *Gay Community News*, May 22–24, 1988 (Julius'). Wockner also claims (without citing sources) that some members of Mattachine "fingered people out to the police." This same view of Stonewall continued to be expounded in the early seventies by the Los Angeles Homosexual Information Center—Don Slater's renamed Tangents group

(Pages 207–215)

("Tangents" was found to be legally reserved by a Nevada company). HIC called the Stonewall uprising "a defensive reaction by a group of jaded, role-playing bar queens who had rejected society . . . emotionally immature, self-ashamed patrons of a gay club . . ." (HIC *Newsletter* no. 21, January 1972, courtesy Scherker Estate).

61. Scherker interview with Wicker, Aug 8, 1988. As a sample of Leitsch's sometime sympathy with the New Left: Leitsch to Mayor Richard Daley, Sept. 5, 1968 (expressing his "horror" at the use of police force during the Chicago Democratic Convention). Leitsch also expressed pleasure at MSNY beginning to draw "a much younger, 'hipper' crowd" (Leitsch to Paul Speier, Feb. 5, 1969), and displeasure at the Annual Reminder's conservative dress code (Leitsch to Barbara Gittings, June 24, 1969; also Leitsch to James K. Mazurek, Nov. 18, 1967). All four letters are in IGIC Papers, NYPL.

    The tape of Isay's *Remembering Stonewall* has Wicker heatedly arguing against mob tactics that "violated everything we thought of as responsible behavior." Wicker later repented; "I had fallen behind the times by 1969 . . . I was a *numbnut*" (Wicker to Duberman, Oct. 10, 1993). Indeed, in 1992 he was back raising public hell at profits from the Christopher Street Festival not going back into the gay community. (*N.Y. Times*, June 26, 1992).

62. Robert Amsel, "Back to Our Future? A Walk on the Wild Side of Stonewall," *The Advocate*, Sept. 15, 1987; Teal, *Gay Militants*, p. 27; Truscott, "Gay Power" (quotation).

63. Truscott, "Gay Power"; Isay show, *Remembering Stonewall* (Pine's comment); phone interview with Nick Browne (at the time a bartender at the nearby Lion's Head), Sept. 12, 1990.

64. Ronnie Di Brienza, "Stonewall Incident," *The East Village Other*, July 1969 (shouts, beatings—though *EVO* erroneously states that July 2 was a Monday, it was a Wednesday); *New York Times*, July 3, 1969 (typically, the *Times* underestimated the crowd at about five hundred people).

65. The quotation ("lawful") is from a packet of material relating to the 1969 Annual Reminder in IGIC Papers, NYPL. It also contains instructions regarding dress that stress the need for a "conservative appearance," and authorizes a three-person committee to "rule off the line those not meeting standards."

66. The quotations from and description of the St. John's meeting are from Tom Burke, "The New Homosexual," *Esquire*, December 1969.

67. Interview with Chuck Shaheen, Nov. 20, 1991. De Martino did make some money by converting the space above the Stonewall into additional apartments. Tommy Lanigan-Schmidt put the Stonewall's closing in heroic terms: "Stonewall died giving birth!" (interview, May 2, 1992). Soon after the closing, Blond Frankie became the doorman at Dr. Feelgood's, the new Mafia-controlled gay bar in the Hotel Earle. But Dr. Feelgood's never caught on (interview with Ryder Fitzgerald, May 5, 1992).

POST-STONEWALL: 1969–70

1. *Time*, Oct 31, 1969; Jim Kepner, *Our Movement Since Stonewall* (IGLA, 1992), p. 2 (Foran).

(Pages 215–219)

2. The quotes in this and the following paragraph are from "Pampered Perverts," Lige Clarke and Jack Nichols's "Homosexual Citizen" column in *Screw*, July 25, 1969; and their article "N.Y. Gays: Will the Spark Dim?" *The Advocate*, Sept. 1969.

3. "Pampered Perverts," *Screw*, July 25, 1969; Madolin Cervantes (MSNY) to David Bird (*N.Y. Times*), July 13, 1969 (IGIC Papers, NYPL); Scherker interview with Wicker, Aug. 8, 1988 (courtesy Scherker Estate). The Queens vigilante incident is described fully in John Gabree, "Homosexuals Harassed in New York," *Guardian*, July 12, 1969. The tree-cutting had come about after ordinary harassment techniques had failed and, as Gabree put it, "had every Freudian in New York chuckling over his morning paper." The Mattachine announcement that it was starting a fund to replace the trees—a cost the Parks Department estimated at $15,000—had led left-leaning gays to mutter about so humble-spirited a response.

4. Toby Marotta, *The Politics of Homosexuality* (Houghton Mifflin, 1981), p. 77.

5. Leitsch to Philip Parris, Sept. 22, 1966 (expressing sympathy for Stokely Carmichael's views but rejecting any association with the Panthers); Leitsch to William Wynne, Feb. 4, 1970 ("none of our damned business"). Both letters are in IGIC Papers, NYPL.

6. Donaldson and Leitsch had recently been at loggerheads. Leitsch accused Donaldson of a gratuitous "personal attack" in the *Clearing House Newsletter* (vol. 1., no. 7); Donaldson accused Leitsch of threatening to walk out of a meeting simply because he (Donaldson) was supposed to say a few words; and the two squabbled angrily over whether the Columbia student homophile group should be allowed to use the name "Mattachine," Donaldson accusing Leitsch of "snobbery" and Leitsch attacking the Columbia group as "apologists" because its members used pseudonyms. (Leitsch to *Clearing House Newsletter*, Sept. 12, Nov. 3, 1967; Donaldson to Herman Slater, March 9, 1968; Leitsch to Gunnison, Oct. 8, 1968; Leitsch to Neil Donovan, Jan 24, 1969—all in IGIC Papers, NYPL).

7. Marotta, *Politics of Homosexuality*, pp. 78–79; Scherker interview with Shelley, June 5, 1989 (tape courtesy Scherker Estate).

8. Two Special Services police reports, dated July 9, 10, 1969 (courtesy Scherker Estate).

9. Marotta, *Politics of Homosexuality*, pp. 78–79.

10. Marotta, *Politics of Homosexuality*, p. 79; Michael Bronski, "Stonewall Stories, Part I," *Gay Community News*, June 11–17, 1989.

11. Interview with Sascha L., Aug. 26, 1991.

12. Interview with Sascha L., Aug. 26, 1991. According to Sascha, the payoffs also stopped—at least for a while—after the Stonewall riots. A number of cops (including, about a year later, Seymour Pine) were transferred.

   The police sweep through the Village gay bars that night was general; at about the same time Tele-Star was raided, Stonewall, too, was hit. Martin Boyce (interview, May 19, 1992) was among the seven or eight people sitting one afternoon, about a week after the riots, at the Stonewall bar (which had not yet closed, but had little business) when the police marched through; it was, as Boyce remembers it, "just a show of muscle; no arrests were made."

   It was a raid more than six months later that would fan the most indignation, and temporarily take on some of the symbolic importance of the Stonewall riots.

(Pages 220–222)

The Snake Pit was an after-hours basement bar on the corner of West Tenth Street, operated, like so many others, without a liquor license. When the police (again led by Seymour Pine) raided it at five one morning, they atypically arrested, along with the employees, all 167 patrons, on charges of "disorderly conduct." Among those patrons was an Argentine national named Diego Vinales, who had never before gone to a gay bar in New York. Brought with the others to the Charles Street police station, Vinales panicked. Terrified that his parents would be notified and that he would be deported, he made a desperate effort to escape by jumping from the second-floor window. He impaled himself on six fourteen-inch iron spikes on the fence directly below, and had to endure agonizing delays while rescue workers, using blowtorches, tried to extricate him. When they finally succeeded, he was rushed into surgery with one piece of the fence still piercing his body. Vinales survived, but barely. Craig was among the many thousands who joined a vigil at the hospital and then marched to the Charles Street police station to protest the Snake Pit raid. The fullest account of the whole affair is in Arthur Bell, *Dancing the Gay Lib Blues: A Year in the Homosexual Liberation Movement* (Simon and Schuster, 1971), pp. 39–49. The *Daily News* put the incident on its front page (March 9, 1970). "Any way you look at it—that boy was PUSHED!!" read a Gay Activists Alliance flyer announcing the protest march (the flyer is included in the Special Services police report of the Vinales incident, dated March 9, 1970, courtesy Scherker Estate).

13. Marotta, *Politics of Homosexuality*, pp. 80–91.
14. Gunnison to Kelley, May 11, 1968, Kelley Papers.
15. Douglas Sanders (the only Canadian delegate), 10 typed pages of Minutes plus Appendices for the August 1968 Chicago NACHO Conference, Kelley Papers. The Homosexual Bill of Rights had been proposed by SIR; in essence, it called for an end to all forms of harassment and discrimination. Beardemphl of SIR had suggested the name "American Conference of Homosexual Organizations" (IGIC Papers, Box 5, NYPL).
16. Fourteen of the twenty-three accredited organizations sent a total of twenty-three delegates to Chicago; and some eighty-five additional people participated as accredited "observers." Of the six organizations turned down by Foster's Credentials Committee on assorted grounds of late fees or recent formation, all six were admitted to the conference by vote of the delegates—a direct slap at Foster, who defended his criteria as "tough—yes, even rigid," but applied with "absolute fairness" (Gunnison to Cromey, May 17, 1968; also Gunnison to Southern California Council on Religion and the Homosexual, June 7, 1968, Gunnison Papers). Shirley Willer on DOB is in Eric Marcus, *Making History* (HarperCollins, 1992), p. 129. On the issue of Mattachine New York's participation, Foster wrote Bill Kelley, soon after the close of the conference, that he was "working with MSNY to bring them into the NACHO, with some success thus far. HOWEVER— my belief is that no organization is God Almighty, and we should not go down on bended knee. . . . And that goes for SIR or any of the others. We are all in this together, and no one organization is going to be the 'hero of the movement' . . ." (Gunnison to Kelley, Nov. 12, 1968, Kelley Papers). In an exchange of letters during 1967–1968, Leitsch vented his anger at the lack of appreciation for MSNY's accomplishments under his leadership, and Foster diplomatically en-

(Page 223)

couraged him not to be "concerned about what anyone else in the movement thinks"—even as he warned Leitsch that "there is a tendency to resent MSNY's being kept out of the general movement," and urged him to join NACHO (Gunnison to Leitsch, Jan. 22, 1967, and Jan. 26, Feb. 9, Oct. 7, 1968; Leitsch to Gunnison, Jan. 23, Feb. 6, 14, Oct. 8, 1968—all in IGIC Papers, NYPL). Privately, Leitsch was writing that "Foster Gunnison himself is responsible for much of the hostility to . . . [the Credentials] Committee . . . his rules, by-laws, whatever they were called, [were] much too authoritarian and exclusionary," and urging that he be replaced with Leitsch's recent ally Jack Campbell, of Cleveland Mattachine (Leitsch to William Wynne, June 5, 1970, IGIC Papers, NYPL). Wynne had been encouraging Leitsch to take over NACHO, writing that he was tired of NACHO being in the grip for so long of those "who do not really represent anyone except themselves" (Wynne to Leitsch, n.d. [1970], IGIC Papers, NYPL).

17. Eight Credentials Committee "Bulletins," March 12, 1969–June 24, 1969, Gunnison Papers; "Marc Jeffers," "Chairman's Interim Report," March 1969; "Jeffers" to Robert Cromey, June 14, 1969 (travel); "Jeffers," "To All NACHO Organizations," n.d., Houston. (The Promethean Society soon reorganized as the Texas Homophile Educational Movement: THEM—all in the Kelley Papers.)

18. "Report of the Committee on Credentials," July 24, 1969, and "Post-Conference Report of the Committee on Credentials," Dec. 10, 1969, Gunnison Papers. "Austin Wade" (Arthur Warner) and Madolin Cervantes, "Report to the Board of MSNY Delegates to ERCHO," n.d., Gunnison Papers. Dick Leitsch had been prepared, this time around, to attend the NACHO conference, but MSNY had refused to vote expense money for him and other potential delegates on the grounds that "the Gay Power movement is on and we're shoveling out dollars like kindling for mimeograph paper." Leitsch had been of two minds about going anyway, and professed not to be disappointed (Leitsch to "Frank," Aug. 19, 1969, IGIC Papers, NYPL).

The Council on Equality for Homosexuals was an organization Gunnison put together with a few members of the West Side Discussion Group; it included David Goldberger, "Sandy Penn," and Barbara Silverglate. ("A little discussion group we had going in New York for a couple of years" was Gunnison's own description during our interviews.) Part of CEH's history is in Credentials Committee "Bulletin #5," May 31, 1969 (Gunnison Papers). Arthur Warner and Madolin Cervantes were among those who attacked CEH as having "no plausible reason for its existence"—other than to garner voting privileges at the NACHO and ERCHO conventions and thereby help to perpetuate the control of the "Kamenyites" (Warner and Cervantes, "Report to the Board of MSNY Delegates to ERCHO." Gunnison Papers).

19. Donaldson to "Young Turks," March 20, 1968; Gunnison to Jeffers, Nov. 13, 1969, to Donaldson, Nov. 22, 1969, and to Kameny, Nov. 22, 1969—all in Kelley Papers.

20. "A Radical Manifesto," dated August 28, 1969 (Kelley Papers), is signed by Scoop Phillips, chair of the 1969 NACHO Arrangements Committee and a Kansas City activist, as well as by Stephen Donaldson. One accompanying document suggests that the age limit for membership on the Youth Committee be

(Pages 225–226)

set at twenty-five, and another set forth a "Bill of Rights" for homosexual stu-
dentson college campuses—both in Kelley Papers.

21. Gunnison to Kelley, Sept. 15, 1969; Gunnison to Jeffers, Nov. 13, 1969; Gun-
    nison to Gittings, Nov. 15, 1969; Gunnison to Kameny, Nov. 22, 1969; Gunnison
    to William Wynne, Dec. 27, 1969—all in Kelley Papers.

22. Gunnison, "Subject: Gay Liberation Front," Nov. 12, 1969, Kelley Papers.

23. Gunnison to Robert Kohler, Dec. 21, 1969 ("rudeness," etc.); Gunnison to Jeffers,
    Nov. 13, 1969 (most dangerous), Kelley Papers.

24. Gunnison, "Proposed Set of Constitutional Aims and Purposes for NACHO,"
    July 24, 1969, Gunnison Papers.

25. Gunnison, "Proposed Set of Constitutional Aims and Purposes for NACHO,"
    July 24, 1969; Gunnison to Teal, n.d. (tactics)—both in Gunnison Papers. Foster
    once rebuked Kameny for being "a bit conservative" about confrontational tactics
    (Gunnison to Kameny, June 4, 1970, Kelley Papers).

26. ERCHO was not an independently formed regional association, as had been the
    case with its regional predecessor ECHO, which it replaced; rather, it was an
    offshoot of NACHO.

27. Rodwell insists to this day that nothing in Mary Baker Eddy's writings can be
    construed as homophobic. Indeed, he insists that Eddy discounted "male" and
    "female" as discrete categories, arguing that all human beings contain aspects of
    both. He further points out that in some of her writings Eddy attacks the insti-
    tution of marriage. But Rodwell is well aware that the Christian Science *church*
    is today "one of the most homophobic institutions in the world." There is a long-
    standing split and constant tug of war between the comparatively liberal pub-
    lishing society, which puts out the *Christian Science Monitor*, and the conservative
    board of directors, which runs the church.

    Beginning in the late seventies, Rodwell helped to organize an action designed
    to awaken the church to the plight of its gay and lesbian members. He and others
    distributed a pamphlet they had written, "Gay People in Christian Science?"
    asking the board of directors to "re-examine their thought on the subject of human
    sexuality . . . and to take whatever loving and practical steps are necessary to
    rectify the present wrongs being done to Gay people in the name of Christian
    Science." Rodwell and his friends mailed out fifteen thousand copies of the
    pamphlet and then decided to attend the annual meeting of the church in Boston
    in June, 1980. Christine Madsen, then a reporter for the *Monitor* but later fired
    for being a lesbian, helped the group with logistical details. Dressed conservatively
    in suits and dresses, they stacked their pamphlets on card tables near the Mother
    Church Center—and put a decorative pot of geraniums on each table. But a unit
    from the Boston Police Department soon appeared, accompanied by the head of
    security for the Mother Church, and told them that if they failed to take the
    tables down at once, they would be arrested "for improper activity on public
    property." The group caucused for a vote; Rodwell voted to go to jail, but a
    large majority voted against him. They took down the tables and then distributed
    the pamphlets by hand. The next day, some of their group stood up during the
    church service to offer silent protest against their treatment; later, outside, they
    displayed signs to the same effect. But from that day to this (1993), the

(Pages 228–230)

board of directors has refused to reconsider its negative attitude toward gays and lesbians.

Rodwell no longer participates in Christian Science services, but does retain "great respect" for Mary Baker Eddy. To an outsider, this allegiance is somewhat perplexing. Toby Marotta, in *The Politics of Homosexuality*, p. 66n., suggests that in its emphasis on "the dignity of all things human and the importance of making things true by believing them so," Christian Science doctrine "inspired Rodwell to work at encouraging homosexuals to think of themselves positively." Perhaps so, but what still needs explaining is why the neo-Platonic insistence in Mary Baker Eddy's writings on the "unreality" of the material world, and the importance of transcending it, did not cause Rodwell (as it did so many other Christian Scientists) to steer clear of any political engagement with that evanescent world. Nor does it explain why Eddy's denigration of the body failed to restrain Rodwell from insisting on his right to bodily pleasure—unorthodox pleasure, no less.

28. Wade and Cervantes, "Report to the Board," Kelley Papers.

29. Austin Wade (Arthur Warner) and Madolin Cervantes, "Report to the Board of MSNY Delegates to ERCHO," n.d. (Nov. 1969); Gunnison to Robert Angell, Nov. 10, 1969 (dissociation); Gunnison to Gittings, Nov. 15, 1969—all in Kelley Papers. The resolutions passed by the conference are summarized and paraphrased in Gunnison to Robert Angell, Nov. 15, 1969; along with the two cited, they included a demand for control over one's own body as an "inalienable right" and a call to defend the "freedom from political & social persecution" of "all minority peoples."

30. Gunnison to Gittings, Jan. 12, 1970 (Lois Hart), Gunnison to Kelley, Nov. 5, 1969, both in Kelley Papers. Arthur Warner insisted that Fouratt had "physically assaulted" Cervantes ("Report to the Board of MSNY Delegates to ERCHO," co-authored with Cervantes, n.d. [Nov. 1969]); but in his interviews with me Fouratt has categorically denied that.

31. Kelley questionnaire response, Nov. 7, 1969, Gunnison to Kelley, Nov. 15, 1969—both in Kelley Papers.

32. Gunnison to Kelley, Jan. 21, 1970, Kelley Papers; Gunnison to Donn Teal, n.d., Gunnison Papers ("thrilled").

33. Gunnison, "Subject: Gay Liberation Front," Nov. 12, 1969, Kelley Papers. By the following summer, after attending many more GLF meetings in New York (and going to a few of their dances), he found even more "exceptions" and had his "fingers crossed" that GLF would "manage to straighten itself out and head off in constructive directions" (Gunnison to William Wynne, July 25, 1970, Kelley Papers).

34. Gunnison, "Subject: Gay Liberation Front," Nov. 12, 1969, Kelley Papers.

35. The quotes in this and the next paragraph are from Gunnison to Kohler, Dec. 21, 1969, Kelley Papers. To Barbara Gittings, too, Foster wrote (Nov. 15, 1969, Kelley Papers), "I do sympathize with them [other social causes] and I am always ready to put the first nickel in the pot for them." But as regards Kohler himself, Foster characterized him to Gittings as "a mealy-mouthed, sad-eyed, con man from way back." Still later, after attending more GLF meetings, Foster once went so far as to say that "there is every possibility that GLF will evolve as a reasonable organization . . . " (Gunnison to Kameny, June 4, 1970, Kelley Papers).

36. Kepner to Duberman, April 29, 1992 ("bad cases"); "Austin Wade" (Arthur Warner) and Madolin Cervantes, "Report to the Board of the MSNY Delegates to ERCHO," and Gunnison to Warner, Nov. 22, 1969—both in Kelley Papers. Foster wrote Kameny that those who opposed him were "nitwits" (Gunnison to Kameny, Nov. 22, 1969, Kelley Papers), and further evidence of Foster's devotion to Kameny is in Gunnison, "General Bulletin" (on Kameny's election to the Executive Board of the D.C. affiliate of the ACLU), Dec. 10, 1969, Kelley Papers. Yet Foster did acknowledge to Warner that Kameny was at times willful and intractable (Gunnison to Warner, June 5, 1970, Kelley Papers).

37. Phillips to Gunnison, Jan. 27, 1970; Gunnison to Bobbi Simpson/Sandy Penn, Nov. 21, Dec. 20, 1969; Gunnison to William Kelley, Jan. 21, 1970—all in Kelley Papers.

38. Bell, *Dancing the Gay Lib Blues*, pp. 20–24; Dennis Altman, *Homosexual: Oppression and Liberation* (Dutton, 1971), pp. 110–116.

39. Gunnison to Kelley, April 9, 1971, Gunnison to Wynne, July 25, 1970—all in Kelley Papers.

40. Marotta, *Politics of Homosexuality*, chapter 6, pp. 134–61.

41. Arnie Kantrowitz, *Under the Rainbow: Growing Up Gay* (Morrow, 1977), pp. 147, 179–80; Kantrowitz to Duberman, May 11, 1992.

42. An interview with "Ernestine Eppinger," conducted by Barbara Gittings and Kay Tobin is in *The Ladder*, June 1966, pp. 4–11. Jim Kepner sums up the role of blacks in the homophile movement this way: "There were usually one or two Blacks, two or three Latins and a very occasional Chinese, around ONE, DOB, Mattachine, and later groups such as Pride and SIR, but, except for Tony Reyes, who, as Don Slater's lover, then and now, was an incorporator of ONE, & long a silent vote on the Board of Trustees, they took no leadership positions." (Kepner, "Blacks & Women in the Early Gay Movement," 24-page typescript, courtesy Kepner.)

43. Joel Hall, "Growing Up Black and Gay," in Len Richmond and Gary Noguera, *The Gay Liberation Book* (Ramparts Press, 1973), pp. 51–56; the manifesto "Third World Gay Revolution (New York City)," is reprinted in Karla Jay & Allen Young, eds., *Out of the Closets: Voices of Gay Liberation* (NYU Press, 2nd ed., 1992), pp. 363–67; Alice Echols, *Daring to Be Bad: Radical Feminism in America, 1967–1975* (University of Minnesota Press, 1989), especially chapter 5. See also the discussion of blacks and gays in Altman, *Homosexual*, pp. 179–94, and Teal, *Gay Militants*, pp. 169–78; and for blacks and feminism, see bell hooks, *Ain't I a Woman: Black Women and Feminism* (South End Press, 1981).

44. Scarpi would also become active, in 1973, in planning the fourth Christopher Street Liberation Day—and would get into a tangle with Foster Gunnison, who was then in the process of disengaging from CSLDC (Scarpi to Gunnison, Jan. 15, April 30, 1973; Gunnison to Scarpi, Jan. 26, 1973; John Paul Hudson to Gunnison, April 12, 1973—all in Gunnison Papers).

45. Arthur Bell Papers, Box 94, IGIC Papers, NYPL.

46. I have written about the 1973 confrontation in *Cures* (Plume, 1992), pp. 278–79 (where—before Sylvia corrected me—I spelled her name "Silvia"). The confrontation was also captured on film; Vito Russo (who was emcee at the 1973

rally) screened it for me shortly before his death. In our interviews, nearly twenty years later, Sylvia was still full of bitterness at Jean O'Leary and at all the other "ingrates" in the movement who despised queens and refused to acknowledge their contribution during and after the Stonewall riots. O'Leary's recantation is in Eric Marcus, *Making History* (HarperCollins, 1992), p. 257.

47. Interview with Kohler, Aug. 20, 1990.

48. See Allen Young, "GLF Memories," *Gay Community News*, June 23, 1979, for the inspirational role Fouratt played in his own coming out. Young, who in late 1969 was a closeted member of the Liberation News Service, also came to live in the Seventeenth Street commune.

49. Leggett is the anonymous author of the moving "Father Knows Best," in Richmond and Noguera, *The Gay Liberation Book*, pp. 165–68. Leggett died of AIDS.

50. The relevant FBI documents, though heavily censored, are now available (I owe special thanks to Duncan Osborne for alerting me to that fact). But since many of the 4,500 pages of documents that I received have been inked out (on the absurd, continuing grounds of "national security"), research into their contents remains sharply limited. For the paragraph above, the relevant materials are SA to SAC, New York, 100-167120-19 through 100-167120-22 (12/10 & 16/69; 1/9 & 13/70); 100-167120-39 (5/22/70: "highly placed"); SA to SAC, Chicago, 100-49116-6 and 100-49116-7 (April 19, July 7, 1970); SAC Albany to Director (Hoover), 100-464380-1 (March 10, 1971 [Transvestites and Red Butterfly]; "gaye" is in April 30, 1970 to Director (100-459225-X). For the FBI and early Mattachine, see Stuart Timmons, *The Trouble with Harry Hay* (Alyson, 1990), pp. 131–32. The information on "Wendy Wonderful" is from an interview with Karla Jay, Aug. 17, 1992.

51. Along with Jim, a man named Lars Larson also came under suspicion in GAA (conversation with Arnie Kantrowitz, Jan. 3, 1992)—though, as in Jim's case, there was never a shred of evidence.

52. *RAT*, v. 3, no. 3, April 4–18, 1970. For the disappointment and anger expressed by other feminists over the results of the action, see Echols, *Daring to Be Bad*, pp. 195–97; and see footnotes 297 and 298 (p. 341) for "Verna Tomasson" probably being a pseudonym and for Karla grabbing Firestone (as well as testimony to the effect that her doing so may have been unnecessary).

53. Echols, *Daring to Be Bad*, p. 213 (Brown); Lois Hart, "Some News and a Whole Lot of Opinion," *Come Out!* (Times Change Press, 1970), pp. 29–32. For more detail, see Marotta, *Politics of Homosexuality*, chapter 9, "Radicalesbians," pp. 229–55. The debate over the lesbian–gay male relationship is well summarized in Rita Mae Brown, "Take a Lesbian to Lunch," and in Gay Liberation Front Women (New York City), "Lesbians and the Ultimate Liberation of Women." Both essays are reprinted in Jay and Young, *Out of the Closets*, pp. 185–95, 201–203.

54. Radicalesbians (New York City), "Leaving the Gay Men Behind," reprinted in Jay and Young, *Out of the Closets*, pp. 290–95.

55. Interviews with Karla Jay; Jay, "The First Lesbian Dance," *Gay Community News*, June 23, 1979. All the material in the next few paragraphs describing the dance comes from these two sources.

56. GAA held a demonstration one night in front of Kooky's to protest the bar's abusive treatment of its own lesbian customers, and their chant was "Kooky's gonna crumble" (Kantrowitz to Duberman, May 11, 1992).

57. Bell, *Dancing the Gay Lib Blues*, pp. 145–46. Sylvia's memory of being turned down is corroborated by the minutes of the GAA general meeting on Nov. 12, 1970 (in IGIC Papers, NYPL). On at least one later occasion, however, GAA did allow STAR to borrow its sound system (minutes, Jan. 14, 1971).

58. Bell, *Dancing the Gay Lib Blues*, pp. 157–58.

59. Interview with Bob Kohler, Aug. 20, 1990; "Rapping with a Street Transvestite Revolutionary: An Interview with Marcia [*sic*] Johnson," reprinted in Jay and Young, *Out of the Closets*, pp. 112–119. On July 6, 1992, Marsha P. Johnson was found floating in the Hudson River, her body badly decomposed; foul play has not been ruled out (*New York Newsday*, July 20, 1992; *New York Native*, July 20, 1992).

60. For example, Gunnison to Martin, April 29, 1970, Kelley Papers.

61. Crompton, "Report of the Religious Committee," December 1969; Kameny, "Workshop on the Federal Government"; Gunnison to Warner, Feb. 20, May 7, 1970; Warner to Kelley, Nov. 2, 1970—all in Kelley Papers.

62. Gunnison to Peters, Jan. 5, 1970 (newsletter); Gunnison to All Homophile Organizations, Feb. 15, 1970 (clearinghouse); Gunnison to members of ERCHO Executive Committee, Feb. 9, 1970 (a sample of his lengthy agenda suggestions); Gunnison to Wynne, Jan. 20, 1970 (losing battle)—all in Kelley Papers.

63. Gunnison letter to *Playboy* (in response to a piece by Stephen Donaldson in the May issue), Aug. 1970, p. 46. A letter responding to Gunnison denounced him for his "intoleration and prudishness" (Ralph Hall, *Playboy*, Dec. 1970).

64. Gunnison to Scoop Phillips, Feb. 11, 1970; Gunnison to Martin, April 29, 1970; Gunnison to Russell Nile, Feb. 21, 1970—all in Kelley Papers. ERCHO did manage to sponsor a meeting in Philadelphia in Nov. 1969, and its executive committee did meet several times in 1970, but by late 1971 Gunnison was himself describing the organization as "moribund" (Gunnison to Canon Clinton R. Jones, Nov. 5, 1971, Gunnison Papers). In his final financial report, Gunnison listed a closing surplus of $88.96 (1971 ERCHO financial report, dated Dec. 31, 1971, Gunnison Papers).

65. Gunnison to Jerome Stevens, March 30, 1970 (lack of will); Gunnison to Kameny, June 4, 1970; Gunnison to Leitsch, Feb. 21, 1970 (Warner); Gunnison to Warner, June 5, 1970—all in Kelley Papers.

At the August 1970 NACHO convention, the Warner/Kameny feud continued unabated. Kameny sent a statement entitled "Austin's Aberration," dated August 28, 1970 (Gunnison Papers), to all the delegates; in it he characterized Warner as having "a well-developed delusional system which is quite impervious to facts," and charged him with contriving "vast, but totally non-existent conspiracies."

Warner's primary loyalty was to Dick Leitsch, and his dislike of Kameny may have been in part a reflection of Leitsch's dislike. And Leitsch's anger at Kameny had, if anything, increased over the years. Six months before the 1970 NACHO convention, Leitsch wrote its chair, Bill Wynne, that Kameny "and his massive ego are a menace to the movement (and the prime cause the movement

(Page 257)

is in such disarray). . . . [Kameny's] roles in NACHO and ERCHO are well-known as divisive. His power plays have shocked and amused all of us. His egocentricity has aroused the sympathy of those of us who are soft-hearted, and the anger of those who are not . . ." (Leitsch to Wynne, Feb. 11, 1970, IGIC Papers, NYPL).

Within the year, Gunnison would draw closer to Warner and somewhat away from Kameny. He still "love[d] Kameny and the old crew . . . as much as ever, believe in them just as much as ever, but am no longer so intimately involved with them. On the other hand I've been able to get much closer to Arthur—he still pisses me off with his tirades—but . . . has begun to take a slightly dim view of MSNY [Mattachine Society New York]. . . . He CAN be objective . . ." (Gunnison to Kelley, April 9, 1971; also Gunnison to Warner, Oct. 13, 1970, Kelley Papers).

66. A useful starting point in salvaging NACHO, Foster thought, might be a change of name. "North American Conference of Homophile Organizations" seemed a little grand, and somehow stodgy; maybe GPU—"Gay Power United"—would sound the right "punchy," contemporary ring. But no sooner had he thought of a new name than he doubted that a change would be a good idea: There was already too much "instability and lack of continuity" in the movement (Gunnison to Jerome Stevens, March 30, 1970 [sponge]; Garrison to Compton, April 10, 1970; Gunnison to Wynne, July 25, 1970 [GPU]—all in Kelley Papers).

67. The quotations in this and the following two paragraphs are from Gunnison to Stevens, March 30, 1970; Gunnison to Wynne, July 25, 1970; Gunnison to Crompton, April 10, 1970; Gunnison, "Bulletins" for March 19, April 10, 1970—all in Kelley Papers. The new gay liberation groups should, in Foster's view, attend the NACHO conference as observers for one or two conferences before being made voting members. And "revolutionary elements" should be kept, if possible, from attending at all; but if admitted, should be contained through a procedural rule that forbade the presentation of any resolution "not directly connected with the homophile cause."

On the central question of whether NACHO should aim at becoming a bridge organization that would link the homophile movement with gay liberation, Foster felt ambivalent. After all, he wrote one of the young militants, NACHO and GLF are "two different groups employing two different philosophies and two different methodologies," and it might be impossible, and even unwise, to try and tether them to a single organization. Yet Foster also believed that the two groups had "the same end in view"—namely, the homophile cause—and he kept open the outside hope that they could combine forces. He made no effort to conceal his own ideological commitment: "I am a gung-ho rightwinger and damn well proud of it, but I struggle against heavy odds to keep an open mind." Sample letters that sum up Gunnison's views are Gunnison to Bob Martin, April 27, 1970; Gunnison to Jim Chesebrough, Aug. 14, 1970 (two philosophies); Gunnison to Jerome Stevens, May 4, 1970; Gunnison to Wynne, July 25, 1970—all in Kelley Papers.

In a letter to Louis Crompton, Gunnison described the GLF–homophile conflict as "the age-old Apollonian vs. Dionysian tug of war," but even in that broad context he continued to indict "the arrogant attitude of some of the older

(Pages 258–261)

groups each of whom thinks it owns the movement lock, stock and barrell [sic], and are [sic] contemptuous and resentful of the newer groups coming along." But beyond the sin of "arrogance," Gunnison also indicted himself and other homophile leaders for having mistakenly devoted so much time at annual conferences to business matters. He felt they had failed to heed "a prime rule of organization management that you keep all business off the floor except where absolutely necessary, and you devote your conferences to programs and activities that will be of interest to all attending" (Gunnison to Compton, April 10, 1970, Kelley Papers).

68. Gunnison to Martin, April 27, 1970; Gunnison to Wynne, May 4, 1970, Kelley Papers. Frank Kameny, among others, would scold Foster for the inappropriate way he substituted "frivolity" for "sobriety." But Foster was "addicted in my belief that life is not one big funeral procession," and went right on signing the occasional letter, "Swish-cerely, 'Kid Basket' Gunnison" (Gunnison to Warner, Nov. 22, 1969, Kelley Papers).

69. As quoted in Marotta, *Politics of Homosexuality*, p. 128.

70. Eldridge Cleaver, *Soul on Ice* (McGraw-Hill, 1968), p. 110.

71. Teal, *Gay Militants*, pp. 167–68; John Murphy, *Homosexual Liberation: A Personal View* (Praeger, 1971), p. 80.

72. Huey Newton, "A Letter from Huey to the Revolutionary Brothers and Sisters About the Women's Liberation and Gay Liberation Movements," *Black Panther*, August 21, 1970. The FBI was also in attendance: Philadelphia to Director, Sept. 5, 1970, 100-65673-12.

73. Echols, *Daring to Be Bad*, pp. 222–23.

74. *Gay Flames*, Sept. 11, 1970; the "Statement" is in Teal, *Gay Militants*, pp. 176–77. During the People's Convention, members of the gay caucus picketed two gay bars for their racist policies (Jim Kepner, *Our Movement Since Stonewall*, L.A. International Gay and Lesbian Archives, 1992, p. 2).

75. Wynne to Leitsch, April 5, 1970 (IGIC Papers, NYPL). Gunnison, "Post-Conference Report of the Committtee on Credentials," Nov. 8, 1970; Gunnison's "Treasure Display"—both in Gunnison Papers.

Minutes of the 1970 convention, signed by Madeline Davis (Kelley Papers). Foster put particular blame for the success of the radicals on the representatives of the revolutionary Socialist Workers Party, accusing them of having "infiltrated" the convention. SWP, in fact, *was* committed to the strategy of infiltration (see Marotta, *Politics of Homosexuality*, pp. 269n., 317), though Jim Kepner, for one, "saw no evidence of SWP presence at the last NACHO conference" (Kepner to Duberman, April 29, 1992).

76. Minutes of the 1970 Convention, signed by Madeline Davis; Gunnison to William Kelley, April 9, 1971 (Leitsch)—both in Kelley Papers. The top vote-getter in the balloting for Conference Committee members was a newcomer, Metropolitan Community Church founder Troy Perry. Foster thought Perry "may become the next great leader of the movement nationwide," though he had heard "mixed reports about him as a person" (Gunnison to Jerome Stevens, March 30, 1970). Jim Kepner of ONE, Inc. (LA), and Sandy Blixton of Homosexuals Intransigent (NYC) were the two candidates who got fewer votes than Gunnison. Of the nine elected to the committee, Frank Kameny got the smallest number of votes.

(Pages 261–266)

Leitsch to Jack Campbell, March 2, 1970. IGIC Papers, NYPL. According to Jim Kepner (Kepner to Duberman, April 29, 1992), "Legg, Leitsch & a few other real conservatives schemed to take over NACHO. . . . That plan included holding the next meeting in New York—but scuttlebutt was that Leitsch merely meant to bury NACHO."

77. William Wynne, "Chairman's Report," August 1970, Gunnison Papers. In the second part of his report, in which he presented his ideas for restructuring NACHO, Wynne adopted many of the suggestions (reshaping committees, keeping business matters off the convention floor, etc.) that Gunnison had earlier sent him (Gunnison to Wynne, July 25, 1970, Gunnison Papers).

78. Gunnison, "Treasury Notes" (1970); Gunnison, "Community Bulletin #5," May 31, 1969; Gunnison to Frank Morgan, Jan. 21, 1970; Gunnison to Bob Martin, April 29, 1970—all in Kelley Papers.

79. The many announcements, bulletins, and press releases relating to *The Directory* are in the Gunnison Papers.

80. Gunnison to Bob Martin, April 29, 1970, Kelley Papers.

81. Teal, *Gay Militants*, pp. 131–32. Koch later denied, in a letter to Dick Leitsch of New York Mattachine, that he had "ever taken the position that homosexuals are creating any special problem in the MacDougal Street area." His concern, he insisted, was with "the increase in violence," which he ascribed to "the increase in the number of young persons flowing into the area .. . who have little or no regard for the community or its residents. . . . What we have is not a homosexual problem but a community problem" (Koch to Leitsch, May 5, 1967, IGIC Papers, NYPL).

82. Bell, *Dancing the Gay Lib Blues*, p. 62.

83. Bell reprinted the article in his book *Dancing the Gay Lib Blues*, pp. 60–64. The quotes in this paragraph are from my interviews with Sylvia. Later, Bell and Sylvia together interviewed Chris Thompson, a black male transvestite; the interview is printed in *Gay Flames*, Nov. 14, 1970.

84. The account of Sylvia's courtroom appearances is drawn in part from my interviews with her, in part from the minutes of GAA general meetings (May 21, 28, June 4, 18, July 2, 9, Sept. 3, 1970) in the Papers of Arthur Bell, Box 93, IGIC Papers, NYPL. By the time of her second appearance in court, Sylvia was represented by Harold Wiener, a lawyer who had volunteered his services. During the drawn-out trial, Sylvia was arrested on a separate charge of "female impersonation," and GAA put up the required fifty-dollar bond (GAA minutes, July 30, 1970).

85. The fullest account of this episode is in Bell, *Dancing the Gay Lib Blues*, pp. 69–73, from which the quotes in this and the next paragraph are taken.

86. Arnie Kantrowitz, an officer in GAA, was also present at the May 13 confrontation with Greitzer; in his recall "Sylvia raised a thick envelope of petitions (too thick to roll up) and threatened Greitzer. I don't believe she actually hit her with them" (Kantrowitz to Duberman, May 11, 1992).

87. For sample GLF feminist analyses, see "Gay Revolution and Sex Roles" (Chicago), in Jay and Young, *Out of the Closets*, pp. 252–59; Marotta, *Politics of Homosexuality*, chapter 9; and Echols, *Daring to Be Bad*, chapters 4 and 5.

(Pages 267–272)

88. Most of the organizing for the "Lavender Menace" action took place in the apartment of Sydney Abbott and Barbara Love, and among the women prominent in it were Micela Griffo (who pulled the fuse box), March Hoffman, Rita Mae Brown, and Ellen Bedoz [Shumsky]. According to Karla, they couldn't figure out what to call themselves, and at first settled on "Lavender Herring" (in response to the dismissive term Susan Brownmiller had used). But the woman responsible for producing the T-shirts misspelled "herring," and to avoid another error they switched to "Lavender Menace." An account of the congress action is also in Echols, *Daring to Be Bad*, pp. 214–16.

89. Yvonne A. Flowers, "Black Goddesses," in The Jamima Collective, *Jamima from the Heart* (1977).

90. Gunnison to Kameny, June 4, 1970, Kelley Papers.

91. Gunnison to Duberman, Jan. 15, 1992. The "guru" quote is from my interviews with Gunnison.

92. Gunnison, "Christopher Street Liberation Day Umbrella Committee . . . Bulletin No. Two—4/10/70," Gunnison Papers.

93. Gunnison, "Two Appeals for Donations—April 10, 1970"; press release, April 28, 1970—both in Gunnison Papers. Gunnison to Kameny, June 4, 1970 (Leitsch), Kelley Papers. Gunnison accused Leitsch of "panicking" as "MSNY's influence in the New York area is ebbing away," and of "a desperate effort to maintain his dominance" by trying to forge an alliance with GLF, by "making Madolin Cervantes a scapegoat for MSNY's past conservatism and pointing to her (and I assume probably Austen [Arthur Warner] as well) as the reason for MSNY's stodginess." Foster offered, in confirmation, that "at the last Christopher St. meeting . . . Bob Kohler astounded all of us by standing up for Leitsch and challenging some negative reports about MSNY's role in bucking the Christopher St. event." Also: Harry L. Phillips, "Meeting of Homophile Leaders in New York" (1970), Gunnison Papers. When "Michael Kotis" became president of MSNY in April, 1970, he was able to persuade the organization's board to participate in the CSLDC and on June 10, 1970 mailed Foster a ten-dollar check—which, ironically, was lost in the mail (Kotis to Gunnison, July 22, 1970, IGIC Papers, NYPL).

94. For the second march in June 1971, another fund-raising strategy proved far more successful. CSDLC (in which both Craig and Foster remained active) arranged with New York University authorities in the immediate aftermath of the first march to put on a series of four gay dances in Weinstein Hall. The first dances drew crowds of up to a thousand; their success was due to an imaginative combination of live bands, twenty-five-cent beer (which Craig and Michael Brown picked up from a wholesaler on Fourteenth Street), side exhibits of photographs and crafts, and "talking areas" for relaxation.

But then, in the summer of 1970, NYU authorities banned any further gay dances in Weinstein Hall. That led to a four-day sit-in in the Weinstein basement in which both Sylvia Rivera and Jim Fouratt took part. Sylvia was by then living on the streets again, having quit her warehouse job; when told of the sit-in, she parked her suitcase and boxes at Craig's bookstore and joined the fifty or so demonstrators. While many of them, including Jim Fouratt, came and went during the four days, Sylvia (and some two dozen others) stayed in the Weinstein

(Pages 274–275)

basement nearly the entire time. Sylvia did her laundry, held consciousness-raising sessions with NYU students, denounced GAA for staying clear of the action, and loudly protested against any suggestion of compromise.

The only time Sylvia left the building was to go to a GAA meeting to ask for support—at least from individuals if not from the organization. That led to a few GAA members showing up at Weinstein. In response to the subsequent series of protests against NYU, the GAA Executive Committee concluded that "since GAA is politically oriented and the demonstrations were called by 'street people,' who are only a small segment of the gay community, it was suggested that members participate as individuals without the organization's commitment in future related actions" (Arthur Bell Papers, and Box 15 of the GAA Papers, both in IGIC, NYPL).

After the NYU administration called in the police, who cleared out Weinstein, injuring several people, an enraged Sylvia at first obstinately refused to leave and had to be carried out; she then led a protest in the streets surrounding the building. Bob Kohler (interview, Aug. 20, 1990) says that Sylvia "was nuts on drugs and almost got us killed," by which he meant, he went on to explain, that when the cops leveled their guns at the demonstrators and gave them ten seconds to leave the building, Sylvia tried to lead them in a cheer, screaming, "Give me a G. . . . Give me an A. . . . Give me a Y. . . . Whadda we have? . . . GAY!" Jim Fouratt, on the other hand, credits Sylvia with being a restraining force when (according to Jim) "a transsexual from Los Angeles" joined the sit-in and brought some firebombs with her. Determined to out-radical everyone else, she then proceeded to plant the firebombs in the building. Jim tried to tell her that burning down the building was not a solution and that the essence of gay consciousness was a determination "not to hurt anyone." He pointed to Sylvia as an example of someone who was loud and angry, and was always willing to "push the boundaries," but did not talk irresponsibly of picking up a gun in order to prove her commitment to the revolution. But that didn't persuade the transsexual either, and finally, according to Jim, he had to follow her and remove every one of the firebombs from the baskets in which she had placed them.

The police action led to a series of protests against NYU and its homophobic policies, with undercover agents present at least once (SSD to Chief Inspector, Oct. 6, 1970, S.S.D. #665-M). The fullest accounts of the Weinstein incident are in *Gay Flames*, no. 5; John Murray, *Homosexual Liberation* (Praeger, 1971), pp. 119–23; Bell, *Dancing the Gay Lib Blues*, pp. 110–119 (which is especially full on Sylvia's role); Teal, *Gay Militants*, pp. 202–209; and the Arthur Bell Papers in IGIC Papers, NYPL, which contain several drafts of his stories on the events at Weinstein.

95. The poster is on the cover of this book. .
96. *RAT*, June 26–July 10, 1970.
97. Murphy, *Homosexual Liberation*, p. 96.
98. The descriptions in this and the following pages about the New York and Los Angeles marches rely on material from my interviews and on Teal, *Gay Militants*, p. 322 (Quakers), 324 (beating), 328 (Panther); Jim Kepner, *Our Movement Before Stonewall* (IGLA, 1989) and *Our Movement Since Stonewall* (IGLA, 1992); Kepner to Duberman, April 29, May 26, 1992; Martin Boyce (interview May 19, 1992) for "suffragette"; Kantrowitz, *Under the Rainbow*, pp. 151–56; Murphy, *Homosexual*

(Page 279)

Liberation, pp. 98–99 (cops reading); *Los Angeles Free Press*, July 3, 1970, and *Hollywood Citizens News*, June 29, 1970.

99. Teletype to Director, June 28, 1970, 100-459225-2. Foster himself, probably for publicity purposes, later inflated the figure to five thousand (Gunnison, CSLDC, "National Bulletin 11-08-70," Gunnison Papers. *Windy City Times*, June 23, 1988 (Chicago); *Gay Times*, June 1989 (London); *Mec* magazine, April 1988 (Paris).

INDEX